Theology and *Game of Thrones*

Theology and Pop Culture
Series Editor: Matthew Brake

The *Theology and Pop Culture* series examines the intersection of theology, religion, and popular culture, including, but not limited to television, movies, sequential art, and genre fiction. In a world plagued by rampant polarization of every kind and the decline of religious literacy in the public square, *Theology and Pop Culture* is uniquely poised to educate and entertain a diverse audience utilizing one of the few things society at large still holds in common: love for popular culture.

Titles in the series
Theology and the Game of Thrones, edited by Matthew Brake
Theology and Spider-Man, edited by George Tsakiridis
René Girard, Theology, and Pop Culture, edited by Ryan G. Duns & T. Derrick Witherington
Theology and Horror: Explorations of the Dark Religious Imagination, edited by Brandon R. Grafius and John W. Morehead
Sports and Play in Christian Theology, edited by Philip Halstead and John Tucker
Theology and Westworld, edited by Juli Gittinger and Shayna Sheinfeld
Theology and Prince, edited by Jonathan H. Harwell and Rev. Katrina E. Jenkins
Theology and the Marvel Universe, edited by Gregory Stevenson

Theology and *Game of Thrones*

Edited by
Matthew Brake

LEXINGTON BOOKS/FORTRESS ACADEMIC
Lanham • Boulder • New York • London

Published by Lexington Books/Fortress Academic
Lexington Books is an imprint of The Rowman & Littlefield Publishing Group, Inc.
4501 Forbes Boulevard, Suite 200, Lanham, Maryland 20706
www.rowman.com

86-90 Paul Street, London EC2A 4NE, United Kingdom

Copyright © 2022 by The Rowman & Littlefield Publishing Group, Inc.

All rights reserved. No part of this book may be reproduced in any form or by any electronic or mechanical means, including information storage and retrieval systems, without written permission from the publisher, except by a reviewer who may quote passages in a review.

British Library Cataloguing in Publication Information Available

Library of Congress Cataloging-in-Publication Data

Names: Brake, Matthew, 1984– editor.
Title: Theology and Game of thrones / edited by Matthew Brake.
Description: Lanham : Lexington Books/Fortress Academic, [2021.] | Series: Theology and pop culture | Includes bibliographical references and index. | Summary: "Theology and Game of Thrones explores themes of religion, institutional norms, and power, Christian ecclesiology, Augustinian thought, religious pluralism and representation, and theology's relationship with sexual violence and death in the HBO television series and the original A Song of Ice and Fire novels"—Provided by publisher.
Identifiers: LCCN 2021037512 (print) | LCCN 2021037513 (ebook) |
  ISBN 9781978707627 (cloth) | ISBN 9781978707641 (paperback) |
  ISBN 9781978707634 (epub)
Subjects: LCSH: Game of thrones (Television program) | Television programs—Religious aspects—Christianity.
Classification: LCC PN1992.77.G35 T44 2021 (print) | LCC PN1992.77.G35 (ebook) |
  DDC 791.45/72—dc23
LC record available at https://lccn.loc.gov/2021037512
LC ebook record available at https://lccn.loc.gov/2021037513

Contents

Preface   vii

Acknowledgments   ix

Introduction: Sex, Violence, and Theology in the World of Ice and Fire   1
Matthew Brake

PART I: POWER AND SACRED INSTITUTIONS IN THE SEVEN KINGDOMS   9

1. Seasons Change and "Winter is Coming": Patterning in *Game of Thrones* and the Hebrew Bible   11
Eric X. Jarrard

2. Targaryen Exceptionalism and Politics in the Sacred Structures of Westeros   39
Mollie Gossage and Edgar Valles

3. Guest Rights and Gods: Historical Hospitium in *Game of Thrones*   61
Katy L. Krieger

PART II: ECCLESIOLOGY OF THRONES   83

4. What is Dead May Never Die: The Drowned God and Jesus' Call to Discipleship   85
Shaun C. Brown

5. Ragamuffins Bound by the Word: The Ecclesiology of the Night's Watch   101
Drew McIntyre

PART III: AUGUSTINE GOES TO WESTEROS — 123

6 Night Kings and Shadow Assassins: Reflections on
   Death, Evil, and Privation — 125
   Mark Wiebe

7 The Faith of the Seven and Faith in the Trinity — 145
   David Mahfood

PART IV: DISPATCHES FROM ESSOS: PLURALISM AND ORIENTALISM IN THE WORLD OF ICE AND FIRE — 165

8 Is Hinduism Present in *Game of Thrones*? — 167
   Jeffery D. Long

9 "To Reach the West You Must Go East": The Empty
   Shadow of Postsecular Orientalism in A Song of Ice and Fire — 191
   Justin KH Tse

10 Comparative Worldview Studies and A Song of Ice
   and Fire: World Religions, Comparison, and Fictional Worlds — 215
   Nathan Fredrickson

PART V: THE NIGHT IS DARK AND FULL OF TERRORS: SEXUAL VIOLENCE, DEATH, AND THE REAL IN *GAME OF THRONES* — 255

11 Concupiscence, Coercion, and the Communion of Persons:
   Reading the Rape of Cersei — 257
   Susan Johnston

12 Valar Morghulis: Late-Modern Imaginaries of Death
   and Nihilism in *Game of Thrones* — 283
   Andrew D. Thrasher

13 Hodor and the Transubstantiation of the Word Made Death:
   The Theological Real in *Game of Thrones* — 301
   Loraine Haywood

Index — 317

About the Editor — 327

About the Contributors — 329

Preface

When I first pitched the *Theology and Pop Culture* series to Lexington, I conceived of this volume as the first to be published. At the time, we were still a year-and-a-half away from the premiere of the final season of *Game of Thrones*. Our collective hopes were high, and the show's immense popularity seemed to me to make it the obvious first choice.

As of the writing of this introduction, the final season of *Game of Thrones* has come and gone. The controversy over the show's writing in its final seasons, as well as its conclusion, call into question the enduring legacy of the show. In many ways, *Game of Thrones* helped define the peak of the Golden Age of Television, yet like others before, it still arguably ended its run as the most popular show on television in disappointment (see also: *LOST*). Likewise, due to both editorial delays on my part and a mandate from the publisher, the first volume in this series was on the intersection of theology and the music and life of Prince. Given the poor reception of *Game of Thrones'* ending, perhaps it was better to start with a much more iconic and enduring pop culture legend.

Still, with two more books in the series forthcoming from Martin, as well as a spin-off coming from HBO, *Game of Thrones* isn't leaving our cultural consciousness anytime soon.

I was a latecomer to *Game of Thrones*. When the Red Wedding premiered, it created a cultural uproar, and I felt I could no longer avoid the bandwagon.[1] During a summer fellowship when I was supposed to be learning Danish and writing about Søren Kierkegaard, I read the first three books in the *A Song of Ice and Fire* series. I was engrossed in the world Martin had built. I found myself having *Game of Thrones*-themed dreams. I was all in! There were times, after I later began watching the show, when I would recall watching certain scenes that in fact I had only read about. The books and the show and the lore all bled together.

I hope that this volume both excites fandom while also bringing a little bit more enchantment to our own world.

Matthew Brake
June 07, 2021

NOTE

1. My goal at that point was to avoid Red Wedding spoilers at all costs. I was unable to do so, thanks to a friend who got a little too detailed in his description of the death of Talisa Stark. He knows who he is, and now, there is a record of his betrayal in writing. The North remembers, Austin!

Acknowledgments

I want to express my gratitude to all of my (patient) contributors. Everything good in this book is to their credit. If anyone finds any problems with the book, I take full responsibility for those. I also want to thank Neil Elliott and Mike Gibson who have given me the opportunity to explore my love for studying the intersection of theology, religion, and pop culture, and to Gayla Freeman for patiently enduring the constant bombardment of emails. Of course, I probably wouldn't have pursued this journey as quickly as I did without a push from my friend, mentor, and brother Jeff Saferite, so he deserves a lot of credit for the existence of this whole book series. My parents probably deserve the most credit for creating the conditions for the possibility of my education, so thank you.

Introduction

Sex, Violence, and Theology in the World of Ice and Fire

Matthew Brake

Game of Thrones was one of the most popular television shows of the last decade, airing on HBO from 2011 to 2019. Based on George R.R. Martin's best-selling fantasy novel series, *A Song of Ice and Fire*,[1] the series captured the cultural imagination during the decade it was on the air. Despite what many saw as a disappointing final season from showrunners David Benioff and D.B. Weiss, *Game of Thrones* introduced Martin's fantasy world to a wider audience, who found themselves captivated by Martin's characters and the intricately created world they inhabited. Some of those who were captivated include the contributors of this volume, who have each found a different facet of Martin's world to explore and elucidate. However, before diving into the chapters contained within, I want to establish the legitimacy of pursuing such a volume to begin with. Many of the theological and religious conversations that take place around *Game of Thrones* concern whether or not devout religious adherents should even watch the show. While I will address those religious reservations, I argue that Martin's world helps us to see our own world more clearly, particularly the questions we have about God, religious devotion, and the world of death, power, and sexual violence the religiously devoted person is confronted with every day. For fans of the show and the books, this volume will reaffirm their interest. For those who may be skeptics, while you may never encounter Martin's world for yourself, I hope you walk away with greater appreciation and respect for those who have made the journey to Westeros and Essos.

WHY *GAME OF THRONES*?

To the question, "Why a volume on *Game of Thrones*?" I could pose a counter question: "Why not?" As a Christian, I have seen plenty of ink spilled on analyses of authors like C.S. Lewis and J.R.R. Tolkien (who, coincidentally, has his own upcoming volume in the *Theology and Pop Culture* series). The theological and religious symbolism is a bit more "on the nose" in Lewis than in Tolkien, but nevertheless, the latter has enjoyed plenty of theological analysis.[2] *Game of Thrones* is as religious, if not more so, than Tolkien's work. That *Game of Thrones* is important for a conversation about pop culture seems obvious. It was, after all, the most popular show on television at its height.[3] But religious audiences themselves are mixed on the show's value for theological investigation.

There is some religious hesitancy about engaging with *Game of Thrones*. Conservative Christian leaders like John Piper express concern over the depiction of sex and nudity in the show, noting that unlike the graphic violence the show portrays, "nudity is not make believe."[4] For Piper, watching such material is a violation of the Christian call to purity, and those who engage in such "public" displays are little better than exhibitionists. Piper places importance on the need for Christians to remain distinct from "the world." He fails to mention that folks in what he would dub "the world" have their own problems with the depiction of sex in *Game of Thrones*. More specifically, they take issue with the multiple depictions of rape, including turning a sex scene from the books into one of rape between Cersie and Jaime Lannister (which Susan Johnston explores in chapter 11). Even more disturbing than the depictions of rape is the real-life exploitation of actress Emilia Clarke, who portrays Daenerys Targaryen. She notes the pressure she faced in early seasons to participate in various scenes of sex and nudity.[5] It is truly unsettling to read about Emilia Clarke crying in the bathroom before doing these scenes.[6]

As we see, conservative Christians are not the only ones who take issue with *Game of Thrones*. David Gibson of the Religion News Service, writing for the more progressive Christian website, *Sojourners*, notes similar concerns as someone like Piper, not just about depictions of sex but also about the violence and moral vision (or lack thereof) of Martin's world, although in this piece, the reaction is more mixed. Some see in Martin's work a rejection of Christian teachings, while others see a story world that calls attention to important ideas, like Reinhold Niebuhr's Augustinian realism, given Martin's tendency to kill off idealistic characters who are unable to get on board with the way the world "really works."[7]

While this volume predominantly leans toward Christian theologizing, it (and the book series as a whole) aims to be inclusive of all religious traditions (a task taken up very well by Jeffery Long, Justin Tse, and Nathan Frederickson in chapters 8–10 in particular), I would be remiss if I didn't mention how other religious traditions have navigated the question of whether their followers should watch *Game of Thrones*. A Google search asking, "Should Muslims watch *Game of Thrones*?" turns up a number of interesting search results, including a message board chastising the show for its content (and seeking to figure out how to get one's wife to stop watching it)[8] and an article about the Turkish army banning *Game of Thrones* and requiring its officers to take courses on Islam.[9] However, one also finds a guide for watching *Game of Thrones* during Ramadan,[10] a wiki style page on Muslim contributions to *Game of Thrones*,[11] and an article noting the love for the show in the Middle East.[12] Typing in "Should Jews watch *Games of Thrones*?" produces similarly mixed results. One finds articles like "8 Jewish Things I Love About '*Game of Thrones*'"[13] or "8 reasons why *Game of Thrones* is so Jewish!"[14] mixed with articles condemning its depiction of nudity and sex[15] or expressing concern about its portrayal of graphic violence (even as a fan).[16]

And yet, despite the chastisement from religious leaders and mixed feelings about the portrayals of sex and violence, people from various religious traditions tuned in to watch Martin's fictional world come to life. Why did religious audiences tune in to *Game of Thrones*? Was it because they were seeking titillation? Was it because they are all sinners rebelling against the wisdom of their spiritual leaders? Were they all deceived? I would surely seek a more nuanced explanation for *Game of Thrones*' popularity among religious adherents. After all, don't popular portrayals of religious and theological ideas say something about how the contemporaneous culture views religion (Andrew Thrasher certainly makes that case in his chapter)? And might the ambiguity and struggle with watching *Game of Thrones* among religious adherents say something about the quality of the world that Martin constructed?

I would argue that the rich, layered world-building present in *Game of Thrones* is what makes the worlds of Westeros and Essos feel so real and makes them so appealing. The vivid and detailed histories help create that world, but so does the complex and varied religious landscape. The show and the books present a pluralistic world with variously credible gods and religious traditions. Some of these gods, like the Seven, appear to lack supernatural power but more than make up for that with the zeal of their followers, while other gods are capable of raising the dead or imparting the ability to shapeshift. The "old gods" send the Stark children direwolves to protect them, while the Lord of Light sends his priests and priestesses to raise up the Prince That Was Promised and to prepare for the battle against the army of the dead. The pluralistic religious context of this world, as well as the varying levels of supernatural power among the different religions, raises important theological and religious questions and considerations about the nature of power, religious piety, religious representation, and violence and death. It is these ideas that brought religious audiences back for more every season (no matter how much this show, or the books, broke our hearts). The World of Ice and Fire speaks to a broad range of human concerns, from politics, to relationships, to sex, and yes, even religion and theology.

THE MAESTERS OF THIS VOLUME

Those of us who are fans of *Game of Thrones* (and the World of Ice and Fire more broadly) all have questions and ways of analyzing Martin's world for the ideas and themes that interest us. This volume contains just a small sampling of such analyses from a group of scholars who are more than up to the challenge and whose insights I believe you will enjoy engaging with!

Part 1 of this book explores various questions about power and the sacred institutions of Westeros. Eric X. Jarrard looks at how certain patterns in the Hebrew Bible show the corrupting power of kingship, which we certainly find at work in *Game of Thrones*, even among some of our most beloved characters. Mollie Gossage and Edgar Valles discuss the integration of the Targaryen kings into the religion of the Seven, and the nature of exceptionalism. Those who were devastated by the Red Wedding may appreciate Katy Krieger's chapter on guest rights and hospitality in Westeros.

Section two visits two of the more remote parts of Westeros: the Wall and the Iron Islands. It is these remote backwaters of the Seven Kingdoms that provide Shaun Brown and Drew McIntyre the opportunity to consider questions of Christian Ecclesiology. Brown looks at the Drowned God of the Iron Islands as an opportunity for reflection on the nature of Christian discipleship, while McIntyre considers the cast of rejects in the Night's Watch as an image of the make-up of the Christian church.

St. Augustine is the subject of section three. Mark Wiebe addresses Augustine's views on evil as privation in the case of the Night King, a living embodiment of privation. David Mahfood considers how the Seven and the Christian Trinity are and are not alike in terms of power and function. He also addresses Augustine's use of the Trinity as a means for analyzing human nature and considers whether the Seven allow for the same analysis.

Section four takes an important look at the religious diversity in *Game of Thrones*, representations of "the East" and Orientalism, and where we might find themes from so-called "Eastern" religions. Jeffery D. Long starts off by asking about the presence of Hinduism in Martin's world and where we might find it, while Justin Tse looks at Orientalism in the World of Ice and Fire and explores how the West has always defined itself against the East. Nathan Frederickson concludes this section with a comparative analysis, in the spirit of Ninian Smart, of the various worldviews one finds across Westeros and Essos.

The final section tackles some of the more visceral themes in Martin's fictional world—sexual violence and death. Susan Johnston asks us to consider the rape of Cersei that was problematically inserted into the television series, and how Catholic theology can contribute to a far more robust understanding of sexuality and the ethics of consent. Andrew Thrasher discusses how Martin has created a medieval world with a late-modern social imaginary. Such an imagination deals with the irrelevance of belief in God for one's everyday life, while enchanting death itself. Finally, Loraine Haywood looks at the death of the beloved character Hodor as a means of considering a type of Lacanian "Theological Real," or the unconscious struggle against death.

This volume is certainly not the final theological or religious analysis of the World of Ice and Fire, but it certainly brings to light many of the ways one might engage with that world and analyze its underlying theological messages. Perhaps by analyzing the religious and theological messages of Westeros and Essos, we might better be able to theologically understand our own world a little better.

NOTES

1. When I use *A Song of Ice and Fire*, I will be referring to the book series, while *Game of Thrones* refers to the TV show. When I say, "the World of Ice and Fire," I'm referring to Martin's world as seen in both the books and the TV show, and will thus not italicize it.

2. See, for example, Fleming Rutledge, *The Battle for Middle-earth: Tolkien's Divine Design in the Lord of the Rings* (Grand Rapids, MI: William B. Eerdmans Publishing Company, 2004).

3. Daniel D'Addario, "*Game of Thrones*: How They Make the World's Most Popular Show." Time. https://time.com/game-of-thrones-2017/. Accessed on May 29, 2021.

4. John Piper, "Should Christians Watch *Game of Thrones*?" Desiring God. https://www.desiringgod.org/interviews/should-christians-watch-game-of-thrones. Accessed May 29, 2021.

5. Roison O'Connor, "Emilia Clarke's awful *Game of Thrones* experience is proof that nude scenes need to change." Independent. https://www.independent.co.uk/arts-entertainment/tv/features/game-thrones-nudity-emilia-clarke-daenerys-sex-scenes-a9213241.html. Accessed on May 29, 2021.

6. Adam White, "*Game of Thrones* star Emilia Clarke says she was pressured to perform nude scenes." Independent. https://www.independent.co.uk/arts-entertainment

/films/news/emilia-clarke-game-thrones-nude-scenes-dax-shepard-daenerys-a9208471.html. Accessed on May 29, 2021. Piper himself comes off as a bit obtuse on the point of rape, exploitation, and the power imbalances that spawn these things. A since-deleted January 2015 tweet that I came across illustrates this point. In it, Piper notes, "The Bible says there are men who rape (Genesis 34:2) and women who seduce (Genesis 39:7). United in sin, distinct in form." To see the tweet (as well as an interesting blog commentary), see "John Piper Steps In It on Rape and Sex." Diary of an Autodidact. http://fiddlrts.blogspot.com/2015/04/john-piper-steps-in-it-on-rape-and-sex.html. Accessed on May 29, 2021 (the blogger does not list their real name on the blog).

7. David Gibson, "Should a Christian Watch *Game of Thrones*?" Sojourners. https://sojo.net/articles/should-christian-watch-game-thrones. Accessed on May 29, 2021.

8. "My wife watches the show *'Game of Thrones.'* How can I convince her to stop?" Ummah. https://www.ummah.com/forum/forum/misc/anonymous-posting-counselling-forum/343398-my-wife-watches-the-show-game-of-thrones-how-can-i-convince-her-to-stop. Accessed on May 29, 2021.

9. JPost.com Staff, "Report: Turkish army bans *Game of Thrones*, requires officers take course on Islam." The Jerusalem Post. https://www.jpost.com/middle-east/report-turkish-army-bans-game-of-thrones-requires-officers-take-course-on-islam-381226. Accessed on May 29, 2021.

10. Mustafa Rashid, "Muslims Guide to *Game of Thrones*." Musty Reviews. http://mustyreviews.com/muslims-guide-to-game-of-thrones. Accessed on May 29, 2021.

11. "Muslim Contributions to *Game of Thrones*." Materia Islamic. http://materiaislamica.com/index.php/Muslim_Contributions_to_Game_of_Thrones. Accessed on May 29, 2021.

12. Kateryna Kadabashy, "How the Middle East reacted to the *Game of Thrones* finale." Arab News. https://www.arabnews.com/node/1499881/lifestyle. Accessed on May 29, 2021.

13. Miriam Anzovin, "8 Jewish Things I Love About *'Game of Thrones.'*" Jewish Boston. https://www.jewishboston.com/read/8-jewish-things-i-love-about-game-of-thrones/. Accessed on May 29, 2021.

14. Francine Wolfsz, "8 reasons why *Game of Thrones* is so Jewish!" Jewish News. https://jewishnews.timesofisrael.com/8-reasons-why-game-of-thrones-is-so-jewish/. Accessed on May 29, 2021.

15. Allison Josephs, "Why We Don't Watch *'Game of Thrones'* (And Other Shows Like It)." Jew is the City. https://jewinthecity.com/2017/07/why-we-dont-watch-game-of-thrones-and-other-shows-like-it/. Accessed on May 29, 2021.

16. Benjamin Resnick, "Should Jews Be Watching *Game of Thrones*?" Forward. https://forward.com/culture/178866/should-jews-be-watching-game-of-thrones/. Accessed on May 29, 2021.

BIBLIOGRAPHY

Anzovin, Miriam. "8 Jewish Things I Love About *'Game of Thrones.'*" Jewish Boston. https://www.jewishboston.com/read/8-jewish-things-i-love-about-game-of-thrones/. Accessed on May 29, 2021.

D'Addario, Daniel. "*Game of Thrones*: How They Make the World's Most Popular Show." Time. https://time.com/game-of-thrones-2017/. Accessed on May 29, 2021.

Gibson, David. "Should a Christian Watch '*Game of Thrones*?'" Sojourners. https://sojo.net/articles/should-christian-watch-game-thrones. Accessed on May 29, 2021.

Josephs, Allison. "Why We Don't Watch '*Game of Thrones*' (And Other Shows Like It)." Jew is the City. https://jewinthecity.com/2017/07/why-we-dont-watch-game-of-thrones-and-other-shows-like-it/. Accessed on May 29, 2021.

JPost.com Staff. "Report: Turkish army bans *Game of Thrones*, requires officers take course on Islam." The Jerusalem Post. https://www.jpost.com/middle-east/report-turkish-army-bans-game-of-thrones-requires-officers-take-course-on-islam-381226. Accessed on May 29, 2021.

Kadabashy, Kateryna. "How the Middle East reacted to the *Game of Thrones* finale." Arab News. https://www.arabnews.com/node/1499881/lifestyle. Accessed on May 29, 2021.

Materia Islamic. "Muslim Contributions to *Game of Thrones*." http://materiaislamica.com/index.php/Muslim_Contributions_to_Game_of_Thrones. Accessed on May 29, 2021.

O'Connor, Roison. "Emilia Clarke's awful *Game of Thrones* experience is proof that nude scenes need to change." Independent. https://www.independent.co.uk/arts-entertainment/tv/features/game-thrones-nudity-emilia-clarke-daenerys-sex-scenes-a9213241.html. Accessed on May 29, 2021.

Piper, John. "Should Christians Watch *Game of Thrones*?" Desiring God. https://www.desiringgod.org/interviews/should-christians-watch-game-of-thrones. Accessed May 29, 2021.

Rashid, Mustafa. "Muslims Guide to *Game of Thrones*." Musty Reviews. http://mustyreviews.com/muslims-guide-to-game-of-thrones. Accessed on May 29, 2021.

Resnick, Benjamin. "Should Jews Be Watching *Game of Thrones*?" Forward. https://forward.com/culture/178866/should-jews-be-watching-game-of-thrones/. Accessed on May 29, 2021.

Ummah. "My Wife Watches the Show '*Game of Thrones*.' How Can I Convince Her to Stop?" https://www.ummah.com/forum/forum/misc/anonymous-posting-counselling-forum/343398-my-wife-watches-the-show-game-of-thrones-how-can-i-convince-her-to-stop. Accessed on May 29, 2021.

White, Adam. "*Game of Thrones* star Emilia Clarke says She Was Pressured to Perform Nude Scenes." Independent. https://www.independent.co.uk/arts-entertainment/films/news/emilia-clarke-game-thrones-nude-scenes-dax-shepard-daenerys-a9208471.html. Accessed on May 29, 2021.

Wolfisz, Francine. "8 reasons why *Game of Thrones* is So Jewish!" Jewish News. https://jewishnews.timesofisrael.com/8-reasons-why-game-of-thrones-is-so-jewish/. Accessed on May 29, 2021.

Part I

POWER AND SACRED INSTITUTIONS IN THE SEVEN KINGDOMS

Chapter 1

Seasons Change and "Winter is Coming"

Patterning in Game of Thrones *and the Hebrew Bible*

Eric X. Jarrard

INTRODUCTION

Although the critical and popular reception of the final season of *Game of Thrones* would ultimately burn with the fiery scorn of, say, a queen unrepentantly torching King's Landing, in the run up to the season premiere, we were optimistic and ignorant to the fate of the show; we were, in the parlance of the series, "sweet summer children." Excited for the return of one of the most celebrated, loyally watched shows of recent memory, meandering dragon rides notwithstanding, critics and fans alike were pleased with the first episode of season eight ("Winterfell"), some even going so far as to claim it was the "best" premiere since the Pilot episode.[1] Kathryn VanArendonk itemized the successfully navigated difficulties of this final season premiere:

> It is hard to pull a juggernaut into port. For *Game of Thrones*, its immense size—sprawling plot, colossal cast, long cultural show—makes that task a particular challenge. It has to create the sense that this huge world is ending, that characters who've been scattered across the map are now, at last, reuniting in meaningful and conclusory ways. It has to feel satisfying, an elusive and unmistakable quality in narrative that relies on a combination of being expected and feeling surprising, and often hinges on long-developing character arcs. And yet, even as the show starts pulling the levers to make this whole thing feel like it's shutting down, it has to maintain some momentum. Slowly and carefully may be the best way to dock an enormous ship, but it's pretty boring to watch.[2]

The sad irony of VanArendonk's praise of the premiere is, of course, that a primary critique of the final season was its virtually nonexistent ability to sustain momentum over the course of the season.

As the season and viewer patience wore on, it became clear that viewers were likely not going to experience the long-awaited resolution they had hoped for, and that pacing, and more specifically momentum, would be chief among the difficulties encountered by the show as it hurtled toward its finale. While the big questions of who would win the "*game of thrones*," and when and how they would accomplish that victory, remained, it became abundantly clear that the ending would likely feel unearned in any real sense of the word, and at the very least would be unevenly paced. In contrast to VanArendonk, this problem was underscored by reviewer Willa Paskin, who commented on the critically unbalanced momentum of the season premiere, or, as she put it, "the idea that we are hurtling toward some conclusion that will explain it all."[3]

In truth, though, the issues of pacing and narrative structure should have been more widely anticipated having plagued the series ever since it departed from the book canon. These problems became especially prominent in the seventh season, reaching a crescendo, for instance, in "Beyond the Wall," when characters completed journeys in a single episode that had taken multiple seasons earlier in the chronology of the show.[4] On this tendency, Nina Shen Rastogi rightly observed,

> Our sprawling tale has lost some of the scaffolds that kept it coherent, like a commitment to logical rules of time and space and a rigorous pairing of action to consequence. But the [story] is still deeply concerned with shapes and patterns.[5]

What Rastogi describes as scaffolds of coherency, however, are fundamentally rooted in the conviction that the pacing and ordering of narrative chronology are self-evident, persistent, and critical elements of storytelling. This is, as a point of fact, not so for at least one other celebrated and fiercely analyzed work: the Hebrew Bible. Indeed, when reviewing the above-cited quote, with only a single, relatively insignificant change—from "show" to "story"—we could apply Rastogi's comments to the Hebrew Bible.

This chapter will explore the notion of narrative scaffolding in these two works—*Game of Thrones* and the Hebrew Bible—as a productive fulcrum of comparison. It argues both works share a preeminent interest in patterning, over and above more commonly accepted forms of plot propellent and resolution, as an effective technique for addressing their mutual pessimism over the failed institution of kingship. Patterning in the final season of *Game of Thrones* demonstrates a tendency to create distinct visual allusions to previous seasons for the purpose of establishing an implicit pattern of cause and effect concerning the ascent and descent of Daenerys Targaryen. Patterning in the Hebrew Bible, especially in the Former Prophets and wisdom literature, similarly forms critiques of leadership with specific reference to what has been called the deed-consequence nexus (*Tun-Ergehen-Zusammenhang*). Finally, both are deeply pessimistic about the human proficiency to self-govern. In sum, this chapter will demonstrate that both stories employ patterning as a mode of storytelling used to establish how the consequences of errant rulers can demonstrably be linked to their earlier actions. Furthermore, it is my contention that this widespread pessimism toward human rulership, blatantly and intentionally theologized in the biblical text, exposes a decidedly more subtle logic of consequence in *Game of Thrones*.

PATTERNING IN *GAME OF THRONES*

The narrative responsibilities of a series finale are tremendous. In some way, the finale must gesture toward the work the show has done in its previous seasons and episodes, resolve—or at least weigh in on—its central questions or themes, but also manage to give closure to its character and plot with a satisfactory resolution. Striking balance between these responsibilities is a formidable task and a good indicator of why series finales can be so incredibly divisive and disappointing. While there is certainly an endless array of techniques to manage these burdens, perhaps the most common devices are the retro- and future-spect, the flashback and the flash-forward.

The difference between flashback and flash-forward is most apparent in the genre of the thirty-minute sitcom. For the use of flash-forward, we could examine the finales of *Parks and Recreation, Veep,* and *How I Met Your Mother*, all of which spent a great deal of time exploring the characters' immediate or distant future. Other shows—*New Girl*,[6] *Big Bang Theory, Seinfeld, Friends,* and *Cheers*—used clip shows, a television device consisting mainly of excerpts from prior episodes, and other devices to look backward into the show's past to instill a sense of nostalgia and to underscore character growth and development.

An emerging third category uses more subtle visual and written clues to achieve both retro- and future-spects. These shows reward the obsessive viewer and careful watcher with subtle, often visual cues that intentionally recollect previous shots without explicitly invoking a clip show device. The future-spect is often relegated to an evocation, a final scene that gestures to the future—or lack of future—of the characters without explicitly flashing forward. This was the case with the crowning achievements of *Breaking Bad, The Americans, The Sopranos, The Wire,* and *Mad Men*. The use of allusion, visual or otherwise, to evoke earlier material is buttressed by the assumption of a highly attentive audience, literate in the chosen medium. Numerous aspects of the final season of *Game of Thrones* indicate that it certainly fancied itself in the model of the high-prestige television comprising this third category.

This subtler approach, however, does demand adroit parsing of the temporal emphases of a given show. That is, in the thirty-minute sitcoms listed above, the amount of time spent in either the past or future unequivocally betrays a vested interest in either recollecting the show's past or projecting its characters' future. In the case of this third category, though, that emphasis is not made explicit, and the interest of the show is left ambiguous. The lingering question of the third approach often gravitates toward character development. These finales interrogate through visual allusion whether the characters persist in their own well-trodden patterns or if they have been able to learn from their mistakes and forge a new, brighter, or at least different future. With very few exceptions, these shows suggest a pessimistic, or perhaps a *realistic*, outlook on the human condition, adumbratively advancing the hypothesis that although people and their surroundings may look different over time, they are determinately and iteratively repeating their old patterns because human beings are decidedly resistant toward, or even incapable of, change.

Winter(fell) is Coming

From the very first episode of the final season of *Game of Thrones* ("Winterfell"), the show is steeped in visual allusions to its previous seasons and, in particular, to its pilot episode ("Winter is Coming") through its presentation of a number of prominent characters. Somewhat predictably, the foci of many of these allusions are the Stark children. In particular, the presentations of Arya and Sansa Stark and Jaime Lannister will serve as noteworthy case studies into the use of visual allusion in the final season of *Game of Thrones*.

The contrasting presentations of Arya Stark in the series and final season premieres serve to remind viewers of the character's self-assuredness, independence, and increasingly tentative ties to House Stark. As the final season premiere opens, a young, dark-haired boy runs through the streets of the city, ducking through parade watchers, trying to catch a glimpse of the royal procession. He climbs a tree to gain a higher vantage point and a better view of the approaching royals. This scene intentionally mirrors the pilot episode, "Winter is Coming," in which another dark-haired child, Arya Stark, bobs and weaves through an assembled mass of onlookers to see the approaching envoy of Robert Baratheon. The parallel is accentuated by the scoring of the scene, in which the theme of House Baratheon is played for both; the House

Baratheon theme is made all the more noticeable in "Winterfell" due to the lack of Baratheons in the Targaryen procession of the final season. One of the primary functions of music, then, is to emphasize the allusion to and contrast with the pilot episode.

The two Aryas are different in numerous ways. First, in the pilot episode, Arya is forced to negotiate her physical position through a crowd of North Men to gain access to the procession, but in season eight, it is a nameless young boy who dodges his way through the crowd. The older Arya, on the other hand, has unobstructed access to the position of her choosing. No longer subjected to the spaces between prominent men, the older Arya aptly maintains her post at the front of the throng of onlookers. Second, by season eight, Arya enjoys greater freedom and evidently prefers the anonymity of a post outside the walls of Winterfell, accentuating her tentative association with her family and, especially, their geographical ties to their family lands, and the North more generally. While she is dressed in the trappings of a Stark, she is not bound by their physical spaces. Finally, lest we think Arya is a fully transformed character, her whereabouts are identically questioned in both episodes with key characters—Catelyn Stark in the pilot, Jon Snow in the season eight premiere—demanding of Sansa Stark, "Where's Arya?" While Sansa is unable to account for her sister's whereabouts in either scene, in the pilot Sansa simply shrugs, a physical embodiment of the abdication of her duties as older sister—yes, Sansa *is* her sibling's keeper—in the latter, though she cannot account for Arya with any degree of precision, her response affirms her confidence in her sister's wellbeing: "Lurking somewhere," she tells Jon. Thus, the visual allusion to the pilot episode serves to underscore the various points of continuity and discontinuity in the development of Arya's character over eight seasons and accentuates the way these developments have influenced her relationships with those around her.

The mirroring of Sansa in both episodes is also worthy of note. Although Sansa Stark is greeted by monarchs in both episodes, the contrast is, well, stark. She is greeted by the reigning monarch in both season premieres, and both offer comments on her physical appearance, but her responses are strikingly different. In the pilot, as Robert Baratheon moves down the line of Stark children, he acknowledges Sansa only with, "Aye, the pretty one." Sansa reacts by blushing and shyly demurring. By the final season, Daenerys greets Sansa with a longer and more flattering greeting. Daenerys's address—"Thank you for inviting us into your home, Lady Stark. The North is as beautiful as your brother claims it to be, as are you"—befits Sansa's obvious change in household stature. Sansa, hardened by her years of abuse and unimpressed with the flattery of equivocating royals, responds with piercing eye contact, sizing up Daenerys by looking at her from head to toe, and replies coolly, "Winterfell is yours, your grace."

In both episodes, special attention is also given to the arrival of Jaime Lannister. Both scenes are similarly framed, with Jaime dismounting his horse and removing his protective headwear. In the pilot, though, Jaime, the golden boy of House Lannister, wears the lavish, gilded armor of the King's Guard, immaculately groomed blonde hair flowing freely as he takes off his helmet, the gold of both hair and helmet functioning as physical manifestations of the opulence and prosperity of House Lannister. The pilot episode culminates with Jaime infamously pushing Bran—who has just witnessed Jaime committing an act of incest with his sister, Cersei—out of a tower window, indifferently remarking, "The things I do for love" ("A Knight of the Seven Kingdoms").[7] In season eight, Jaime's golden armor is swapped for black rags and a leather hood, the removal of which reveals his hair is dark, and his rugged beard is streaked with gray. Jaime pauses to survey the courtyard of Winterfell, his eyes eventually coming to rest on Bran, poised in the wheelchair to which he has been confined due to the paralysis precipitated by his fall in the pilot episode. Bran, who has apparently been waiting in the same spot for days in anticipation of Jaime's arrival, stares meaningfully at Jaime, his assailant, who looks back in horror at the physical evidence of his abhorrent attempt to cover up his incestuous relationship with Cersei. The scene marks the first time the two have seen each other since their fateful encounter at the end of the pilot. Their final interaction is left utterly devoid of meaning without the context of the pilot purposely activated by the visual allusion.

Finally, the gruesome corpse patterns created by the White Walkers in both episodes visually parallel each other. The penultimate scene of "Winterfell" depicts an envoy from the North on a mission to Last Hearth, the seat of House Umber. This group, Tormund Giantsbane, Beric Dondarrion, and the remaining delegation from the Night's Watch, eventually discovers the house and its inhabitants have been destroyed by the Night King. The members of the household are entirely gone, presumably turned into wights—members of the army of the dead—save the young Lord Ned Umber, who is nailed to the wall, surrounded in an elaborate, spiral configuration of cadaver limbs. Ned Umber awakens, shrieking, with the trademark blue eyes of the wight army. Dondarrion sets him on fire to destroy him, engulfing the entire spiral in flames. This intricate design, of course, mirrors the first scenes of the pilot episode in which members of the Night's Watch encounter a similarly intricate and mysterious configuration of severed wildling limbs with a child nailed to a tree.

Such pronounced visual allusions in the season eight premiere are intended to cultivate a specific disposition within viewers. Primarily, an overwhelming sense begins to emerge that the final season has a corollary in what has preceded it and that the eventual ramifications of those previous actions are only elucidated by examining previous episodes. For instance, if we grant that the final scene depicting the ignoble arrival of Jaime Lannister in Winterfell visually alludes to Jaime's first imposing appearance in the same place from the pilot episode, we can also observe that his antagonizing reception by Bran recalls the pilot episode and, pointedly, Jaime's attempted murder of Bran. This mode of storytelling prioritizes the relationship of the present season to past episodes, thereby forming a direct link between a character's earlier deeds and actions to the manifested consequence of those actions in the final season. So, in the case of Jaime and Bran, the difference in the physical appearance and reaction of both characters—the consequence—is elucidated only through the allusion to Jaime pushing Bran out of the tower window—the action or deed—from the same pilot episode.

The deliberate introduction of frames with such a high degree of visual similarity establishes a specific expectation for viewers that the present season can and should be compared to what has come before it, and that patterns and similarities are consequential and worthy of analysis. The sum total of these allusions and callbacks allows the viewer to recognize visual and dialogue patterns within the episodes and draw conclusions based on those patterns. Moreover, these similarities make it apparent that the viewer is intended to draw potential conclusions based on those differences. As an example, the visual allusion formed through the similar presentations of a young child dodging his or her way through a crowd to observe approaching royalty is intended to draw attention to the similarities and, critically, the differences between the two presentations of Arya Stark. The Arya of "Winterfell" is intentionally presented as both similar and dissimilar to the Arya of "Winter is Coming." By pursuing those differences, one must begin to account for Arya's change in stature, location, and disposition, and draw conclusions concerning why those differences exist. Critically, the repeated use of visual allusion and callbacks in the premiere of season eight ratify pattern recognition as an authorized mode of viewership; they achieve their effectiveness by training the viewer to recognize and analyze patterns between seasons.

The Ascent and Descent of Daenerys Targaryen

These early allusions in the season premiere primarily serve as a precedent for interpreting the more complex allusions marking the ascent of Daenerys to power and her purported descent into madness. Indeed, cultivated attention to allusion is essential to understanding the depiction of Daenerys Targaryen's siege of King's Landing in the penultimate and final episodes of the series, "The Bells" and "The Iron Throne," respectively. In these episodes, we witness the descent of Daenerys into perceived madness. The speed and degree of this decline, though, is entirely contingent upon one's ability to recall and link certain behaviors with earlier episodes of Daenerys's rise to power and dominion over Essos.

Several implicit indications of Daenerys's propensity to follow in the fiery footsteps of her father, Aerys II Targaryen, the Mad King, can be traced throughout the series. These might include her emotionless reaction to the execution of her brother, Viserys, by Khal Drogo ("A Golden Crown"); the punishment of her would-be assassin; and looking on lustfully and approvingly as Khal Drogo promises to reclaim Westeros in recompense:

> I will take my khalasar west to where the world ends and ride wooden horses across the black sea as no khal has done before. I will kill the men in iron suits and tear down their stone houses. . . . I swear before the mother of mountains as the stars look down in witness. ("You Win or You Die")

To this we might also add her impassioned threat to Qarth ("We will take back what was stolen from me and destroy those who have wronged me. We will lay waste to armies and burn cities to the ground." ["Garden of Bones"]); the execution of Dickon and Randyll Tarly ("Eastwatch"); or the promise to Varys that if he ever betrays her, she will burn him alive ("Stormborn"). Even so, Daenerys's behavior all felt earned in the moment, or at least matched Daenerys's perception of justice; the incidents are only indicative of a slow descent into "madness" in hindsight.

Rather, it is precisely Daenerys's unflagging pursuit of justice, and in particular its culmination in her final victory speech delivered at the top of the stairs to the Red Keep after laying waste to King's Landing, which is the focal point of allusion for Daenerys in season eight. This entire scene is an intricate matrix of allusion to similar declarations made by Daenerys throughout the course of the show. This speech can be roughly separated into three addresses, the first to the Dothraki khalasar, a second to the Unsullied troops, and a third general address.

Her address to the Dothraki is strongly evocative of similarly impassioned speeches delivered to various khalasari throughout the show. As she stands at the top of the stairs, she proclaims to her gathered Dothraki troops: "Blood of my blood, you kept all your promises to me. You killed my enemies in their iron suits. You tore down their stone houses. You gave me the Seven Kingdoms" ("The Iron Throne")! These opening lines recall several important earlier scenes. First, the iconic, if somewhat hackneyed, visual framing of Daenerys between Drogon's wings visually recalls a similar speech given between the wings of a dragon in season six, when she made the entire Khalasar her *dothrakhqoyi* (blood riders):

I will ask more of you than any khal has ever asked of his khalasar. Will you ride the wooden horses across the black sea? Will you kill my enemies in their iron suits and tear down their stone houses? Will you give me the Seven Kingdoms, the gift Khal Drogo promised me before the Mother of Mountains? ("Blood of My Blood")

In both addresses, the speech is punctuated visually and audibly by the intimidating roar of Drogon. Second, her positioning at the top of the stairs is a clear visual allusion to several earlier scenes involving khalasari in Vaes Dothrak and Lhazar. The most obvious of these is her emergence at the top of the stairs of the burning Temple of the Dosh Khaleen in Vaes Dothrak ("Book of the Stranger"), but we must also recall in the finale of the first season her emergence from fire in Lhazar, having murdered Mirri Maz Duur for her perceived role in the death of Khal Drogo ("Fire and Blood"). Daenerys's rabble-rousing of the Dothraki in the finale, then, serves both to fulfill and to extend their commitment to their Khaleesi.

The allusions continue as she addresses the Unsullied. She reminds them, "Unsullied, all of you were torn from your mothers' arms and raised as slaves. Now, you are liberators! You have freed the people of King's Landing from the grips of a tyrant, but the war is not over" ("Iron Throne"). They respond in turn by rhythmically beating their spears on the ground in unison, the camera panning from a few beating spears to reveal a sea of beating spears. The scene audibly and visually mirrors her speech delivered to free the unsullied when she proclaims to them, "Unsullied! You have been slaves all your life. Today you are free . . . Will you fight for me? As free men?" to which they slowly respond with the approving, methodical thrum of their spears in the Astaporian dirt ("And Now His Watch Is Ended"). The callback to their emancipation serves to elongate an arc for the unsullied troops activated in season three, from enslaved soldiers, to free men, to liberators of other slaves.

Finally, she concludes her speech with an allusion to the imagery of a broken wheel. She announces to the entire assembled army, "We will not lay down our spears until we have liberated all the people of the world! From Winterfell to Dorne, from Lannisport to Qarth, from the Summer Isles to the Jade Sea, women, men, and children have suffered too long beneath the wheel. Will you break the wheel with me" ("Iron Throne")? Her impulse to "break the wheel" recollects her commitment to Tyrion inside the Great Pyramid of Mereen. When Tyrion interrogates the ascending queen about her plans to conquer Westeros, she responds:

Lannister, Targaeryn, Baratheon, Stark, Tyrell, they're all just spokes on a wheel. This one's on top, then that one's on top, and on and on it spins, crushing those on the ground . . . I'm not going to stop the wheel. I'm going to break the wheel. ("The Winds of Winter")

By invoking the broken wheel, she is able to conscript her remaining army into a longer, more violent goal. She affirms their fulfillment of their earlier pledges, while simultaneously reenlisting them to another, separate tour of duty. Their victory at King's Landing is only a first victory in a much larger war she plans on waging.

Perhaps the most interesting visual feature of this matrix of allusions is the depiction of Daenerys's ascent to power and the escalating violence accompanying that power. Beginning with the first allusion to her first-season emergence from the funeral pyre, Danaerys moves from the ground, to horseback in Astapor, to the top of the ten stairs of the Temple of the Dosh Khaleen, to the back of the imposing and growing Drogon, to the royal quarters of the Great Pyramid of Mereen, and finally to the top of the stairs of the Red Keep in the elevated city of King's Landing. Thus, if we plot out these visual allusions over time, we see Daenerys's physical stature mounting at a commiserate rate with the threat of her power. As the physical height of her platform increases, so, too, does her metaphorical power, and her conviction that her pursuits are noble; as Daenerys grows taller, she also grows more dangerous.

Commensurate with this ascension and the increasing threat posed to Essos and Westeros has been her ostensible commitment to a notion of justice that is irreconcilable with mercy. By her calculation, these many destroyed cities, their rulers, and their citizens have received a measure of earned punishment; they have reaped only the consequences for their actions. Indeed, her siege of King's Landing is preceded by yet another exchange with Tyrion on the eve of battle in which he begs her to give the city an opportunity to surrender. She scolds him for what she perceives as a disloyalty:

> [The resident of King's Landing] are in a tyrant's grip. Whose fault is that? Mine? . . . Your sister knows how to use her enemies' weaknesses against them. That's what she thinks our mercy is. Weakness . . . She's wrong. Mercy is our strength. Our mercy towards future generations who will never again be held hostage by a tyrant. ("The Bells")

This false dichotomy between justice and mercy was a frequent point of contention between Daenerys and her advisors. It recalls another contentious debate between the young queen and Barristan Selmy, when Daenerys expresses her intent to repay the crucifixion of 163 Meereeneese slave children in kind by crucifying 163 of the remaining masters of Meereen. Selmy cautions her, "Sometimes it is better to answer injustice with mercy," to which she responds, "I will answer injustice with justice" ("Oathkeeper").

Likewise, in her exchange with Jorah Mormont, when she resolves to kill every slave master in Yunkai, Jorah warns her, "It's tempting to see your enemies as evil, all of them. But there's good and evil on both sides in every war ever fought" ("Mockingbird").

The final episodes' visual allusions and explicit callbacks to multiple episodes from earlier seasons allow us to compare the analogous ascents, as well as the proportionate commitments to justice, of Daenerys and her father, the Mad King Aerys II Targaryen. Daenerys's pursuit is remarkably like her father's, in that both view their power as inextricably linked to their pursuit of justice and the retribution of injustice. For the elder and younger Targaryen rulers, mercy is understood as the antithesis of justice, and thus to be merciful is to be disempowered. Selmy, the former Lord Commander of Aerys's King's Guard, points out the potential liability of the elder Targaryen's approach to kingship for Daenerys. Although Daenerys never knew her father, Selmy witnessed first-hand his descent into what was called madness. So, he explains to her, "When the people rose and revolted against him, your father set their towns and castles aflame. He murdered sons in front of their fathers. He burned men alive with wildfire and laughed as they screamed" ("The House of Black and White"). Selmy's foreboding admonition to Daenerys is that the Mad King's descent into "madness" was not perceived as such by the king himself. He understood the countless executions as measured *justice*, as appropriate punishment for acts of treason and rebellion. His only madness, then, was the belief in an absolute good and evil and the presumption that he was capable of adjudicating between them.

George R. R. Martin explores the relative nature of the concepts of good and evil at length, to the extent that these may, in fact, be a crux of the series. Martin has made clear that, unlike the vast majority of fantasy works, he has an interest in establishing the difficulty of adjudicating between good and evil.

> I think the struggle between good and evil is central to fantasy and, indeed, in some ways, central to most fiction. It's certainly a worthy subject for fiction. But I regard the struggle between good and evil as being waged within the individual human heart . . . You know, the greatest monsters of history, as we look back on them, thought they were the heroes of the story. You know, the villain is the hero of the other side, as sometimes said. That doesn't mean that it's all morally relative. That doesn't mean that all things are equally good and evil. I think there is good and there is evil in the world. But you know, it's sometimes a struggle to tell one from the other and to make the right choices.[8]

Thus, the measure of justice demanded by the Targaryens of their victims, and any critical evaluation of their respective rules, according to such a rubric, is potentially circumstantial.

Daenerys's final speech on the stairs of the Red Keep establishes through visual allusion and explicit callbacks an entrenched pattern displaying the measures the Queen has taken to surround herself with a revolving door of backers who support and bolster her claim to the Iron Throne—armies, advisors, and benefactors. These backers-cum-abettors frequently demonstrate their allegiance to the would-be Queen of Westeros through their staunch and unflappable support of their queen's commitment to the notion of justice. Occasionally, this almost exclusively male cohort offers measured dissent, as witnessed in the recommendations of Selmy and Mormont, but she heeds their counsel with irregularity.

Her remarkable dynamism and conviction, though, have fatal consequence in the finale. Daenerys's attempt to "break" the wheel only sets the perilous wheel in motion. Her resolute commitment to justice and her assemblage of a group of enablers has the unintended effect of hoisting the would-be queen by her own petard. Because she has surrounded herself with people equally committed to the belief in absolute good and evil and an individual's ability to adjudicate between them, she ends up paying the ultimate price by becoming a victim of her own measure of justice. As with Aerys II Targaryen, she is blind to the fact that good and evil and the ability to adjudicate between them requires nuance and moral distinctions, and just as her father before her, she is stabbed in front of the Iron Throne, assassinated by the person self-sworn to protect her.

The conviction that humans somehow reap what they sow is, of course, not unique to *Game of Thrones*. The Hebrew Bible shares with *Game of Thrones* the view that actions and their consequences are inextricably correlated over a person's lifetime, and this correlation affects the capacity of humans to rule over each other. Indeed, the Bible exhibits similar uses of patterning to form critiques of leadership and may thus shed important light on the correlation between deed and consequence in *Game of Thrones*.

PATTERNING IN THE HEBREW BIBLE

In his seminal essay "Gibt es ein Vergeltungsdogma im Alten Testament? (Is there a Doctrine of Retribution in the Old Testament),"[9] Klaus Koch assessed whether the Hebrew Bible generally espouses a direct correlation between action and its consequences and coined the term deed-consequence nexus (*Tun-Ergehen-Zusammenhang*) to describe that correlation. To establish the deed-consequence nexus, Koch's study focused primarily on the book of Proverbs and identified a foundational assumption, "a construct which describes human actions which have a built-in consequence . . . [that] reflects on and articulates the close connection between the Good

Action-Blessings-Construct and the Wicked Action-Disaster-Construct as this applied to individuals."[10] What this process envisions is a self-perpetuating system, designed by the deity, in which consequence is systematically commensurate with human action. So we see, for instance, "The one digging a pit will fall into it, and a stone will come back onto the one who rolls it" (Prov 26:27).[11] In this illustrative example, neither result is punitive, according to Koch, but simply presented as a factual description of probable outcome or statistical likelihood.[12] Although important nuance has been added to Koch's original proposal,[13] the basic idea that the Hebrew Bible attests to a correlation between action and consequence has withstood critique.

The deed-consequence nexus is by no means limited to Proverbs; it, in fact, undergirds most of the sapiential literature of the Hebrew Bible and ancient Near East. Indeed, Koch identifies the author's inability to discern the correlation between action and consequence as a unifying element in Qohelet (Ecclesiastes). Throughout much of Qohelet, the apparent radical reevaluation of a correlation between action and consequence suggests the ubiquity of the concept throughout the ancient Near East.[14] So, for instance, when the author laments: "I have seen everything in my futile days. There is a righteous man who perishes in his righteousness and there is a wicked man who lives long in his evildoing," (Qoh 7:15) what renders the days of the author futile is the lack of consistency with the widely upheld correlation between action and consequence. Righteous people should live long lives, while wicked people should perish, and the author finds the observable exceptions to the paradigm unpalatable.

The nexus is especially prominent, too, in the so-called Deuteronomistic History (DtrH).[15] In the book of Deuteronomy, for instance, the action–consequence nexus is most plainly evident in the blessings and curses in the conclusion of the book (Deut 27–30). In the literary fabula, after summarizing much of the narrated history of the Torah and submitting a sizeable new legal corpus, the nexus is presented by Moses as a choice between life—obedience and blessing—and death—disobedience and curse. Thus, the blessings and curses at the end of the book constitute a list of potential positive and negative consequences that correspond to the Israelites' relative obedience to the previously stipulated covenant.

Predictably, this nexus also has significant ramifications in the related composition of Samuel–Kings,[16] concerning which scholars have long upheld the importance of patterning. Patterning is a particularly strong component in the book of Samuel, which tells the story of the rise and fall of King Saul and King David. For instance, the songs of Hannah (1 Sam 2) and David (2 Sam 22) have been identified as structural bookends of the larger composition.[17] Linguistically, we have strong evidence to suggest these two songs are related in some way; in particular, the repetition of several key words including exult (*'alaṣ/ramah*), enemies (*'ōyēḇ*), rock (*ṣûr*), king (*mlk*), and anoint (*mšḥ*) in both songs. Famously, Brevard Childs understood the canonical function of the two songs to indicate "an interpretive key for this history which is, above all, to be understood from a theocentric perspective."[18] Childs, thus, read these songs as typological episodes in a more significant and predictable pattern of divine action, or, as he put it: "God exalts the poor and debases the proud."[19] Robert Polzin, building on the work of Childs, finds a significant number of additional linguistic features shared between the two songs, ultimately arguing that the two "form a poetic inclusion" for the book of Samuel.[20]

Many of these structural parallels also reflect the deep ideological ambivalence toward kingship in ancient Israel. A good example of this is the dual prophecies of Nathan concerning construction of the Jerusalem Temple (2 Samuel 7) and his condemnation of David's murder of Uriah (2 Samuel 12), framing the rise and fall of David, respectively. The former marks a high point in David's reign, with the king presuming to replace the existing tent storing the ark of the covenant with a permanent temple (literally "house"; *bayit*) for the deity. God declines David's offer, but responds in kind by promising to build an everlasting line (again, "house"; *bayit*) for David. This is in resolute contrast to Nathan's rebuke of David after his affair with Bathsheba and execution of her husband, Uriah. Strikingly, although the overall tone of the first prophecy is positive and the latter is negative, both preserve a certain dubiety about the monarchical institution. As Rosenberg notes of the 2 Samuel 7 prophecy:

> Nathan seems simultaneously to say yes and no to David's proposal . . . .The Temple will be built, but by a successor to David, not by David; the dynastic successors of David will have everlasting rule (the house indeed survived in exile and passed from there into Jewish messianism) but will also suffer punishments for their moral failings; the throne will be secure, but it will also be vulnerable; it will survive the onslaughts of others, but it will not be protected from itself.[21]

A similar ambivalence can be observed in the second prophecy, too, wherein the child conceived in their affair is condemned to death, and the house of David will be subjected to external threats, but not destroyed. David's mourning also encapsulates this duality: he sorrowfully repents, but the first child still dies, and through the ensuing rituals over their lost child and the comfort David offers Bathsheba, she conceives a second son, Solomon, David's successor. Importantly, we can observe the wrought relationship between action and recompense, and that the threats to the Davidic line are consequences born out of their own actions.

The use of the relationship between actions and their consequences to emphasize an ambivalence toward the institution of the monarchy can be further observed in two additional examples from Saul and David. These intertwined stories depict the transition from the period of the judges to monarchy in Israel under the leadership of its first two kings. Although both rulers hold considerable promise at the beginning of their rule, through a series of misguided choices, their reigns ultimately end in utter ruin. The first example—the two condemnations of Saul by Samuel (1 Sam 13–15 and 1 Sam 28–31)—demonstrates how the ascent and descent of monarchs in Samuel is contiguous with the correlation of actions and their consequences. Rosenberg described "conspicuous symmetries" between these two sections of 1 Samuel,[22] including several smaller structuring units: first, the doublet of David's refusal to kill Saul (1 Sam 24, 26) around the story of David's impulsivity toward Nabal (1 Sam 25); and, second, the three appearances of Samuel (1 Sam 16, 25, and 28) interspersed at the beginning, middle, and end of the core of the macro structure. These two structural elements—David's (lack of) constraint and the appearances of Samuel—are framed by Saul's brazen act of disobedience by fighting the Philistines (1 Sam 13) and his ultimate defeat and death at the hands of the Philistines (1 Sam 30–31). In this way, the structural presentation of the protracted demise of Saul and the simultaneous rise of David can be seen as a consequence of the earlier act of disobedience.

As a second example, scholars have long pointed to the symmetries between David's sexual misconduct with Bathsheba (2 Sam 11) and its reflex in the incestuous rape of Tamar (2 Sam 13) by her brother, David's son, Amnon.[23] Among those who have granted the similarities between the two stories, Jan Fokkelman described Amnon as a "chip off the old block,"[24] replicating many of his father's fundamental character flaws; namely, impulsivity and sexual deviancy.[25] In this way, the story of Tamar's rape by Amnon may function as a partial fulfillment of Nathan's prophetic response to David's sexual transgression with Bathsheba (2 Sam 12:1–14). That is, the structural parallels between David's actions (2 Sam 11) and the story of Tamar and Amnon (2 Sam 13) suggest that the latter is a consequence of the former and should be understood as the first glimpse of a fulfillment of Nathan's prophecy to David:

> The sword will never depart from your house because you have despised me by taking the wife of Uriah the Hittite to be your wife . . . and I will raise up evil against you from within your own house. (2 Sam 12:10–11a)

To further underscore the ubiquity of the deed-consequence paradigm, a final example from the book of Esther is also instructive. In this story, the villain, the King's advisor Haman, devises a genocidal plot to kill all the Jews in Persia, including Mordecai, the cousin and adoptive father of Esther. As part of this plot, Haman erects a pole on which Mordecai will be impaled, but, through the intervention of Esther, the King thwarts Haman's nefarious scheme and, learning of the pole Haman had erected for Mordecai, he resolves to have Haman executed on it instead. Thus Haman, not unlike David and Saul, is hoisted by his own petard. On this point, Jon Levenson has observed: "Ironically, it is Haman's gigantic self-regard and his exaggerated fear of disgrace that puts him on the course that will result in his most ignominious disgrace, and, finally, self-destruction (7:1–8:2)."[26]

Curiously absent from the book of Esther and the demise of Saul's and David's households is the active presence of God. With reference to the stories of Saul and David, Gerhard von Rad argued that

> God's activity is not experienced now as something miraculous and intermittent, as in the old "holy wars." It is hidden to the natural eye, but is understood to be more continuous and all-embracing. God works in every sphere of life, public as well as private, in profane matters no less than in religious ones.[27]

The deity is even more conspicuously absent from the entire book of Esther, save for, perhaps, a single oblique reference by Mordecai that help may arise for the Jews from "another quarter" if Esther refuses to act on their behalf ("If you remain silent at this time, relief and deliverance will arise from another quarter, but you and the house of your father will perish. And who knows? Maybe it is for this occasion that you have come into the royal estate"; Esth 4:14). On this point, Levenson supports a theological understanding of the verse on the basis of the expression "who knows" (*mî yôdēaʿ*), citing other places in the Hebrew Bible where it is used to entreat the deity for deliverance from punishment. One of these places, in fact, is David's hope to stymie God's plan to kill the son conceived through his affair with Bathsheba (2 Sam 12:22).[28] If Levenson is right, it is possible that "another quarter" in Esth 4:14 is a "theological affirmation."[29] Still, the reference is evasive about the direct intercession of the deity in the doling out or prevention of punishments.

From the examples presented, we can distill six key points. As is made abundantly clear in the work of Klaus Koch and those that follow his assertion of the deed-consequence nexus, (1) the existence of consequence is decidedly *not* divine retribution. The examples of Saul and David demonstrate how the book of Samuel is structured to present the downfall of the reigning monarchs of Israel as tied to their negative behavior. Moreover, these examples demonstrate that (2) Kings and nobility are not exempt from and may be even more tightly bound to the consequences of their action. (3) The presentation of kingship in the Hebrew Bible suggests a general ambivalence about the capacity of humans to rule over each other. Encoded within the first fledgling institutions of human leadership in ancient Israel is the overall sense that the entire enterprise of humans ruling other humans is simply doomed to fail. Noticeably, (4) these failures are often commensurate with an ascent to power, suggesting that ruling may, in fact, distort one's judgment and promote a tendency to prioritize the amassing of influence and dominance. (5) Theological activity is often ambiguous or implicit, and in many of the examples reviewed, curiously absent in the deed-consequence nexus. This may be in part due to the sense that action and consequence work themselves out within the parameters of the due course established by the deity. Perhaps most important, though, is the critical assertion that (6) exceptions to the deed-consequence nexus exist. This insistence is the fundamental basis of, for instance, Qohelet and Job, but it is also embedded within texts that challenge the correlation between action and consequence; for example, the plight of Job, or the "better than" Proverbs: "Better is a poor man who walks in his integrity than a rich man who is crooked in his ways" (Prov 28:6). Were the deed-consequence nexus consistently true, a man with integrity should not be poor, and a crooked man should not be rich. Thus, we must be exceedingly cautious when retrospectively ascribing actions to perceived consequences.

In reviewing the use of patterning in *Game of Thrones* and the Hebrew Bible, a number of thematic affinities begin to emerge between these two works. The remainder of this chapter will consider these key affinities, paying special attention to their resonance with these six key points about the deed-consequence nexus in the Hebrew Bible.

THE SHAME OF THRONES

Almost immediately following the tragic beheading of Missandei, Daenerys's Naathi translator,[30] speculation was rampant about the imminent transformation of Daenerys's into the Mad Queen.[31] While some of this speculation engaged unhelpful, misogynistic expectations of how a woman should (not) behave in certain contexts,[32] many looked for indications of Daenerys's decline in earlier episodes and similarities in behavior to her father's.[33] This search for logical patterns and evidence from previous episodes was essentially performing the task viewers had been trained to do throughout the season.

This resolute determination to divulge and synthesize patterns in the downfall of monarchs has notable affinities with our discussion of the Hebrew Bible. The idea that Daenerys's present and future consequences can somehow be determined and better understood through a thorough investigation of her past actions, is, of course, strikingly consistent with Klaus Koch's articulation of the deed-consequence nexus. In both instances, the failings of

Saul and David in Samuel, and the tragic decline of Daenerys Targaryen, the consequences of errant rulers are demonstrably linked to their earlier actions. Curiously, though, for all the explicit discussion about the involvement of deities and their ability to intercede and influence the fate of humankind, in both works, an explicitly articulated theology is noticeably absent. It is truly remarkable that while both works establish ample precedent for the active role of deities, and have an apparent vested interest in establishing a correlation between the actions of rulers and the consequences of those actions, there is no real sense that any deity—whether YHWH, Rhallor, or the Old or the New gods—has a specific role in doling out those consequences; or, as the book of Esther would have it, the sense is that they arise from a self-sustaining system that requires no divine intervention.[34] Thus, just as the Hebrew Bible establishes that Kings and nobility have no exemption from the deed-consequence nexus, both texts also resist a notion of divine retribution.

Both works also demonstrate a deeply held pessimism about human proficiency to self-govern, which may have been evident in its title. When George R. R. Martin's fantasy series made the enormous leap from page to screen, HBO assumed the title of the first book, *A Game of Thrones*, as its series title—indefinite article notwithstanding—and eschewed the title of the fantasy series, *A Song of Ice and Fire*. The title of the HBO series and the first book is, of course, derived from Cersei Lannister's ominous warning to Eddard (Ned) Stark in the gardens of the Red Keep: "In the *game of thrones*, you win, or you die." Likely due to the title of the HBO series, this may be one of the more famous mottos from the story.[35]

Cersei's ostensibly wise counsel, however, is patently contradicted throughout the show in a number of important ways. Examples abound throughout the show of men who die chiefly because they are kings, declaring themselves rightful King of the Seven Kingdoms and then almost immediately meeting their demise. By episode seven—the aptly titled "You Win or You Die"—when Cersei warns Ned, we are already painfully aware of the events of Robert's Rebellion, including the murder of the Mad King Aerys II Targaryen at the hands of the King Slayer, Jaime Lannister, and the subsequent usurpation by Robert Baratheon.[36] Moreover, by the end of "You Win or You Die," Robert Baratheon succumbs to the hunting wounds he sustained—as result of the treasonous plotting of Cersei Lannister—with the line of his succession cast in doubt by the yield of Cersei's incestuous affair with her brother Jaime. These examples, and many others,[37] suggest that in the *game of thrones*, kings and queens win and die anyway.

Indeed, nowhere in the series is this tension felt more prominently than in its final episodes, where we see, in rapid succession, the somewhat shocking deaths of three presumed winners of the *game of thrones* who are summarily executed: the annihilation of the Night King after laying waste to Winterfell ("The Long Night"), the death of Queen Cersei after the siege of King's Landing ("Bells"), and the murder of Daenerys Targaryen mere moments after realizing her destiny and touching the Iron Throne for the first time ("Iron Throne"). These three deaths deeply betray Martin's assertion that the most significant struggles for power happen on the periphery of political machinations, but also undercut the Cerseian logic of the *game of thrones*.[38] Thus, a considerate view of Westerosi rulership might be more closely summarized as, "In the *game of thrones*, you win *and then* you die," or, more simply, with the ubiquitous Braavosi greeting, "*Valar Marghulis*" ("All men must die"). Which is to say, perhaps the deeds of kings and queens are only tangentially related to their consequence if at all.

To undercut the integrity of the enterprise of power acquisition and maintenance so severely attests to a more deeply held pessimism about human proficiency to self-govern as the cynosure of the series, a concern, as we have seen, that is witnessed in both secular *and* sacred literature. Examples of such pessimism concerning the capacity for human beings to rule over one another include, for instance, the acknowledged parallels between Martin's *A Song of Ice and Fire* series and the seven-part series of historical novels, *Les Rois maudits* (*The Accursed Kings*), which chronicles the failures and skullduggery of the French monarchy during the fourteenth century.[39] But to stop at Druon would be, historically speaking, shortsighted.

Nearly all the examples we have examined concerning Saul and David betray an ambivalence about the capacity of humans to rule over each other similar to what we can observe in *Game of Thrones*. As an example, we can recall that even when David receives Nathan's prophecy foretelling the promise of a perpetual Davidic line (2 Sam 7), that same prophecy captures both the endurance and the vulnerability of that promise equally. Moreover, just as the Hebrew Bible recognizes that failures and their related consequences are often commensurate with a monarch's ascent to power, we see strikingly similar downfalls in the kings and queens of Westeros.[40] This may suggest that both works perceive a negative correlation between power and self-awareness. Just as the Hebrew Bible reveals ways in which power has the potential to distort one's judgment and promote the amassing of influence and dominance, we see an almost identical impulse in the various rulers of Westeros.

Over the course of eight seasons, Daenerys amasses armies and allies that share her notion of justice, but when she most strongly exhibits those principles by destroying King's Landing, she ignites the very sense of justice that attracted Jon Snow to her; recalling the forewarning of Proverbs 26:27 (cited above), in her ardent pursuit to crush the wheel, the wheel rolls back to crush her. Tragically, just as Daenerys realizes her dream of the Iron Throne, she is murdered before it by Jon Snow, in his own pursuit of justice, in recompense for her destruction of King's Landing.

Interestingly, both the Hebrew Bible and *Game of Thrones* also suggest a significant disjuncture in an audience's expectation and tolerance for incoherence within a canonical corpus.[41] As the Hebrew Bible developed over time and space, Bible scholars posit that the redaction process created evidence of multiple perspectives—theological, political, and so on—exerting themselves in the textual compilation process. Thus, we find, for instance, a certain level of dissatisfaction in the incoherence of biblical texts in the tendency of Bible scholars to attest and parse the existence of multiple sources within and across multiple books to account for inconsistent textual features. So, for instance, biblical scholars are loathed to read the bookending songs of Hannah (1 Sam 2) and David (2 Sam 22), discussed above, as continuous with the narrative material between them. They are an inconsistent, secondary creation. The ostensible lack of continuity, though, presented apparently far fewer problems during the historical redaction process. Consequently, we can attribute the perception of discontinuity as being specific to a particular audience's expectation of an individual work. When a theologically oriented audience expects a continuous, uniform, perhaps even divinely inspired narrative, exceptions to that expectation must be methodologically explained.[42]

This modern commitment to finding continuity in biblical literature is also, to some extent, at the root of the development and identification of the deed-consequence nexus. Scholars often posit that it arose in large part during the exilic and post-exilic period to explain why the Israelites had been forcibly deported from the land that was promised to them. The exile was the observable consequence and so its concomitant deed must be discernable in the covenant disloyalty demonstrated by previous generations of Israelites. Thus, to the extent that a deed-consequence nexus does exist in the Hebrew Bible, the very nature of the relationship between actions and their consequences likely arose out of and benefited from a sort of retrospective view of history at the same time that the canon itself was being negotiated.

Game of Thrones as a series, on the other hand, had no such luck. The show runners, and Martin himself, were actively negotiating the ideas of narrative content and canon as both series—book and show—progressed. Some of that tension naturally developed through the migration of Martin's story from page to screen. It manifested nowhere more clearly than in the post-canonical world of Benioff and Weiss in the final three seasons of the show where a disjuncture was created by its passing through multiple hands. Once those multiple perspectives became discernibly palpable, audience dissatisfaction in the unambiguous disunity became evidenced in the precipitous decline in audience satisfaction with the ending of the show.[43] Audiences desired continuity and their fandom—its own sort of religious or theological devotion—created an expectation not met by the show.

CONCLUSION

Both the Hebrew Bible and *Game of Thrones* point to ways in which our ethical systems are often far more relative than we, or Daenerys Targaryen, or King David, would choose to admit. What furthers our own interests is judged to be objectively "good," whether it be Daenerys Targaryen launching an all-out, scorched earth campaign against King's Landing, or Saul's waging war against the Philistines. Consequently, no ruler, mad or otherwise, ever thinks of themselves as evil. Rather, what the ascent and descent of Daenerys suggest is that given the options, rulers—and nearly all humans—will always choose what is in their own best interest, and often surround themselves with enablers who will promote those interests. Indeed, what the sum total of the show suggests is that humans have an enormous propensity for ethical relativism, and even those characters judged to be morally upright are capable of heinous acts when believed to be in the service of some greater, or personal, good.[44]

Our review of the deed-consequence nexus in the Hebrew Bible also offers important nuance for *Game of Thrones*. The pervasive intentional patterning between episodes serves an obvious artistic function, but the use of patterning to predict and foreshadow outcomes has distinctively theological underpinnings—whether intentional or not. This is not to say that *Game of Thrones* takes its notion of the relationship between cause and effect from the Hebrew Bible, but rather the belief that actions are somehow linked to consequences requires, in some way, an orchestrator of the system. In the Hebrew Bible, this link is intentionally theologized for obvious reasons, but the surprising but inescapable presence of a correlation between action and consequence in *Game of Thrones* exposes a subtle theological logic for the show as well. This subtly reaffirms what can be observed in the biblical text, that theological activity is often ambiguous or implicit in the relationship between action and consequence, as is the case with Esther or the sapiential literature of the Hebrew Bible.

Finally, *Game of Thrones* redirects our attention back to an important characteristic of the deed-consequence nexus within Hebrew Bible; namely, that there are obvious exceptions to the relationship between actions and consequences. As we discussed above, the persistence of the so-called heterodox wisdom of Qohelet and Job, but also the "better than" proverbs, demonstrate the ways in which the observable universe is often incompatible with our expectations of the speed and viability of the attested pattern. Accordingly, while *Game of Thrones* does point to an extended propensity for the use of patterns to discern and account for consequence, we are also reminded that, according to the Hebrew Bible at least, not every action has its appropriate reaction. Perhaps Daenerys of the House Targaryen, the First of Her Name, The Unburnt, Queen of the Andals, the Rhoynar and the First Men, Queen of Meereen, Khaleesi of the Great Grass Sea, Protector of the Realm, Lady Regent of the Seven Kingdoms, Breaker of Chains and Mother of Dragons, was never fully bound to a pattern to begin with.

NOTES

1. Kathryn VanArendonk, "This Is the Best *Game of Thrones* Premiere Since the Pilot," Vulture.com, 14 April 2019, https://www.vulture.com/2019/04/game-of-thrones-season-8-premiere-review.html.

2. VanArendonk, "Best *Game of Thrones* Premiere."

3. Willa Paskin, "Last Call in Westeros," *Brow Beat*, Slate.com, 14 April 2019, https://slate.com/culture/2019/04/game-of-thrones-season-8-premiere-review.html.

4. Kathryn VanArendonk, "Is Time a Problem for *Game of Thrones*?" Vulture.com, 21 August 2017, https://www.vulture.com/2017/08/game-of-thrones-season-7-timeline-chronology-problems.html; Julia Alexander, "*Game of Thrones*' Main Problem This Season Can Be Explained in a Few Maps," Polygon.com, 22 August 2017, https://www.polygon.com/2017/8/22/16180630/game-of-thrones-season-7-episode-6-pacing-distance-maps; Christopher Hooton, "*Game of Thrones* season 7 pacing: Episode 6 director admits 'there was some effort to fudge the timeline a little'," Independent.co.uk, 22 August 2017, https://www.independent.co.uk/arts-entertainment/tv/news/game-of-thrones-season-7-episode-6-beyond-the-wall-director-pacing-speed-raven-gendry-the-wall-a7905961.html.

5. Nina Shen Rastogi, "The Real Purpose of Spirals on *Game of Thrones*," Vulture.com, 16 April 2019, https://www.vulture.com/2019/04/game-of-thrones-season-8-spiral-shapes.html. The original quote has "show" instead of "story"; I have changed it for reasons that will be clear imminently.

6. It should also be noted that often New Girl creates entirely new scenes to participate in this genre or trope. That is, it does not include clips from previous episodes but rather creates pasts for its characters and sequences them into montages.

7. The apothegm is explicitly recalled by Bran when Jaime appeals to Daenerys and the Starks to allow him to fight on their behalf against the Night King's army.

8. George R. R. Martin, "George R. R. Martin talks to David Shuster," interview by David Shuster, 13 November 2014, 2014, AlJazeera America, http://america.aljazeera.com/watch/shows/talk-to-al-jazeera/articles/2014/11/13/george-rr-martintalkstodavidshuster.html.

9. Klaus Koch, "Gibt es ein Vergeltungsdogma im Alten Testament?," *ZTK* 52 (1955): 1–42. For an abbreviated English translation, see Klaus Koch, "Is There a Doctrine of Retribution in the Old Testament," in *Theodicy in the Old Testament*, ed. James L. Crenshaw, IRT 4 (Philadelphia: Fortress Press, 1983), 57–87.

10. Koch, "Is There a Doctrine of Retribution in the Old Testament," 64.

11. For further discussion on act and consequence in Proverbs with a particular focus on its implications for interpreting death in the Second Temple period, see Samuel L. Adams, *Wisdom in Tradition: Acts and Consequence in Second Temple Instructions*, JSOTSup 125 (Leiden: Brill, 2008), 53–100.

12. Important critiques of Koch's work focus primarily on his lack of attention to the sociological function of sapiential instruction in the ancient Near East, the passivity of YHWH in bringing about consequence, and the appropriateness of the concept of *Vergeltung* ("retribution"); see Carl-Albert Keller, "Zum sogenannten Vergeltungsglauben im Proverbienbuch," in *Beiträge zur alttestamentlichen Theologie: Festschrift für Walther Zimmerli zum 70. Geburtstag*, ed. Herbert Donner, Robert Hanart, and Rudolf Smend (Göttingen: Vandenhoeck & Ruprecht, 1977), 223–38; Jan Assmann, *Ma'at: Gerechtigkeit und Unsterblichkeit im alten Ägypten* (Munich: Beck, 1990); Lennart Boström, *The God of the Sages: The Portrayal of God in the Book of Proverbs*, CBOTS 29 (Stockholm: Almqvist and Wiksell International, 1990); Bernd Janowski, "Die Tat kehrt zum Täter zurück: Offene Fragen im Umkreis des »Tun-Ergehen-Zusammenhangs«," *ZTK* 91 (1994): 247–71; Elizabeth Huwiler, "Control of Reality in Israelite Wisdom" (PhD diss., Duke University, 1988), 64. For two recent applications see Adams, *Wisdom in Tradition*; Georg Freuling, *»Wer eine Grube gräbt...« Der Tun-Ergehen-Zusammenhang und sein Wandel in der alttestamentliche Weisheitliteratur*, WMANT 102 (Neukirchen-Vluyn: Neukirchener Verlag, 2004).

13. See Hans H. Schmid, *Gerechtigkeit als Weltordnung*, BHT 40 (Tübingen: Mohr, 1968); Ronald E. Murphy, *The Tree of Life: An Exploration of Biblical Wisdom Literature*, 3rd ed. (Grand Rapids: Eerdmans, 1990); Michael V. Fox, "World Order and Ma'at: A Crooked Parallel," *JANESCU* 23 (1995): 37–48.

14. Adams treats the existence of the paradigm in Egyptian literature at length; see Adams, *Wisdom in Tradition*, 15–52; and also Fox, "World Order and Ma'at," 37–48.

15. The Deuteronomistic History is a scholarly construct established by Martin Noth that groups the books of Deuteronomy with the Former Prophets (Joshua, Judges, Samuel, and Kings) on the basis of similar language, style, and content. Martin Noth, *Überlieferungsgeschichtliche Studien: Die sammelnden und bearbeitenden Geschichtswerke im Alten Testament*, Schriften der Königsberger Gelehrten Gesellschaft Geisteswissenschaftliche Klasse 18 (Tübingen: Max Niemeyer, 1943). Noth's work builds on the earlier work of W. M. L. de Wette; Wilhelm Martin Leberecht de Wette, *Beiträge zur Einleitung in das Alte Testament* (Halle: Schimmelpfennig, 1807). For recent explanations of the corpus as well as the challenges and potential problems with treating it as a single literary work, see Thomas Römer, *The So-Called Deuteronomistic History: A Sociologica, Historical, and Literary Introduction* (Edinburgh: T & T Clark, 2007); Richard Coggins, "What Does 'Deuteronomistic' Mean?" in *Those Elusive Deuteronomists: The Phenomenon of Pan-Deuteronomism*, ed. Linda S. Schearing and Steven L. McKenzie, JSOTSup (Sheffield: Sheffield Academic Press, 1999), 22–35; Douglas A. Knight, "Deuteronomy and Deuteronomists," in *Old Testament Interpretation; Past, Present, and Future; Essays in Honour of Gene M. Tucker*, ed. James Luther

Mays (Edinburgh: T & T Clark, 1995), 61–79; Richard Elliott Friedman, "The Deuteronomistic School," in *Fortunate the Eyes That See: Essays in Honor of David Noel Freedman in Celebration of His Seventieth Birthday*, ed. Astrid B. Beck et al. (Grand Rapids, MI: Eerdmans, 1995), 70–80; Moshe Weinfeld, *Deuteronomy and the Deuteronomic School* (Winona Lake, IN: Eisenbrauns, 1992).

16. The most comprehensive treatment of patterning in Samuel can be found in Jan P. Fokkelman, *Narrative Art and Poetry in the Books of Samuel: A Full Interpretation Based on Stylistic and Structural Analyses*, 4 vols., SSN 20, 23, 27, 31 (Assen: Van Gorcum, 1981–1993).

17. Concerning the structural importance of 2 Samuel 22, Joel Rosenberg has also commented on its contrast to the following chapter and its use to "epitomize" the first part of David's career; Joel Rosenberg, "1 and 2 Samuel," in *The Literary Guide to the Bible*, ed. Robert Alter and Frank Kermode (Cambridge, MA: Belknap Press, 1987), 140.

18. Brevard S. Childs, *Introduction to the Old Testament as Scripture* (Philadelphia: Fortress Press, 1979), 274.

19. Childs, *Introduction*, 278. Walter Brueggemann expanded Childs's work to adjacent chapters, see Walter Brueggeman, "1 Samuel 1: A Sense of a Beginning," *ZAW* 102 (1990): 33–48. Randall Bailey granted the structural framing of the two songs, but denied their historical function and instead argued that they serve to present an orthodox presentation of the deity, Randall C. Bailey, "The Redemption of YHWH: A Literary Critical Function of the Songs of Hannah and David," *BI* 3 (1995): 213–31.

20. Robert Polzin, *Samuel and the Deuteronomist: A Literary Study of the Deuteronomic History Part Two, 1 Samuel* (New York: Harper & Row, 1989), 31. See also the work of Rolf Carlson who identifies Deuteronomic links between the two works, Rolf A. Carlson, *David, the Chosen King* (Stockholm: Almquist & Wiksell, 1964).

21. Rosenberg, "1 and 2 Samuel," 142.

22. Rosenberg, "1 and 2 Samuel," 129.

23. Theory about the literary unity and cohesion of large parts of the book of 2 Samuel, and in particular the Succession Narrative, was shaped in large part by Leonhard Rost, who argued that the royal succession was a unifying element of sections of 2 Samuel and 1 Kings 1–2, Leonhard Rost, *Die Überlieferung von der Thronnachfolge Davids*, BWANT 3 (Stuttgart: Kohlhammer, 1926). The main points of Rost's argument have been largely maintained in the more recent work of R. N. Whybray, *The Succession Narrative: A Study of II Sam. 9–20 and I Kings 1 and 2*, SBT 2/ 9 (Naperville, IL: Allenson, 1968); James W. Flanagan, "Court History or Succession Document? A Study of 2 Sam 9–20 and 1 Kings 1–2," *JBL* 91 (1972): 172–81; Charles Conroy, *Absalom Absalom! Narrative and Language in 2 Sam 13–20*, AnBib 8 (Rome: Biblical Institute, 1978), 1–13; P. Kyle McCarter, Jr., "'Plots, True or False.' The Succession Narrative as Court Apologetic," *Interpretation* 35 (1981): 355–67; P. Kyle McCarter, Jr., *2 Samuel: A New Translation with Introduction and Commentary*, AB 9 (New York: Doubleday, 1989), 9–16; Arnold A. Anderson, *2 Samuel*, WBC 11 (Waco: Word, 1989), xxv–xxxvi.

24. Jan P. Fokkelman, *Narrative Art and Poetry in the Books of Samuel: A Full Interpretation Based on Stylistic and Structural Analyses (Sam 9–20 & Kings 1–2)*, vol. 1, SSN 20 (Assen: Van Gorcum, 1981), 99.

25. This view is upheld to a greater or lesser degree by, i.a., Hans Wilhelm Hertzberg, *I and II Samuel: A Commentary*, OTL (Loondon: SCM Press, 1964), 322; John Mauchline, *1 and 2 Samuel* (London: Oliphants, 1971), 259; David M. Gunn, *The Story of King David*, JSOTSup 6 (Sheffield: JSOT Press, 1978), 100; Howard F. Vos, *1, 2 Samuel* (Grand Rapids: Zondervan, 1983), 133; Regina M. Schwartz, "Adultery in the House of David: The Metanarrative of Biblical Scholarship and the Narratives of the Bible," *Semeia* 54 (1991): 47–49; Danna N. Fewell and David M. Gunn, *Gender, Power, and Promise: The Subject of the Bible's First Story* (Nashville: Abingdon Press, 1993), 157; Mark Gray, "Amnon: A Chip off the Old Block? Rhetorical Strategy in 2 Samuel 13.7–15 The Rape of Tamar and the Humiliation of the Poor," *JSOT* 77 (1998): 39–54.

26. Jon D. Levenson, *Esther: A Commentary*, OTL (Louisville: Westminster John Knox Press, 1997), 69.

27. Gerhard von Rad, "The Beginnings of Historical Writing in Ancient Israel," in *The Problem of the Hexateuch and Other Essays* (Edinburgh: Oliver and Boyd, 1966), 202.

28. See also Joel 2:14 and Jonah 3:9.

29. Levenson, *Esther*, 81.

30. A separate but important critique levied after this scene aired focused on the massacres of the Unsullied and Dothroaki armies in "The Long Night," and Missandei's death, pointing out nearly all characters of color had been unceremoniously eviscerated from the show. See Ben Philippe, "How *Game of Thrones* Failed Missandei," VanityFair.com, 6 May 2019, https://www.vanityfair.com/hollywood/2019/05/game-of-thrones-missandei-death-season-8-episode-4; Aja Romano, "*Game of Thrones*' Missandei Controversy, Explained," Vox.com, 6 May 2019, https://www.vox.com/2019/5/6/18530526/game-of-thrones-season-8-episode-4-death-who-died-missandei-daenerys; Kathryn VanArendonk, "*Game of Thrones* Did Brienne and Missandei Dirty," Vulture.com, https://www.vulture.com/2019/05/game-of-thrones-brienne-missandei-last-of-the-starks.html; Gretchen Smail, "Missandei's Death On '*Game Of Thrones*' Was Tragic In More Ways Than One," Bustle.com, 6 May 2019, https://www.bustle.com/p/missandeis-death-on-game-of-thrones-was-tragic-in-more-ways-than-one-17305617.

31. Alex Abad-Santos, "*Game of Thrones*' Mad Queen Theory, Explained," Vox.com, 5 May 2019, https://www.vox.com/2019/5/5/18530451/game-of-thrones-season-8-episode-4-daenerys-dracarys-mad-queen; Nate Jones, "Is Daenerys Doomed to Become the Mad Queen on *Game of Thrones*?," Vulture.com, 7 May 2019, https://www.vulture.com/2019/05/game-of-thrones-theory-daenerys-mad-queen.html.

32. Joanna Robinson, "Is *Game of Thrones* Really Setting up the Battle of the Mad Queens?," 5 May 2019, https://www.vanityfair.com/hollywood/2019/05/game-of-thrones-season-8-episode-4-daenerys-mad-queen-villain-twist; Zack Sharf, "'*Game of Thrones*': Daenerys' Mad Queen Twist Enrages Fans, Megan Ellison and More Slam Writers," IndieWire.com, 13 May 2019, https://www.indiewire.com/2019/05/game-of-thrones-daenerys-mad-queen-reactions-sexist-1202140198/.

33. Jennifer Vineyard, "At the Red Keep, '*Game of Thrones*' History Repeats Itself," NYTimes.com, 13 May 2019, https://www.nytimes.com/2019/05/13/arts/television/game-of-thrones-red-keep.html.

34. On the self-sustaining system in Job, see Tsevat Matitiahu, "The Meaning of the Book of Job," *HUCA* 37 (1966): 73–106.

35. Excluding, perhaps, "Winter is coming"—the oft-cited words of House Stark—and Ygritte's taunting jibe, "You know nothing, Jon Snow."

36. The details of Robert's Rebellion are revealed throughout the course of the show. The earliest detailed discussion can be found between Robert Baratheon and Ned Stark in "The Kingsroad" (season 1, episode 2).

37. To these we could also add the commitment of Khal Drogo to take the Iron throne, followed by the injury that leads to his death ("You Win or You Die"; "Fire and Blood"); the fratricide of Renly Baratheon by the conjured shadow ("The Ghost of Harrenhal"); the murder of Robb Stark at the Red Wedding ("The Rains of Castemere"); Olenna Tyrell's ensuing poisoning of Joffrey Baratheon at the Purple Wedding ("The Lion and the Rose"); the siege of Castle Black by Mance Rayder and his resulting his death sentence ("The Wars to Come"); Stannis Baratheon's presumed decapitation by Brienne of Tarth ("Mother's Mercy"); Tommen's suicide upon witnessing the murder of his wife, Margaery Tyrell, at the hands of the Wildfire explosion set by Cersei ("Winds of Winter"). While one might rightfully object to a number of these examples on the more technical grounds of succession rights, the vast majority recount seemingly lawfully, acknowledged, installed kings and queens of Westeros and beyond.

38. Martin, "George R. R. Martin Talks."

39. The earlier work, in fact, was so acutely influential on the latter series that Martin called it the "original *game of thrones*" in his forward to the reprinted translation, George R. R. Martin, foreword to *The Iron King*, by Maurice Druon (New York: HarperCollins, 2013).

40. For examples, see esp. n. 36, above.

41. For a recent treatment of how modern readers perceive (in)coherence in an ancient texts, see D. Andrew Teeter and William A. Tooman, eds., *Standards of (In)coherence in Ancient Jewish Literature*, *HBAI* 9 (2020): 90–261.

42. To be sure, attempts to explain discontinuity in the Hebrew Bible significantly predate modern biblical criticism. In fact, they can be seen within the biblical canon itself as well as early Jewish biblical interpretation, for example, midrash, which is characterized by its attention to detail, specifically the verbal, phonetic, and orthographic features of the text. As David Stern observes common characteristics between inner-biblical and post-biblical interpretation nothing that both tend to "harmonize conflicting or discordant verses; to reemploy and reapply biblical paradigms and imagery to new cases; to reinvent 'old' historical references with 'new' historical contexts; and to integrate non-historical-portions of the Bible within the larger context of biblical history." Both inner-biblical and post-biblical interpretation, then, share a sort of "prenatural sensitivity"—to use Stern's term—for discordance in scripture. David Stern, "Midrash and Midrashic Interpretation," in *The Jewish Study Bible* (Oxford University Press, 2004), 1865, 1870. See also, my own discussion of the

differences between traditional and modern midrashim, Eric X. Jarrard, "'Midrash? More like *Midtrash*!': Jewish Identity and Biblical Exposition in the Oeuvre of Darren Aronofsky." *Harvard Divinity Bulletin* 46 (2018): 69–76.

43. Seasons 5–8 received audience scores of 93, 82, and 30 percent on Rotten Tomatoes.

44. Recall that Ned Stark helps Robert Baratheon usurp the throne and lies to everyone to protect his nephew from that same man who he knows will murder an infant; Sansa declaring the secession of the North from the Seven Kingdoms to reclaim the autonomy of the North under her rulership; Bran remains silent in the wake of the desolation of the North to the Night King, and the South to Daenerys, so that he can be appointed the new king of Westeros.

WORKS CITED

Childs, Brevard S. *Introduction to the Old Testament as Scripture*. Philadelphia: Fortress Press, 1979.

Fokkelman, Jan P. *Narrative Art and Poetry in the Books of Samuel: A Full Interpretation Based on Stylistic and Structural Analyses (Sam 9–20 & Kings 1–2)*. Vol. 1. SSN 20. Assen: Van Gorcum, 1981.

Koch, Klaus. "Gibt es ein Vergeltungsdogma im Alten Testament?" *ZTK* 52 (1955): 1–42.

Levenson, Jon D. *Esther: A Commentary*. OTL. Louisville: Westminster John Knox Press, 1997.

Martin, George R. R. "George R. R. Martin talks to David Shuster." interview by David Shuster. 13 November 2014, 2014. *AlJazeera America*. http://america.aljazeera.com/watch/shows/talk-to-al-jazeera/articles/2014/11/13/george-rr-martintalkstodavidshuster.html.

Paskin, Willa. "Last Call in Westeros." *Brow Beat*. Slate.com. 14 April 2019. https://slate.com/culture/2019/04/game-of-thrones-season-8-premiere-review.html.

Polzin, Robert. *Samuel and the Deuteronomist: A Literary Study of the Deuteronomic History Part Two, 1 Samuel*. New York: Harper & Row, 1989.

Rastogi, Nina Shen. "The Real Purpose of Spirals on *Game of Thrones*." Vulture.com. 16 April 2019. https://www.vulture.com/2019/04/game-of-thrones-season-8-spiral-shapes.html.

Rosenberg, Joel. "1 and 2 Samuel." Pages 122–45 In *The Literary Guide to the Bible*. Edited by Robert Alter and Frank Kermode. Cambridge, MA: Belknap Press, 1987.

Teeter, D. Andrew, and William A. Tooman. "Editorial Introduction: Standards of (In)coherence in Ancient Jewish Literature." *HBAI* 9 (2020): 91–93.

VanArendonk, Kathryn. "This Is the Best *Game of Thrones* Premiere Since the Pilot." Vulture.com. 14 April 2019. https://www.vulture.com/2019/04/game-of-thrones-season-8-premiere-review.html.

von Rad, Gerhard. "The Beginnings of Historical Writing in Ancient Israel." In *The Problem of the Hexateuch and Other Essays*. Edinburgh: Oliver and Boyd, 1966.

Chapter 2

Targaryen Exceptionalism and Politics in the Sacred Structures of Westeros

Mollie Gossage and Edgar Valles

Why has *Game of Thrones* struck such a chord with fans, bringing in many viewers who had never read the books or who had never been fans of fantasy before? Perhaps the first reason that comes to mind is the series' uncommon dedication to a kind of realism, especially in terms of violence and its unpredictability. Unlike more traditional fantasy series—or even unlike most popular fiction in general—the heroes do not have a protective bubble shielding them from tragic or even meaningless anticlimactic ends. Because the show is like real life—sociopolitically complex and uncertain—viewers can be shocked by the plot's twists and turns while still finding them convincing. Characters' strategies to make sense of such a chaotic world are similarly dynamic and profound. In short, despite its magical elements, the show succeeds in feeling *real*, and is meaningful because of it. This has compelled a host of unlikely fantasy fans to become deeply invested in the series.

An inclination to take this fantasy *realistically* fuels on-going debates among fans over to what degree the characters within the story represent real behavioral possibilities. The show, unsatisfyingly to many, questioned and forefronted whether the Targaryens are insane (or not), and to what extent this insanity is genetic (i.e., the result of generations of incest). After all, the negative effects of isolated gene pools are now common knowledge. However, to carry on a debate over the scientific basis of Targaryen madness and their behavior in general is a form of perspectivism driven by our modernist insistence that there is just one objective version of reality and tendency to think that the only hidden structures worth pondering are material ones. Though to some extent it is unavoidable, projecting the rationalism of our own worldview into the *A Song of Ice and Fire* universe resists the more profound, troubling, and (we argue) relevant conclusions that arise when regarding Targaryen behavior in its socioreligious context. Why not use Martin's complex narrative, in particular the history of Targaryen rule, as a thought experiment for addressing the current political moment across pertinent sociocultural themes?

We take the Targaryen saga as an anthropological exploration of political authority in relation to religious structures. The house's rise and fall in Westeros may seem a mere contest of strength on the surface, but all the conflicts therein were fueled by the Targaryens' constant struggle to perform an awkward form of divinity despite the possibility of their common humanity. Westerosi citizens' openness or even need to believe in the divinity of their kings went hand-in-hand with Targaryen self-understanding and propelled an ultimately dangerous narrative of inherent superiority.

Much like the idealistic European immigrants who left religious persecution and traditional political structures of Europe aiming to create better, more liberal forms of governance in colonial and early America, Aegon I tried to set a foundation for stable, just, and tolerant Targaryen rule that was far removed from the dragonriders' conquesting and enslaving ways in Essos. Unable to claim authority based on autochthony in their foreign homes, the political legitimacy of each group of newcomers simultaneously demanded new logics and had to rely upon more deeply rooted institutions and existing senses of the world. Over time, structures of power conflated with religion to become hegemonic, acquiring a sense of self-evidentiality. Ignoring the religious foundations that initially made and continue to uphold authority blinds us to the fact that kings (or politicians) are but normal people and dangerous to the extent that they have come to internalize the structures that were used to set them apart. Governance through a central figure is therefore a confluence of intersecting interests working to convince the governed that subjugation and reverence toward leadership is the nature of the relationship.[1]

EXCEPTIONAL OUTSIDERS

The categories sacred and profane, insider and outsider do not occur naturally but are distinctions humans create to make sense of the world and our place within it. Considering the construction of such distinctions is important to understanding the fundamental ordering of society across both our own history and that of Westeros. In the *A Song of Ice and Fire* universe, perhaps the ultimate outsider category is inhabited by the Targaryens, the last dragonriders in the known world (while their relationship to the sacred is more complex and will be explored further below).

Many lines of dragonlords (and ladies) collectively dominated the eastern continent of Essos for thousands of years in the form of the "Valyrian

Freehold." Ruthless to all opposers, tolerant only to the submissive, they wreaked havoc on other civilizations from the back of their dragons. Such conquest was rationalized on the claim that they were "descended from dragons and were kin to the ones they now controlled."[2] Thus some Westerosi historians see it as a form of divine retribution that the Freehold was wiped out entirely through a mysterious cataclysm known simply as the Doom, which left Valyria uninhabitable even centuries later.

Interestingly, just *one* line of dragonlords was spared that fate. Daenys "the Dreamer" Targaryen foresaw the Doom of Valyria and her father's house relocated to Dragonstone in Westeros. Three sibling descendants of Daenys—Visenya, Aegon, and Rhaenys, along with their three dragons—would alter the history of their transplanted home, conquering Westeros and uniting its "Seven Kingdoms" for the first time. This act was not a mere continuation of power struggles either in the mode of Essos or Westeros. It established a new reckoning of space and time as well, with the date of Aegon's coronation by the High Septon in Oldtown marking year one in a new, sanctified calendar. The rule of the dragonlords in Westeros would be different than the reign of terror enacted by the Freehold. It was the Targaryens' status as outsiders in Westeros—as *exceptional* outsiders—that would define both the basis *and* the limits of their authority.

We argue that the saga of Targaryen reign (and here we will concentrate on that portion detailed in Martin's 2018 book *Fire and Blood*) is best understood as a negotiation of their own divine[3] status within and against the religious structures of Westeros. At the time of the Conquest, Westeros was already complexly pluri-religious, but the Andals' religion—the Faith of the Seven—was hegemonic among them, defining the social–moral order for the richest and most populated regions of Westeros. A small family with only a small foothold in the continent, the Targaryens could not merely employ the religious tolerance strategy of their erstwhile Valyrian kin, but had to submit themselves to the Andals' religion to win the support of its institution ("the Faith," headquartered in Oldtown) and its many followers. This submission was ever partial and incomplete, however, because the Targaryens' unique qualities—exemplified particularly in their dragon-bonding—meant that they could only truly relate to this cosmological order as elevated beings themselves set apart from all other humans. Rather than externalizing the sacred as in the many aspects of the Seven-Faced God, the Targaryens internalized the sacred and transcended common humanity. This performance constituted their legitimacy in the form of charisma, but produced constant tensions with the existing religious order, ultimately contributing to the loss of the dragons and loss of the throne.

THE SACRED IN WESTEROS: FROM ANIMISM TO EXTERNALIZATION

A series of migrations which preceded the Targaryens' brought different peoples from Essos to Westeros, breeding hostilities between distinct religio-cultural groups but eventuating in a majority assimilating to the Faith of the Seven. We further recognize the Faith of the Seven as the dominant religious structure due to its power to anoint, and thus formally legitimate, the one ruler of the Seven Kingdoms and designate him as both King of the Andals *and* the First Men. This foundational act served to conflate the Faith's divine power as mouthpieces for the gods with the Targaryens' more mysterious claims of suprahumanity, thereafter confounding the Faith's monopoly on power to make consecrated judgments and allowing for new arrangements of individual will, institutional power, and morality.

To better understand the Targaryen mystique, it helps to review the early confrontations between the different belief systems as they came into contact on the continent. We can glean from what legends tell that the indigene of Westeros—the giants and Children of the Forest—understood the world far differently from the human species that would supplant them. Their animistic[4] beliefs had no formal institutional manifestation but elevated nature as an object of sacred reverence. For later inhabitants of Westeros, this magic was far beyond the realm of either believability or acceptability, and the carved "heart trees" remain frightening to those whose religions turned away from the apparent crudeness of animism to more social-institutional models. Thus as humans came to Westeros and the so-called First Men moved up the continent, their razing of the weirwoods incited prolonged conflicts with the children. After many years, "The Pact" established a truce by which the First Men ultimately came to revere the animated environment that the children held sacred as well.[5] For the children and the First Men who adopted their beliefs, the gods—which became synonymous with the weirwoods over time—were in direct witness of and communication with the world, but there was never an institution that governed, passed judgment, or spoke on behalf of some more distant and transcendent order of beings. The migration of the Andals to Westeros and proliferation of the "new gods" would introduce by force a completely foreign structure for human-divine relations.

The religion of the Andals maintains there is one true god and that it can be known through seven personified aspects (colloquially referred to as "gods" themselves). The seven points, or aspects, are all idealizations of social roles and experiences—the Warrior, the Smith, the Mother, the Crone, the Father, the Maiden, and the Stranger—together exemplifying the great potential contained within an individual. But the Seven did not only reflect; they *demanded* certain behavior and qualities, which all were expected to strive toward (lest they be doomed to the seven hells). The culture and institutions of the Andals were dependent upon the moral compass of the Seven-Faced God, set down in their holy text *The Seven-Pointed Star*, to justify the sacred and delineate between the righteous and the abominable. Like the Targaryens who would come later, it was the Andals' inability to make autochthonous claims in Westeros that made the codification, and thus transportability, of their religion so imperative. Andal religion and culture came to dominate the Westerosi continent, not as the sole way of believing, but by the far reach of its institutional authority. For example, noble houses would employ septas to teach their children, and weddings and funerals were overseen by Sept officials wherever possible. These practices imbued the Faith's morals with deep sentimental value and a common sense rationality, well-entrenched by the time of the Conquest.

The Targaryens, as open practitioners of incest and polygamy, could not claim to adhere to this moral universe. Even if they could be persuaded to abandon these, they could not abandon their dragons, who were their own kin. But the pantheon of the Andals had no conceptualization of dragon or dragonrider, the essential relationship at the heart of Targaryen identity. Thus, Aegon I and his descendants negotiated a distinct relationship to the Faith of the Andals, positioning themselves as both insiders—believers who had renounced their Valyrian gods—but also, and primarily, outsiders—and thus unbeholden to the same customs, laws, and judgments as other Westerosi. Although many of Aegon's progeny would demonstrate their devotion to the Seven, their Valyrian ways would never fully conform. The coronation of Aegon I in Oldtown essentially meant that they didn't have to: for the first time, under this new relationship, the boundaries of the acceptable could be reinterpreted—incest could be celebrated, women could be held in (nearly) as high esteem as men, and (certain) people could fly.

The truth was, the Faith and the crown needed one another to survive. The spectacle of the Conquest had irreversibly altered the imagined reality of Westeros, but the meaning and longevity of this alteration were somewhat inscrutable. Merging with the Faith made the Targaryens somewhat more intelligible to their subjects and provided a basic moral and social structure by which to govern and hold the kingdom together—which seemed in the interests of both parties. Mobilizing the population of Westeros into state-crafting was never the goal of the Targaryens. Local rule and custom, in general, remained the instrument to convince the majority of Westerosi that new lordship did not interrupt familiarity with ruling institutions.[6] Power structures of the Targaryens seen through the station of the monarch were complicated by drama created within the household due to problems of succession unique to their incest and their exceptional capabilities.

As the Targaryens unprecedentedly centralized power, the Faith was further strengthened through its connection to the crown, and Oldtown acquired an even firmer grip across the continent. But at the same time, the sudden addition of dragonlords into an Andal-dominated Westerosi cosmology presented a new set of problems for the Faith. Not since the children and First Men still held the continent had there been such a threat to the Andals' envisioned promised land, where all was understood and ordered among humanity according to the will of the Seven-Faced God. The dragons indicated a return to the strange and magical, and just as with the children, this arcane power was secret, restricted to the few. The Targaryens, meanwhile, would likewise continue to struggle defining their new role in tenuous dependency on the Seven.

As may already be apparent, the Faith of the Seven is analogous to the structure found in Christianity. Ludwig Feuerbach's treatise on Christianity analyzes this religion not as based in a natural truth but in a constructed ideal—particularly in Christ, the anthropomorphized incarnation of an otherwise infinite and unfathomable God. To know God is not really *to know* some ultimate, but to know the best possible version of ourselves. The drive to create an external ideal stems from our basic human nature. For humans, Feuerbach claims, our essence lies in our ability to reflect on our own qualities and their significance; unlike an animal, a human ponders over the mystery of their own existence, refers to themselves in the first and second person, and responds to the queries that they pose themselves. Feuerbach calls this inner dialogue our species-consciousness, which is separate from the mere biological capacity to perceive and judge stimuli. As humans are inescapably social creatures, our species-consciousness is informed not only by self-knowledge, but knowledge of others, which accumulates into a conversation about what it means to be human. The conclusion inevitably reached is that *any individual* is hopelessly limited and imperfect, unable to achieve the range of great qualities that some humans might at some times display. Humans thus transcend their limited individual existence by imagining a limitless and perfect human, that is, a god. Feuerbach contends that this is the "object of religion . . . Religion is the consciousness of the infinite; hence it is, and cannot be anything other than, man's consciousness of *his* own essential nature, understood not as a finite or limited, but as an infinite nature."[7] Because no one person could realistically internalize and possess all the great human qualities, we must instead consolidate these into an externalized representation, a mirror-like image. In relating to the mirror, humans come to know the best of themselves.

The Seven constitute such an externalization, a mirror to many situations and manifestation of many ideal traits. The Seven represent dualities and extremes such as tenderness and brute strength, masculinity, and femininity, as well as the life cycle from birth to old age and death; thus, they provide guidance for the faithful according to whichever characteristic needs to be invoked. Similarly, God the Father and Jesus the Son, as manifestations of the divine within Christianity, are anthropomorphisms constructing an image of man that is all-seeing, all-knowing, and all-loving. At the same time, in humbly submitting to their own infinite creation, humanity relinquishes the power of ultimate judgment, at least to those who speak on God's behalf. The Faith of the Seven—like Christianity—manifests as an oppressive structure in its definitive separation of the sacred from the profane, and furthermore the abominable.

Once agreed upon through an institutionalization of the faith, then the infinite and sacred not only represent unlimited good, but wickedness becomes associated with everything human, attributed to all as a characteristic essence of our limited nature. Feuerbach states:

> The lamentation over sin is found only where the individual does not recognize himself as a part of mankind, but identifies himself with the species, and for this reason makes his own sins, limits and weakness, the sins, limits, and weaknesses of mankind in general.[8]

The defeating move to define evil as inherent to every human is solutioned among the Andals by adherence to the laws and rulings of a religious order headed by the High Septon. Thus are a set of cultural norms and values externalized and enforced back upon the populace, purportedly for their own good (even salvation). Officials of the Sept had the sole power to interpret the divine text and decree its implications, standing in for the Seven-Faced God to pass judgment on the sinful, or abominable. This term would be reserved for the worst sins, and at times applied to the Targaryens' own incestuous unions, polygamy, bastards, and at least at one point, even the mere existence of their dragons. Therefore, in legitimizing and symbolically merging with the (Targaryen) crown, the Faith (perhaps unknowingly) relinquished power to define all possible divine ideals as well as pass credible judgments of sin. During and after the Conquest, Aegon I and his queens did overt homage to the Faith, but by their nature as exceptional outsiders also cast doubt upon the Faith's theretofore exclusive right to define good and evil. Two contradictory entities began to operate in tandem, opening up space for a kind of charismatic leadership that was both sacred *and* abominable.

CHARISMATIC LEADERSHIP

When Queen Visenya placed a Valyrian steel circlet, studded with rubies, on her brother's head and Queen Rhaenys hailed him as, "Aegon, First of His Name,

King of All Westeros, and Shield of His People," the dragons roared and the lords and knights sent up a cheer . . . but the smallfolk, the fishermen and fieldhands and goodwives, shouted loudest of all.[9]

Why do the smallfolk cheer for this fearsome outsider who had married his own sisters, and, from the back of a fire-breathing beast, just wreaked havoc upon all who resisted him? Shouldn't they have been afraid? Perhaps, and maybe they were. But clearly Targaryen authority did not derive from sheer terror alone. Their negotiations with the Faith were part of a broader negotiation of consent with the general populace. The Targaryens' intrusion and accommodation into the sacred landscape of Westeros structurally situated them in an elevated position, conflating them with an anthropomorphic imagination of divinity; furthermore, as living, dragonriding beings, the Targaryens were more directly inspiring figures than the abstracted Seven. The form of consent the common people of Westeros entrusted to the Targaryens thus bordered on the irrational, inseparable from a religious ecstasy. Targaryen governance was then able to mix cruelty with generosity as befitting the needs of lordly sovereignty. And it seems that Aegon I understood well how to compel the public to this effect.

Aegon is an enigmatic figure, and his motivation for claiming dominion over the Seven Kingdoms is similarly obscure in the available histories. We can clearly observe, however, that the Conquest was not the grasping of a man desperate for either power or destruction: Aegon "took no pleasure in feats of arms" and exacted only as much force as was necessary to take and retain the Seven Kingdoms.[10] On the contrary, the Conquest was a confident and calculated performance of Targaryen superiority and acknowledgement of domestic structures.

While existing kings had reason to begrudge bending the knee, and had to be sorted through military offensives, it was the smallfolk who seemed to love Aegon I most effortlessly. The absence of a rational explanation for their devotion suggests that they had been swept up in the panic and also pleasure of collectively witnessing and recognizing a superior form of humanity, and besides that a monarch who was able to situate his line within the power structures of most of Westeros. Unearthly and beautiful, descending from the skies on impossible creatures and commanding their flames as though dragon and rider were one, the Targaryen siblings were far from comparable to any of the existing kings, and thus delegitimized them all. Through the absolute spectacle of the Conquest, the Westerosi population became persuaded that the unprecedented Targaryen claim was nevertheless justified. Consent to rule came in part from fear, but also wonder, joy, and a mysterious attraction. Thus, the Targaryens derived their legitimacy not only by Aegon's anointing by the Faith but also through their charismatic authority.

Preeminent sociologist Max Weber analyzed "charismatic authority" in contrast to the authority commanded from either longstanding tradition or from bureaucratic organization. Within the latter two ideal types, legitimacy and power derive from a permanent office—either by appeals to custom (under traditional authority) or rational, legal regulation (under a bureaucracy)—in a large sense independent of the individual officeholder. In contrast, the charismatic leader commands recognition from their following by right of their personal qualities and the demonstration of abilities that normal people do not possess:

> The subjects may extend a more active or passive "recognition" to the personal mission of the charismatic master. His power rests upon this purely factual recognition and springs from faithful devotion. It is devotion to the extraordinary and unheard-of, to what is strange to all rule and tradition and which therefore is viewed as divine. It is a devotion born of distress and enthusiasm.[11]

Weber's classic examples of charismatic leadership are the prophet and the warlord. It is through their seemingly superhuman attributes and demonstration of divine favor that these leaders incite fervent emotions and compel a following. But because charisma is subjective and irrational, must exist outside of office and routine to maintain its magical allure, and must constantly be performed to be convincing, it is inherently unstable. At any moment, charisma may fail and followers retract their support. Charismatic movements therefore tend to seek to establish themselves in more fixed, institutional forms. This was the case, Weber contended, with the early Christian church. At first glance, it seems that Targaryen authority adheres to this trend of increased formalization, particularly by the reign of Jaehaerys I. However, though the office did develop more regulated and stabilizing elements, charisma remained paramount. If the populace ever believed that a non-Targaryen was special enough to sit on the throne, then the whole narrative behind the institution would also fall away, and the kingdoms would fracture again.

For the moment, it is beside the point whether or not the Targaryens *actually* possessed godly traits and were thus divinely chosen to conquer Westeros and rule over all its inhabitants. What matters is whether or not such ideologies became accepted as common sense among the subjects, and the histories reveal that this was indeed the case. Strikingly, when recounting the debate over the customary right of "first night" exercised by many lords throughout the kingdoms, Archmaester Gyldayn comments:

> Though the first night was greatly resented elsewhere . . . such feelings were muted upon Dragonstone, where Targaryens *were rightly regarded as being*

closer to gods than the common run of men. Here, brides thus blessed upon their wedding nights were envied, and the children born of such unions were esteemed above all others. (italics added)[12]

Further persuasive evidence of Targaryen divine favor or suprahumanity was plentiful, including the capacity among some for prophetic dreams, the line's resulting exemption from the Doom of Valyria, a surpassing and unique physical beauty, high tolerance for heat and even flames, presumed immunity to some illnesses or disease, a general extraordinariness of character—across the spectrum from virtuous to diabolical—and most of all, their affinity with dragons and for dragonriding.

Other noble houses decorated their sigils with totems, oftentimes animals, with which they identified and felt pride. But the Targaryens were clearly different. They *had* dragons: majestic animals and the most powerful weapons in all of Westeros, yet Targaryens literally grew up with them from the cradle. The relationship between dragon and rider was ideally a lifelong bond, such that the lines between each became blurred. Indeed, the Targaryens often spoke of their own blood as "the blood of the dragon," and in keeping the customs of Valyria, were expected to marry within the family to keep this bloodline "pure."[13] Behind their dragon sigil were real, (fire-)breathing dragons, and both the Targaryens and their subjects came to recognize, if never fully fathom, Targaryen kings' divine position through this animal form.

As stated previously, however, charismatic authority is inherently unstable. The fervor of the Conquest, the freshness of its memory, the novelty of the Iron Throne and the dragon king upon it, could not last. It is likely that no king would have been able to fill the vacancy left by Aegon I, but his and Rhaenys's indecisive son Aenys fell far short of the task. It was once he took up his father's throne that serious challenges to Targaryen rule began to emerge. These challenges largely stemmed from the incompatibility of Targaryen custom with the Faith's strict cosmology of righteousness and sinfulness they now claimed to follow. Despite the incest of the founding siblings, no forceful objections were raised until Aegon's sons themselves came to power and began to refute these strictures of the Seven. Aenys completely lost the support of the Faith and much of the general population by wedding two of his children. After his untimely death, Aenys's half-brother Maegor "the Cruel"—who himself took six wives—waged a ruthless war against the "Faith Militant," a militia roused in protest of Targaryen immorality following his young niece and nephew's union.

Thus was the state of crown-Faith relations when succession passed to the only surviving son of Aenys I—Jaehaerys. It was under the long reign of Jaehaerys I ("Jaehaerys the Conciliator") that the charismatic authority of his house was codified as an explicit doctrine, and thereby reconciled crown with Faith. This was a truly amazing feat considering Jaehaerys and his sister Alysanne's own uncompromising resolve to wed, despite their mother's fervent opposition. But far from the fate of their war-inspiring older siblings, Jaehaerys and Alysanne's love story would be celebrated as one of the most romantic in Westeros history.

This was thanks in large part to King Jaehaerys and Queen Alysanne being as strategic about their reign as they were headstrong about their romance; from the beginning, Jaehaerys strove to model his reign off of Aegon the Conqueror's. He and his queen traveled widely—with their dragons—performing Targaryen superiority and re-inspiring the devotion and support of their subjects. And to those particularly astute subjects who knew the precepts of *The Seven-Pointed Star* and would question the propriety of Targaryen traditions, Jaehaerys and his loyal septons devised an answer that proved satisfactory, and came to be known as the Doctrine of Exceptionalism. While the laws of the Seven were made for the Andals—and were also appropriate for those who had assimilated into the transplanted culture of Andalos—the Targaryens were obviously a different kind of human altogether:

> A man had only to look at them to know that they were not like other men; their eyes, their hair, their very bearing, all proclaimed their differences. *And they flew dragons.* They alone of all the men in the world had been given the power to tame those fearsome beasts, once the Doom had come to Valyria (italics in original).[14]

Thus the Targaryens, rulers over the Andals, could not be judged according to the same laws as an Andal, nor even be judged by the Seven-Faced God of the Andals, for they were exceptional to that entire cosmology. In truth, the doctrine was but an explicit formulation of that widely (if not firmly) held sentiment which Targaryen legitimacy had always hinged upon.

Jaehaerys I and Alysanne also set in place a common code of law, built a system of roads, abolished the custom of "first night," entrusted the tricky matter of Jaehaerys's succession to a vote among the lords of the realm,[15] disbanded the Faith Militant, and normalized relations with the Starry Sept, enjoying a lengthy, peaceful reign. But though counted among their triumphs, making Targaryen Exceptionalism explicit may also have had negative consequences for Targaryen identity and legitimacy down the line. After all, the Targaryens were in fact but mortal human beings, and contradictions between their idealized and actualized selves were always bound to arise. In those moments when charisma inevitably faltered, disgruntled detractors now had a clear target: a doctrine upon which Targaryen legitimacy to rule relied. Meanwhile the Targaryens had an exceptional, now codified, standard to live up to, yet one for which the limits were not made clear. If, for the Targaryens, idealized being was not limited even to the Seven, then the question of what it really *meant* to be exceptional—and where those limits lied—remained open.

DANCE, DESTRUCTION, AND DECLINE

The inherent conflict plaguing Targaryen being—the very same exceptionalism generating their legitimacy—played out in two ways: first, externally, in the "Dance of Dragons," and afterward, internally, as the lineage experienced metaphysical decline accompanied by ever-deeper forays into madness. The dragons themselves are useful proxies for understanding the trajectory of Targaryen fortune. Before growing smaller, weaker and disappearing from Westeros entirely, they gave their most beautiful—and terrible—performance. When at their most self-destructive, human Targaryens likewise performed their charismatic authority; if this was hard to define in code, it was identifiable enough when witnessing firsthand. The Dance of Dragons was much more than a family quarrel or Targaryen madness; it was the culmination of a cultural conflict in a Targaryen-ruled Westeros, a war over the meaning and limits of exceptionalism even as this ideology competed with a more stable and "sensible" socio-religious order in the Seven. The details of the Dance are complex, and need not concern us here in much nuance, but a brief account of the civil war's background is required to illustrate this grander point.

Jaehaerys I was succeeded by his son, Viserys I, who for many years produced no male heirs. Instead of naming his mercurial brother Daemon as his successor, Viserys I went against the precedent of his own succession, instead naming his beloved daughter, Rhaenyra, as heir to the Iron Throne. Although it seemed Rhaenyra and her uncle Daemon desired one another, they were deliberately kept apart, each wed to other members of the extended Targaryen family. Meanwhile King Viserys, after the death of Rhaenyra's mother Aemma Arryn, remarried to Alicent Hightower, who bore him three sons and a daughter. Thereupon, two factions developed at court: Rhaenyra and her children (who were rumored to be bastards)—their supporters known as "the blacks"—against Queen Alicent, her children, and their supporters—"the greens." After their respective spouses each passed away, Rhaenyra and Daemon finally wed one another, and had children of their own. By this time, Viserys and Alicent's eldest son, Aegon "the Elder,"[16] had come of age, married his sister Heleana, and they had had three children. Despite the increasing strength of Aegon the Elder's claim (as Viserys's firstborn son with his own male heirs of undisputed parentage), King Viserys never retracted his pronouncement of Rhaenyra as heir, even upon his deathbed.

When Queen Alicent found Viserys I had passed away, the greens acted quickly to claim the Iron Throne for Aegon the Elder (now "King Aegon II") instead. As news of the new king spread, Rhaenyra prepared to defend her right and Aegon II prepared to resist her; each faction gathered and recruited allies; blood was soon spilled, revenge swiftly enacted. It was Targaryen against Targaryen and dragon against dragon in a war of unprecedented scale and unmatchable devastation. But beyond political intrigue, family drama, and military campaigns, what came to be known as the "Dance of Dragons" demonstrated the instability inherent to the doctrine of exceptionalism, a charismatic spectacle that broke out along deep lines of cultural friction.

Sex constituted one area of cultural friction. As each faction quickly sought to de-legitimize the other, they were also pitting the more lax, ambiguous relations between sex and power from Old Valyria against the longstanding Andalos tradition of male inheritance. Valyrian women were not restricted from riding dragons, the most important avenue to power within the Valyrian Freehold. When adapting their rule to the customs of Westeros, the Targaryen kings conformed to succession through the male line, but it was ever a de facto conformity rather than de jure, a result of specific circumstances even when appearing as a set rule. The Great Council of 101 was convened to settle a *specific* matter of succession, and only in retrospect was the result taken to definitively mean that the line of succession could pass neither to, nor through, a woman. The vote was the will of the majority of the lords of the realm, not an expression of Targaryen beliefs.

Thus, the Targaryens—as charismatic rulers *and* outsiders with different cultural sensibilities—would have some difficulty abiding by their own apparent regulations of office. From the Conquest, women had played major roles in both governance and—as dragonriders—military campaigns. Moreover, a charismatic ruler emerges as a result of their personal abilities and qualities of character. True to this form, as a young girl and young woman, Princess Rhaenyra was renowned throughout the kingdom for her beauty, intelligence, and particularly her bravery; she began riding her dragon at about seven years of age. When Viserys I named her his heir, no immediate protest followed and many lords swore their oaths of fealty to her, though some remained uneasy with the proclamation, its discordance with the Great Council—and thus its discordance with idealized gender qualities as externalized in the Seven. The debate around Rhaenyra's planned ascension to the throne was therefore the culmination of a cultural debate over the propriety of female leadership rooted in a deeper religious sensibility. This was helped in no part by the ambiguous state of Targaryen authority: would they rule by force, by Andal custom, or by their own exceptional magic, the limits of which were yet unknown?

Ironically, Aegon II, the male competitor for the throne, was a temperamental and rather uninvolved king; throughout the war he was, in effect, a figurehead for his mother's will. Indeed, the increasing infiltration of other noble houses into the Targaryen family generated both overt political scheming as well as more metaphysical challenges to Targaryen legitimacy. Although Targaryen royals had previously wed into the Velaryon and Baratheon houses, these lines were still extended relatives with some "blood of the dragon" in them. Viserys I was the first king to marry into a house with no blood ties to his own, in his second marriage to Alicent Hightower.[17] Not only did the Hightowers[18] come to play a crucial and instigative role in the events leading up to and throughout the Dance of Dragons, but their newfound positions of power lessened the symbolic distance between the Targaryens and other noble houses. As Targaryen exceptionalism, and thus their right to rule, was premised on their unbridgeable distance from other humans, for an outsider to join the royal family as kin weakened these claims of exclusivity. We might also consider Rhaenyra's eldest three children as another case challenging the uniqueness of Targaryen abilities.

It was widely believed (if never spoken too loudly) that the three boys from Rhaenyra's first marriage were not the sons of her husband and kinsman, Leanor Velaryon, but bastards fathered by Ser Harwin Strong. Queen Alicent, though seemingly willing to accept the Targaryens' incestuous practices, condemned bastards as "monstrous by nature"—a view inculcated by the Faith of the Seven—and infected her own children with this loathing for Rhaenyra's heirs.[19] Many others shared her misgivings, seeing these brown-eyed, brown-haired boys as not truly the blood of the dragon. Lacking the characteristic Targaryen features put the boys under further stress to prove themselves as true "dragons." However, that the eggs placed in each of their cradles all hatched may have done little to help the Targaryen cause overall; if these bastards, hated by the Seven-Faced God, could ride dragons, then maybe it was not such an exclusive, divine capability. Indeed, as there were more dragons on the blacks' side than able dragonriders, more lowborn bastards populating Dragonstone (known as "dragonseeds") came forward from among the smallfolk to claim their command; some of these baseborn dragonriders, such as the girl Nettles, did not even claim to have Targaryen blood. Although desperate times called for these desperate measures, after the war it could no longer be claimed that a dragon would only listen to its Valyrian kin—a serious blow to Targaryen exceptionalism. However, there would be no chance for the full implications of this realization to spread, as by the end of the Dance, the population of dragons would shrink from over twenty to just four.

Even discounting its dragon members, House Targaryen had more casualties than any of the great houses of Westeros. Yet it is fair to say that the war was most catastrophic for the smallfolk, caught between the chaos of battle and plunder, the constant threats of either burning alive or starving upon burned fields. Residents of King's Landing faced the fear of dragonfire most acutely with Rhaenyra barring the gates upon retaking the city, allowing none to enter or leave. They were trapped, knowing that sooner or later the war would be upon them. Perhaps an uprising was inevitable under such pressures, but the distinctly religious form that it would take demonstrates that discontent with the Targaryens was not borne of these circumstances alone.

Under the stress of war, desperate souls turned to their faith for guidance, their need for salvation from both fires of dragon and hells only making clear the ultimately irreconcilable discordance between Targaryen custom and Andal morality. With these sentiments brewing, even a simple person could garner impassioned followers. Thus, a tattered commoner known simply as "the Shepherd" emerged to preach against the evils of the royalty of Westeros, convincing growing crowds that

> Dragons were unnatural creatures . . . demons summoned from the pits of the seven hells by the fell sorceries of Valyria, "that vile cesspit where brother lay with sister and mother with son, where men rode demons into battle whilst their women spread their legs for dogs."[20]

Under this interpretation of the Faith, every deed and even the presence of a Targaryen was an affront to the gods. The Targaryens went from occupying an elevated gray space in the cosmology of Westeros to being the dark force at total odds with the Seven.

A multitude of followers or "lambs" gathered around the Shepherd, his words sweeping them into a millenarian fervor that culminated in storming the Dragonpit. They managed—though at great cost to themselves—to slay the dragons there, and in one decisive night significantly reduce the great power of the Targaryens. Though the dragons in King's Landing were at least somewhat more likely to protect the city than turn against it, it was a matter of what they represented—as the Targaryens' living sigils and basis of their untouchability—that could no longer be allowed to stand. In the universe of sin and punishment inhabited by the faithful, Targaryen exceptionalism itself was the only transgression profound enough to explain the horror of the Dance. This war was not a political power struggle in the eyes of the Shepherd and his lambs but a sign of the gods' wrath, and the lambs' own participation was not for power or glory, but in hopes of delivering a world on the brink of damnation.

"Never have I seen a sight more terrible, more glorious." These are reported to be the words of Rhaenyra as, from a (marginally) safe distance, she observed the assault on the Dragonpit and resulting inferno engulfing

King's Landing.[21] Such destructive capacities of dragons, the sheer irrationality of such violence, had never been witnessed in full before, not on Westeros. The Dance of Dragons stands as the epitome of Targaryen greatness and its ultimate unsustainability. Emboldened by their exceptional status, and by all appearances at peace with the Faith, it is as though the Targaryens lost sight of the truth—that their right to rule was ever tenuous, dependent upon the constant recognition from and devotion of the people—many of whom first and foremost answered to the Seven—rather than something in fact, guaranteed by their "fire and blood." With the loss of the dragons, however, the Targaryens would only grasp at this illusion more fiercely.

GREATNESS AND MADNESS

The end of the war and insignificance of its surviving dragons did not bring about an age of peace and prosperity, but a six-year winter. Winters ever after the Dance, it seemed, would last longer, an observation attributed to the dragons' extinction.[22] A wonderful yet terrible magic had been lost to the world. Aegon III, who succeeded Aegon II, knew only too well how terrible: he had looked on helplessly as his own mother Rhaenyra was devoured by his predecessor's dragon, and thereafter he refused to have anything to do with them. Happily for "Aegon the Unlucky," it was within his reign that the last of the dragons perished. The Targaryens' living sigil was dead. Moreover, the imposed cultural particularities of the Targaryens lost much of their justification without the fire of the dragons to back them. Yet this point of weakness only served to inflame the Targaryens' drive to perform exceptionalism with all they had—their limited humanity. The actual *dragons* had perished, but the Targaryens believed themselves to be dragons by blood as well, and strove to compensate for the loss of their kin. All of Targaryen identity which had once taken physical form in their dragons was now internalized, incorporated into vessels that were human in form—but in thought and practice, had to be much more.

And so they were. Daeron "the Young Dragon" ambitiously brought Dorne into the realm; Baelor "the Blessed" walked barefoot to and from Dorne to secure peace, performing a number of "miracles" en route and thereafter; Aemon the Dragonknight is reputed as "the noblest knight who ever lived";[23] Aegon IV "the Unworthy" was exceptionally insatiable, legitimizing his many bastards upon his deathbed to result in "blood and fire for five generations" as his progeny continuously vied for the throne;[24] Daeron "the Good" finally solidified peace with Dorne; Aerion Brightflame drank wildfire to fulfill his dream of literally becoming a dragon; Aegon V became obsessed with resurrecting dragons and perished in a feat of pyromancy; finally, Aerys

II ("the Mad King") succumbed to such paranoia that he began to burn alive anyone who aroused his suspicions and took steps to destroy all of King's Landing with wildfire. Aerys II, who most definitively lost the legitimacy of rule, is the hallmark example of Targaryen madness. As Ser Barristan Selmy explains to Aerys II's exiled daughter Daenerys:

> Every child knows that the Targaryens have always danced too close to madness. Your father was not the first. King Jaehaerys once told me that madness and greatness are two sides of the same coin. Every time a new Targaryen is born, he said, the gods toss the coin in the air and the world holds its breath to see how it will land.[25]

But rather than Jaehaerys II's dualistic conceptualization of Targaryen qualities as either-or, we can understand them as *both-and*: madness-greatness was the manifestation of internalizing a previously externalized, sacred ideal. This was ever the Targaryens' means of asserting legitimacy (conforming to Westerosi cosmology through association with the Seven yet retaining an ineffable charismatic power through their dragons), but the internalization process intensified after the loss of their dragons.

From an anthropological standpoint, belief and behavior should be understood contextually, from an insider's perspective as well as an outsider observer's. What seems like "insanity" to the one might be respected as sacred from the other. Shamanistic trance, for instance, has been categorized as a kind of dissociative psychological episode from the point of view of modern science. But experientially, this labeling does little explanatory work. A culturally immersive analysis would show how the shaman is able to access a spiritual power due to a particular structuring of the sacred in relation to human bodies, including the separation of ritual time and space from that of the mundane. This separation is necessary for the trance, through which a "normal" human may perform the spectacular or experience the inexplicable. Yet just like the fervor of charisma, ritual space and the performances within it are limited; one cannot live forever in a trance.

For the Targaryens, to try and live continuously upon an elevated plane of charisma and exceptionalism, fire and blood, was to attempt the impossible. They came as exiles to a continent dominated by a religious institution incongruous with the customs core to their identity. Like Christianity, the Faith of the Seven magnified and elevated certain human ideals while denigrating humankind itself as sinful. This dichotomy of good and evil conflated with the dragonlords' deeply felt sense that they were special among humankind. Moreover, they had the charismatic authority, at times, to convince Westeros of their divine superiority as well, both through violence and in spite of such abominable behavior. This notion of divinity-made-flesh was legitimated through the Conquest and particularly the coronation at Oldtown. Even then, like the terrible beauty of the dragons in flight, Targaryen behavior could be said to simultaneously exhibit a respectable glamor *and* a twisted darkness. For many of the Targaryen kings who would follow Aegon I, this exceptional status simply became taken for granted as the structure of reality. But all this elevation rested ultimately on an illusion—for the Targaryens were but mortals, and not even the only ones who could command a dragon. To protect the fantasy of exceptionalism, the limits of Targaryen greatness demanded constant performance and ever-deeper exploration; while for a time, this burden could be shared by their reptilian kin, the weight of living out an imagined ideal finally culminated in self-destructiveness. To inhabit the divine roles available to them as rulers of the Seven Kingdoms, the Targaryens indeed outperformed "normal" humanity, but at the cost of spectacular violence to themselves and to their kingdom. In the end, it becomes impossible to say where insanity ended or began—in the blood of the dragon, or in the exceptional status the dragonlords were acknowledged as having?

THE DANGEROUS CONFLATION OF CHARISMATIC WITH MORAL AUTHORITY

Beyond mere entertainment, the *Game of Thrones* world gives us a massive thought experiment from which to ponder human relations and in particular the nature of leadership. There are at least some noteworthy parallels between Targaryen exceptionalism and real-world doctrines, including the exceptionalism at the heart of Western politics. The metanarrative of hegemons' uniqueness (and, it is at least implied if not explicitly emphasized, superiority) and an individualistic, personality-based understanding of leadership further stokes internalized feelings of superiority and divine providence among leaders and those who idealize them. Political logic becomes confounded with unattainable ideals. Where we no longer have sovereigns, the relationship between state and religion throughout history has set a moral basis for society and its leaders with polarized notions of good and evil. This structure comes into conflict with the unstable cult of charismatic leadership to irrational effects. However, the confusing relationship between our complex systems of religion and supposedly secular leadership take on a kind of common sense and limit clarity of perception from within a society. There is no pure play of power, no "*game of thrones*," unshaped by institutional conflicts. Still, authority rests upon consent. To whom then do we grant the power to reinterpret what is unquestionably good (sacred) and what should be resolutely condemned (abominable)?

The Song of Ice and Fire series and its companion works have inspired many conversations covering all manner of topics based in the narrative's realism. The decline of the television series' popularity following the final season is evidence of that discourse, where many former fans lost their connection to the story when it seemed that the showrunners cut character exposition and ignored previous character development to speed progress toward the finale. Some of the realism was lost. However, the moment that the show created by bringing fantasy into the mainstream proved the strength of cerebral, humanistic fantasy as a thought experiment for exploring our gendered, social, political, and religious realities and potentialities. Leadership and governance lean on myriad social structures to help justify ideologies and national narratives. The intrigue in George R. R. Martin's creation remains a point of reference for understanding our own roles as subjects in a world of unequal power.

NOTES

1. Machiavelli, Niccolò, Gauss, C., and Ricci, L., *The Prince* (New American Library, 1952); Foucault, Michel, "Governmentality" In *The Foucault Effect: Studies in Governmentality*, edited by G. Burchell, C. Gordon, and P. Miller (Chicago: University of Chicago Press, 1991).

2. George R. R. Martin, Elio M. Garcia, Jr., and Linda Antonsson, *The World of Ice & Fire: The Untold History of Westeros and the Game of Thrones* (New York: Bantam, 2014), 13.

3. By divine we mean godly—of or like a god. In the known world of *A Song of Ice and Fire,* many forms of divinity are known if not mutually acceptable as true: from the "old gods" to the "new gods," as well as many foreign gods.

4. Animism is a theory that even nonhuman elements of the natural world are inhabited with living spirits and first-person perspectives. Taking an ontological approach as in the work of Viveiros de Castro, we can consider the weirwoods in the *Game of Thrones* universe as subjects acting in the world rather than just a system of belief.

5. Ibid., 7–9.

6. This approach to governance, brought into conversation through the Middle Ages by Machiavelli, and subsequently critiqued for its focus on the prince (as by Foucault), centers the sovereign as the point from where to justify rule.

7. Ludwig Feuerbach, *The Essence of Christianity,* trans. George Eliot (California: MSAC Philosophy Group, 2008), 6.

8. Ibid., 119.

9. George R. R. Martin, *Fire & Blood: 300 Years Before A Game of Thrones* (New York: Bantam, 2018), 10.

10. Ibid., 9.

11. Max Weber, "The Sociology of Charismatic Authority," in *From Max Weber: Essays in Sociology*, edited and translated by Hans H. Gerth and C. Wright Mills (New York: Oxford University Press, 1946), 249.

12. George R. R. Martin, *Fire & Blood: 300 Years Before A Game of Thrones* (New York: Bantam, 2018), 440.

13. Ibid., 53.

14. Ibid., 192–193.

15. This would be known as the "Great Council of 101," wherein the two most hopeful claimants to the throne were Viserys Targaryen, son of Jaehaerys's late son Baelor, and Laenor Velaryon, whose mother was the daughter of Jaehaerys's firstborn son. The council decided in favor of Viserys, who had the advantages of age (twenty-four years against Laenor's seven) and descent through his father rather than his mother.

16. Alicent's Aegon was known as "Aegon the Elder," to distinguish him from Rhaenyra and Daemon's son "Aegon the Younger." They would each sit the throne, and thus come to be known as Aegon II and Aegon III, respectively.

17. Although Viserys I's first marriage was to Aemma Arryn, Aemma's mother was Daella Targaryen, Viserys's own aunt.

18. Alicent Hightower was the daughter of Viserys' Hand. It is of interest to note that the Hightower seat is Oldtown, so the house had particularly close ties to the Faith.

19. Ibid., 396.

20. Ibid., 494.

21. Ibid., 522.

22. George R. R. Martin, *A Knight of the Seven Kingdoms* (New York: Bantam, 2015), 18.

23. Martin, García, Jr., and Antonsson, *The World of Ice & Fire*, 94.

24. Ibid., 96.

25. George R. R. Martin, *A Storm of Swords* (New York: Bantam, 2003), 987.

BIBLIOGRAPHY

Feuerbach, Ludwig. *The Essence of Christianity*. Translated by George Eliot. California: MSAC Philosophy Group, 2008.

Foucault, Michel. "Governmentality." In *The Foucault Effect: Studies in Governmentality*, edited by G. Burchell, C. Gordon, and P. Miller. Chicago: University of Chicago Press, 1991.

Machiavelli, Niccolò, C.Gauss, and L. Ricci. *The Prince*. USA: New American Library, 1952.

Martin, George R. R. *A Storm of Swords*. New York: Bantam, 2003.

———. *A Knight of the Seven Kingdoms*. New York: Bantam, 2015.

———. *Fire & Blood: 300 Years Before A Game of Thrones*. New York: Bantam, 2018.

Martin, George R. R., Elio M. García Jr., and Linda Antonsson. *The World of Ice & Fire: The Untold History of Westeros and the Game of Thrones*. New York: Bantam, 2014.

Viveiros de Castro, Eduardo. "Cosmological Deixis and Amerindian Perspectivism." *The Journal of the Royal Anthropological Institute* 4, no. 3 (September 1998): 469–88.

Weber, Max. "The Sociology of Charismatic Authority." In *From Max Weber: Essays in Sociology*, edited and translated by Hans H. Gerth and C. Wright Mills, 245–52. New York: Oxford University Press, 1946.

Chapter 3

Guest Rights and Gods
Historical Hospitium in Game of Thrones
Katy L. Krieger

Strangers are often seen in dichotomous terms when they arrive on our doorstep; they are either guest-friend or hostile-enemy.[1] People have always been skeptical of outsiders because such "radical otherness of people" causes individuals to hesitate, though they still seem to abide by social customs when welcoming and eventually hosting a visitor.[2] Such hospitality includes a warm welcome, food, shelter, and some form of conversation or entertainment.[3] The idea of hospitality is as applicable today as it was in all of the previous historical periods, and its customs are universal to the point that they have been written into literature. This chapter first aims to provide an understanding of hospitality through its historical and theological roots and elaborate on how George R. R. Martin created the world of *Game of Thrones* so that it (a) relies on the subversion of how honorable people are treated, (b) utilizes violent vengeance, and (c) simultaneously upholds these ideas alongside traditional hospitality. Specifically, this chapter will explore the pivotal Red Wedding in the *Game of Thrones* series and will primarily focus on the HBO television show version of this shockingly gruesome break in hospitality rituals.[4] Finally, this chapter proposes larger questions about divine agency for retributive justice as the Many-Faced God of Death and the faceless assassins manifest to exact vengeance on behalf of their god (or those that pay enough to their god).

HISTORICAL AND UNIVERSAL HOSPITIUM

Guest friendship, in ancient and classical Rome and Greece, was called *xenia* or *hospitium privatum*.[5] *Hospitium privatum* focuses on the agreements between men as individuals instead of between representatives of an official state. In establishing the rules of *hospitium* in *Game of Thrones*, Martin is able to utilize the agreements established by hosts and guests as a plot device. For example, at the Red Wedding, Lord Walder Frey offers his hospitality to the entire Stark family, their bannermen, and the entire Stark army. In doing so, the Freys invoke *hospitium privatum*, and the two houses forge a personal bond that aims to eventually develop a more public, outward-facing alliance.[6]

Historically, relationships built on guest friendship were held in high esteem and placed guest above friend when they resided under the host's roof.[7] This extended to criminal behavior against another being, and a crime against a stranger was seen as worse than an attack on a fellow citizen.[8] The reasoning behind this elevated status was likely because guests represented vulnerability and temporary weakness since they were at a disadvantage by being at their host's mercy. However, strangers also present issues of their own. Guests, upon entering the home to stay, represent the possibility to consume the host's resources and consume the actual hosts by means of expelling, overthrowing, or killing.[9] Thus, mysterious guests were frequently written into stories to be used as lessons about (mis)trusting strangers.[10]

Once the invitation for guests to reside in the host's home had been made, guests had basic rules to follow, in that they would not usurp the host nor would they refuse their offerings of any kind.[11] Likewise, hosts were expected to refrain from insulting or dishonoring the guest, unnecessarily questioning the guests, and providing any and all means of protection to these people while they were staying in the home.[12] The laws of hospitality in *Game of Thrones* also appear to follow these same guidelines and encourage proper courtly behavior by both guests and hosts. For example, at the Red Wedding, the audience knows that the Freys, Boltons, and Lannisters have severely violated *hospitium*, which creates in the audience the drive for some kind of retribution on behalf of the fallen Starks.[13] However, Martin also constructs narratives where the audiences' knowledge of the supposed rules gets them into trouble. Walder Frey, and his accomplices, take advantage of the Stark's trust in the code of guest rights during their Red Wedding visit, and use this advantage to execute their plan and the entire Stark army.[14] This episode also capitalizes on the audience's trust in the laws of hospitality and betrays this trust. Martin's goal is to demonstrate that sometimes (well, most of the time) moral and just characters do not win and very frequently die.[15]

Martin also built his world in reflection of the medieval worlds that shaped our modern society. Westeros is clearly an honor society where vengeance is sought through means of warfare, trial by combat, and invoking the gods in your name to defeat your enemies. This noble ethos is drawn from traditional Christian chivalric code that relies on protecting the weak and using this system to show class status.[16] This is where the Freys, often referenced as lacking social distinction, are seen as breakers of the chivalric code. However, Old

God or New God vengeance is rarely seen in the books and show but can easily be analyzed in the human action on screen and on page.[17] In pulling from historical and literary references, Martin relied on the universality of the laws of hospitality to be understood and honored by his series' audience.[18] Martin's narrative world seems to punish its honorable inhabitants, and yet divine retribution consistently operates on those who violate hospitality throughout the series.

Judith Still, like most scholars, suggests that hospitality is one of our most universal concepts and can be termed "Kantian universal human hospitality" because of its shared nature.[19] For example, in applying for asylum, conventional and universal signs have always been used to identify oneself as needing safety.[20] As seeking asylum can happen to anyone in any country, the importance of the process being universally accepted is paramount to all humans feeling as though safety is possible. Though it is a fictional world, *Game of Thrones* has a similar belief in the universal signs of asylum, which is obvious when Daenerys Targaryen goes on her journey through the Red Waste and arrives at the doorstep of Qarth seeking asylum.

Furthermore, in the ancient near east, and many other countries, hospitality was also seen as a temporary alliance between two parties and each party was obliged to perform their role.[21] This alliance was forged through relational bonds and backed by godly might. In the *Game of Thrones* universe, hospitality is extended to others in order to join the forces of houses together and take on common enemies. For example, Lady Olenna Tyrell sails to Dorne to join forces with Ellaria Sand to eventually fight against the Lannisters, the Greyjoys request hospitality with Daenerys Targaryen in an effort to combat their uncle's fleet, and the Starks turn to the Freys to combine their houses' strength and beat Tywin Lannister in the War of the Five Kings.

THEOLOGY AND *HOSPITIUM*

Though some variations in *hospitium* exist because of religious differences, one of the universal tests of morality is being faced with a stranger at your door and responding to them by being kind and offering shelter.[22] In a biblical context, many people believe that strangers may very well be God, Jesus, or angels in disguise. Turning away a stranger might mean turning away someone very high up in the religious order and disgracing your own religious beliefs. Similarly, Greco-Roman beliefs thought gods might be disguised or watching omnipotently from above to pass judgment on hosts and guests.[23] Here, *Hospitium* begins to move from a social discussion to one of theology when questions of morality take shape around the treatment of others and is primarily a devotional set of customs that represent a tangible, focused belief in religious power, divine protection, and godly punishment. In *Game of Thrones*, the laws of hospitality and guest rights exist similarly to those in our world. Bonds of guest rights are forged in the name of the gods, are overseen by the gods, and are punishable by the gods.

Some scholars consider hospitality to be a biblically driven practice, which involves the love and benevolence of God, no mutual benefit to the host, and the idea that God is acting on behalf of humans' best interests.[24] In this sense, hospitality is about graciousness, charity, and modeling one's own hospitality after God's hospitality as the ultimate host.[25] Hospitality should also be extended to strangers because Christ can be viewed as the ultimate stranger who should be willingly accepted into one's heart to build belief and offered a place in one's home.[26] In the Old Testament, God represented the initial host who epitomized the protector of those who upheld the laws of hospitality and punished the violators.[27] Hospitality was a response to the presence of a stranger and served as a "nationalistic mark" to demonstrate group identity within a religious community.[28] In the New Testament, however, hospitality is a means of charity as demonstrated by the stories of Luke, and extending hospitality to a stranger is equivalent to extending hospitality to Jesus. Biblical literature also captures stories of hospitality; Hebrews 13:2 discusses the unknowing benefits to the entertainment of angels when hospitality was extended to strangers, and the biblical tales of Sodom's inhospitable treatment of the angels in disguise shows the clear retribution of God for being unwelcoming to strangers.[29] Like mythological lore, the treatment of strangers is used as a lesson to teach kindness, humility, fairness, consideration, and care. Furthermore, Christianity and Judaism used ideal models of the host to teach their flocks how to live.[30]

Polytheism also dedicated a handful of gods to overseeing hospitality.[31] Private hospitality in these societies was extra-legal and deeply rooted in divine law and inherently tied to the natural world and home space.[32] Based on these connections, Hestia (Greek) or Vesta (Roman) was the goddess of the home and hearth and provided protection for those inside the home whether they were host or guest.[33] In *Game of Thrones*, the New Gods represent a direct link to nature and can easily be associated with the hospitable comforts of the home. The Seven, on the other hand, are more removed from the natural world and the figure of the Mother might oversee aspects of hospitality; however, the Stranger is also an apt choice to handle matters of hospitality, since it is the deified representation of the unknown guest.[34]

Similar to biblical hospitality, Roman and Greek hospitality took on legal definitions, but was "hallowed by religion" and viewed as god-watched.[35] This meant that providing hospitality was a belief more so than a choice, but that hospitality was also an obligation and violators could not escape without the gods' wrath.[36] For this reason, people did not violate the laws of hospitality.[37] However, for most, it was based on honor, duty, and religious devotion instead of formal agreements, and for these reasons personal, spiritual investment in the process of *hospitium* was intensely powerful.[38] Such theological underpinnings of hospitality are also present in *Game of Thrones* and draw on similar religious structures as mentioned above.[39]

VICIOUS VIOLATORS OF *HOSPITIUM* AT THE RED WEDDING

The "Red Wedding" episode, also known formally as the "Rains of Castamere" episode, racked in 5.9 million illegal downloads, which makes it the most illegally downloaded episode ever.[40] This episode is vital to the storyline, marks one of the most violent death sequences in the series, and is an extensive example of *hospitium* violation.[41] As the episode "The Rains of Castamere" opens, the audience is privy to a conversation between Robb Stark and his mother, Catelyn, we find out that the Starks will go ahead with their plan to attack the Lannister holding of Casterly Rock.[42] However, this plan hinges on "if Walder Frey cooperates" ("The Rains of Castamere"). Already, the Starks are aware of Walder Frey's inability to follow the social codes of Westeros. The scene cuts to the arrival of the Stark army with Grey Wind, Robb Stark's direwolf, leading the charge and the Stark banners flying high as they enter the Twins. Following Steve Reece's categorization of the phases of *hospitium*, the audience has now seen the official arrival of the guests and is being moved through the rest of the *hospitium* process.[43] The framework of this episode also reestablishes for the audience the presence of medieval chivalric codes and the status of the Starks as visitors to the Twins.

The next scene sets the tone for the practice of *hospitium* where the passing of the traditional salt and bread bowl represents the forging of a bond between hosts and guests. The bowl moves from Robb Stark to Catelyn Stark and then to his new bride, Talisa Stark.[44] In the meantime, Walder Frey says, "my honored guests be welcome within my walls and at my table ... I extend to you my hospitality and protection in the light of the Seven" ("The Rains of Castamere"). When the bowl reaches Lord Frey, he dips the bread in the salt and slowly chews the offering. In sharing in the traditional salt and bread ritual, the two groups are then bound in brotherhood, and *hospitium* is fully established by Lord Frey's words and actions.[45]

Up to this point, the episode does not deviate from the traditional steps of *hospitium*, and Robb Stark, after taking the offering from the Freys, begins to prostrate himself to Lord Frey. He gives thanks, apologizes, and asks for forgiveness for his previous wrongdoing of breaking the oath his mother swore on his behalf to marry one of Lord Frey's daughters. In response, Lord Frey suggests that Robb apologize to the Frey girls, since they are the ones who lost out from Robb's betrayal of the oath. Robb claims, "All men should keep their word, kings most of all" ("The Rains of Castamere"). This seems like an interesting hint of what is to come when Lord Frey will break his oath to protect his guests under his roof.[46] To close the scene, Lord Frey says, "The wine will flow red and the music will play loud and we'll put this mess behind us" and he stands from his throne ("The Rains of Castamere"). Finally, the audience is given the full reception of the *hospitium* tradition and can move on to the subversion of the traditional marriage ceremony and reception feast.

After the Edmure-Roslin wedding ceremony takes place in the show, the Red Wedding montage opens with a deep focus on the musicians at the feast.[47] This should alert the audience to the role of the musicians, which will become more apparent throughout the progression of the scene. Overall, the tone of the feast is celebratory, and offers the audience a touchstone from Reece's categorization where entertainment is provided to please the guests and suggest that the Freys are offering more than the fulfillment of needs.[48] However, with some extensive close reading, we can see that the Stark guests are having their fill of food, drink, and entertainment, while the Frey and Bolton factions appear alert.[49] Lord Frey calls for the bedding of Edmure and Roslin, and King Robb responds in deference to his host's desires.[50] Up until this point in the episode, the audience is lulled into a false sense of security in the hospitality system at work between the Starks and Freys. Perhaps this is because the focus of the camera and of hospitality is often on the guests and their behavior.[51] In response to King Robb's acquiescence to the bedding ceremony, the Freys escort Roslin and Edmure out of the hall, which leaves only the essential Freys and all of the Starks present in the space.[52] Once the hall has emptied, one of the Freys closes the doors, and the camera pans back to the musicians as they begin to play the "Rains of Castamere."[53] Though the action has not started, all signs of an impending attack are present, and the looming violation of *hospitium* is palpable in this moment.

The tipping point of the violation comes when Lord Frey holds his hand up, the music ceases, and he tells King Robb that he has been "remiss in my duties . . . [I] haven't shown you the hospitality you deserve" ("The Rains of Castamere"). As he speaks these words, Catelyn pulls back Roose Bolton's sleeve to reveal armor. A rapid array of events then takes place: Lord Frey states that he owes Queen Talisa a wedding gift, Catelyn yells for Robb to run, Lothar Frey stabs Talisa's pregnant stomach numerous times, the Freys pull out knives and begin to slit the throats of the Stark men, and the musicians-turned-assassins throw aside their instruments and take up crossbows to shoot Robb and his bannermen. Outside of the hall, Arya Stark arrives to see the first Stark men die as they dine and will then witness the hostile shooting of the defenseless Grey Wind in the Frey pens.[54] Though Arya Stark is no stranger and no god, her future role as an assassin of the Many-Faced God suggests that her viewing this massacre is important because she personally witnesses these deaths and will take on violent vengeance toward these traitors. She also represents the "watching god" that is ever-present in the world of *Game of Thrones*. As Arya served the God of Death in the series, she can be interpreted as a human representation of the god's impending retribution. The remainder of the Red Wedding events inside and outside of the hall is a mess of stabbings, throat-slitting, and repetitive arrow shooting. In addition, Lord Frey is drinking his wine, laughing, and watching the scene unfold, which demonstrates his flagrant disrespect of the established laws of hospitality and openly mocks the gods.

For a second time, Lord Frey holds his hand up and the music ceases as Robb Stark rises to go to the dying Talisa. At this point, Catelyn takes Lord Frey's young wife as a hostage and begs him to let Robb leave the hall unharmed or she will murder the girl. She claims, "I swear we will forget this by the Old Gods and the New . . . we will take no vengeance" ("The Rains of Castamere"). This moment shows the removal of human punishment that Catelyn is offering to Lord Frey, though this does not keep him from divine punishment. However, Lord Frey rejects this last attempt to show *hospitium* to his guests and demonstrates his deep indifference for the killing of his wife. The final moments of the episode show the ultimate betrayal of *hospitium* when Robb Stark is killed by Roose Bolton, who stabs him once more and states, "The Lannisters send their regards" ("The Rains of Castamere"). Though this is a standard phrase from House Lannister, it seems inappropriate given that they, along with Houses Frey and Bolton, just committed one of the most heinous crimes in the eyes of the people of the realm and the gods. As Catelyn Stark wails over her son's death, Black Walder slits her throat and the episode ends. Until the last second of this episode, the extent of the violation being committed can be seen by the audience. There is no question of the atrocity that was committed nor the theological implications of the violation for the perpetrators.

GRUESOME RESULTS AND GODLY REVENGE

Carolyne Larrington, at the point where the show left off in 2016, makes the claim that the Freys are not served justice and that no executive power can penalize the Freys for their violation of guest rights.[55] However, two plus years later and an added few seasons shows us that the Freys, Lannisters, and Boltons all receive their punishment. It is the nature of this punishment that is most apt and clearly indicates the theological basis of guest rights. Unlike other moments of punishment for violators (i.e., Daenerys' revenge on Xaro

Xhoan Daxos), this act of vengeance appears to be linked to the gods in numerous ways.

In the aftermath of the Red Wedding, the small council meets with King Joffrey in King's Landing. The entire council, except for Tyrion Lannister, celebrates and mocks the deaths of the Stark family. This includes Joffrey's request that the head of Robb be sent to him so that he can serve it to Robb's sister, Sansa, on his upcoming wedding day feast.[56] Once the small council empties, Tyrion and Tywin are left alone, and Tyrion tells his father that, "The northerners will never forget" ("Mhysa") and that "Walder Frey gets all the credit, or the blame, I suppose, depending on your allegiance" ("Mhysa"). Tyrion is pointing out that human blame will depend on house alliances, but his comments miss that the punishment of the Old Gods and the Seven is not as wavering for those who break guest rights.[57] Regardless of the Lannister's beliefs, the gods serve retributive justice in Tywin's death by Tyrion's hand when he is on the latrine. Not only is this patricide, but it is an equally cursed offense of kinslaying by his son. Furthermore, it speaks of the poetic irony that Tywin is slain by a crossbow, when most of the high-ranking Stark leaders are killed at the Twins by the crossbow-bearing musician assassins. In Tywin's mind, the gods have always punished him in the form of Tyrion's birth as a dwarf, and his own death by the hands of his "monster" son is suggestive of the god's mocking his belief.

In the episode titled, "Mhysa," Arya Stark and her captor, the Hound, come upon a group of Frey soldiers re-enacting the Stark deaths and discussing their roles in the massacre. Not only did the Boltons, Lannisters, and Freys murder the Starks as their guests but they also desecrated their bodies. This included throwing Catelyn Stark into the river and merging the body of Robb Stark with his direwolf's head.[58] The Freys and their partners go beyond the typical violation of guest rights and flaunt their disregard for the gods' potential punishment.[59] In this scene, Arya Stark seeks a seat around the fire of some Frey soldiers and food; however, they violently rebuke her as a potential guest, and she takes her revenge on the soldier who was discussing his part in the desecration of Robb's body. The violation of *hospitium* is doubled down on in this moment, and the immediate punishment of the soldier by Arya should indicate what lies in wait for Lord Frey. Furthermore, it should demonstrate the volatile vengeance that comes with betraying the trust that hospitality laws have established in this society.

As though Arya's actions against the soldier weren't enough to foreshadow the retribution of the gods, the tale of the "Rat Cook" told by Bran Stark solidifies not only the impending deaths of Lord Frey and Lord Bolton but also substantiates the theological power behind the law of hospitality in Westeros. Bran's story about the Rat Cook opens with the cook of the Night's Watch being angry at the king of Westeros for a reason he cannot recall.[60] The king visits the Nightfort and the cook kills the king's son and cooks him into a pie. The Rat Cook then serves the pie to the king and he devours not one but two slices because of the delicious taste. The gods are angry with the cook and turn him into a giant white rat that must haunt the Nightfort forever and consume his offspring but never be full. Meera Reed questions the veracity of Bran's tale by suggesting that it is ridiculous for the gods to punish all killers by turning them into giant white rats. However, Bran rebukes her claim and says, "it wasn't for murder the gods cursed the Rat Cook or for serving the king's son in a pie. He killed a guest beneath his roof. That's something the gods can't forgive" ("Mhysa"). Immediately after saying these words, the scene cuts to a close-up of Lord Walder Frey eating and drinking as his hall is cleaned after the Red Wedding. If the audience listens closely, they can also hear the squeaking of rats in the hall.[61] The scene ends with Lord Frey toasting to the Starks, drinking in their honor, and howling like a wolf. Together, Frey and Bolton mock and celebrate the demise of the Starks and their sudden wealth of titles, lands, and income.[62]

The end of the sixth season brought complete and violent closure to the violators of *hospitium* at the Red Wedding.[63] In the penultimate episode of season six, Roose Bolton, who played the pivotal traitor of the North in the Red Wedding, is murdered by the hand of his own son, Ramsay Bolton.[64] Similar to Tyrion Lannister, Ramsay Bolton commits patricide and kinslaying, which are both attributed to the gods' punishment. This moment also echoes of Roose Bolton's murder of Robb Stark through one strong blow from a close-range knife stab. Again, the gods appear to be doling out retributive justice to the violators of *hospitium* through rather ironic, symmetrical means. Furthermore, the vengeance of the gods goes beyond mere punishment. Both Tywin Lannister and Roose Bolton, who committed one of the biggest crimes in betraying their guests, are served their deaths through the equally heinous crimes of kinslaying and patricide. To the audience, this might also read as poetic, humorous justice being served to the worst of offenders.

Finally, in the episode titled, "The Winds of Winter," the audience sees justice served to the biggest perpetrator of the laws of hospitality.[65] Contextually, the Freys are entertaining the Lannister army after their joint victory at River Run.[66] At the celebration, Lord Frey and Jaime Lannister have a conversation where they distinguish between men who fight and men who win battles by other means. Jaime looks down on and mocks Lord Frey for his lack of killing; however, Lord Frey tells him that he can mock and laugh at him like the Tullys and Starks did and see where that gets him in the long run.[67] Again, there is a clear show of no remorse by Lord Frey, and makes it evident that he will happily break *hospitium* again if it means his houses' survival. This might also be a conversation overheard by Arya Stark, who is disguised at the feast, to remind her of the atrocities committed by this man.

Later, Walder Frey finishes off a slice of meat pie and is served a second slice by a young girl who shows up early at the Lannister-Frey celebration.[68] After this, Lord Frey asks about the whereabouts of his children, Lothar Frey and Black Walder, and the girl repeats twice that the sons are there in the hall with Lord Frey. When Lord Frey does not understand her meaning, the serving girl moves the pie plate in front of him and repeats again that the male heirs are in front of him. Lord Frey lifts back the top of the pie crust to reveal a cooked finger. As Lord Frey is gagging, the serving girl comments that both sons were hard to carve, especially Black Walder. Lord Frey looks up at the girl, she pulls off her face, and Arya Stark reveals herself and claims her Stark name. Arya proceeds to grab Lord Frey's head and slit his throat. Similar to Lord Frey's reaction at the Red Wedding, Arya shows little emotion other than satisfaction by smiling while he dies.

In this moment, it is important to understand that Arya serves two functions—Arya as a Stark and Arya as an assassin trained by the Faceless Men. In the first role, Arya exacts violent revenge on her house's enemies. She witnessed the murder of her family and is now calling on the violator to pay for his actions. This is an intimate form of vengeance that speaks more to retributive justice that is exacted on those who violate *hospitium*. In her second role, Arya's actions mean far more for the might of the gods and the actual power behind the laws of hospitality in the world of *Game of Thrones*. Arya, in her arduous journey from Westeros to the Free Cities, is received in the House of Black and White, which is a place of worship for the God of Death or the Many-Faced God. Under Jaqen H'ghar's tutelage, Arya is trained as an assassin for the Faceless Men who serve the Many-Faced God and kill on contract.[69] Though Arya leaves the Faceless Men, she takes her training and ideals back to Westeros. It is in this episode where we see Arya's assassin training come to life in Westeros and her use of the face disguise to get into the celebration suggests her representation of godly retribution. However, her removal of the face and the deliberate identification of herself to Lord Frey suggest that she transitions in her vengeance from godly agent to personal agent. Arya's connection to the Many-Faced God complicates the theological basis of the laws of hospitality. This god hails from Essos, not Westeros, and the god's name is never invoked during the guest rights ritual of the Red Wedding. Thus, Arya's killing of Lord Frey spins an intricate web of questions related to the gods' role in punishing Lord Frey. Some aspects of consideration here are that Arya's training will always align her with the God of Death and the God of Death may correlate to the Stranger god from the Faith of the Seven.[70] It is also interesting to consider that the Old Gods of the North and the Seven failed to punish the Freys for their violation of *hospitium* and the retribution of a new god, the Many-Faced God, is necessary to fulfill the notion of godly agency and power. No matter the interpretation of Arya's representation in this moment, the role of the gods in punishing all the violators of *hospitium* is clear, complete, and powerful.

This consideration of new godly power in Westeros leads into the conversation we see take place after the death scene of Lord Frey. The episode moves the audience to a landscape view of the Winterfell weirwood, where Sansa is sitting in front of the heart tree. Petyr Baelish asks Sansa if he is interrupting her prayers, and Sansa tells him that she is done with that sort of thing (prayer). Sansa then tells the story of praying every single day to the Old Gods about taking her away from Winterfell. It appears Sansa has given up her belief in the Old Gods because they answered her prayers and brought her to the horrific adventures in King's Landing that she endured for seasons. Similarly, while at King's Landing, Sansa appears to have taken up belief in the Seven to get her out of the situation of marrying Joffrey and getting her away from the Lannisters. However, the Seven did not answer her prayers until it was too late, and she was then married off to worse stock in the form of Ramsay Bolton.[71] In all, the Old Gods and Seven failed Sansa precisely because they answered her prayers but in a literal and uncompassionate manner or because they remained inactive and ignored her prayers. In response, the audience and scholars are left to consider if perhaps the strength and exacting manner of the Many-Faced God of Death appears to have been the real underlying power behind the laws of *hospitium* in the *Game of Thrones* universe. If true, this would mean that guest rights should continue to be upheld above all other laws, even during a time in Westeros (post-Red Wedding) when faith in *hospitium* is failing in places like the Riverlands. Also, it means that violators should give serious pause to their actions because of the swift, ruthless, vengeful nature of this new god. The retributive justice that slowly moves through the series becomes ever-present with the arrival of the Many-Face God, and the audience is left to wonder how divine agency now functions in the face of hired assassins.

CONCLUSION

By drawing on the historical extent and nuance of the laws of *hospitium*, Martin constructs a familiar set of socially governed rules. However, similar to the real-world laws of hospitality, the fictional world of *Game of Thrones*' laws of *hospitium* are substantiated through their theological roots. The bonds of guest rights are forged in the name of the gods and are to be upheld to show piety and respect for the gods' power. Violators, like those who plotted the infamous Red Wedding, are dealt with through godly, violent vengeance that often reflects punishments of irony, rough justice, and wrathful exaction. Though religion in the series is often represented as either dogmatically followed or radically imposed, it appears that the role of the gods in *Game of Thrones* is vital, and that divine retributive justice is the tie that binds all of the religions in Martin's narrative world together. Furthermore, for any single leader to win the game, it seems evident that the gods will play a part in the process and that following the laws of *hospitium* and demonstrating faith in the theologies of their kingdom(s) is essential to establishing rule in the universe of *Game of Thrones*.

NOTES

1. Christoph Auffarth, "Protecting Strangers: Establishing a Fundamental Value in the Religions of the Ancient Near East and Ancient Greece," *Numen* 39, no. 2 (1992): 195.

2. Clifford Ando, "Aliens, Ambassadors, and the Integrity of the Empire," *Law and History Review* 26, no. 3 (2008): 501.

3. Kevin D O'Gorman, "Dimensions of Hospitality: Exploring Ancient and Classical Origins," In *Hospitality: A Social Lens*. United Kingdom: Routledge, 2007: 17–32.

4. This chapter will also pull in various minor examples from the series to substantiate claims about hospitality. Furthermore, this chapter will only use references to the book version of *Game of Thrones* to show deviations from the television show.

5. Oscar E Nybakken, "The Moral Basis of Hospitium Privatum," *The Classical Journal* 41, no. 6 (1946): 248.

6. Though *hospitium publicum* could be possible here, the fact that both the Freys and the Starks hail from the North suggests that there is little differentiation between the geographical locations of their houses. The Starks are calling on the Freys to become part of the Northern bannermen and serve the King of the North. However, the Red Wedding visit is not portrayed in the same *hospitium publicum* manner that King Robert Baratheon's visit to Winterfell (in season one) is with the pomp, circumstance, and proper process.

7. See Nybakken, "The Moral Basis of Hospitium Privatum," 249.

8. Ibid.

9. Randi Pahlua, "Hospitality and the Natural World Within an Ecotheological Context in William Shakespeare's *Much Ado About Nothing* and Jane Austen's *Pride and Prejudice*," (Doctoral dissertation, Kent State University, 2015: 50. ProQuest Number: 3739311).

10. Calvo, 49.

11. H. Mark Ashworth. "Hospitality as Informing Image for Christian Community: A Study in Theological Ethics," (Doctoral dissertation, Baylor University, 1997), 12–13, UMI Number: 9734352.

12. Ibid., 13–21.

13. Carolyne Larrington, *Winter is Coming: The Medieval World of Game of Thrones*, Vol. 20151021 (London and New York: I.B. Tauris), 2016: 36–38. See

Larrington, 36–38. Though the Red Wedding catches viewers by surprise because of its ruthless execution of guests, a similar story of guests dying at dinner is told in Chaucer's Man of Law's Tale where the newly married couple and their guests are murdered during a wedding feast. Historical equivalents of the Red Wedding also exist. The most notable are the Black Dinner in 1440 and the Glencoe Massacre 1692.

14. Felix Schröter, "The Game of *Game of Thrones*. George RR Martin's A Song of Ice and Fire and Its Video Game Adaptations," *Media Convergence and Transmedial Worlds (Part 3)/ Medienkonvergenz und transmediale Welten (Teil 3)*. Special Issue, *IMAGE* 22 (2015): 65–82.

15. Larrington, 38. *Game of Thrones* also demonstrates moments where the good guys consider breaking guest rights. For example, Jon Snow goes into Mance Rayder's tent with the intent of killing him, but quickly changes his mind as they share a meal together. This moment of potential violation is given a full stop in the episode likely because Jon was raised in the North as a Stark child and he was taught to honor the principles of guest rights. As Jon took his Night's Watch oath under the heart tree outside of Castle Black, we also know that his belief in the Old Gods might sway his decision to not attack his host because of the sacredness of guest rights under the gods. *Game of Thrones* lore suggests that heart trees know when someone is lying, which is why oaths, prayer, and marriage all happen in a godswood in front of one of the trees. This suggests that Jon truthfully upholds his beliefs in the Old Gods and abides by their absolute rule.

16. Ibid., 121.

17. Ibid., 42.

18. See Kavita Mudan Finn, *Fan Phenomena: Game of Thrones*, (Chicago: The University of Chicago Press and Intellect Books, 2017). This text provides additional reading on materiality in *Game of Thrones*, fan reactions and communication about the show, and analysis of the show and books related to current theories.

19. Judith Still, *Derrida and Hospitality*, Edinburgh: Edinburgh University Press, 2012: 27; 205.

20. Auffarth, "Protecting Strangers," 204–5.

21. Ashworth, "Hospitality as Informing Image," 11–12.

22. Christoph Auffarth. "Protecting Strangers: Establishing a Fundamental Value in the Religions of the Ancient Near East and Ancient Greece." *Numen* 39, no. 2 (1992): 199.

23. O'Gorman, "Dimensions of Hospitality," 20.

24. Pahlua, "Hospitality and the Natural World," 18.

25. Ibid., 18–19.

26. See Felicity Heal's discussion on Christian charity and hospitality. Felicity Heal, "The Idea of Hospitality in Early Modern England," *Past & Present* 102 (1984): 66–93. Also, for a longer discussion of the Host, host, and guest connection of God's hospitality, see Pahlua, 53. Furthermore, see Auffarth, 198 for a discussion on the laws of Israel and how these laws view the protection of strangers as a deed that God performed first and that others merely follow.

27. The God of the Old Testament was complicated and could equally provide mercy and wrath to his followers.

28. Ashworth, "Hospitality as Informing Image," 41.

29. Still, *Derrida and Hospitality*, 187.

30. Ibid., 206. Still discusses how in both faiths, Abraham, as the saint of hospitality, gathered followers who patronized him by acting as good hosts to others and offering their hospitality to all strangers.

31. For example, Jupiter/Zeus was often seen as the overseer of strangers and could dole out the full might of godly punishment to violators. As the practice of *hospitium* relied on *fides*, or faith in word, the goddess Fides would be deified and have a cult of her own to honor the essential part of faith in oaths (Nybakken, "The Moral Basis of Hospitium Privatum," 249).

32. Nybakken, "The Moral Basis of Hospitium Privatum," 249; Pahlua, "Hospitality and the Natural World," 45–50.

33. Janis Jennings, "Hestia, Goddess of the Hearth: Fire at the Center," (Doctoral Dissertation), Pacifica Graduate Institute, 2003: 44; 164. UMI Number: 3128820. Jennings discusses that Hestia also heavily protected the male lineage of those in the home and due to her nature, she sought to reject others, put up boundaries, and sustain the host's bloodline over her protective duties of the guest.

34. Characters often reference the Mother's mercy, which suggests godly intervention on the behalf of those that commit wrongs of any kind.

35. O'Gorman, "Dimensions of Hospitality," 25.

36. Calvo, 49.

37. Ignoring hospitality customs meant offending the gods and receiving their vengeance (Nybakken, "The Moral Basis of Hospitium Privatum," 250–52). Violating unwritten rules of hospitality was considered one of the grossest of crimes and perhaps provides a reason as to why so few violations occurred because the penalties were so severe. Violations of hospitality were sometimes slated into the categories of *xenodaites* or guest-eating monsters (e.g., Cyclops who devoured guests) or *xenoktonos* or those who slayed guests. Both kinds of offenders were condemned by humans and punished by the gods. Such violations and punishments include Cyclops' blindness as a result of ignoring the hospitality laws and the series of earthquakes created by Zeus for major breaks in *hospitium*. Other examples can be found in the great literary work of Ovid's *Metamorphoses*. Ovid recounts the tale of Jupiter and Mercury wandering around earth seeking a place to stay. After being turned away, the gods are finally invited in by Baucis and Philemon. After completing their host duties, the gods whisked Baucis and Philemon up to a high vantage point to watch their home be transformed into a temple and a flood take the homes of those in the valley who turned the gods away.

38. Ibid., 55.

39. For example, in Westeros, guilt of the gods watching was often invoked to scare people off, however, violations of guest rights happen in both Westeros and Essos. Thus, throughout the entire *Game of Thrones* universe, all guests are vulnerable. In Qarth, Daenerys loses her dragons and members of her *khalasar* are murdered even though she is the guest of Xaro Xhoan Daxos. Though Essos may not have as strong of social laws guiding hospitable interactions as Westeros, there is a universality inherent in guest rights that suggests this violation of Daenerys's

status of guest will come with retribution. In the North, the Old Gods are a collective entity who are undemanding of their followers and do not have buildings or official leaders. For example, Tyrion Lannister states, "I confess, I know little of the Old Gods. Perhaps someday you might enlighten me. I could even accompany you." In response, Sansa Stark says, "No. You ... you are kind to offer, but ... there are no devotions, my lord. No priests or songs or candles. Only trees, and silent prayer" (*A Storm of Swords,* chapter 53). However, the New Gods (often called the Seven) all play specific roles, have places and leaders of worship, and have many "rules." One of the Seven, the Stranger, is often referenced in relation to guest rights and Walder Frey invokes their name during the bonding ritual of the Red Wedding. However, the Stranger is also always seen as being feared because he represents the unknown and possibility of death (Larrington, *Winter is Coming,* 132). Both the Old Gods and the Seven put stock into the laws of hospitality, which means that both sets of gods should uphold and punish any violations of guest rights in the *Game of Thrones* universe.

40. Gierzynski, Anthony. "*Game of Thrones,* House of Cards and the Belief in a Just World." *Annual Meeting of the Midwest Political Science Association,* 2015: 6. This count does not include the legal downloads and HBO subscribers who accessed the episode on its air date.

41. Up to this point, the execution of Ned Stark likely held this title because of its abrupt nature, severe consequences, and brutal violence against a loved character of the series.

42. This plan is devised in a previous episode and discussed between Robb Stark and his wife, Talisa.

43. Steve Reece, *The Stranger's Welcome: Oral Theory and the Aesthetics of the Homeric Hospitality Scene,* (Michigan: University of Michigan Press, 1992). Steve Reece provides a categorization of the Homeric hospitality scenes whose calculated steps inform our understanding of the *Game of Thrones* process of hospitium. Reece, in analyzing all of the Homeric episodes, came up with the following phases of the hospitality ritual: arrival, reception, seating, feasting, identification, bedding down, bathing, gift giving, and departure. This is a fairly fixed-order process in Homer's episodes and involved similarly planned substeps. Of Reece's 38 sub-scenes of hospitality, the most relevant to this chapter are the phases of reception including hesitation of the host and the feast including the preparation, consumption, and conclusion. In receiving the guest, the host often sees the visitor, hesitates to see them as a friend or enemy, rises to greet them, and approaches for the official meeting. Reece's work also discusses how many guests in the Homeric episodes are often introduced to the host in a supplicant position where they are on bent knee begging for shelter and welcome. This leads the host to then raise them from this status to the role of guest of honor. The process of hospitium is similar to a well-rehearsed dance, and any deviation from the social script should cause some sort of hesitation in the hosts or guests. In the feast step of the process, the focus is on the preparation of the food and only short one-line comments make up the consumption and conclusion of the feast activities. In *Game of Thrones* and in the historical periods referenced in the texts, feast sharing is viewed as an intimate practice and the main locus of participation between hosts and guests.

Therefore, it seemed fitting to focus on the Red Wedding episode as a site of analysis and application of the hospitality discussion.

44. It is then passed around to the remaining high-ranking guests, and finally given over to the Frey family. All guests must partake in this ritual, and in having the bannermen take the bread and salt, an extension of hospitality is being offered to the entire Stark army.

45. For a discussion of the Eucharistic notions behind this ritual, see Larrington, *Winter is Coming*, 24.

46. Immediately following, there is an extensive moment of Lord Frey inspecting Queen Talisa as Robb's new wife, which can easily be interpreted as the "hesitation of the host" period that is easily dismissed with Lord Frey's supposed understanding of Robb's reasons for breaking the marriage promise.

47. Queen Talisa leans over to one of the Freys and comments on the good playing of the musicians. In response, Lothar Frey tells her they should be good because of how much they cost.

48. Unlike Reece's categories, the audience does not receive the standard lengthy feast preparation. This is likely because a modern audience would not find this as action-packed and interesting as the events of the Red Wedding. This might also be part of the unforeseen nature and lack of revealed planning on the part of the Freys, Boltons, and Lannisters. The less information given to the audience about this new alliance, the more shocking the deaths will be for them.

49. In the episode, Catelyn Stark notes Roose Bolton's refusal of the cup bearer's refill to his wine goblet. Bolton answers her questioning by mentioning that drink dulls the senses.

50. Lord Frey employs melodic, rhyming language in this moment. His request for the official bedding part of the ceremony is met with cup banging from around the hall, the starting up of the music, and the chants of "to bed."

51. A similar sense of guest-focus is given to the audience of Shakespeare's *Macbeth*. However, Shakespeare (unlike Martin and the *Game of Thrones* television show writers) provides numerous scenes of preparation and plotting on the end of the hosts. Thus, the audience is fully expecting the murder of the guest, King Duncan, by his hosts, Lord and Lady Macbeth.

52. As the hall empties, Roose Bolton and Catelyn Stark discuss her marriage to Ned Stark and his intolerance for the bedding ceremony. Catelyn says that Ned forbid the bedding from taking place because he thought "it wouldn't be right if he broke a man's jaw on our wedding night." Roose's reaction is to scoff at this remark and walk away from Catelyn. Though this is a bit of an odd moment for Catelyn, she is immediately drawn to watching her son and his wife share a passionate kiss and her suspicions (and those of the audience) are once again mitigated. See *Game of Thrones*, season three, episode nine, "The Rains of Castamere."

53. When the music begins, Grey Wind is shown whining and howling in warning from inside an outdoor pen. In front of Grey Wind's cage, the Stark men are laughing, drinking, and enjoying the revelry of the feast. The Hound and Arya Stark arrive into this scene by way of a stolen pig-selling cart. The Hound is stopped by Frey men and told the feast is over, though he rebukes their claim by stating that the feast does not

sound like it is over. In the background, Arya sees armed Frey men entering the hall and the "Rains of Castamere" can be heard loudly from within the castle.

54. However, in the books, this moment has Grey Wind running through the camp and taking some Frey men down before being killed. The lack of agency in the television version suggests a completely helpless Stark direwolf and a parallel being drawn between Robb Stark and his companion animal.

55. Larrington, *Winter is Coming*, 38.

56. As possible godly retribution, Joffrey will actually die at his wedding day feast from poisoned wine after he feasts on a pie; this moment echoes the Red Wedding deaths and the breaking of *hospitium* on the end of the guest in killing their host king.

57. This is likely because Tyrion is not a believer in either set of gods, however, he does know that human punishment (i.e., the Northerners) for the violation will likely make the perpetrators pay. This moment is then followed by a conversation between the two men about the nobility of murdering a large number of people in battle versus killing a few key players at a dinner. Tyrion says he is all for "cheating" during wartime, however, he disapproves of the killing of people at a wedding feast. This suggests that Tyrion adheres to the Westerosi law of hospitality, but that his father does not honor the same code of hospitality. This is a striking difference as Tywin is a high lord and was likely trained up (like all Westerosi knights) to respect and fear the Seven and their rule.

58. The desecration of Catelyn Stark's body is only discussed in the book (see *A Storm of Swords*) and leads to her becoming Lady Stoneheart and returning to the *Game of Thrones* series. Fans and scholars are still wondering if the final season will have Lady Stoneheart appear, though this is unlikely.

59. See *Game of Thrones*, season one, episode seven, "You Win or You Die," created by David Benioff and D. B. Weiss, aired May 29, 2011, on HBO. This might be fueled by the lack of the Seven's capacity to be seen as active agents in this society. This is most notable in the switching of religions by many of the characters. For example, Lord Commander Mormont asks if any of the Night's Watch recruits still keep the Old Gods. In response, Jon Snow stands and states that he does. This where Mormont suggests that Snow will want to take his vows in front of the sacred heart tree like his missing uncle did when he swore his oath. The commander says, "You'll find a weirwood a mile north of the wall and your Old Gods, too, maybe." In this moment, Samwell Tarly asks Lord Commander Mormont to take his vows with Jon Snow in front of a heart tree. Allisor Thorne, a fellow man of the Night's Watch and trainer of the new recruits, asks Sam, "Why would you forsake the Gods of your father and your own house?" In response, Sam states, "The Seven have never answered my prayers, perhaps the Old Gods will" and he is granted his request. After Sam makes his request, Mormont appears skeptical that House Tarly holds the Old Gods, but Sam's response convinces him to accept the notion. Other examples of the abandonment of the Old Gods and the Seven might include the acceptance of the Lord of Light by characters such as Stannis Baratheon and the Brotherhood without Banners.

60. This suggests that, similar to Lord Frey's reasons behind the Red Wedding, the Rat Cook's reasons were petty and weak and do not justify his retaliation.

61. From there, Lord Frey recounts to Roose Bolton the mockery he has faced at the hands of the Starks and Tullys and how they often called him late, laughed at him, and that the high lords thought of him as a lesser man. In all, Lord Frey appears to be justifying his actions at the Red Wedding by suggesting the lords of the North thought they were better than him and he managed to outwit them and survive.

62. Lord Frey receives the new title of Lord of River Run, which was once held by Lord Tully (the freshly deceased father of Catelyn Stark). Similarly, Roose Bolton will receive the title of Warden of the North because of his efforts at the Red Wedding.

63. See the episode titled, "Battle of the Bastards."

64. See *Game of Thrones*, season six, episode nine, "Battle of the Bastards," created by David Benioff and D.B. Weiss, aired on June 19, 2016, on HBO.

65. *Game of Thrones*, season six, episode ten, "The Winds of Winter," created by David Benioff and D.B. Weiss, aired on June 26, 2016, on HBO.

66. Lord Frey tells Jaime Lannister that he cannot kill Edmure Frey because he is his son by law. Frey claims that it wouldn't be "right," and it would "give the family a bad name." All of these things he says in a tongue-in-cheek manner as if he knows that killing Edmure is the least of the offenses he could or has already committed. See *Game of Thrones*, season six, episode ten, "The Winds of Winter."

67. In this moment, Lord Frey calls himself and Jaime Lannister kingslayers. This is not to be confused with kinslayers, where families kill one another. Instead, kingslaying is the act of murdering one's sworn king. Both acts are cursed by the Old Gods and New Gods and seen as heinous crimes against the gods.

68. In the interim of this scene, Lord Frey asks the young serving girl if they are related—something she denies—and he smacks her backside in a sexual manner.

69. Martin draws on medieval historical assassin groups that served whomever was paying their contract. See Larrington, *Winter is Coming*, 57.

70. As Martin's religions often reflect historical religions, the similarities between Westeros and Essos religions become more apparent over the seasons. In the same way that the Lord of Light's following has spread from Essos to Westeros, the belief in the Many-Faced God might also be travelling to Westeros and is an easy substitute for the Seven's figure of the Stranger. This idea is further substantiated by the failure of the Seven to protect those in King's Landing from dying from Cersei Lannister's wildfire massacre.

71. Ramsay Bolton repeatedly beat and raped Sansa during the brief period they were married.

BIBLIOGRAPHY

Ando, Clifford. "Aliens, Ambassadors, and the Integrity of the Empire." *Law and History Review* 26, no. 3 (2008): 491–519.

Ashworth, H. Mark. "Hospitality as Informing Image for Christian Community: A Study in Theological Ethics" (Doctoral dissertation, Baylor University, 1997), 1–212, UMI Number: 9734352.

Auffarth, Christoph. "Protecting Strangers: Establishing a Fundamental Value in the Religions of the Ancient Near East and Ancient Greece." *Numen* 39, no. 2 (1992): 193–216. www.jstor.org/stable/3269906.
Benioff, David and Weiss, D. B. *Game of Thrones* (Warner Bros. Studio, HBO, 2011). Television.
Bremmer, Jan. "Scapegoat Rituals in Ancient Greece." *Harvard Studies in Classical Philology* 87 (1983): 299–320. www.jstor.org/stable/311262.
Cadwallader, Alan. *Earth as Host or Stranger?: Reading Hebrews II from Diasporan Experience.* Sheffield, England: Sheffield Academic Press, 2002.
Calvo, Ana María Manzanas. "Junot Díaz's "Otravida, Otravez" and Hospitalia: The Workings of Hostile Hospitality." *Journal of Modern Literature* 37, no. 1 (2013): 107–23.
Davetian, Benet. *Civility: A Cultural History.* Toronto, Canada: University of Toronto Press, 2009.
Del Sapio Garbero, Maria. "'A Goodly House": Memory and Hosting in Coriolanus', in *Shakespeare in Europe: History and Memory,* ed. by Marta Gibinska and Agnieszka Romanowska. Krakow: Jagiellonian University Press, 2008.
———. *"Fostering the Question 'Who Plays the Host?'." Identity, Otherness and Empire in Shakespeare's Rome.* United Kingdom: Routledge, 2016: 105–118.
Derrida, Jacques. "Hostipitality." *Angelaki: Journal of Theoretical Humanities* 5, no. 3 (2000): 3–18.
Finn, Kavita Mudan. *Fan Phenomena: Game of Thrones.* Chicago: The University of Chicago Press and Intellect Books, 2017.
Forcier, Eric. "Re (a) d wedding: A Case Study Exploring Everyday Information Behaviors of the Transmedia Fan." *Proceedings of the Association for Information Science and Technology* 54, no. 1 (2017): 93–101.
Game of Thrones, season one, episode seven, "You Win or You Die," created by David Benioff and D.B. Weiss, aired May 29, 2011, on HBO.
———, season three, episode nine, "The Rains of Castamere," created by David Benioff and D.B. Weiss, aired June 2, 2013, on HBO.
———, season three, episode ten, "Mhysa," created by David Benioff and D.B. Weiss, aired on June 9, 2013, on HBO.
———, season six, episode nine, "Battle of the Bastards," created by David Benioff and D.B. Weiss, aired on June 19, 2016, on HBO.
———, season six, episode ten, "The Winds of Winter," created by David Benioff and D.B. Weiss, aired on June 26, 2016, on HBO.
Gierzynski, Anthony. "*Game of Thrones*, House of Cards and the Belief in a Just World." *Annual Meeting of the Midwest Political Science Association.* 2015. www.researchgate.net/publication/283908504.
Heal, Felicity. "The Idea of Hospitality in Early Modern England." *Past & Present* 102 (1984): 66–93.
Hartinger, Brent. "A Different Kind of Other: The Role of Freaks and Outcasts in A Song of Ice and Fire." In *Beyond the Wall. Exploring George RR Martin's A Song of Ice and Fire.* Dallas: BenBella Books, 2012: 153–67.

Jennings, Janis. "Hestia, Goddess of the Hearth: Fire at the Center," (Doctoral Dissertation, Pacifica Graduate Institute, 2003. UMI Number: 3128820.

Jones, Andrew Zimmerman. "Of Direwolves and Gods." In *Beyond the Wall: Exploring George RR Martin's A Song of Ice and Fire, from A Game of Thrones to A Dance with Dragons.* Dallas: BenBella Books, 2012: 108–22.

Larrington, Carolyne. *Winter is Coming: The Medieval World of Game of Thrones.* Vol. 20151021. London and New York: I.B. Tauris, 2016.

Lowder, James. *Beyond the Wall: Exploring George R.R. Martin's A Song of Ice and Fire.* Dallas: BenBella Books, 2012.

Martin, George R. R. *A Game of Thrones.* New York City and United Kingdom: Bantam Spectra and Voyager Books, 1996.

———. *A Clash of Kings.* New York City and United Kingdom: Bantam Spectra and Voyager Books, 1998/9.

———. *A Storm of Swords.* New York City and United Kingdom: Bantam Spectra and Voyager Books, 2000.

Nybakken, Oscar E. "The Moral Basis of Hospitium Privatum." *The Classical Journal* 41, no. 6 (1946): 248–53. www.jstor.org/stable/3291725.

O'Gorman, Kevin D. "Discovering Commercial Hospitality in Ancient Rome." *Hospitality Review* 9, no. 2 (2007): 44–52. https://strathprints.strath.ac.uk/5846/.

———. "Dimensions of Hospitality: Exploring Ancient and Classical Origins." In *Hospitality: A Social Lens.* United Kingdom: Routledge, 2007: 31–46. https://strathprints.strath.ac.uk/6012/.

Ogletree, Thomas W. *Hospitality to the Stranger: Dimensions of Moral Understanding.* Westminster: John Knox Press, 2003.

———. "Hospitality to the Stranger: Reflections on the Role of the" Other" in Moral Experience." Selected Papers from the Annual Meeting of the American Society of Christian Ethics: Georgetown University Press, 1977.

Pahlua, Randi. "Hospitality and the Natural World Within an Ecotheological Context in William Shakespeare's *Much Ado About Nothing* and Jane Austen's *Pride and Prejudice.*" Doctoral dissertation, Kent State University, 2015: 1–214. ProQuest Number: 3739311.

Pohl, Christine D. "Hospitality From the Edge: The Significance of Marginality in the Practice of Welcome." *The Annual of the Society of Christian Ethics* 15 (1995): 121–36. www.jstor.org/stable/23559674

Reece, Steve. *The Stranger's Welcome: Oral Theory and the Aesthetics of the Homeric Hospitality Scene.* Michigan: University of Michigan Press, 1992.

Schérer, René. Zeus Hospitalier: Éloge de L'Hospitalité: Essai Philosophique. trans. A. Colin, 1993.

Schröter, Felix. "The Game of *Game of Thrones.* George RR Martin's A Song of Ice and Fire and Its Video Game Adaptations." *Media Convergence and Transmedial Worlds (Part 3)/ Medienkonvergenz und transmediale Welten (Teil 3).* Special Issue, *IMAGE* 22 (2015): 65–82.

Schubart, Rikke, and Anne Gjelsvik. *Women of Ice and Fire: Gender, Game of Thrones and Multiple Media Engagements.* New York: Bloomsbury, 2016.

Still, Judith. *Derrida and Hospitality*. Edinburgh: Edinburgh University Press, 2012.

Vaught, Susan. "The Brutal Cost of Redemption in Westeros. Or, What Moral Ambiguity?" In *Beyond the Wall: Exploring George RR Martin's A Song of Ice and Fire*. Dallas: BenBella Books, 2012: 89–106.

Weber, David P. "Law of the *Game of Thrones*." 2018: 1–4. www.dspace.creighton.edu

Westmoreland, Mark W. "Interruptions: Derrida and Hospitality." *Kritike: An Online Journal of Philosophy* 2, no. 1 (2008): 1–10.

Part II

ECCLESIOLOGY OF THRONES

Chapter 4

What is Dead May Never Die

The Drowned God and Jesus' Call to Discipleship

Shaun C. Brown

In *The Great Code: The Bible and Literature*, Northrop Frye demonstrates the pervasive influence of the Bible upon Western art and literature. Frye says that he initially came to have an interest in this topic when teaching William Blake and John Milton to his students. He realized that even his most conscientious students have difficulty understanding much of Blake and Milton apart from some knowledge of the Bible.[1] Frye notes that translations of the Bible like Martin Luther's German Bible "were powerful generators of narrative, allusion, and other forms of verbal articulateness in their cultures."[2] Other translations, like the King James Version in English, served a similar function within other cultures.

Not all art and literature draw upon the Bible in the same way. Some writings, such as John Bunyan's *Pilgrims Progress* or C. S. Lewis' *The Lion, The Witch, and The Wardrobe*, draw constructively upon the Bible and biblical imagery in order to tell distinctly Christian stories. Others, however, use biblical language or imagery in order to subvert it (e.g., Philip Pullman's *His Dark Materials*), because it is a part of the common language of people within a given culture (Abraham Lincoln's Second Inaugural), or to escalate the significance of a conflict (the film *Tombstone* or the television series *Sleepy Hollow*).

George R. R. Martin's *A Song of Ice and Fire* also draws upon imagery from the Bible, either directly or indirectly due to Martin's indebtedness to other Western authors.[3] An example of this can be seen in his description of the people of the Iron Islands, who do not worship the Seven nor the old gods, but the Drowned God, who creates and makes kings, sets apart the people of the Iron Islands, and drowned on their behalf.[4] It is unclear whether or not he draws upon this imagery to comment upon Christianity, but it is clear that he does so in order to develop the mythology of Westeros. Martin also derived inspiration for the ironborn from the Vikings.[5] This can be seen in their use of longships, practice of raiding, and so on. Martin, of course, is not the only fantasy author to draw upon both biblical imagery and Norse mythology, as J. R. R. Tolkien exemplifies.

In his work on the New Testament use of the Old Testament, Richard Hays distinguishes between a quotation, allusion, and echo. A quotation is a direct, verbatim quotation, usually of a sentence or more, of source material. An allusion, according to Hays, "usually imbeds several words from the precursor text, or is at least in some way explicitly mentions notable characters or events that signal the reader to make the intertextual connection."[6] If readers miss an allusion, then they have a much weaker grasp of a text. An echo, the "least distinct" of the three categories, "may involve the inclusion of only a word or phrase that evokes, for the alert reader, a reminiscence of an earlier text." Hays says,

> Readers who hear an echo will discern some semantic nuance that carries a surplus of significance beyond the literal sense of the text in which the echo occurs; ordinarily, however, the surface meaning of the text would be intelligible to readers who fail to hear the echoed language.[7]

There are no quotations of the Bible in *A Song of Ice and Fire*, though one can see some allusions and echoes to the Bible within the series. This essay will reference other instances of biblical echoes and allusions in Martin's description of the Drowned God, but it will primarily focus on the parallels between faith in the Drowned God and Jesus' call to discipleship. While both call upon people to die to themselves, these two calls differ in *telos*—the ironborn die to themselves so they may bravely fight in battle and disciples of Jesus die to themselves so that they may serve God and neighbor.

THE DROWNED GOD

The ironborn describe the Drowned God as the "Lord God who drowned for us,"[8] just as Paul says "Christ died for us" (Rom 5:8). The people of the Iron Islands believe that the Drowned God has watery halls beneath the sea.[9] They hope to find their way to these halls after their death, so they return their dead to the water ("Home").[10] They do not fear drowning or dying at sea. When this happens, they enter the watery halls where "mermaids attend to [their] every want."[11] They thus maintain, "There is no joy but in the Drowned God's watery halls."[12] They, however, also sometimes execute people by drowning them, so the water can symbolize both salvation and judgment.[13]

The Drowned God is, according to the people of the Iron Islands, opposed by the Storm God, a "malignant deity who dwells in the sky and hates men and all their works."[14] The Storm God, as his name implies, sends storms to thwart the work of people. The ironborn blame the Storm God for misfortune, such as death, that arises, as well as for disagreements that arise among them.[15]

This Drowned God "makes men,"[16] and he gives every person a gift.[17] The ironborn, however, see themselves as unique. While others claim to be the "first men," the people of the Iron Islands claim to be a people set apart. They see themselves as a chosen and elected people, like Israel does.[18] While other people came to Westeros from across the seas, the priest Sauron Salt-Tongue says, in words reminiscent of the priestly creation narrative in Genesis, "We came from beneath those seas, from the watery halls of the Drowned God who made us in his likeness and gave us dominion over the waters of the earth."[19] The faith of the Andals, with their septas and septons and the preaching of the Seven, has been tolerated on occasion among the ironborn, largely due to intermarrying with the Andals, but only in co-existence with the worship of the Drowned God. It did not catch on in the Iron Islands the same way that it did elsewhere.

The World of Ice & Fire says, "The Drowned God has no temples, no holy books, no idols carved in his likeness, but he has priests aplenty."[20] These itinerant, mendicant priests preach from their oral traditions and denounce the worship of other gods, as well as perform marriages and other sacred duties.

The Drowned God, like the God of the biblical text (e.g., Dan 2:21; John 19:11; Rom 13:1–2), also makes kings. The legends of the priests say that during the Age of Heroes, the ironborn were ruled by their first king, the Grey King. The Grey King married a mermaid so that his children could live above or below the sea. He taunted the Storm God and slayed the great sea dragon Nagga. He ruled for one thousand years. After that time, as his skin turned grey from old age, he set his crown aside and descended into the sea and took his place at the right hand of the Drowned God, the inverse of Jesus ascending to the right hand of the Father.[21]

During the time that the ironborn had kings, a prophet would convene a kingsmoot, a meeting in which all the men who owned boats would deliberate and listen to the waves in order to discern the Drowned God's will for who should be king. The devout, like Aeron, insist that a godless person cannot serve as king, and the people know that the Drowned God may cast down faithless kings. This practice ended due to a great conflict among the ironborn, but the priest and prophet Aeron Greyjoy convened a kingsmoot after the death of his brother Balon.[22]

WHAT IS DEAD MAY NEVER DIE

The ironborn have a common motto: "What is dead may" or "can never die, but rises again, harder and stronger."[23] Priests like Aeron call upon the ironborn to commit themselves to the Drowned God.[24] If they are already dead, then their foes cannot kill them. They say, "We are born to suffer, that our sufferings make us strong."[25] They believe that the Drowned God leads the people of the Iron Islands to "reave and rape, to carve out kingdoms and write their names in fire and blood and song."[26] Priests ask the Drowned God to "bless [their] swords," to lead them with strength into battle,[27] and the people pray that the Drowned God will return their warriors safely from battle.[28] Within the television series, we see Theon invoking this maxim to motivate his troops.

Theon: We die today, brothers. We die bleeding from a hundred wounds, with arrows in our necks and spears in our guts . . . but our war cries will echo through eternity! They will sing about the Battle of Winterfell until the Iron Islands have slipped beneath the waves! Every man, woman and child will know who we were and how long we stood. . . . What is dead may never die!
Soldiers: What is dead may never die! ("Valar Morghulis")[29]

They also use the saying after they lose men in battle ("Home").

The theology and practice of the people of the Iron Islands has some parallels with Jesus' call to discipleship, and in particular, his call for disciples to take up the cross. Within Matthew's Gospel, Jesus begins to call his disciples in chapter 4.[30] There we see him initially call two sets of brothers. He says to Simon Peter and Andrew, "Follow me, and I will make you fish for people," and, "Immediately they left their nets and followed him" (4:19–20). Shortly after, he came upon the sons of Zebedee, James and John, and they, and like Peter and Andrew, "Immediately they left the boat and their father, and followed him" (4:22). Later, Jesus comes upon Matthew, a tax collector. Jesus says, "Follow me," and "[Matthew] got up and followed him" (9:9). Dietrich Bonhoeffer notes that the text does not provide psychological explanations of why these disciples obeyed the call to follow Jesus. He argues that "there is only one good reason for the proximity of call and deed: *Jesus Christ himself.*"[31]

We later learn that Jesus called twelve disciples, and that he "gave them authority over unclean spirits, to cast them out, and to cure every disease and every sickness" (10:1). He sent them out to preach to the "lost sheep of the house of Israel," proclaiming to them that "[t]he kingdom of heaven has come near" (10:7). While some decline to follow after Jesus (8:18–22; 19:16–22), these disciples, as Peter remarks, "left everything" in order to follow Jesus (19:27).[32]

Jesus warns them as well that persecution will come to them because they follow him, but he reassures them that they will be aided in what to say to their persecutors by the Spirit of God (10:16–20) and that "the one who endures to the end will be saved" (10:22b). Jesus, however, does not encourage them to foolishly remain where they are rejected, but to go to the next town (10:23). They should not fear those who can only destroy their bodies, but rather "fear him who can destroy both the soul and the body" (10:28). He will acknowledge before God the Father those who acknowledge him and deny those who deny him (10:32–33).

Jesus then tells his followers that his coming will bring about divisions, even among family members (10:34–36). It is in this context that he first likens following after him to taking up the cross. He says,

> Whoever loves father or mother more than me is not worthy of me; and whoever loves son or daughter more than me is not worthy of me; and whoever does not take up the cross and follow me is not worthy of me. Those who find their life will lose it, and those who lose their life for my sake will find it. (10:37–39)

Jesus then repeats his call to take up the cross in Matthew 16:24–26:

> If any want to become my followers, let them deny themselves and take up their cross and follow me. For those who want to save their life will lose it, and those who lose their life for my sake will find it. For what will it profit them if they gain the whole world but forfeit their life? Or what will they give in return for their life? (cf. Mark 8:34–36; Luke 9:23–27, 14:27)[33]

In these passages within the Gospels, we see Jesus arguing that taking up one's cross, dying to oneself, leads to life. What dies in Christ may never truly die but is "born again" or "born from above" (John 3:3–5).

As the ironborn connect their commitment to the Drowned God with endurance in the face of suffering, so does Jesus in his call to discipleship. Bonhoeffer argues, "The call to discipleship is connected here with the proclamation of Jesus' suffering. Jesus Christ has to suffer and be rejected."[34] So Jesus here does not simply suffer, for he could have suffered and been admired for his suffering. Jesus, however, was also rejected, and this rejection "removed all dignity and honor from his suffering."[35] While Jesus did suffer and undergo rejection on behalf of others, he did not do so in order that his followers may avoid the same fate. Bonhoeffer concludes of Jesus' call to discipleship, "Whenever Christ calls us, his call leads us to death."[36]

This does not mean that disciples are left to suffer alone. Rather, "The cross is suffering *with Christ*."[37] Suffering is not optional for disciples of Jesus, but is "the identifying mark of a follower of Christ."[38] This is true not only of individual believers, but of the church as a whole. In this, Bonhoeffer follows Martin Luther, who places suffering and persecution as his seventh mark of the church.[39]

While the ironborn see this endurance in the face of suffering as giving them strength in battle and raids, Christians have through the centuries seen the strength that comes from dying to oneself in Christ as giving them strength in the face of persecution and death. Suffering for Christ, even to the point of martyrdom, does not bring misery for the believer, but is rather "the greatest joy and blessedness of his community."[40] On this point, Philip Ziegler quotes Ulrich Zwingli, who argues that "Christianity is something for which one must be prepared to die."[41] Ignatius of Antioch illustrates this in his letter to the Romans. There he expresses a willingness to die a martyr's death, saying that if he were to die and his remains eaten by the wild beasts, "Then I will truly be a disciple of Jesus Christ, when the world will no longer see my body."[42] He contends that he is only now, as he faces the possibility of death, truly becoming a disciple of Jesus. While he tells the Roman Christians not to wish for his death, he expresses a willingness to face all kinds of torture, from fire and crosses to the breaking of bones and the devil's tortures, in order to follow Christ. Christians like Ignatius recognize that it is through taking up their cross that they overcome suffering, and this was also the case for Jesus. Jesus prays in Gethsemane that the cup pass from him (Matt 26:39, 42), and while some may believe that Jesus' prayer went unanswered, Bonhoeffer argues, "The cup of suffering will pass from Jesus, but *only by his drinking it.*"[43]

There is an asymmetrical relationship between Jesus and disciples, which can be seen in the narratives in which Jesus calls his disciples discussed above. Jesus Christ, as Lord and Savior, calls disciples to follow him, to imitate him in a life of service. Jesus shows his disciples how to pray, how to love, and serve God and their neighbors. Before Jesus is an exemplar, however, he is Savior and Lord. One sees in looking at the person and work of Jesus Christ, especially his death on the cross, the goodness of God—that Christ acts on my behalf (*pro me*). As Luther says,

> If you have Christ as the foundation and chief blessing of your salvation, then the other part follows. Then you take him as your example and give yourself in service to your neighbor just as you see that Christ has given himself for you.[44]

So both Christians and the ironborn see dying to themselves as a way of pledging their allegiance to Jesus and the Drowned God, respectively, which is exemplified in their practices of baptism.

BAPTISM AS COMMITMENT TO THE DROWNED GOD

The people of the Iron Islands practice a form of baptism, and their holy water is sea water.[45] They recognize, as noted previously, that the Drowned God drowned "for us." They then, in imitation of the Drowned God, drown people and then resuscitate them with something resembling CPR. While this may seem odd, since this is a fantasy series, Martin gives this description of the drowned men resuscitating a boy named Emmond:

> His drowned men formed a circle around the dead boy, praying. Norjen worked his arms whilst Rus knelt astride him, pumping on his chest, but all moved aside for Aeron. He pried apart the boy's cold lips with his fingers and gave Emmond the kiss of life, and again, and again, until the sea came gushing from his mouth. The boy began to cough and spit, and his eyes blinked open, full of fear.[46]

Upon raising Emmond, Aeron Greyjoy says to him, "Rise. You have drowned and been returned to us. What is dead can never die." Then Emmond, struggling to speak, replies, "But rises. Rises again. Rises again. Harder. And stronger." Aeron tells him, "You belong to the god now." Emmond is welcomed by drowned men, and then Aeron continues, "You belong to the sea now, so the sea has armed you. We pray that you shall wield your cudgel fiercely, against all the enemies of our god." They see it as "a sign of the Drowned God's favor" when they resuscitate someone, though every priest but Aeron has lost people from time to time.[47] Aeron preaches, "We were born from the sea, and to the sea we all return,"[48] which echoes the words from Genesis, "you are dust, and to dust you shall return" (3:19). While Christian baptism takes place only once,[49] the ironborn sometimes repeat their baptisms, which can be seen in the example of Tarle the Thrice-Drowned.[50]

Game of Thrones depicts the practice in a different context. Euron Greyjoy comes to a kingsmoot and claims the throne for himself, saying that he will go with a fleet and convince Daenerys Targaryen to marry him. A priest then baptizes him, saying as Euron is held underwater:

> May Euron, your servant, be born again from the sea as you were. Bless him with salt. Bless him with stone. Bless him with steel. Listen to the waves. Listen to the god. He is speaking to us and he says, "We shall have no king but Euron Greyjoy." Let the sea wash your follies and your vanities away. Let the old Euron drown. Let his lungs fill with seawater. Let the fish eat the scales off his eyes. What is dead may never die, but rises again harder and stronger. ("The Door")

Unlike the depiction given in *A Feast for Crows*, they then simply lay Euron's body on the shore and wait to see if he wakes. When he does, the witnesses cheer.

It is a custom of the people of the Iron Islands to give a newborn child to the Drowned God. While some priests, like Aeron, believe that the infant should be drowned in a similar manner to what we see with Emmond, more often the people simply dip their children into a tub of seawater, slightly getting their heads wet. Not all agree with this accommodates practice. Aeron says of these dips, "That is no true drowning. He that does not die in truth cannot hope to rise from death."[51]

In addition to the practice of drowning described in *A Feast for Crows*, we see in *A Clash of Kings* that the ironislanders also practice a kind of consecration for those recommitting themselves to the Drowned God. As Theon returns from his time as a ward in Winterfell, his uncle Aeron, now a priest of the Drowned God, instructs him to kneel and bow his head. Aeron then pours some seawater upon Theon's head and says, "Let Theon your servant be born again from the sea, as you were." He then adds, "Bless him with salt, bless him with stone, bless him with steel." He asks Theon if he remembers the words, and Theon answers, "What is dead may never die," to which Aeron replies, "What is dead may never die, but rises again, harder and stronger."[52]

Within the television series, Theon's consecration is set in a slightly different context. Like in *A Clash of Kings*, he returns home to the Iron Islands not to the celebration he expects. Instead, his father, Balon Greyjoy, ridicules him as a traitor, as someone who has become a Stark, the family responsible for his older brothers' deaths. Though Theon is the oldest remaining son, Balon has given much trust and authority to his daughter, Yara (named Asha in the books). While he sends Yara off with thirty longships to plunder the north, he only gives Theon one ship with which to raid fishing villages.[53] Theon tries to convince Balon to pledge fealty to King Robb, arguing that if they do, they will be given Casterly Rock as a prize, and Robb will also make them an independent kingdom, giving Balon a crown. Balon angrily reminds Theon, "We are ironborn. We're not subjects. We're not slaves. We do not plow the fields or toil in the mine. We take what is ours. Your time with the wolves has made you weak."

Theon reminds his father that he did not volunteer to go to be a ward to the Starks. He says, "You gave me away! Your boy! Your last boy! You gave me away like I was some dog you didn't want anymore. And now you curse me because I've come home." His sister then also accuses Theon of spilled loyalty because he wants Balon to swear loyalty to the Starks. While he argues, "I have no other family," she tells him, "Don't you? Make your choice, Theon, and do it quickly. Our ships sail with our without you." Theon proceeds to write a letter to Robb explaining that his father has rejected his offer, but he burns the letter instead of sending it.

In the next scene, a priest asks him, in a visible, public ceremony in front of his father and sister and some soldiers with flags, "Theon of the house Greyjoy, you would this day consecrate your faith to the Drowned God?" He replies, "I would." He is instructed to kneel, and then the priest prays, "Let Theon your servant be born again from the sea as you were." As the priest pours water over Theon's head, he says, "Bless him with salt. Bless him with stone. Bless him with steel." Theon then responds, "What is dead may never die," and the priest repeats those same words, and adds, "but rises again harder and stronger" ("What is Dead May Never Die").[54]

BAPTISM AS UNION WITH CHRIST'S DEATH

In the Pauline letters, baptism is described as union with Christ's death. While some have stressed the differences in the teaching of Paul and Jesus, sometimes to the point of placing them in opposition to one another, Bonhoeffer emphasizes the continuity in how the Gospels and Pauline literature discuss the relation between disciples and Jesus Christ. While the Synoptic Gospels, in particular, stress the language of discipleship in discussing this relation, Paul often uses a different set of terms. Bonhoeffer says this is because of Paul's goal, which is not to describe Jesus' earthly life, but to proclaim Jesus' "presence as the risen and glorified Lord, and his work for us."[55] "To express the full witness of Christ requires more than a single set of terms," he argues. "Paul's terminology thus confirms that of the Synoptic Gospels and vice versa."[56]

Paul does, however, also speak of the need for followers of Christ to die to themselves. He says in Romans 8:13, "if you live according to the flesh, you will die; but if by the Spirit you put to death the deeds of the body, you will live." He echoes this sentiment in Galatians by arguing that he has been crucified with Christ, and because of that, "it is no longer I who live, but it is Christ who lives in me" (2:20; cf. Gal 5:24; 6:14). This is not possible due to any action on his part, but because of Christ's action on his behalf.

Paul discusses this death to oneself in connection with baptism. As Bonhoeffer argues, "What the Synoptics describe as hearing and following the call to discipleship, Paul expresses with the concept of *baptism*."[57] Baptism is a visible, passive act of obedience in which the Christian is claimed by Christ.[58] Paul demonstrates this in Romans 6, where he begins the chapter by raising a question. If grace abounds with the increase of sin, should people continue living lives of sin so that grace may continue to abound? Paul answers this, "By no means!" He reminds the Roman church that they have, in fact, died to sin through baptism. The baptism of the ironborn depicts this death in graphic detail. He says,

> Do you not know that all of us who have been baptized into Christ Jesus were baptized into his death? Therefore we have been buried with him by baptism into death, so that, just as Christ was raised from the dead by the glory of the Father, so we too might walk in newness of life. (6:3–4)

Here Paul correlates baptism with the death and burial of Christ and new life with Christ's resurrection.

According to Paul, those in Christ, those who have been baptized into him, should live differently than they had previously. As Paul argues,

> We know that our old self was crucified with him so that the body of sin might be destroyed, and that we might no longer be enslaved to sin. For whoever has died is freed from sin. But if we have died with Christ, we believe that we will also live with him. We know that Christ, being raised from the dead, *will never die again*; death no longer has dominion over him. The death he died, he died to sin, once for all; but the life he lives, he lives to God. So you also must consider yourselves dead to sin and alive to God in Christ Jesus. (6:6–11)[59]

People cannot bring about this death themselves, rather Christ makes this break possible, and it is made present to them through baptism. Through baptism they are set free from sin. Paul thus contends that they should not let sin rule them, but instead "present your members to God as instruments of righteousness" (6:13). Indeed, Paul tells them that true freedom does not come simply from being set free from slavery to sin, but from becoming "obedient from the heart to the form of teaching to which you were entrusted" (6:17); from becoming "slaves of righteousness" (6:18; see 19–22). Individuals are baptized, for as Bonhoeffer says, "We die in Christ alone; we die through Christ and with Christ."[60] At the same time, however, this baptism initiates people into community with Christ's body, the church.

Just as those who are baptized in Christ should live differently than they did before, we learn that before Aeron became a priest of the Drowned God, he was a partyer and a gambler. He was then captured when Stannis Baratheon trapped the ship that he sailed upon, and he spent the rest of the war in chains. He says,

> The god took me deep beneath the waves and drowned the worthless thing I was. When he cast me forth again he gave me eyes to see, ears to hear, and a voice to spread his word, that I might be his prophet and teach his truth to those who have forgotten.[61]

Aeron calls others to devote themselves to the Drowned God.[62]

The connection of baptism with Christ's death also fits with the watery imagery used of Christ's death in the Gospels, which is echoed in Martin's depiction of the Drowned God. Jesus, for example, compares his death and resurrection to Jonah spending "three days and three nights in the belly of the sea monster" (Matt 12:40; cf. 16:4). Jesus also describes his death as "the baptism with which I am baptized," and he tells his disciples that they will undergo the same baptism (Mark 10:39; cf. Luke 12:50). As Bonhoeffer says, "The cross of Christ is the gracious death, which we die once for all in our baptism; the cross to which we are called is our daily dying in the power of the death accomplished by Christ."[63]

CONCLUSION

There are various parallels and similarities between the faith of the ironborn in the Drowned God and Jesus' call to discipleship; echoes of scripture in Martin's depiction. They both have a belief in God acting *pro me*: the Drowned God drowned for us and Jesus dying for us. They both say by dying to oneself one has life, by drowning like the Drowned God or by taking up one's cross, by uniting to Christ's death in baptism. This act of baptism brings them into community with God and their community. They are also both assured that suffering will come and that it builds strength and endurance (Rom 5:3–5). This makes them willing to face death. They also have hope in new life, both in this life and the next.

There are of course also differences. While those of the Iron Islands die and are raised to become great in battle, Jesus tells his disciples that "unless you change and become like children, you will never enter the kingdom of heaven" (Matt 18:3). He calls upon them to be humble and argues that the one who is humble like a child is "the greatest in the kingdom of heaven" (Matt 18:4). Jesus declares that "many who are first will be last, and the last will be first" (19:30). And again,

> whoever wishes to be great among you must be your servant, and whoever wishes to be first among you must be your slave; just as the Son of Man came not to be served but to serve, and to give his life a ransom for many. (20:27–28)

While the ironborn valorize those in their midst who reave their enemies, Jesus calls upon his disciples to not retaliate (5:38–42) and to "[l]ove your enemies and pray for those who persecute you" (5:44). Bonhoeffer says of this, "Loving one's enemies leads disciples into the way of the cross and into communion with the crucified one."[64]

NOTES

1. Frye, *The Great Code*, xii.
2. Ibid., 5.
3. Martin argues he used the middle ages as a model for developing the mythology of the series, so the use of biblical language and imagery could come indirectly from that as well. See "Religions of Westeros."
4. The books depict the worship of the Drowned God as distinct to the people of the Iron Islands, but within the television show, the House of Black and White in Braavos includes a depiction of the Drowned God as one aspect of the Many-Faced God ("The House of Black and White," "The Sparrow").
5. "House of the Seven Kingdoms: Minor Houses."
6. Hays, *Echoes of Scripture in the Gospels*, 10.
7. Ibid., 10.
8. Martin, *A Feast for Crows*, 32.
9. Martin, García, Jr., and Antonsson, *The World of Ice & Fire*, 179; Martin, *A Feast for Crows*, 21, 23, 24, 28, 30, 334, 533, 534, 539; Martin, *A Dance with Dragons*, 345, 350, 674, 748, 749, 824, 833.
10. Martin, *A Dance with Dragons*, 257, 345. Some express concern that traveling to other lands may place them out of the jurisdiction of the Drowned God (674, 742).
11. Martin, *A Feast for Crows*, 28. Here it says, "Lord Quellon never returned from his last voyage; the Drowned God in his goodness granted him a death at sea." See also "Religions of Westeros."
12. Martin, *A Dance with Dragons*, 748.
13. Martin, *A Clash of Kings*, 405, 543.
14. Martin, *The World of Ice and Fire*, 175.
15. Martin, *A Feast for Crows*, 23, 343. Their understanding of the Storm God is thus not only a moral dualism, but a metaphysical one. This is reminiscent of Manicheism or Zoroastrianism.
16. Martin, *A Clash of Kings*, 127.
17. Martin, *A Feast for Crows*, 29.
18. Ibid., 27.
19. Martin, *The World of Ice and Fire*, 175. The narrator of *The World of Ice & Fire*, Maester Yandel, notes that some ironborn doubt this and consent to the more commonly accepted view of the descent of people. He says, "Certainly, we cannot seriously accept the assertions of the ironborn priests, who would have us believe that the ironmen are closer kin to fish and merlings than other races of mankind." The master does acknowledge, however, that the ironborn have different practices and beliefs than others in the land.
20. Ibid., 175.
21. Ibid., 178–79. Maester Yandel says that while this is present within the legends that, "History tells a different tale."
22. Ibid., 179, 182; Martin, *A Feast for Crows*, 27–33, 320, 333.
23. E.g., Martin, *A Feast for Crows*, 33.
24. Ibid., 21.

25. Martin, *A Feast for Crows*, 28.

26. Martin, *A Clash of Kings*, 129. While the people of the Iron Islands believe this, they did not always practice it. Aegon the Dragon, the first king of the Seven Kingdoms, banned the practice of stealing women and "forbade the reavers to prey upon his own domains." Martin, *The World of Ice & Fire*, 178. Some kings, like King Harmund, banned the practice of reaving with the support of the septons, but he was overthrown for his opposition (184).

27. Martin, *A Clash of Kings*, 297.

28. Martin, *A Dance for Dragons*, 333.

29. Of course, immediately after his speech, one of Theon's men, Dagmer, hits him over the head with a spear, knocking him out.

30. I will primarily engage with Matthew's Gospel because this is the one Bonhoeffer pays the most attention to in *Discipleship*.

31. Bonhoeffer, *Discipleship*, 57. See also Boring and Craddock, *The People's New Testament Commentary*, 24.

32. See Bonhoeffer, *Discipleship*, 59. Here Bonhoeffer defines discipleship as "commitment to Christ."

33. See Boring and Craddock, *The People's New Testament Commentary*, 215. In his version of this saying, Luke adds the words "daily," as a reminder that this call to discipleship continues throughout one's life (9:23).

34. Bonhoeffer, *Discipleship*, 84.

35. Ibid., 85.

36. Ibid., 87. The previous translation famously says, "When Christ calls a man, he bids him come and die" (87n11).

37. Ibid., 87. Emphasis added. See Romans 8:17 and Colossians 1:24; Ziegler, *Militant Grace*, 197.

38. Bonhoeffer, *Discipleship*, 89. Bonhoeffer carries on the Reformation emphasis on the call of discipleship being upon all Christians, not just a select group within the church. He says,

> [T]he decisive mistake of monasticism was not that it followed the grace-laden path of strict discipleship, even with all of monasticism's misunderstandings of the contents of the will of Jesus. Rather, the mistake was that monasticism essentially distanced itself from what is Christian by permitting its way to become the extraordinary achievement of a few, thereby claiming a special meritoriousness for itself (47). See Ziegler, *Militant Grace*, 188–89

39. Luther, "On the Councils and the Church Part III," 375–76. Luther's other first six marks or "holy possessions" of the church are: the word of God, baptism, the altar/Eucharist, the keys (Matt 18:15–20), offices, and worship practices like prayer, praise, and thanksgiving (366–75).

40. Bonhoeffer, *Discipleship*, 89.

41. Ziegler, *Militant Grace*, 196.

42. Ignatius, "To the Romans," 4 in Holmes, 171.

43. Bonhoeffer, *Discipleship*, 90. Emphasis original.

44. Martin Luther, "A Brief Instruction on What to Look For and Expect in the Gospels," 73.

45. "Religions of Westeros."
46. Martin, *A Feast for Crows*, 25.
47. Ibid., 25.
48. Ibid., 30, 32, 332, 334.
49. *Baptism, Eucharist and Ministry*, § 13. The statement says here, "Baptism is an unrepeatable act. Any practice which might be interpreted as 're-baptism' must be avoided." In practice, however, this is not always observed. See also Bonhoeffer, *Discipleship*, 211–12.
50. Martin, *A Feast for Crows*, 20.
51. Ibid., 21. In "Religions of Westeros," Martin does not mention this dispute and simply assumes that Theon and others among the ironborn were drowned as children. This description of this dispute resembles debates in the Christian tradition over modes of baptism.
52. Martin, *A Clash of Kings*, 133.
53. In *A Clash of Kings*, Balon gives Theon eight ships (297).
54. When we next see Theon, he is gathering a raiding party to rape and pillage fishing villages ("The Ghost of Harrenhal"). He, however, soon comes up with a plan to take Winterfell while Robb has his army away from the city in order to prove himself to his father ("The Old Gods and the New," "And Now His Watch is Ended"), which leads to his downfall.
55. Bonhoeffer, *Discipleship*, 205.
56. Ibid., 205.
57. Bonhoeffer, *Discipleship*, 207. Emphasis original.
58. Ibid., 207, 210.
59. Emphasis added.
60. Bonhoeffer, *Discipleship*, 208.
61. Martin, *A Feast for Crows*, 33.
62. Ibid., 21.
63. Bonhoeffer, *Discipleship*, 208–9.
64. Ibid., 141. Interpreters of Bonhoeffer, especially in North America, have argued that during World War II Bonhoeffer abandoned his "idealistic" pacifism and exchanged it for a position of "realism" similar to Reinhold Niebuhr's. I follow after interpreters who allow for development in his work but see more "substantial continuity" between the Bonhoeffer of *Discipleship* and his work as seen in *Ethics*. See Harvey, *Taking Hold of the Real*, 7–8, passim.

BIBLIOGRAPHY

Baptism, Eucharist and Ministry. Faith and Order Paper No. 111. Geneva: World Council of Churches, 1982.

Bonhoeffer, Dietrich. *Discipleship*. Edited by Geffrey B. Kelly and John D. Godsey. Translated by Barbara Green and Reinhard Krauss. Dietrich Bonhoeffer Works 4. Minneapolis, MN: Fortress Press, 2003.

Boring, M. Eugene, and Fred B. Craddock. *The People's New Testament Commentary*. Louisville, KY: Westminster John Knox Press, 2004.

Frye, Northrop. *The Great Code: The Bible and Literature*. Toronto: Academic Press Canada, 1982.

Harvey, Barry. *Taking Hold of the Real: Dietrich Bonhoeffer and the Profound Worldlines of Christianity*. Eugene, OR: Cascade Books, 2015.

Hays, Richard B. *Echoes of Scripture in the Gospels*. Waco, TX: Baylor University Press, 2016.

"House of the Seven Kingdoms: Minor Houses." Bonus Feature. *Game of Thrones* Season 1. Blu ray. Home Box Office.

Ignatius. "To the Romans." In *The Apostolic Fathers: Greek Texts and English Translations*, Updated edition, edited by Michael W. Holmes, 167–177. Grand Rapids, MI: Baker Books, 1999.

Luther, Martin. "A Brief Instruction on What to Look For and Expect in the Gospels." In *Martin Luther's Basic Theological Writings*, Third Edition, edited by Timothy F. Lull and William R. Russell, 71–75. Minneapolis, MN: Fortress Press, 2012.

———. "On the Councils and the Church—Part III." In Martin Luther's Basic Theological Writings, Third Edition, edited by Timothy F. Lull and William R. Russell, 363–383. Minneapolis, MN: Fortress Press, 2012.

Martin, George R. R. *A Clash of Kings: Book Two of A Song of Ice and Fire*. New York: Bantom Books, 1999.

———. *A Dance with Dragons: Book Five of A Song of Ice and Fire*. New York: Bantom Books, 2011.

———. *A Feast for Crows: Book Four of A Song of Ice and Fire*. New York: Bantam Books, 2005.

Martin, George R. R., Elio M. Garcia, Jr., and Linda Antonsson. *The World of Ice & Fire: The Untold History of Westeros and The Game of Thrones*. New York: Bantom Books, 2014.

"Religions of Westeros." Bonus Feature. *Game of Thrones* Season 2. Blu ray. Home Box Office.

Ziegler, Philip G. *Militant Grace: The Apocalyptic Turn and the Future of Christian Theology*. Grand Rapids, MI: Baker Academic, 2018.

Chapter 5

Ragamuffins Bound by the Word

The Ecclesiology of the Night's Watch

Drew McIntyre

In *Game of Thrones*, the Christian church shows up in an unexpected place. Of course, the various religions of Westeros and the outer territories play a significant role in George R. R. Martin's sweeping narrative. The faith of the Seven contains allusions to Catholicism and other Christian communions, and the vicious belief system centered on the mysterious Lord of Light echoes the Manicheanism that marked St. Augustine's early life. Nevertheless, the closest institution to the church is not found in any of the organized religions in Martin's universe.

This is true not just on an institutional level but also on a personal level. While few of Martin's characters—in particular, the priests—would qualify as pious in any real or imagined world, supernatural elements are portrayed as an important aspect in the lives of many characters. Here one might think of Catelyn Stark, who prays at the heart tree, or Davos, who despite his own agnosticism has a gnawing sense that the Red Woman represents a dark force that should be resisted. And yet, these and other devout individuals do not offer the closest analog in *Game of Thrones* to followers of Jesus. The community in *A Song of Ice and Fire* which most resembles what Christians call church is not represented by septs, corrupt priests, heart trees, Maesters, or fiery sacrifices. Instead, this chapter will contend that there are significant parallels to the communion of saints in the order known as the Night's Watch. Like the Body of Christ, the Watch is a motley collection of sinners, saints, and outcasts whose commitments free them to serve together in a distinctive mission[1] for the benefit of those who do not believe in their cause.

RAGAMUFFINS ON THE WALL

The Night's Watch is composed of men drawn from the length and breadth of Westeros.[2] Some, like Jon Snow, volunteer for the Watch, while many others flee or are banished to the Wall after committing a crime. Ned Stark, for instance, was told he could "take the black," that is, join the order, in lieu of punishment for his purported treason. (As it turns out, one ought not trust a Lannister.) While it amounts to a kind of exile in practice, many characters are seen choosing life on the Wall instead of execution. This means that the Night's Watch, while in some ways an esteemed brotherhood, is composed of many ruffians, murderers, and thugs. To be sure, there are noble men as well—Maester Aemon, the reader eventually learns, is technically royalty, and Sam the lovable coward is highborn—but, predominantly, the Night's Watch is composed of outcasts and worse.

Like the Night's Watch, the church has often been understood as a haven for the lost and broken.[3] As a well-beloved sermon illustration puts it, the Body of Christ is called to be a hospital for sinners, not a museum for saints. Though followers of Jesus often fail this in practice, community in the way of Christ means (in its ideal form) finding grandmothers side by side with criminals, addicts, refugees, the infirm, and all manner of other people society deems shameful or valueless. At its most faithful, Christians believe that the church should welcome all such people, not as mere depositories of charity, but as sisters and brothers.[4]

The constant refrain of Jesus' most vocal enemies, the religious professionals, is instructive here: "This fellow welcomes sinners and eats with them."[5] When true to its founder, the church has imitated him in this radical welcome. Centuries ago, the Pietist leader Philip Jacob Spener argued, "We do not understand the perfection which we demand of the church in such a way that not a single hypocrite is any longer to be found in it."[6] Spener's insight makes clear that the failure of the church to live up to the ideals of Jesus is nothing new. Full of what he called "wheat and tares," the community called together in Jesus' name is always composed of a mixed bag of people struggling toward redemption.[7] While this chapter will focus on the church as it should be, any reader of history or headlines is aware of the ways it has often fallen short of the radical hospitality found in the biblical mandate.

The New Testament church was initially composed primarily of the marginalized, many of whom were, because of their faith, separated from their families. Similar to the Night's Watch, except for a few people of high birth, the early church was predominantly a poor people's movement. Note what St. Paul says to the community in Corinth:

> Brothers and sisters, think of what you were when you were called. Not many of you were wise by human standards; not many were influential; not many

were of noble birth. But God chose the foolish things of the world to shame the wise; God chose the weak things of the world to shame the strong. God chose the lowly things of this world and the despised things—and the things that are not—to nullify the things that are, so that no one may boast before him.[8]

"Not many" were influential or of noble birth, but that is precisely the point. Jesus spent his earthly ministry among the sick, unclean, and demon-possessed, a whole disreputable slew of humanity often summed up in the gospels as "tax collectors and sinners."[9] One of Jesus' final acts before his torture and execution was to forgive a thief who was crucified next to him and promise him the Kingdom. The church which takes the witness of Jesus seriously here often finds itself in similarly mixed company offering radical reconciliation. Like the church that Jesus envisioned, the Watch is a perplexing mix of people, ranging from noble (in character if not title) to brutish.

This means not only that the church draws those the world deems unimpressive, but that the scandal of hypocrisy remains a constant. In the early centuries of the church, conflict erupted into schism over the question of whether clerical sin ruined the efficacy of sacraments. In subsequent discussions of the church's sins and virtues, the issues raised in this scandal, known as the Donatist Controversy, continue to be relevant. Peter Brown, one of Augustine's pre-eminent biographers, explains how the saint's Neo-Platonist insights aided his defense of the Catholic Church against the Donatists' critiques:

> The whole world appeared to him as a world of "becoming" as a hierarchy of imperfectly realized forms, which depended for their quality, on "participating" in an Intelligible World of Ideal Forms. This universe was in a state of constant, dynamic tension, in which the imperfect forms of matter strove to "realize" their fixed, ideal structure, grasped by the mind alone. It was the same with Augustine's view of the Church. The rites of the church were undeniably "holy," because of the objective holiness of a Church which "participated" in Christ . . . [t]hus, the men who received and administered these rites merely strove imperfectly to realize this holiness, "according to a certain shadow of the reality."[10]

Even the most tacit reading of church history, from Augustine until today, reveals that imperfect striving continues to be the norm, rather than the exception, for every Christian communion. Similarly, the Night's Watch is presented as a hazy reflection of its ideals. Some of the brothers are selfless and brave, and serve with honor, while others are cruel, petty, or lazy. Little in Martin's world is neat or clean, and this includes the ancient order guarding the Wall.

In the world of contemporary fiction, such complexity carries the virtue of authenticity. But in the church, this distance between ideal and reality has troubled Christian leaders since at least Paul's letters. One way of reading this situation, however, is to reframe the gap between the church as it should be and the broken church one often encounters as a continuing sign of God's mercy. The late Brennan Manning, a former Catholic priest who had struggled with faith and addiction, wrote of the scandalous grace at the heart of Jesus' message. Grace, which Christian grammar describes as God's undeserved love, means that God loves "ragamuffins," to use Manning's term. He describes Jesus' ministry this way:

> The sinners to whom Jesus directed His messianic ministry were not those who skipped morning devotions or Sunday church. His ministry was to those whom society considered real sinners. They had done nothing to merit salvation. Yet they opened themselves to the gift that was offered them. On the other hand, the self-righteous placed their trust in the works of the Law and closed their hearts to the message of grace.[11]

The radical hospitality of God, revealed in and made available to all through Jesus, is still shocking today when it is realized.

That is exactly the point. Christians believe that, simply put, this is God's character, revealed in the witness of Jesus. John Newton could sing of God's "amazing" grace, because he experienced it. As a former slave trader turned evangelical Christian, he marveled that even a scoundrel like him was invited to participate in God's redemption story. But in truth, this is in keeping with God's actions across the arc of Scripture: using murderers (Moses), adulterers (David), prostitutes (Rahab), persecutors (Paul), and doubters (Thomas) to fulfill divine intentions. Even today, one could argue God still only has sinners with whom to work. As Joseph Ratzinger wrote,

> We are tempted to say, if we are honest with ourselves, that the Church is neither holy nor catholic . . . so deeply aware are we all of the sinfulness of the church.[12]

The scandal of grace, from a Christian point of view, is that God is also deeply aware of the church's faults, and yet continues to call prodigal children into communion with God and one another.

Likewise, men who join the Night's Watch, even the most grotesque criminals and traitors, are given a clean slate, welcomed into a community and trained—perhaps even *discipled*—into an honorable way of life. Kinslayers, thieves, and turncloaks alike are given new identities once they join the Watch. Whatever they were before, they now become part of a brotherhood held together by mutual promises. Here, Samwell Tarly is an excellent example. Despised by his father for his perceived weakness, the highborn Sam is forced to take the Black. In his old life, he would have lived in luxury, but in the Watch he eventually finds his calling as a scholarly Maester. Though Sam likely would not have forsaken his birthright willingly, among the Watch, which makes space for his bookish pursuits, he discovers fulfillment that would have been denied to him as the eldest son of a nobleman and military commander. This new community shapes Sam into something he would not have been had he remained just another elite Westerosi son.

YOU SAID THE WORDS: A COMMUNITY BOUND BY PROMISES

As Sandra Richter argues, Scripture's metanarrative can be helpfully understood as a succession of covenants, sacred agreements through which God honors a relationship with a particular people. This pattern—covenant, infidelity, mercy, renewed (and sometimes expanded) covenant—can be seen throughout the biblical texts, culminating (from a Christian perspective) with the new covenant inaugurated by the life, death, and resurrection of Jesus.[13] In many Christian traditions, one enters this narrative by baptism, a sign-act that makes public the covenant between the individual (as a member of the church) and the Triune God. In baptism, as practiced within most communions, the new convert renounces sin, expresses trust in Christ, and is marked with water (either sprinkled, poured, or immersed therein). This symbolic drowning—paralleled in the religion of the Iron Islands, in which postulants are drowned and resuscitated in a public ritual—represents a spiritual burial from which one rises to new life. It is widely held that baptism, and the promises attached to this act, generates a new humanity, joining those who were once strangers together into a new family. "The act of believing," Paul Minear says, "creates a new [person] who lives in a new community in a new age. It would be contradictory indeed if believers did not find themselves bound together with quite new bonds."[14] Baptismal vows create the tendons of a body called church.

The Night's Watch is also a community bound by covenant to something more significant than the individual members; the whole is greater than the sum of its parts. The vows, like marital promises, are for life. Deserters, as we learn in the opening minutes of the series, are executed without hesitation. This—the permanent nature of the vows—is the chief distinction between a contract and covenant.

Most modern people live in a world of contracts, whether formal or informal. One person, group, or organization agrees to do something, and another party agrees to do some action in return. Tom agrees to pay Netflix ten dollars a month, and thus Tom gets the pleasure of watching *Daredevil* and *Ozark*. If Tom stops paying Netflix, Tom's shows stop as well. Contracts dissolve when one party does not hold up its end.[15] Covenants are distinct because they are permanent, and as such, are often considered sacred. Outside of marriage, the closest common parallel may be joining the military. There is a reason becoming a member of the armed forces is often called "signing your life away." The difference, of course, is that military service will normally end after a set period, while covenants (like, say, ordination, marriage, or baptism) mark the inauguration of permanently life-altering relationships. The Night's Watch is thus a covenantal order.

In such a community, promises matter. Consider the common refrain by Jon and Sam: "You said the words." When Jon threatens to leave, this recollection of their shared oath is exactly how Sam jogs his memory.[16] For members of the Watch, it becomes part of their internal dialogue and part of their communal culture. Thus Jon, about to break his vows with the wildling woman Ygritte, tries to exercise self-control (unsuccessfully) by reminding himself of his oath.[17] Even when lived imperfectly—as is seen throughout both the books and the HBO series—these vows constitute the brotherhood. Similarly, in Christian discipleship, baptismal vows will need to be revisited from time to time in seasons of repentance (such as Lent, the forty-day period of fasting before Easter). Christians are not made overnight, and neither are brothers of the Watch.

Given the brutal and violent nature of life in the Night's Watch, the vows that shape their common life are critical for cohesion and loyalty. When that loyalty is broken, such as when Jon is betrayed, the tragedy is heightened because—like Caesar and Brutus—suffering originating from a disloyal friend stings more than when it comes from a known foe. Such bonds are no less important in the church, which also faces divisive forces within and without, and who is composed of wide variety of people (noted above). Dietrich Bonhoeffer, a pastor and scholar who founded a seminary for the Confessing Church (which stood against Nazi Germany), wrote to his pastors in training, "Christians, too, belong not in the seclusion of cloistered life but in the midst of enemies."[18] The enemies among whom followers of Jesus find themselves, both in and outside of the community, ensure the promises that bind the church are all the more critical.

Near the end of his storied career, Yale theologian and ecumenist George Lindbeck spoke in an interview about how outside pressures heighten the need for visible Christian unity. Such unity is found chiefly in celebrating commonalities between ostensibly divergent communions and confessions; for instance, recognizing that the baptismal seal that United Methodists and Lutherans share (to cite just one of many possible avenues) is stronger than anything which divides them. Both have "said the words," pray to the Triune God, and celebrate the eucharist. In an increasingly post-Christian West, rediscovering this kinship would be a vital step toward a renewed witness. Given that historical forces may yet force divided Christians to come together once more, Lindbeck remarks that he is "quite willing to leave this life" still hopeful about the visible unity to which he dedicated much of his career.[19] Here, the unexpected alliances into which the Watch enters in the later seasons offer a parallel to Lindbeck's foxhole ecumenism. The community, made internally cohesive by its covenants (and perhaps given urgency by fraught external circumstances), can confidently enter into relationships with other groups and extend their fellowship when mutual interests align.

Like the vows which make one a brother, the promises made at baptism mark the entry into a new family, a community to which one is bound for life. However, a question that gets asked in several ways throughout Martin's drama parallels a query which haunts contemporary Western culture: is it possible to be free if one is bound to something—a person, a community, or an institution—outside of themselves?

SNOW KNOWS NOTHING (OR DOES HE?)

Jon Snow's encounter with the Free Folk raises a significant conflict for him and for the audience: does life north of the Wall represent a more pristine, authentic freedom than what is offered by the Night's Watch? After Jon allows himself to be captured, he is taken to the King Beyond the Wall, Mance Rayder. On the way, we get a foreshadowing of much that will follow from a brief exchange with Ygritte:

Ygritte: D'ya think you're the first crow ever flew down off the Wall? In your hearts you all want to fly free.
Jon: And when I'm free . . . will I be free to go?
Ygritte: Sure you will . . . It's dangerous being free, but most come to like the taste o' it.[20]

Upon arriving at their destination, we learn that Mance was once himself a brother of the Night's Watch. When pressed about his own desertion, Jon challenges Mance to exchange stories of oathbreaking. Mance asks Jon if he has heard rumors, and Jon replies yes: "Some say it was for a crown. Some say for a woman. Others say that you had the wildling blood."[21] All of these, however, miss the mark.

Mance had been hunting with some brothers and was wounded. A wildling woman sewed up both his skin and his black cloak, the latter using a fine red thread. Upon returning to camp, Mance was given a new cloak and told, by his superior, to burn the old one. This was his breaking point. Rayder tells Snow, "I left the next morning . . . for a place where a kiss was not a crime, and a man could wear any cloak he chose."[22] For all of its noble intentions, Rayder experienced the covenant of the Watch as a curse rather than a gift.

These conversations echo a concern at the heart of modern (and postmodern) life: What does it mean to be free? For twenty-first-century Western culture, the binary question of freedom versus repression is more an unspoken worldview than a conscious moral or philosophical inquiry. Consider the multitude of other examples of this paradigm from popular culture, such as (to name only two) the class-conscious peasants in *Monty Python and the Holy Grail*, or William Wallace's cries for freedom before dying in *Braveheart*. Thus, the interaction between the Jon and the Free Folk provides a fresh occasion for a classic argument about the nature of human flourishing. This debate, critical to people of all faith traditions, is a common trope in books, television, and film. Martin portrays Mance sympathetically, and the HBO series follows suit. As usual, *Game of Thrones* does not offer its audience a simple resolution.

Perhaps this suggests there is a balance to be found, a virtue, that is neither a selfish, libertarian anarchy, nor stultifying obedience. As much as contemporary Western culture loves to romanticize freedom, another possible reading is that this purported freedom is more akin to a perpetual adolescence. Joseph Ratzinger, later Pope Benedict XVI, made exactly this claim, referring to the newfound bias against commitments as the "countermorality":

> Only one rule holds in the new moralism of the countermorality: Everything that serves the destruction of obligations and thus the struggle for freedom is good, everything that preserves obligations is bad.[23]

Thus, it is interesting to observe that, while nuanced, Martin does not overly romanticize life among the Free Folk. Mance's truce among various wildling factions is tenuous, and without a strong-arm leader like him to unite them, it seems plausible that life north of the Wall would be, as Hobbes described the state of nature in *Leviathan*, "nasty, brutish, and short."[24] That is a freedom few would desire.

The Christian tradition offers a different vision of human flourishing rooted in holy obligations. For centuries, the devout have found freedom in monastic orders where their lives, outside of swordplay, dragons, and the living dead, closely resemble the Night's Watch. One can recognize what sounds like classic monastic vows of poverty and chastity in the oath that every new recruit takes when joining the order:

> Night gathers, and now my watch begins. It shall not end until my death. I shall take no wife, hold no lands, father no children. I shall wear no crowns and win no glory. I shall live and die at my post. I am the sword in the darkness. I am the watcher on the walls. I am the shield that guards the realms of men. I pledge my life and honor to the Night's Watch, for this night and all the nights to come.[25]

The "shall nots" are all in service to a higher good; in denying many of the pursuits than animate others, members are thus able to fully give themselves to the brotherhood, without any encumbrances that would hinder their duty or divide their loyalty and focus. Paul Minear writes of a similar transformation in the apostolic church which set a precedent for the later vow of poverty. "Among the results of participation in this power and grace," he notes, "was a transformation in the idea of property." Such concerns were subsumed by both the larger goal of their fellowship and the greater needs of the community.[26]

As noted in Ratzinger, Christians (and quite possibly those of other faith traditions) may notice a familiar vision of mature personhood echoed in Martin's depiction of the Night's Watch; in this vision, freedom is best understood not in opposition to commitment, but as its sibling. After all, these are covenantal communities. Promises are the DNA of their life together. The kind of liberty proffered here is not, therefore, chiefly freedom *from* any outside determination, but freedom *for* a vocation worthy of sacrificing one's life (Whether individual members of the community recognize the value of that mission and/or live up to its disciplines is another matter). Jon, after all, joins the Watch in part, because he was looking for family and purpose he could not find by remaining at Winterfell.

This modern worldview that places freedom and commitment in opposition also impacts views of Jesus. Contemporary Christian writers often portray Jesus as a reflection of modern countercultural sentimentalities: on many readings, Jesus is a rebel, a line-stepper, a rule-breaker.[27] Ratzinger, in a tantalizing observation, argues that this is to choose Jesus Barabbas (a lawless bandit) rather than Jesus Christ from the gospels, just as did the crowds who called for his execution when given an opportunity to set Jesus free.[28] This portrayal of Jesus as a late-modern rebel continues to fill sermons and books. But is it possible that such visions transform a first-century countercultural rabbi into a mere pastiche of twenty-first-century sensibilities?

Another reading is worth attempting. If one endeavors to lay down contemporary Western habits of mind, it becomes plausible that Jesus liberated humanity from sin and death not by following his own private vision of freedom, or being his so-called authentic self, detached from any external influence, but through obedience. Jesus, on this view, was faithful to the mission for which he had been sent and died for those who despised him.

This radically obedient Jesus may thus inform contemporary visions of Christian discipleship, such that this pattern—the path of other-regarding love and selfless service—becomes the mark of any freedom that can rightly be called Christian. This would fit with what Paul says to his wayward Galatian church:

> For you were called to freedom, brothers and sisters; only do not use your freedom as an opportunity for self-indulgence, but through love become slaves to one another. For the whole law is summed up in a single commandment, "You shall love your neighbor as yourself."[29]

Freedom may therefore be reclaimed according to the pattern that Christ lived and taught: self-denial and costly love. "The goal of the Exodus is Sinai," as Ratzinger put it. The *telos* of liberation is a new life under God's gracious rule.[30] God's people are set free to enjoy a covenant. This means that Christians cannot live just any way they choose (though various communions will disagree on the precise shape of faithful lives). As Paul Minear observes, "the Gospels record blunt utterances in which Jesus lays down the requirements for being a disciple" which are "stated without qualifying or ameliorating conditions."[31] But for Christians freed from captivity to modern cultural norms, these demands can be experienced as *gospel* (good news), precisely because they mark the contours of a life lived within a story that is more significant than their own personal stories.

Jon Snow's character arc illustrates this dynamic well. Though he is tempted, first by the Free Folk and later by Stannis, to lay aside his vows for a very different kind of life; ultimately, however, Snow decides he is bound by duty and by the promises (read: covenant) he has made to his brothers. Jon will not be able to do everything that he might like to do, but he will get to be true to a noble and worthy calling. This rendering of freedom is reminiscent of General George S. Patton's famous speech to the Third Army, immortalized by George C. Scott in *Patton*. The original speech concludes,

> There is one great thing that you men will all be able to say after this war is over and you are home once again. You may be thankful that twenty years from now when you are sitting by the fireplace with your grandson on your knee and he asks you what you did in the great World War II, you won't have to cough, shift him to the other knee and say, "Well, your Granddaddy shoveled shit in Louisiana."[32]

The soldiers of the Third Army might have avoided the danger and inconvenience of war, but they did get a great (albeit costly) benefit: they will look back on their life and know they gave it to something worthy.

Both disciples of Jesus and the Night's Watch live into a similar sort of freedom, one that is significant because it is not selfish. Like Jon and his brothers, disciples are not free to do anything they please, but they are free to live with others in a covenant community dedicated to a sacred calling. In this communion, Christians believe they experience God's grace as they forfeit their independence to the interdependence of mutuality and service.

The life of St. Francis of Assisi offers a beautiful portrait of this grace in action. Francis was born to a wealthy, aristocratic family in Italy. By any measure, he was part of the 1 percent of his day, possessing a life of luxury and affluence by birthright. But Francis rejected it. He had what he described as a powerful encounter with Christ, and, to his wealthy father's great vexation, Francis sold all his belongings and gave the money to the poor. He became a wandering, homeless preacher. Over time, he attracted other people to his simple way of life, and the Pope eventually gave them permission to form an official order.

St. Francis is often depicted as rebellious, akin to portraits of the radical Jesus discussed above. Such sketches are, at best, only partially true. In his *Testament*, a compilation of the saint's final instructions to his order, Francis points out that he would never preach in parishes in which the priest did not welcome him.[33] Though he possessed a special charism (spiritual gift), he still viewed his ministry as in concert, rather than in competition, with other religious leaders. He was also quite direct about his high standards for the members of the community. "I strictly command all my cleric and lay brothers, through obedience," Francis says, "not to place any gloss upon the Rule or upon these words."[34] Of course, it is prudent to avoid proof-texting Francis to make him either a libertine or a legalist. As one recent biographer put it:

> If the profound fidelity of Francis toward the church is not to be doubted, that does not imply, however, any renunciation of his own vocation. He sought till the end of his life to maintain a balanced relationship—respectful, but neither servile nor always on call—with respect to the ecclesiastical hierarchy.[35]

Thus St. Francis, who followed Jesus' teachings quite literally in selling all his possessions and giving them to the poor, found freedom by giving up his old life and living instead for Christ with a community of others dedicated to the same. Their communal life was shaped by a covenant to which even the radical Francis asked strict fidelity. Such rule-bound orders still exist today in various Christian communions.

This amalgamation of faithfulness and critique sounds much like Jon Snow's own relationship to the traditions and practices of the Night's Watch. Jon honored the Watch, but was not slavish to its traditions, as evidenced by his relationship with Ygritte and his treatment of Mance. Perhaps, then, Jon

Snow is more free than is obvious at first glance. As a brother of the Watch, he has taken vows to which he must be loyal upon pain of death. And yet, Jon sought out this covenant, dissatisfied with his life in Winterfell, and perhaps seeking a community to which he, as a bastard not fully accepted by his adoptive family, could belong. In that sense, the Watch offers freedom not as autonomy, but purpose. Similarly, it is worth pondering whether those enamored by self-focused and banal visions of freedom are not so liberated as they imagine. Joseph Ratzinger has another name for this freedom that is not shaped by a sense of community or mission:

> By "freedom" one generally understands today the possibility of doing everything one wants and of doing only what one would like. Thus understood, freedom is arbitrariness.[36]

The Night's Watch, like the church in its most potent form, hereby offers glimpses of a freedom that, while not palatable to everyone, is anything but arbitrary. In fact, the Watch's integrity is maintained as much by the actions it avoids, as it is by those it undertakes.

REFUSING TO TAKE SIDES

A final parallel between the Body of Christ and the Night's Watch is that, to fulfill its unique mission, the Watch takes no sides. The reader (or viewer) encounters this refrain about the brotherhood from the beginning; as a rule, new recruits are taught at the outset of their training. Their duty is to protect the realm from enemies north of the Wall, so they take no part in conflicts to the south. This is not out of cowardice, but rather out of a commitment to their primary calling.

Similarly, the church serves most effectively when it avoids partaking in secular conflicts on their own terms. It is no accident that some of the worst epochs in the history of the church—periods of corruption, persecution, scandal, and such—occurred when institutional Christianity was wedded to state power in some form. Looking back to examples like the Constantinianism of the late Roman Empire, in which citizenship became coterminous with baptism, or Puritan New England's witch hunts, two inferences can be drawn. The church is at its most faithful when, first, it is not consumed by secular concerns and, second, when its power is not joined to Caesar's. As Hauerwas and Willimon[37] argue,

> The fundamental issue . . . is not whether we shall be conservative or liberal, left or right, but whether we shall be faithful to the church's peculiar vision of what it means to life and act as disciples.[38]

The Night's Watch similarly possesses what Rodney Clapp, describing the church, also names a "peculiar vision." The Watch, like the Body of Christ, is a motley collection of people who have agreed to abandon the world's power schemes and "recognize that they are no longer in control."[39]

The temptation to exercise overt power can be strong, however. Just as various forces in Westeros desire the Night's Watch to intervene at certain times—such as Stannis late in the series—the Watch has a particular vocation that no else can fulfill. They are "the fire that burns against the cold," "the horn that wakes the sleepers," and "the shield that guards the realms of men."[40] Though many in the south believe that the Watch guards against little more than myth and superstition, and while queens and kings often ignore their calls for resources and fresh recruits, the Watch (like the North) remembers. Because of this memory, the order knows what could happen to Westeros if they shirk their duty even for a brief period.

Similarly, the church has a long memory, which is critical for its faithfulness. As Gerhard Lofhink says, "The Church's memory is thus not simply a clinging to the old and the eternal yesterday. It is a kind of life insurance."[41] The church remembers not to enjoy the narcotic effects of nostalgia, but out of a desire for fidelity to its Lord. And if it is life insurance, it is a policy not only for the Christian community but for the whole world.[42]

The church has often failed in its vocation to "take no sides." Some notable exceptions stand out, however. Bonhoeffer, mentioned previously, died for his witness standing up against the Nazi regime which had, except for a small Confessing group, co-opted most pastors and congregations in Germany. Oscar Romero, Roman Catholic Archbishop of El Salvador, was assassinated while celebrating the Mass because he dared to question government corruption and violence. Thousands of other martyrs fill the annals of church history because they refused to submit to emperors and despots.

This should make clear, then, that "take no sides" here does not mean a mealy mouthed, faux neutrality. Martin Luther King Jr. condemned moderates during the American civil rights struggle for being more problematic than the out-and-out racists.[43] No, the church has a voice and must be heard, but it must always be a distinctive voice. At their best, Jesus-shaped communities stand up for justice and peace, but not by selling themselves wholly to a regnant ideology or party. On this score, the rightist agenda of evangelical groups and the leftist agenda of Mainline Protestantism in recent years share much in common. T. S. Eliot sounded the alarm when he wrote,

> The Church cannot be, in any political sense, either conservative or liberal, or revolutionary. Conservatism is too often conservation of the wrong things: liberalism a relaxation of discipline; revolution a denial of the permanent things.[44]

Imagine how odd it would be if the Night's Watch suddenly became a tannery, or started a mercenary-for-hire service, or taught all the brothers to make pies and opened a bakery in a nearby town to raise money. This would be foolish, not because any of those tasks are immoral or valueless in themselves, but because these activities would chip away at the singular mission of the Night's Watch. This calling is not merely the only task to which they are bound by covenant, but a vocation for which only they are equipped.

At issue is the discipline that Steven Covey famously named "keeping the main thing the main thing."[45] The church often loses its identity not simply by aligning with secular causes, but in trying to do many valid activities while neglecting their primary calling. Recall here Jesus' advice to the sisters Mary and Martha, in Luke 10, about the one thing truly needed. Jesus visits the house of some friends, and while Mary sits at his feet as he talks, Martha is busy with many tasks. When she rebukes her sister, Jesus corrects the anxiously busy Martha, and reminds her that only one thing is needed, which Mary has chosen.

Like the Night's Watch, there is a charge that only the church can fulfill: to baptize, celebrate the eucharist, and form disciples. There are thousands of churches in the United States, and doubtless in Canada and Europe as well, which have many wonderful service projects and community outreach events, but who have not baptized a single person in years. Still other churches become just another social service agency in their community, or worse, a country club that exists only to benefit the members and thereby exclude their neighbors. In an interview about the revitalization of what had been a declining, downtown church, Andrew Forrest of Munger Place Church in Texas said this:

> Every dying church in America has a community garden. Every dying church in America has a co-working space. What do I mean by that? I have no problem with community gardens; a garden is a beautiful thing. And I don't have any problem with co-working spaces. But Jesus didn't tell us to start a community garden, and he didn't tell us to start co-working spaces; he told us to make disciples. That's literally the mission of the church. The problem is not the gardens. I'm being provocative to make a point. The problem is that we often want to substitute secondary and tertiary concerns for the primary concern of discipleship.[46]

The crucial question here, as Forrest names, is the distinction between the primary and tertiary. The Night's Watch has kept the realm safe for countless ages, because they have never veered from their chief vocation. The church, sadly, cannot say the same for much of her history.

At her best, the church is a "sacrament of the world's salvation."[47] By rejecting all sides in culture wars, by refusing to be distracted from the primary mission, the church can be faithful to the mission that only it can fulfill. On the other hand, when the church becomes a thermometer rather than a thermostat, the Body of Christ is in danger of bowing before the wrong lord. New Testament scholar Leander Keck, writing about the decline of Mainline Protestantism, describes the danger well:

> The churches' identity and mission seemed to be determined less and less by the resources of the gospel and their tested wisdom and more and more by extraneous agendas. That their identity and mission always, and inevitably, were forged in interaction with their circumstances is a truism, but that "the world sets the agenda" is sheer capitulation.[48]

Just as the Night's Watch can only serve Westeros faithfully by refusing to engage in lesser conflicts, instead setting its own priorities, so too the church best fulfills its mission in and to the world when the world does not set the terms of their engagement.

This is risky, of course. The world rewards the church when it veers off-course. Caesar (and Cersei) will always offer scraps from the table if one bends the knee, as Robert Jeffress has repeatedly displayed.[49] But there is another path. N.T. Wright puts the choice—pardon the pun—starkly:

> I have known economics faculties and history faculties and others too, where half the professors are Marxists and half are not, or where half are committed postmodernists and half are not. Where should the Christian be in such a case? You may well believe that the gospel commits us to one side of the debate, though these things are rarely that easy. But my suggestion is that you see it as a call to be in prayer where your discipline [or, the world] is in pain ... And out of that prayer discover the ways of being peacemakers, of taking the risk of hearing both sides, of running the risk of being shot at from both sides. Are you or are you not a follower of the crucified Messiah?[50]

Like the Watchers on the Wall, the church is at its most faithful when it refuses to engage in partisan battles or second-order activities that do not relate to its primary purpose.

THE NIGHT'S WATCH AS THE FAMILY OF GOD

Similar to the Night's Watch, the Body of Christ is a community of people from many different backgrounds bound by a lifelong covenant to a unique calling that is more significant than personal desires or external conflicts. The church, like the sentries who guard the Wall, are called out of the world for the sake of the world,[51] to a mission that only the church can accomplish:

> But you are a chosen race, a royal priesthood, a holy nation, God's own people, in order that you may proclaim the mighty acts of him who called you out of darkness into his marvelous light.[52]

Followers of Christ are thus commissioned, like the Night's Watch, to take up (spiritual) arms in a conflict that the world does not believe exists, to fulfill a mission that those outside her ranks do not find valid. Just as the Wall must be defended even though many to the south do not recognize what is truly at stake, so too Christians recognize there are malevolent forces at work in the world which must be faced:

> "For our struggle is not against enemies of blood and flesh, but against the rulers, against the authorities, against the cosmic powers of this present darkness, against the spiritual forces of evil in the heavenly places."[53]

The church, as it faithfully proclaims the gospel and wrestles against the principalities and powers, is the sole community who can fulfill this vocation.[54] Churches can do many helpful activities, such as clothing closets, soup kitchens, and community gardens, but if the church forgets the primary duty to which only it has been called, these all amount to window treatments on the *Titanic*. If the faithful are not recruiting new members into the servant community, neglecting to disciple people to live a truly free life—liberated from sin and in covenant with Christ—then no matter how many activities fill their calendars, the church's calling has been deserted. In the same way, if the Watch stopped recruiting and training its Brothers, or if they all decided to take a holiday rather than guard their posts, it would be overrun when the worst happens and the realm they had been entrusted to guard could fall.

The most significant parallel, therefore, between the church and the Night's Watch is that both organizations exist to benefit those outside of their community. To be a follower of Jesus is to give up oneself in service to God and others. Likewise, when a new brother joins the Watch, no matter how vile their old life, they henceforth servant an order which makes sacrifices to benefit those who neither support them nor even believe their cause worthwhile. The church and the Watch are both communities called to live chiefly for the sake of outsiders. "Where the life of the Church is exhausted in self-serving," wrote Karl Barth, "it smacks of death."[55] In portraying the Night's Watch as a community of scoundrels who are free precisely because they are bound by sacred vows to other-directed service, *Game of Thrones* offers a compelling, if unexpected, depiction of the church.

NOTES

1. While ecclesiology (the study of the church) and missiology (the study of mission) are distinct categories, this chapter presumes a tight link between the nature of the church and its purpose. In the same way that the Watch is organized and trained solely for its particular mission, the church exists, on this reading, for its God-given mission. Its activity and its ontology are distinct but inseparable.

2. *Game of Thrones* is rightly praised for its portrayal of powerful and interesting female characters. Of course, this is not reflected well in a chapter focusing on the Night's Watch, and it is also a reminder that too often the church, like the Night's Watch, has been dominated by men.

3. Here I am inspired by Andrew Walker's account of his own faith journey from Pentecostal, to atheist, to Russian Orthodox convert and theology professor. See Andrew G. Walker, "Notes from a Wayward Son," in *Notes from a Wayward Son* (Eugene: Cascade Books, 2015).

4. See Galatians 3:28, for instance.

5. Luke 15:2, Harold W. Attridge, Wayne A. Meeks, and Jouette M. Bassler, *The HarperCollins Study Bible: New Revised Standard Version, with the Apocryphal/Deuterocanonical Books* (San Francisco: HarperOne, 2006).

6. Philipp Jacob Spener, *Pia Desideria*, ed. Theodore G. Tappert (Philadelphia: Fortress Press, 1989), 81.

7. See Matthew 13:24–30.

8. 1 Corinthians 1:26–29, *HarperCollins Study Bible*.

9. Mark 2:15, *HarperCollins Study Bible*.

10. Peter Brown, *Augustine of Hippo: A Biography* (Berkeley: University of California Press, 1969), 221–222.

11. Brennan Manning, *The Ragamuffin Gospel* (Colorado Springs: Multnomah Books, 2015), 43.

12. Joseph Ratzinger, *Introduction to Christianity* (San Francisco: Ignatius Press, 2004), 339.

13. Here I am giving broad outlines of Sandra Richter's excellent work. See Sandra L. Richter, *The Epic of Eden: A Christian Entry into the Old Testament* (Downers Grove: IVP Academic, 2008).

14. Paul S. Minear, *Images of the Church in the New Testament* (Louisville: Westminster John Knox Press, 2004), 140.

15. I am indebted to my teacher, Douglas Campbell, for his stress on the important distinction between contract and covenant. See Chapter 8, "The Contractual (JF) Construal of Paul's Gospel," in Douglas A. Campbell, *The Quest for Paul's Gospel: A Suggested Strategy* (Edinburgh: T and T Clark, 2005).

16. George R. R. Martin, *A Dance with Dragons: Book Five of a Song of Ice and Fire* (New York: Bantam Books, 2011), 102.

17. George R. R. Martin, *A Storm of Swords: Book Three of A Song of Ice and Fire* (New York: Bantam Books, 2000), 296.

18. Dietrich Bonhoeffer, *Dietrich Bonhoeffer Works, Volume 5: Life Together and Prayerbook of the Bible* (Minneapolis: Fortress Press, 2005), 27.

19. George A. Lindbeck, David B. Burrell, and Stanley Hauerwas, *Postliberal Theology and the Church Catholic: Conversations with George Lindbeck, David Burrell, and Stanley Hauerwas*, ed. John W. Wright (Grand Rapids: Baker Academic, 2012), 74–75.

20. Martin, *A Storm of Swords*, 75.

21. Ibid., 84.

22. Ibid., 85.

23. Joseph Ratzinger, *Church, Ecumenism, and Politics: New Endeavors in Ecclesiology* (San Francisco: Ignatius Press, 2008), 243.

24. Thomas Hobbes, *Leviathan* (New York: Barnes & Noble Books, 2004), 92.

25. George R. R. Martin, *A Clash of Kings: Book Two of a Song of Ice and Fire* (New York: Bantam Books, 2005), 711.

26. Minear, *Images of the Church*, 141.

27. Evangelical and progressive Christians have distinct versions of this. For a popular evangelical take, see John Eldredge, *Wild at Heart—Discovering the Secret of a Man's Soul* (Nashville: Thomas Nelson Publishers, 2011).

28. Ratzinger, *Church, Ecumenism, and Politics*, 243.

29. Gal. 5:13–14, *HarperCollins Study Bible*.

30. Ratzinger, *Church, Ecumenism, and Politics*, 248.

31. Minear, *Images of the Church*, 147.

32. Andrew Carroll and Robert G. Torricelli, *In Our Own Words: Extraordinary Speeches of the American Century* (New York: Kodansha International, 2000), 143.

33. Andre Vauchez, *Francis of Assisi The Life and Afterlife of a Medieval Saint* (New Haven: Yale University Press, 2014), 338.

34. Ibid., 339.

35. Ibid., 286.

36. Ratzinger, *Church, Ecumenism, and Politics*, 243.

37. For a helpful critique of Hauerwas and Willimon's postliberalism, see Robert P. Jones and Melissa C. Stewart, "The Unintended Consequences of Dixieland Postliberalism" *CrossCurrents* 55, no. 4 (Winter 2006).

38. Stanley Hauerwas and William H. Willimon, *Resident Aliens: Life in the Christian Colony Expanded 25th Anniversary Edition* (Nashville: Abingdon Press, 2014), 69.

39. Rodney Clapp, *A Peculiar People: The Church as Culture in a Post-Christian Society* (Downers Grove: InterVarsity, 1996), 193.

40. Martin, *A Storm of Swords*, 12.

41. Gerhard Lohfink, *Does God Need the Church? Toward a Theology of the People of God* (Collegeville: Liturgical Press, 1999), 251.

42. Insofar as the New Covenant, on Richter's reading, is expanded to include all people. See Richter, *The Epic of Eden*.

43. See Martin Luther King, Jr., "Letter from a Birmingham Jail," University of Pennsylvania African Studies Center. Accessed January 16, 2019, https://www.africa.upenn.edu/Articles_Gen/Letter_Birmingham.html.

44. T. S. Eliot, *The Idea of a Christian Society* (New York: Harcourt, Brace, and World, 1940), 102.

45. Covey, Stephen, Merrill, Roger, and Merrill, Rebecca, *First Things First* (New York: Free Press, 1994), 75.

46. Benac, Dustin D. "Andrew Forrest: Every Dying Church in America Has a Community Garden." Ministry Matters. April 19, 2017. Accessed January 15, 2019. https://www.ministrymatters.com/all/entry/8114/andrew-forrest-every-dying-church-in-america-has-a-community-garden.

47. Geoffrey Wainwright, *Doxology: The Praise of God in Worship, Doctrine and Life: A Systematic Theology* (New York: Oxford University Press, 1984), 146.

48. Leander Keck, *The Church Confident* (Nashville: Abingdon Press, 1993), 16.

49. Graham, Ruth. "The Pundit Pastor: How Robert Jeffress Became One of the Most Influential Trump Supporters in Christendom." *Slate Magazine*. May 14, 2018. Accessed January 15, 2019. https://slate.com/human-interest/2018/05/robert-jeffress-has-became-one-of-trumps-most-powerful-supporters.html.

50. N. T. Wright, *The Challenge of Jesus: Rediscovering Who Jesus Was and Is* (Downers Grove: IVP Books, an Imprint of InterVarsity Press, 2015), 191.

51. See Peter L. Berger and Richard John Neuhaus, *Against the World for the World: The Hartford Appeal and the Future of American Religion* (New York: Seabury Press, 1976).

52. 1 Peter 2:9, *HarperCollins Study Bible*.

53. Eph. 6:12, *HarperCollins Study Bible*.

54. There are resonances here with what Avery Dulles refers to as a "servant ecclesiology." See Avery Dulles, *Models of the Church: Expanded Edition* (New York: Doubleday, 1987), 93.

55. Karl Barth, *Dogmatics in Outline*. (New York: Harper, 1959), 146.

BIBLIOGRAPHY

5th Armored Division Online. Accessed January 15, 2019. http://www.5ad.org/Patton_speech.htm.

Attridge, Harold W., Wayne A. Meeks, and Jouette M. Bassler. *The HarperCollins Study Bible: New Revised Standard Version, with the Apocraphal/Deuterocanonical Books*. San Francisco: HarperOne, 2006.

Barth, Karl. *Dogmatics in Outline. With a New Foreword by the Author*. New York: Harper, 1959.

Benac, Dustin D. "Andrew Forrest: Every Dying Church in America Has a Community Garden." Ministry Matters. April 19, 2017. Accessed January 15, 2019. https://www.ministrymatters.com/all/entry/8114/andrew-forrest-every-dying-church-in-america-has-a-community-garden.

Berger, Peter L., and Richard John Neuhaus. *Against the World for the World: The Hartford Appeal and the Future of American Religion*. New York: Seabury Press, 1976.

Bonhoeffer, Dietrich. *Dietrich Bonhoeffer Works, Volume 5: Life Together and Prayerbook of the Bible*. Minneapolis: Fortress Press, 2005.

Brown, Peter. *Augustine of Hippo: A Biography.* Berkeley: University of California Press, 1969.

Campbell, Douglas A. *The Quest for Paul's Gospel: A Suggested Strategy.* Edinburgh: T and T Clark, 2005.

Carroll, Andrew, and Robert G. Torricelli. *In Our Own Words: Extraordinary Speeches of the American Century.* New York: Kodansha International, 2000.

Clapp, Rodney. *A Peculiar People: The Church as Culture in a Post-Christian Society.* Downers Grove: InterVarsity, 1996.

Covey, Stephen, Roger Merrill, and Rebecca R. Merrill. *First Things First.* New York: Free Press, 1994.

Dulles, Avery. *Models of the Church.* New York: Doubleday, 1987.

Eldredge, John. *Wild at Heart - Discovering the Secret of a Man's Soul.* Nashville: Thomas Nelson Publishers, 2011.

Eliot, T. S. *The Idea of a Christian Society.* New York: Harcourt, Brace and World, 1940.

Graham, Ruth. "The Pundit Pastor: How Robert Jeffress Became One of the Most Influential Trump Supporters in Christendom." *Slate Magazine.* May 14, 2018. Accessed January 15, 2019. https://slate.com/human-interest/2018/05/robert-jeffress-has-became-one-of-trumps-most-powerful-supporters.html.

Hauerwas, Stanley, and William H. Willimon. *Resident Aliens: Life in the Christian Colony (Expanded 25th Anniversary Edition).* Nashville: Abingdon Press, 2014.

Hobbes, Thomas. *Leviathan.* New York: Barnes & Noble Books, 2004.

Jones, Robert, and Melissa Stewart. "The Unintended Consequences of Dixieland Postliberalism." *CrossCurrents* 55, no. 4 (Winter 2006): 506–21.

Keck, Leander. *The Church Confident.* Nashville: Abingdon Press, 1993.

King, Martin Luther, Jr. "Letter from a Birmingham Jail." University of Pennsylvania African Studies Center. Accessed January 16, 2019. https://www.africa.upenn.edu/Articles_Gen/Letter_Birmingham.html.

Lindbeck, George A., David B. Burrell, and Stanley Hauerwas. *Postliberal Theology and the Church Catholic: Conversations with George Lindbeck, David Burrell, and Stanley Hauerwas.* Edited by John W. Wright. Grand Rapids: Baker Academic, 2012.

Lohfink, Gerhard. *Does God Need the Church? Toward a Theology of the People of God.* Collegeville: Liturgical Press, 1999.

Manning, Brennan. *The Ragamuffin Gospel.* Colorado Springs: Multnomah Books, 2015.

Martin, George R. R. *A Clash of Kings: Book Two of a Song of Ice and Fire.* New York: Bantam Books, 2005.

———. *A Dance with Dragons Book Five of a Song of Ice and Fire.* New York: Bantam Press, 2011.

———. *A Storm of Swords: Book Three of A Song of Ice and Fire.* New York: Bantam Books, 2000.

Minear, Paul S. *Images of the Church in the New Testament.* Louisville: Westminster John Knox Press, 2004.

Ratzinger, Joseph. *Church, Ecumenism, and Politics: New Endeavors in Ecclesiology.* San Francisco: Ignatius Press, 2008.

———. *Introduction to Christianity*. San Francisco: Ignatius Press, 2004.
Richter, Sandra L. *The Epic of Eden: A Christian Entry into the Old Testament*. Downers Grove: IVP Academic, 2008.
Spener, Philipp Jacob. *Pia Desideria*. Edited by Theodore G. Tappert. Philadelphia: Fortress Press, 1989.
Vauchez, Andre. *Francis of Assisi: The Life and Afterlife of a Medieval Saint*. New Haven: Yale University Press, 2014.
Wainwright, Geoffrey. *Doxology: The Praise of God in Worship, Doctrine and Life: A Systematic Theology*. New York: Oxford University Press, 1984.
Walker, Andrew G. *Notes from a Wayward Son*. Eugene: Cascade Books, 2015.
Wright, N. T. *The Challenge of Jesus: Rediscovering Who Jesus Was and Is*. Downers Grove: IVP Books, 2015.

Part III

AUGUSTINE GOES TO WESTEROS

Chapter 6

Night Kings and Shadow Assassins

Reflections on Death, Evil, and Privation

Mark Wiebe

In the opening moments of *Game of Thrones*, the audience glimpses the artfully arranged bodies of a group of wildlings north of the Wall, whose mysterious demise is soon followed by the death of the investigating rangers. The scene introduces creatures and forces that do not fall within the narrow limits of mortal capacities. From the beginning, George R. R. Martin makes it clear that the real conflict at the heart of his story has little to do with who will sit on the Iron Throne. The real fight is between the living and the dead, between darkness and light. "There is only one war that matters—the Great War," Jon Snow later says to Queen Cersei ("The Dragon and the Wolf").[1] And it is this facet of Martin's world that I wish to explore and consider. This will involve fleshing out Martin's depiction of evil and death in the world of *Game of Thrones* by way of an analysis of two key figures—the Night King and the Shadow. I will then lay out some of the strengths and weaknesses of the notion of evil they seem to embody. This kind of analysis will require not only an examination of these two characters and their world, but of a larger network of arguments tracing back to the third-century CE, and surrounding the religious and philosophical movement known as the Manichaeans. The Manichaeans maintained a dualistic vision of good and evil, which the fourth-century Christian philosopher and theologian Augustine forcefully critiqued. Ultimately, following Augustine, I will argue that although *Game of Thrones* exhibits figures like the Night King and the Shadow as physical or substantive manifestations of evil, in fact, they can be seen ultimately to illustrate a privative or negative view of the nature of all things evil.

EVIL AND ENCHANTMENT IN THE REALM OF THE SEVEN KINGDOMS

What we have in the realm of the Seven Kingdoms is something philosopher Charles Taylor would describe as an enchanted cosmos.[2] This is a world where the various elements, physical, spiritual, supernatural, and magical are intertwined and have intrinsic meaning and power. To put it another way, the assorted elements, qualities, and potencies of this cosmos comprise a united whole which exists and operates independently of anyone's particular belief set or religiosity, and which, in this way, shapes the meaning and values of everyone's lives. This is a world where the spirits of the dead can be summoned to dance and yield some wretched, twisted form of life back to the deceased corpse of Khal Drogo. It's a world where comets are tied to and, as a young wildling girl recognizes, signal the return of dragons. A world where Dragon Glass and Valerian Steel are not simply physical or chemical materials, but have a mysterious potency to fend off the living dead, even to extinguish the simulacrum of life they possess.

In the enchanted world of *Game of Thrones*, evil has many manifestations. Two exemplary figures stand out from among this wide array, revealing most clearly the *nature* of evil in this story's "known world." The first figure that I would like to highlight is the Shadow—a murderous figure deployed by Melisandre in support of King Stannis. Melisandre gives birth to this character, if we can use that term for it, and deploys it as a tool to kill Stannis' brother Renly. By doing so, she helps remove one of the claimants to the throne in the wake of Robert Baratheon's death. The second figure I want to focus on is the Night King. This character only appears in the televised adaptation of Martin's *A Song of Ice and Fire*. The Night King arrives early on in *Game of Thrones*, riding his war-horse and leading the army of the dead. Later on, the audience learns that he and the others like him were originally created by the Children of the Forest.[3] The Night King and his army are a haunting presence throughout the narrative, though mostly in the background hunting, building their ranks, and waiting for their day to come. But what stands out about the depiction of these figures is not simply that they are antagonistic, inhabiting and representing the side of evil, but that they evidently *are* what they represent. Evil is all they seem to be. Aside from this there does not seem to be anything else to them. They are revealed as visceral, substantive, time-space-continuum-occupying constituents of evil in the world of the Seven Kingdoms, able to do things like pierce the heart of King Renly Baratheon, fling spears of ice at flying dragons, and demolish the great northern wall.

In the world of the Seven Kingdoms, evil is depicted as a tangible and physical substance taking up space and existing in fundamental and total opposition to goodness and life. This is a kind of opposition that goes beyond the clashes between the various claimants to the throne of swords in King's Landing. One way to see this is to note that, despite their political disagreements, figures like Cersei Lannister and Daenerys Targaryen are able to forge a sort of bond together around the shared value of self-preservation and a mutual (though ultimately mutually exclusive) desire to create a united kingdom. In contrast, there is no possibility of identifying a common good valued by both the living and the dead. There is no negotiating or sitting down for peace talks with the Night King; indeed, he and the other living dead do not seem to speak at all. In any case, the white walkers and their leader are not inclined to build, sustain, or protect anything. They are single-minded, appearing to have almost no thought or will aside from that of destroying life wherever they find it.

What I've described so far amounts to a dualistic portrayal of the nature of evil. On one side are goodness and light and life, and on the other, quite literally, death and evil. As Melisandre says to anyone who will listen, "there are two gods—darkness and light."[4] Here, evil is palpable, a part of the universe alongside the other things, the good's opposite and equal. Yet why might one conceive of evil in this way? What reasons could there be to adhere to this sort of metaphysical framework? What arguments can be made in favor of it or against the alternatives?

One of the main strengths of a dualistic view of evil is that it seems to reflect our experience of suffering. One might reasonably ask whether alternative ways of defining the nature of evil can effectively capture the physical experience of pain or certain types of extended suffering like depression, the ongoing effects of trauma, and forms of illness like cancer. The suggestion that these things are, for example, illusions, can strike the one who experiences them as a description that is deeply insufficient if not obscene. These things have a sense of reality and presence to them, an is-ness.

In *Game of Thrones,* the figures of the Night King and the Shadow Assassin mirror evil's apparent quality of solidity, each in their own way. For instance, in the case of the Night King, in addition to his bodily presence and aggression, there is his tendency to leave a stylistic arrangement of his victims' bodies—"always the artists," Mance Raider says sardonically about this gruesome practice ("Walk of Punishment").[5] Superficially, this is a generative act and yet it is really only a physical monument to death, a reveling in and exhibition of the Night King and his army's being consummately evil. In this and other ways, the Night King is depicted as an agent—a dynamic, willfull force. In him, death itself actively confronts the human realm. We can see something comparable to this with regard to the Shadow. While explaining the fundamentals of her religiosity and referencing the Shadow assassin indirectly, Melisandre declares, "We have the power to make life and light and cast shadows" ("Sons of the Harpy").[6] Aware of Melisandre's role in the death of Renly Baratheon, the audience understands that she is not using the phrase "cast shadows" in its more common metaphorical sense. Rather, certain kinds of Shadows can quite literally be cast and directed. We see in the Shadow a depiction of murderous intent that might seem commensurate with our sense of it as an active and malignant force. Along this line, as Mark Ian Robson puts it regarding various sorts of evil, they seem to have "fairly obviously, a foothold on reality."[7]

Moreover, this kind of approach to evil and suffering also has an ancient pedigree. Manichaeans, named after the Mesopotamian gnostic Mani, are among the most well-known proponents of a substantive and dualistic view of good and evil.[8] Their dualistic cosmology and the related practices, which I will discuss in more detail momentarily, were in stark contrast to those of their fourth-century Christian contemporaries. Instead of thinking of evil as a substance in the universe, the equal and opposite of goodness, early Christian patristic writers tended to think of evil as a privation. One of the most prominent defenders of this view was the late fourth-century north African bishop Augustine.

AUGUSTINE THE MANICHAEAN AND AUGUSTINE THE CHRISTIAN

In 354, Aurelius Augustine was born in Thagaste, on the edge of north central Africa, in what is now Liberia. He would go on to become the bishop of Hippo and one of Christianity's most formidable and influential thinkers, shaping not only Christian thought but also Western culture. From a time early in his life, he was drawn to profound questions about human wholeness, the nature and source of evil, and also the relationship between evil and God. These questions would linger with him throughout his life and surface in a wide range of contexts within his writings. In his late teens, he was inspired by the writings of Cicero on human happiness and, by contrast, found the available Latin translation of the Bible to be crude, uncivilized, and offensive to his senses of rhetorical and moral taste.[9] As he was discarding the writings of the Christians, he was also picking up those of Mani. At the time, he found them deeply persuasive.[10]

Following the teacher after whom their tradition was named, the Manichaeans believed the cosmos to be divided in half between the substances of light and darkness. These two substances were locked in an eternal struggle against each other. In *Game of Thrones,* we see something parallel to this most clearly and explicitly in the faith associated with the "Red God." Just before burning Mance Raider alive, Melisandre sums it up, declaring, "everyone must choose the true God or the false one, light or dark" ("The Wars to Come").[11]

The Manichaeans also saw themselves as the true followers of Christ, rejecting many of the teachings and practices of the orthodox Christian church, and denying in particular any connection between Christianity and Judaism, which they saw as favoring a positive view of both the Creator and of creation itself.[12] The Manichaeans believed that, following an ancient attack by the side of darkness, particles of light had become trapped within the various elements and creatures of this world. Some things contained more particles, especially vegetables and fruit such as cucumbers and melons, and other things less or none, such as meat or wine.[13] To solve this problem, what was needed was an escape plan. The light particles must somehow be extracted so that they might return to their source, the kingdom of light. This extraction occurred, according to the Manichaeans, via the digestive tracts of the members of the highest echelon within the religion—the Elect. By eating their vegetarian diet, they were able to help free particles of light from their bondage within the dark bodies that had trapped them.

For the better part of ten years, as Augustine swam deeper and deeper into the teachings and practices of the Manichaeans, serving as a "Hearer," he was convinced he had found the answers he had been seeking. The Manichaeans offered a clear explanation of the source and nature of evil. Their explanation seemed to correspond well to the reality of evil in the world. And it had a certain tight logic to it in comparison to the overly simple and occasionally barbaric teachings and texts of the orthodox Christians.

As they reasoned, evil must have come from somewhere, and there were a limited number of possible sources. Either God had created evil, or evil was something that had existed independently and eternally of itself. The former possibility was unacceptable. And so it followed for the Manichaeans that evil had no beginning, but was instead on an ontological par with goodness.[14] As he neared age thirty, however, Augustine began to be unsatisfied with the answers Manichaeism offered to his questions on these subjects. He started interrogating Manichaean leaders, who again and again failed to supply him with adequate replies.[15] At the heart of his dissatisfaction was the notion that evil was an independent substance with its own ontology, its own being, in opposition to goodness. Eventually, his dissatisfaction grew to the point that he could no longer consider himself a Manichaean. Through Augustine's interactions with Christians, like Ambrose and Simplicianus, he also came to recognize more sophisticated ways of reading biblical texts that he had previously found objectionable. In all this, he had a growing sense of God acting to draw him toward orthodox Christianity, and at the age of thirty-two he was baptized by Ambrose in Milan. Over the course of his subsequent writing career, he continued to identify more and more objections to the dualistic Manichaean cosmology, some metaphysical and some theological.

AUGUSTINE'S CRITIQUES OF MANICHAEISM

For Augustine, one of the reasons why the Manichaeans failed to discern the real source and nature of evil was because their investigation started in the wrong place: "Out of time and out of order, he [Mani] began with inquiring into the origin of evil, without first asking what evil was; and so his inquiry led him only to the reception of foolish fancies."[16] Contrastingly, Augustine's first step was to ponder the nature of evil by reflecting on various instances of it. He came to the conclusion that these instances are not primary and independent realities, but rather privations, the lack of what should be the case: "For evil is not a positive substance: the loss of good has been given the name of 'evil.'"[17] We can see more clearly what he and other proponents of this view mean by considering an example. Think of a perforation generated by rust in the side of a car. The gap or hollow itself is not a substantial thing; it is precisely the absence of something that should be there. And it is that loss itself that is the evil in this case. Likewise, wounds and other sorts of harm, loss, and corruption are all cases of a good thing suffering some sort of deprivation. Augustine summarizes his thinking in this area in his *Enchiridion*:

> In the bodies of animals, disease and wounds mean nothing but the absence of health; for when a cure is effected that does not mean that the evils which were present—namely, the diseases and wounds, go away from the body and dwell elsewhere: they altogether cease to exist; for the wound or disease is not a substance, but a defect in the fleshly substance—the flesh itself being a substance, and therefore something good, of which those evils—that is, privations of the good which we call health—are accidents.[18]

Elsewhere, he provides a more technical explanation, saying that the God Christians worship is the source of all measure, form, and order in creation, and has created the cosmos to contain beings with widely varying levels of these three things. These, he says, are the "generic goods in things made by God, whether in spirit or in body."[19] To possess these things in any degree is to possess goodness, and thus to suffer the loss or corruption of any of these three is to suffer evil, to move away from goodness. Evil is "nothing else than corruption, either of the measure, or the form, or the order, that belong to nature."[20] It is important to emphasize at this point the language of accidents versus substances. Evil is always an accident, according to Augustine. Thus, he is not saying good things cease to be good and become evil things instead. Rather, when we are speaking of a specific instance of evil, what we are really referring to is a good thing that has become less good, but which is still good in so far as it retains its own proper measure, form, and order.

Returning to the example of the perforation in the car's side or Augustine's examples of diseases and wounds, we can see not only that these are privations, but also that evils are always dependent on the existence of some particular good. It would, accordingly, not be possible to move the car and leave the perforation behind. Or to put it another way, to resolve the evil of the corruption in the car is to make it cease to exist. "There can be no evil where there is no good."[21] Making the same point with the examples of pain, war, and even the Devil, Augustine says,

> Just as there is life, then, without pain, whereas there can be no pain when there is no life, so there is peace without any war, but no war without some degree of peace. This is not a consequence of war as such, but of the fact that war is waged by or within persons who are in some sense natural beings—for they could have no kind of existence without some kind of peace as the condition of their being. There exists, then, a nature in which there is no evil, in which indeed, no evil can exist; but there cannot exist a nature in which there is no good. Hence not even the nature of the Devil himself is evil, in so far as it is a nature; it is perversion that makes it evil.[22]

Evils are secondary to and parasitic upon some prior good thing. From this it also follows that there can be no maximally and purely evil thing. As Augustine points out in his *On the Morals of the Manichaeans*, "But if this is granted [that evil is a privation], the consequence seems plain. In that race which you take for the chief evil, nothing can be liable to be hurt, since there is no good in it."[23] That is, there can be no infinite, ultimate, or chief instance of evil or darkness, because there would be no good left to suffer harm. Thus, contrary to the teachings of the Manichaeans, evil cannot be a first principle, a primary substance, or an independently existing thing.

That every case of evil is apt to be described as a case of privation or absence constitutes a good reason for denying the sort of dualism that the Manichaeans affirmed. There are other reasons, both metaphysical and moral, for denying that sort of dualism. Augustine articulates some of them in his writings. Several more recent thinkers have continued to flesh out the Augustinian tradition and have provided further objections to the sort of cosmological dualism to which the Manichaeans adhered. Among them C. S. Lewis and Reinhold Niebuhr are especially significant.

THE PRIVATIVE VIEW IN MODERN THOUGHT: FOOTNOTES TO AUGUSTINE

In his essay "Evil and God," C. S. Lewis argues that only a non-dualistic view of evil is capable of providing a solid explanation for the existence of a finite cosmos containing good or evil, or a foundation for a sound theory of morality. This is because, were evil and good on par with each other, equals and opposites, there would be no way to distinguish or explain the existence of the two. There would be no reason to call one "good" or the other "evil" aside from an arbitrary preference for one over the other. Thus, for example, it would be impossible to make any real distinction between Hodor's self-sacrificial love, on the one hand, and the deadly animosity of the Night King or the Lannisters' unmitigated misanthropy, on the other. This is a distinction I assume most would be inclined to make at the most basic level of moral intuition. Yet, Lewis argues, for there to be a clear and absolute distinction of this sort requires that there be a first principle that can be *identified* with the Good and which exists in a way that is unlike the existence of anything other than itself. Likewise, to assign any sense of *being* at all to goodness and evil requires that they be unequal, since for them to be equal would entail that neither could be the ground or explanation for the other. As Lewis puts it, assuming a form of cosmological dualism to be the case,

> More ultimate than either of them is the inexplicable fact of their being there together. Neither of them chose this *tete-a-tete*. Each of them, therefore, is *conditioned*—finds himself willy-nilly in a situation; and either that situation itself, or some unknown force which produced that situation, is the real Ultimate. Dualism has not yet reached the ground of being.[24]

Both Lewis and Reinhold Niebuhr comment on the further significance of this moral point. Under dualism, the unavoidable tendency would be to paint the world in black and white, to carve out an unbridgeable chasm between those on the side of evil and those on the side of good. From Lewis' perspective, while it is tempting to frame the world in this way, one problem this creates is that it is self-defeating. It is to "have lost the power to condemn. If a taste for cruelty and a taste for kindness were equally ultimate and basic, by what common standard could the one reprove the other?"[25]

An argument could be made here that to cast the enemy as *naturally* evil rather than a corrupted good is to invalidate one's ability to judge or evaluate them as evil, since one does not condemn in another that for which she is not willfully responsible. Indeed, Augustine makes this point against the Manichaeans, using the example of an unconscious subject to prove his point: "whoever has done anything evil by means of one unconscious or unable to resist, the latter can by no means be justly condemned."[26] Thus, the Manichaean position, which posits a substantial evil as the cause of human sin, undercuts the possibility of holding people responsible for their sin in the same way that we would not generally hold a person responsible for what they were compelled to do apart from or in opposition to their will.

Elsewhere, Augustine makes the same point again saying, in so far as one is "wanting in a movement of mind free both for doing and not doing, if finally no power of abstaining from their work is conceded to them; we cannot hold that the sin is theirs."[27] Contrastingly, when a person consciously and willfully intends to commit some sin, it is natural for them to be held responsible for it. It follows that sin is not something that can be attributed to our flesh or to some evil substance within us. Rather sin must be attributed to a misused free will. To put this within the framework of the world of *Game of Thrones*, Cersei Lannister is arguably more worthy of censure than the Night King or the Shadow. After all, Cersei is willfully wicked, while the latter two seem to be naturally so. Cersei is literally and intentionally malevolent (from *male* and *velle*—"willing that which is bad"), while the living dead do not really seem to have *chosen* to incline whatever little will they possess toward murder and mayhem. The latter is better compared to a virus or disease—harmful, but not intentionally so.

However, Lewis' reason for saying that judgment would be undermined by dualism does not have much if anything to do with responsibility, but rather, again, metaphysics. Under dualism, the ultimate moral foundation would be absent and thus, being on moral par, neither "good" nor "evil" would be in a position to condemn each other. Of course, this is a point that one is not likely to take much time to consider while fighting or fleeing an army of the living dead. Nevertheless, it is worthy of some reflection.

A related set of arguments appears in the writings of Niebuhr, a prominent twentieth-century theologian and political philosopher. He traces out why this network of abstract claims about the nature and location of evil is deeply important for the realms of moral and political philosophy in the modern world. As Niebuhr repeatedly points out, one flaw in the Manichaean form of dualism is that it tends to encourage a failure to recognize the limits and egotism of the self. From a neat division of the moral world and the identification of the enemy with unalloyed wickedness, it tends to follow that one identifies oneself with unalloyed goodness. And this is never either an accurate or a practically effective way of framing conflict and disagreement.

Niebuhr's rejection of this sort of dualism in moral philosophy helped shape the stance that would ultimately define his thinking—realism—and he traces this primarily to Augustine. For Niebuhr, realism means, first, that the actual problem most in need of solving is not out there in some excizable foreign object, some wholly evil substance that needs to be extracted or from which the real, pure self needs to escape. And second, what's required is a recognition "of the seat of evil being in the self."[28] Christianity, he says, is a combination of views. It affirms a high view of creation—if evil is merely a corruption of some good, it follows that nature itself is good. And in particular, human beings have a deep value; they are, according to the Christian heritage, created in the *Imago dei*. At the same time, Christianity adds to this a "low estimate of human virtue . . . Man is a sinner."

> The Christian estimate of human evil is so serious precisely because it places evil at the very centre [sic] of human personality: in the will. This evil cannot be regarded complacently as the inevitable consequence of his finiteness or the fruit of his involvement in the contingencies and necessities of nature . . . In Christianity it is not the eternal man who judges the finite man; but the eternal and holy God who judges sinful man.[29]

The problem that needs resolution is not our nature or even a particular part of our nature, but rather the willful misuse of our nature. Another way of putting this, along Augustinian lines, is that we must recognize that evil is not to be identified with our flesh or with some substantial part of the cosmos. Rather evil in the form of human vice is the twisting and corruption of a good thing, the will, away from what it should be. This recognition, not of the self's limits *per se,* but of the various tendencies to *deny* those limits is crucial, Niebuhr argues. More specifically, it is vital to recognize that sin has its seat in the misuse of freedom itself—sin is a spiritual problem, rather than a problem rooted in finitude or flesh.[30] The failure to recognize this can itself exacerbate the human tendency to overestimate the extent and accuracy of our knowledge, along with the purity of our judgments and actions. Likewise, one reason why it is important to recognize the real source of our troubles along with our various limits is that this recognition precludes certain overly optimistic or overly simple assessments either of our own goodness or our enemies' wickedness. This makes conflict at the individual and at the broader political level more complex, but rightly so:

> The fact that the two impulses [the will-to-live-truly and the will-to-power], though standing in contradiction to each other, are also mixed and compounded with each other on every level of human life, makes the simple distinctions between good and evil, between selfishness and altruism, with which liberal idealism has tried to estimate moral and political facts, invalid.[31]

Practically, this means that it is never possible to conceive of the self as purely on the side of the good and the enemy as being entirely on the side of evil, since to be purely evil would be not to be at all. Instead, the truth is that on each side of all conflict are human beings possessed of, in the language of Augustine, measure, form, and order. And on each side are human beings who have made free and willful choices to fall away from these goods in varying ways and degrees. Several different figures in *Game of Thrones* bring this important insight to life for us.

As the plot winds its way across Westeros and Essos, the perspective frequently shifts, moving from the wildlings north of the Wall to the Night Watch soldiers guarding it, from the Lannisters at King's Landing to Daenerys Targaryen on her way to take the throne. Through all of these shifts and many others, it is difficult for the audience member to resist toggling back and forth between loathing and sympathy for these characters. This happens because each character is complex and still (at least minimally) human. In Niebuhr's language, both sides of every conflict are populated by people whose lives, at every level, are characterized and shaped by both a will-to-live-truly and a will-to-power. This excludes simple arrogance or an overly "easy conscience" on the part of the self, as well as absolute condemnation of the enemy. Alternatively, recognizing the complexity of the moral life on both sides of any conflict makes it possible to conceive of resolution and transformation in ways that are not available under a more dualistic framework. This is because the dualistic framework tends to identify the person himself with the evil he commits, "reduc[ing] a person to crime," as Kathleen Ray puts it, and excluding the notion of that person being or becoming anything else.[32] Instead, "human experience is simply not divisible in this way, and it is time our conceptions of good and evil responded to, rather than ignored, the uncompromising ambiguity of life in a finite world."[33]

OBJECTIONS TO THE PRIVATIVE VIEW

I have identified several justifications for rejecting anything like the Manichaean form of dualism as a viable option and have also drawn out some of the implications for affirming cosmological monism. Some of these arguments are traceable to Augustine and some to later thinkers writing in Augustine's shadow. Yet there are powerful objections to the privative view as well that we have not considered at length. Obviously, given the focus and scope of this chapter, it will only be possible to graze in this part of the conversation about the privative view of evil. So I would like to focus only on a couple of objections, which are significant and also relevant to the material upon which this chapter concentrates. The most prominent, as mentioned above, is the assertion that the privative view does not sufficiently reflect the way that evils sometimes seem to be quite concretely, powerfully present. Arguably, a privative view does not do justice to the experience people have of evil and pain along this line. We might call this the phenomenological objection to the privative view of evil. The other major objection is that the defenders of the privative view affirm propositions concerning evil that are inconsistent with each other, and thus that the view lacks cogency.

According to the first objection, the privative view of evil does not do justice to people's experience of evil as having its own being, causal power, and presence. One version of this objection comes from Mark Robson in a response to Brian Davies' work on this subject. Robson cites depression as a counterexample to the notion that all evils are properly describable as privations or absences. Using the example of a woman struggling with depression, he says "it seems difficult to equate a feeling of mind-numbing horror with absences . . . The notion that something, e.g., a horrible feeling of utter dread, is actually identical with nothing does not seem to make any sense."[34] On a related note, though she rejects "absolute dualism," Kathleen Ray argues that the powers of evil are "pervasive and potent," and evil's presence in the world must be recognized.[35] Perhaps George R. R. Martin had something comparable to this in mind when he crafted creatures like the white walkers or the Shadow assassin. These kinds of figures certainly do a good job of exemplifying the perceptibility and actuality that can sometimes seem to characterize evil. And arguably, a privative view of the nature of evil might fail in this regard since evil, on such a view, has no real presence whatsoever.

The second objection to the privative view that I have noted above claims that the view is not logically consistent or cogent. Mark Robson has offered a version of this critique as well. His argument can be summed up as follows. The defenders of the privative view of evil assume both that evil is an absence and that evil has causal power to do things like cause pain, suffering, and ruin. And yet only substantive things have these sorts of causal powers. Thus, if evil is identical with nothing, it can have no such causal powers. As he puts it, under the privative view, "Evil cannot be causally effective at all since . . . it is an absence, a kind of nothing. Only things—'substantial' parts of reality—can do things . . . Evil is consigned to powerlessness"[36] From this, as Robson declares, it follows that one cannot affirm both that evil is a privation and that evil has any sort of causal potency.

How can a proponent of a privative view respond to these arguments? Regarding the first objection, it is important that any view of evil take into consideration the actual experience people have with various kinds of evil. However, if there are good reasons to reject alternative ways of conceiving of evil and, likewise, good reasons to affirm that evil is an absence, then what follows is that we have good reason to look for a way to render the privative view compatible with the apparent reality and power of evil. Along the same lines, if our impressions of evil imply a view of the nature of evil that lacks cogency, then we have good reason either to reject the validity of those impressions or to reconsider their precise import. Since the experience of evil as having causal power and as having a sort of reality to it seems to be so widespread, and since we have several good reasons to reject views of evil other than a privative view, it follows that we should pursue the possibility of upholding both a privative view along with the validity of those experiences. What I am defending is the position that this is indeed possible.

First, to say that evil is a privation is not to say that it is absolutely nonexistent, a point relevant to both objections. A shadow is an absence, and yet it has a certain reality and presence to it. We can point at and refer to shadows. We can speak of them as being in a particular place and time, and as having a certain length or size. Similarly, we frequently speak of losses and privations in terms that impute to them a certain sort of reality and causal power. This is not to say that absences are themselves possessed of the same sort of causal power that we attribute to independently existing and acting things. Rather, as Brian Davies puts it in reply to Robson, using the example of negligence to make his point,

> Negligence can enter into an account of how certain events come about, not because there is something to be named "negligence" that has a life of its own and is able to wreak havoc, but because not paying attention to something can sometimes (and sometimes culpably) leave the way open to something able to wreak havoc. In this sense, a lack can be referred to as significant when it comes to the coming about of evil or badness and is not a mere illusion.[37]

Applying this to the second objection, we can say that just as there is no inconsistency in affirming both that negligence is a form of absence and that we can attribute a sort of causal potency to negligence, so also there is no inconsistency in affirming more generally both that evil is an absence or privation and that evils have a certain sort of causal potency. And to the first objection, we can say that there is no incompatibility in affirming the evident reality of, for example, pain and suffering while also upholding the notion that what we are referring to when we describe these sorts of things as "evils" is a type of absence—the absence of some good that we would naturally desire and expect to have. And what's more, as Davies also points out, were these evils not, at bottom, the loss of some prior good, we would have no basis for describing them as evil.

> We do not understand what is being said when told that something is a bad x unless we have a sense of what it would be to be a good x. If rotten apples were the norm, we would not understand what a bad apple is.[38]

DEATH, EVIL, AND PRIVATION IN *GAME OF THRONES*

Returning our attention to death and evil as it is portrayed in *Game of Thrones*, if what I have argued thus far is correct, then it might seem to follow that evil such as that depicted by the figures of the Night King and the Shadow assassin is, in the end, beyond even the realm of conception. That is, the privative view might appear to entail that the real evils for which we should be on the lookout are those that are not so conspicuous or, in particular, substantive. Or to put the point otherwise, perhaps we should be more on our guard against evil in the form of, as Hannah Arendt famously put it, banality.[39] That is, we must be wary of coming to think that evil is always obvious, striking, arresting. From the recognition that evil is a privation, rather than an independent and pure Ultimate, follows the recognition that evil manifests itself in varied and mixed forms. In other words, from a privative view of evil, it follows that instead of suffering from evil as some particular thing "out there" or as some sort of obvious, excizable element of the self, the truth is that good things suffer all sorts and degrees of deprivation. But this also means that in the real world, evil is not always easily recognizable. It is not always donning an evil grin or wielding an ice spear. Rather, it is something that can get worn in slowly and quietly so that it becomes mundane, ordinary, and difficult to notice. What's more, it is something that can wear the veil of virtue.

Many figures in the world of *Game of Thrones* exhibit for us various ways of being vicious under the cloak of virtue. For example, we can observe this in Queen Daenerys' inability to perceive the savagery of using her dragon to execute without trial Randyll and Dickon Tarly, who surrendered to her after a battle. It's visible in the Lannisters who, for the sake of protecting the family or the kingdom, commit heinous acts like tossing Bran from the tower or using wildfire to burn an enemy naval fleet alive. Many other examples from as many other characters could be supplied. What's important to note is not just that these are vicious acts, but that the agents behind them do not even perceive them as such. Instead, they have painted over them with a veneer of virtue or used them to achieve an end so valuable to the character that it justifies absolutely any means. This point about the banality and inconspicuousness of evil is also easy to forget or reject because the last thing one wants to recognize in oneself, one's culture, or the systems and institutions of which one is a part, is some form of engrained evil and vice. And so we are in constant need of being reminded of Arendt's insight.

Yet the figures we have been focusing on from *Game of Thrones* like the Night King and the Shadow hold a lasting significance of their own for a couple of reasons. First, it's interesting to note that although the two figures I have examined and others like them seem to be intended to represent some ultimate form of substantial evil, there is also an inescapable contingency and deprivation to them. The Shadows are not self-sustaining and cannot exist by themselves. Rather, as the "Red Woman" says, they are ultimately "children and servants of the light" ("Garden of Bones").[40] And of course, despite their appearance as a substantive force, like other shadows, they remain an *absence* of light. The white walkers, including their leader the Night King, are the work of Children of the Forest, who created them as instruments of war. The army of the dead is composed of once-living people who have been twisted and degraded into their current form. The Night King and the dead army are ultimately not intrinsic and pure evils, but are rather corrupted goods. It seems, then, that even in the apparent attempt to portray evil as something pure and ultimate, its privative nature inevitably shows through. Of course, this is a construal of evil that Augustine and the later Christian tradition would still reject, since even though evil in the world of the Seven Kingdoms is contingent and in a sense privative, it is also somehow a substance and, more importantly, is actively *created* or *generated*. In the Christian tradition, contrastingly, evil is indeed a servant of God, yet one of the primary reasons why this is so is because evil is purely a privation, having no substantive being of its own. As Karl Barth declares, commenting on this tradition,

> Whatever evil is, God is its Lord. We must not push our attempt to take evil seriously to the point of ever coming to think of it as an original and indeed creative counter-deity which posits autonomous and independent facts competing seriously with the one living God and striving with Him for the mastery. Evil is a form of that nothingness which as such is absolutely subject to God.[41]

Precisely because evil has no autonomy of its own, it follows for Barth and others in this tradition that God is not its source *and* that it is subservient to God. What's more, this does not diminish its seriousness. Along this line, dramatic, concrete figures like the Night King and the Shadow are important and even helpful for the same reason that figures like the dragon or the various beasts and monsters of apocalyptic literature are important and helpful: they provide us with a means of depicting the gravity and enormity of evil. They highlight the reality and potency that evil, even as a privation, retains.

CONCLUSIONS

The world George R. R. Martin has created for *A Song of Ice and Fire* is a lively and complex one that merits sustained exploration. I have only begun the process of surveying the landscape, engaging in reflection on figures that represent, quite literally, death and evil. I have also briefly examined one of the most prominent views of the nature of evil in the Christian heritage, considered a couple of the most significant objections and critiques of this view, and provided some initial replies and defenses. There is much more to say on each of these points, but I believe I have offered several good reasons to affirm a privative view of evil, several good reasons to reject alternative ways of construing the nature of evil, and provided some solid defenses of the privative view in the face of objections. I have also argued that attending carefully to evil within a privative view involves taking into account people's experience of it and, at the broader level, recognizing evil's multitudinous forms. The night is dark and full of terrors, Melisandre repeatedly reminds us, but it turns out that those terrors appear in a wide assortment of manifestations. Evil is horrendous and devastating and dreadful. Evil is banal and mundane, and often difficult to perceive. In all its forms, it has a certain sort of reality, presence, and causal potency to it. And as tangible and concrete dramatic figures, the myriad characters of *Game of Thrones* give unique expression to this.

NOTES

1. HBO Entertainment; co-executive producers, George R. R. Martin, Vince Gerardis, Ralph Vicinanza, Guymon Casady, Carolyn Strauss; producers, Mark Huffam, Frank Doelger; executive producers David Benioff, D.B. Weiss; created by David Benioff & D.B. Weiss; Television 360; Grok! Television; Generator Entertainment; Bighead Littlehead. *Game of Thrones.* New York: HBO Home Entertainment, 2012. Season Seven, Episode Seven. Directed by Jeremy Podeswa. From here on the show *Game of Thrones* will be cited in abbreviated form as *GOT*.

2. Charles Taylor, *A Secular Age* (Cambridge: Belknap Press, 2007), 59–61.

3. *GOT,* Season Six, Episode Five: "The Door." Directed by Jack Bender.

4. *GOT,* Season Four, Episode Two: "The Lion and the Rose." Directed by Alex Graves.

5. *GOT,* Season Three, Episode Three: "Walk of Punishment." Directed by David Benioff.

6. *GOT,* Season Five, Episode Four: "Sons of the Harpy." Directed by Mark Mylod.

7. Mark Ian Robson, "Evil, Privation, Depression, and Dread," *New Blackfriars*, 94, no 1053 (Sep 2013) 557.

8. Henry Chadwick, "Introduction," in *Confessions.* Trans. Henry Chadwick (Oxford: Oxford University Press, 1991) xiv.

9. G.R. Evans, "Evil," in *Augustine Through the Ages: An Encyclopedia* (Grand Rapids: William B. Eerdmans, 1999) 340.

10. Chadwick, "Introduction," xiv.

11. *GOT,* Season Five, Episode One, "The Wars to Come." Directed by Michael Slovis.

12. J. Kevin Coyle, "Mani, Manicheism," in *Augustine Through the Ages: An Encyclopedia* (Grand Rapids: William B. Eerdmans, 1999) 524.

13. Henry Chadwick, *Augustine: A Very Short Introduction* (Oxford: Oxford University Press, 1986) 13.

14. William E. Mann, "Augustine on Evil and Original Sin," in *Cambridge Companion to Augustine.* Ed. Eleonore Stump and Norman Kretzmann (Cambridge: Cambridge University Press, 2001) 40.

15. Chadwick, *Augustine*, 15.

16. Augustine, *Against the Epistle of Manichaeus*, in *Nicene and Post-Nicene Fathers*, Vol. 4: *Augustin: The Writings Against the Manichaeans, and Against the Donatists,* ed. Philip Schaff (Peabody: Hendrickson Publishers, 2004) ch. 36, § 41, 147.

17. Augustine, *City of God*, trans. Henry Bettenson (London: Penguin, 1972) XI.9, 440.

18. Augustine, *Enchiridion*, ch. 11, 240.

19. Augustine, *Nature of Good, Against the Manichaeans*, in *Nicene and Post-Nicene Fathers*, Vol. 4: *Augustin: The Writings Against the Manichaeans, and Against the Donatists,* ed. Philip Schaff (Peabody: Hendrickson Publishers, 2004) ch. 3, 352.

20. Augustine, *Nature of Good, Against the Manichaeans*, in *Nicene and Post-Nicene Fathers*, Vol. 4: *Augustin: The Writings Against the Manichaeans, and Against the Donatists,* ed. Philip Schaff (Peabody: Hendrickson Publishers, 2004) ch. 4, 352.

21. Augustine, *Enchiridion, Nicene and Post-Nicene Fathers:* Vol. 3: *Augustin: On the Holy Trinity, Doctrinal Treatises, Moral Treatises*, ed. Philip Schaff (Peabody: Hendrickson Publishers, 2004) ch. 13, 241.

22. Augustine, *City of God*, XIX.13. 871.

23. Augustine, *On the Morals of the Manichaeans*, in *Nicene and Post-Nicene Fathers*, Vol. 4: *Augustin: The Writings Against the Manichaeans, and Against the Donatists,* ed. Philip Schaff (Peabody: Hendrickson Publishers, 2004) 70.

24. C.S. Lewis, "Evil and God." in *God In the Dock: Essays on Theology and Ethics*, ed. Walter Hooper (Grand Rapids: William B. Eerdmans, 1970) 22.

25. *Ibid.*, 23.

26. Augustine, *On the Morals of the Manichaeans*, in *Nicene and Post-Nicene Fathers*, Vol. 4: *Augustin: The Writings Against the Manichaeans, and Against the Donatists,* ed. Philip Schaff (Peabody: Hendrickson Publishers, 2004) ch. 10, §12, 102.

27. Augustine, *Two-Souls, Against the Manichaeans*, in *Nicene and Post-Nicene Fathers*, Vol. 4: *Augustin: The Writings Against the Manichaeans, and Against the Donatists,* ed. Philip Schaff (Peabody: Hendrickson Publishers, 2004) ch. 12, §17, 105.

28. Reinhold Niebuhr, "Augustine's Political Realism," in *The Essential Reinhold Niebuhr: Selected Essays and Addresses,* ed. Robert MacAfee Brown (Yale, 1986) 124.

29. Reinhold Niebuhr, *The Nature and Destiny of Man*, Vol. 1 (New York: Charles Scribner's Sons, 1949) 16.

30. Niebuhr, *Nature and Destiny*, Vol. 1, 120.

31. Niebuhr, "Children of Light and Children of Darkness," in *The Essential Reinhold Niebuhr: Selected Essays and Addresses,* ed. Robert MacAfee Brown (Yale, 1986) 171.

32. Kathleen Darby Ray, "Undermining Evil," in *Deceiving the Devil: Atonement, Abuse, and Ransom* (Cleveland: Pilgrim, 1998) 126.
33. *Ibid.*
34. *Ibid.*, 556.
35. Ray, "Undermining Evil," 132–4.
36. Robson, "Evil, Privation, Depression, and Dread," *New Blackfriars*, 94 no 1953 (Sep 2013) 555.
37. Brian Davies, "Reply to Robson on Evil as Privation," *New Blackfriars*, 94 no 1953 (Sep 2013) 565–8.
38. Davies, "Reply to Robson," 567.
39. Hannah Arendt, *Eichmann in Jerusalem: A Report on the Banality of Evil* (New York: Penguin Books, 1963).
40. *GOT*, Season Two, Episode Four. Directed by David Petrarca.
41. Karl Barth, *Church Dogmatics*, IV.1, *The Doctrine of Reconciliation*, eds. G.W. Bromiley and T.F. Torrance (Peabody: Hendrickson Publishers, 1956) 408.

WORKS CITED

Arendt, Hannah. *Eichmann in Jerusalem: A Report on the Banality of Evil*. New York: Penguin Books, 1963.

Augustine. *Against the Epistle of Manichaeus*, in *Nicene and Post-Nicene Fathers: Vol. 4: Augustin: The Writings Against the Manichaeans, and Against the Donatists*. Ed. Philip Schaff. Peabody: Hendrickson Publishers, 2004.

———. *City of God*. Trans. Henry Bettenson. London: Penguin, 1972.

———. *Enchiridion*, in *Nicene and Post-Nicene Fathers: Vol. 3: Augustin: On the Holy Trinity, Doctrinal Treatises, Moral Treatises*. Ed. Philip Schaff. Peabody: Hendrickson Publishers, 2004.

———. *Nature of Good, Against the Manichaeans*, in *Nicene and Post-Nicene Fathers: Vol. 4: Augustin: The Writings Against the Manichaeans, and Against the Donatists*. Ed. Philip Schaff. Peabody: Hendrickson Publishers, 2004.

———. *On the Morals of the Manichaeans*, in *Nicene and Post-Nicene Fathers, Vol. 4: Augustin: The Writings Against the Manichaeans, and Against the Donatists*. Ed. Philip Schaff. Peabody: Hendrickson Publishers, 2004.

———. *Two-Souls, Against the Manichaeans*, in *Nicene and Post-Nicene Fathers, Vol. 4: Augustin: The Writings Against the Manichaeans, and Against the Donatists*. Ed. Philip Schaff. Peabody: Hendrickson Publishers, 2004.

Barth, Karl. *Church Dogmatics*, IV.1, *The Doctrine of Reconciliation*. Eds. G.W. Bromiley and T.F. Torrance. Peabody: Hendrickson Publishers, 1956.

Chadwick, Henry. *Augustine: A Very Short Introduction*. Oxford: Oxford University Press, 1986.

Coyle, J. Kevin. "Mani, Manicheism." In *Augustine Through the Ages: An Encyclopedia*. Grand Rapids: William B. Eerdmans, 1999.

Davies, Brian. "Reply to Robson on Evil as Privation." *New Blackfriars*, 94 no. 1953 (Sep 2013).

HBO Entertainment; co-executive producers, George R. R. Martin, Vince Gerardis, Ralph Vicinanza, Guymon Casady, Carolyn Strauss; producers, Mark Huffam, Frank Doelger; executive producers David Benioff, D.B. Weiss; created by David Benioff & D.B. Weiss; Television 360; Grok! Television; Generator Entertainment; Bighead Littlehead. *Game of Thrones.* New York: HBO Home Entertainment, 2012.

Lewis, C.S. "Evil and God." In *God In the Dock: Essays on Theology and Ethics.* Ed. Walter Hooper. Grand Rapids: William B. Eerdmans, 1970.

Mann, William E. "Augustine on Evil and Original Sin." In *Cambridge Companion to Augustine.* Ed. Eleonore Stump and Norman Kretzmann. Cambridge: Cambridge University Press, 2001.

Niebuhr, Reinhold. "Augustine's Political Realism." In *The Essential Reinhold Niebuhr: Selected Essays and Addresses.* Ed. Robert MacAfee Brown. New Haven: Yale University Press, 1986a.

———. "Children of Light and Children of Darkness." In *The Essential Reinhold Niebuhr: Selected Essays and Addresses.* Ed. Robert MacAfee Brown. New Haven: Yale University Press, 1986b.

———. *The Nature and Destiny of Man*, Vol. 1. New York: Charles Scribner's Sons, 1949.

Ray, Kathleen Darby. "Undermining Evil." In *Deceiving the Devil: Atonement, Abuse, and Ransom.* Cleveland: Pilgrim, 1998.

Robson, Mark Ian. "Evil, Privation, Depression, and Dread." *New Blackfriars*, 94, no 1053 (Sep 2013).

Taylor, Charles. *A Secular Age.* Cambridge: Belknap Press, 2007.

Chapter 7

The Faith of the Seven and Faith in the Trinity

David Mahfood

THE SEVEN: ERSATZ TRINITY?

On the continent of Westeros, at least during the events of *A Song of Ice and Fire*, the dominant religion is known as the faith of the Seven. This religion appears to be, in many respects, inspired by the Roman Catholic Church in medieval Europe. Like the Catholic faith of medieval Europe, the faith of the Seven is not native to Westeros but was brought over from elsewhere and ultimately displaces faith in the Old Gods (which appears roughly analogous to what Christians would call pagan religions). Like medieval Catholicism, the Church of the Seven seems to build ornate places of worship in which well-defined liturgies are carried out by ordained clergy. Like Catholicism, the Church of the Seven seems to include ascetic or monastic orders (including controversial new ones; the Sparrows perhaps bear some resemblance to the medieval Franciscans), and organized in a hierarchical fashion with an individual cleric functioning as head of the entire church in a way similar to the papacy. And, of course, there is the vision of God as Trinity, three and yet one, which seems to be a clear inspiration for the idea of a deity who is seven and yet one. Like the Christian Trinity of Father, Son, and Holy Spirit, the Seven are thought of (at least officially) by those who believe in them as one God, in this case seven rather than three.

Martin's use of medieval Christianity as a model is cleverly done, but it raises some theological questions from the point of view of Christian faith. How well does the Seven function as a theological analog to the Trinity? Could these seven names serve the same theological functions which Father, Son, and Spirit are supposed to serve? Is seven, after all, just as good as three, or perhaps even better, as a way of thinking about God? What, if anything, does Trinity do that the Seven couldn't, and vice versa? The comparison turns out to be instructive for understanding Christianity, because it helps us see more clearly how the doctrine of the Trinity functions both for how Christians think about God, and for how they think about human beings as creatures who bear the image of the Triune God.

We will see that in fact the most plausible interpretation of the Seven based on the material we have seems to conflict with some basic Christian doctrinal commitments. The theology of the Seven seems likely to involve a form of modalism, the persons seem to be distinguished primarily by what kinds of benefits they provide to creatures rather than in relation to one another, and it implies a kind of fragmentation within the deity, as both life and death seem to be intrinsic aspects of the Seven. In conversation with St. Augustine's reflection on the human psyche as an image of the Trinity, we can then see how this differing picture of God might imply a different spiritual vision of humanity—one which, I will argue, is less likely to prize the contemplative life as the highest spiritual calling, and instead to be more focused on activity within a well-ordered society capable of successfully responding to external challenges.

TRINITY: A BASIC PRIMER

To make a comparison between the idea of God as Trinity and the Westerosi Seven, we first need to understand some basic elements of trinitarian theology.[1] With the doctrine and its history clearly in view, we will be able to make a detailed comparison to what we know about the doctrine of the Seven and its history. We can begin by thinking about the fundamental premises that motivated the doctrine in the first place. These are the basic criteria that the doctrine is designed to fulfill, and which any account of God must meet in order to be successful from a trinitarian point of view. Relatedly, we need to get a basic historical sense of how the doctrine of the Trinity came about. What events or experiences fundamentally motivated Christians to think and speak about God this way? This will enable us to ask whether the Seven as they're presented in *A Song of Ice and Fire* could meet the same or similar criteria or whether it could have arisen out of a similar history.

It took Christians some centuries to arrive at the doctrine, after all. It isn't an idea that Jesus or a biblical author articulated in a finished way which Christians thereafter universally accepted. Many basic elements of trinitarianism are arguably expressed by the biblical authors, but it took time, and a good deal of trial and error, for Christians to arrive at this particular way of describing the God they worship. Getting a sense of this history is essential for understanding what the doctrine means. As we'll see, we don't have much hint of a similarly lengthy process for the doctrine of the Seven, but seeing clearly what led to the doctrine of the Trinity will enable us to raise questions and speculate about the doctrine of the Seven.

We can start by noting that Christianity arose out of first-century Judaism. Jesus was a Jew, and his followers believed him to be the Jewish Messiah, the one through whom Israel's God would ultimately rescue God's people from their oppression. This means that Christians inherited the Jewish scriptures (which they came to call the Old Testament) as well as a bedrock commitment to some key theological claims early Christians understood to be taught in these texts. Central among these is the claim that there is one God who created the world and everything in it, and this God alone is worthy of worship.[2] To worship other beings besides this God is idolatry. This is the only God in whom salvation is found, the only one who has authority to forgive sins.

Christians, along with many first-century Jews, believed this God to be transcendent, eternal, immortal, immaterial, perfectly good, all-powerful, all-knowing, unchanging, and perfectly self-sufficient. All of these claims were themselves products of complex development and interpretation, and some early Christians tried to excise some of them from the Christian faith—but by and large, what became the orthodox, trinitarian Christian faith insisted on retaining them. We can sum up these ideas by saying early Christians held onto *Jewish monotheism* as they understood it. Christians believed that this God, the Jewish God, is the one who sent Jesus and whom Jesus faithfully proclaimed. This is the God Jesus identified as his Father.

On the other hand, Christians saw Jesus as standing in a unique relationship to the Father. In the Old Testament, of course, various human beings played mediating roles between God and humanity: prophets spoke for God, priests offered sacrifices on the people's behalf, and kings represented God in ruling and protecting the people. But for Christians, Jesus was linked even more intimately with God than anyone who had come before. In Jesus, they had met the Father's *only* Son. Moreover, the early Christians came to attribute to Jesus things which belong only to God. In the Gospels, Jesus forgives sins and exercises authority over nature. For instance, he taught as one who had authority of his own, not simply as an interpreter of the Law of Moses. John's Gospel proclaims him to be the Word through which God created all things. Elsewhere in the New Testament, he is called the image of the invisible God, in whom the fullness of God dwelled.

So, the early Christians faced a profound intellectual problem. Utterly committed to the proposition that there is one God, the Father, who created all things, who alone is worthy of worship, who alone can forgive sins and save creatures from death, they nonetheless came to see *Jesus* as worthy of worship, and as the agent of both creation and of salvation. In the third and fourth centuries, the status of the Son (Jesus) relative to the Father became a subject of protracted controversy. All agreed that the Son was highly exalted, nearer to God than anything else, but there were significant factions within Christianity that felt it necessary to insist that the Son was not eternal along with the Father, but a product of the Father which at one time did not exist and then later came into being.

At the same time, Christianity had become increasingly widespread in the Roman Empire, and the emperor Constantine had made it a legal religion (though it wasn't until the time of Theodosius that Christianity became the official religion of the empire). Constantine called a council of the church's bishops to try to address this ongoing religious dispute (among others of slightly less theological importance) within his empire. The council met at Nicaea in 325, and ultimately produced a creed meant to resolve the controversy. The Nicene Creed emphatically insisted on Jesus's divine status, confessing him to be "God from God, light from light, true God from true God, . . . consubstantial with the Father,"[3] and condemned as heretical the proposition that there was some time at which the Son did not exist.

Over time it became clear that Christians faced the same situation with respect to the Holy Spirit. The Spirit, St. Paul had written, reveals the deep things of God, things which God alone knows. He claimed that the Spirit pours out the love of God in the hearts of believers and makes them into adopted sons and daughters of the Father along with Jesus. The church was said to be the Body of Christ, and it was the Holy Spirit (also described in the New Testament as the Spirit *of Christ*) who was said to make them into that one Body. Jesus and the Holy Spirit also came to be incorporated into the early Christian experience of worship and salvation in a thoroughgoing way. Baptism, for instance, which was the rite by which one entered the church, was done in the name of the Father, the Son, and the Holy Spirit. So perhaps it isn't surprising that, after the council at Nicaea, there was controversy about the status of the Spirit similar to the earlier (and indeed ongoing) controversy about the Son.

In 381, a second council met at Constantinople to resolve both new and continuing controversies. The council produced a new version of the Creed, reaffirming the divine status of the Son proclaimed at Nicaea, but expanding on the status of the Spirit as well. Where the Nicene Creed had said only, "And [we believe] in the Holy Spirit,"[4] the Creed of Constantinople proclaims the Holy Spirit to be "the Lord, and the Life-giver, that proceeds from the Father, who with the Father and Son is worshipped together and glorified together."[5] At Constantinople, then, the bishops declared the Holy Spirit to be divine, like the Son and the Father. In the case of the doctrine of the Seven, we don't have much evidence suggesting it arose from this kind of historical process of theological disputation, though it certainly could have done so. But noticing the historical process in the case of Christianity can help us see the boundaries or constraints that apply in the case of the Trinity, and we can then ask whether or not the doctrine of the Seven fits within similar boundaries.

In the case of Christianity, we can now see the basic shape of the problem to which Trinity is the solution. By the late fourth century, what would become orthodox Christianity seemed to believe that the Father, Son, and Holy Spirit each do what only God can do, and so each rightly receive the honor only God can receive. And yet, the idea that these are three separate Gods (*tritheism*) is ruled out by the commitment to monotheism they understood themselves to receive from Judaism. With this much in view, one might think another solution presents itself: perhaps there is one God who simply appears in these three roles, like an actor putting on different masks, playing different characters at different times while remaining in reality a single person. But this option (now usually called *modalism* because it envisions God as one person appearing in three different "modes") was also rejected by the mainstream of Christianity. Orthodox trinitarianism insists that the Father is God and the Son is God and the Spirit is God, but the Father is not the Son, the Son is not the Spirit, and the Spirit is not the Father. These three are really distinct from one another even though they are one and the same God. Modalism and tritheism represent boundaries or constraints on the Christian understanding of God. Avoiding tritheism means Christians needed a way to say God is genuinely one, but avoiding modalism meant they needed a way to say God is genuinely three.

There's an obvious risk of straightforward contradiction here: "There are exactly three apples in this basket" and "There is exactly one apple in this basket" can't both be true at the same time. For the sake of basic coherence, what was needed was a way to say that God is three in one sense but one in another sense—one X, but three Ys. There's no contradiction in saying "Here are eleven people, but they are one football team." By and large, orthodox Christianity arrived at the language of *essence* to describe God's oneness, and the language of *person* to describe the distinction of the three. So, there is one God, because there is a single divine essence, but this essence is shared by three distinct persons. Whatever the three persons share that makes them God will be part of the essence. For example, to have the divine essence is to be all-powerful, all-knowing, eternal, worthy of worship, and so on. Father, Son, and Holy Spirit each fully possess the divine essence. Whatever distinguishes the Father, Son, and Holy Spirit from one another—what they *do not* have in common—will be what makes them each a distinct person.[6]

What, then, makes these three persons distinct? It can't be anything that goes with being God—they must share everything in that regard. That means the Father, Son, and Spirit share equal authority and power and are alike eternal. Moreover, they must be united in everything they will and do toward creatures—being divided in will or action would break the unity of essence.

Creation and salvation must be the common action of all three, since being the Creator and the sole source of salvation both go with being the one God. They can play distinct roles within these acts, but they cannot be separated or opposed in any way. For instance, it's the Son, and only the Son, who Christians believe became incarnate in the human being Jesus—this is distinctly the Son's mission—but he is *sent* in this mission by the Father, and he carries it out in the Spirit (through whom he is born of Mary, and by whom he was empowered throughout his earthly life). In this way, the incarnation is the common act of the Trinity, though we can distinguish the way the persons relate to one another in that common act. The same is true of the act of creation: the Father creates *by* his Word (Word being another biblical name of the Son) and Spirit. These examples provide the clue as to how the persons are distinguished: not by anything that is necessary to being God and not by their actions toward creatures, but *by their relations to one another*. The Father is the Father, because he begets the Son rather than being begotten; the Son is the Son, because he is begotten by the Father rather than begetting; the Spirit is not begotten but breathed forth, and thus proceeds from the Father.[7] The way the Triune God acts toward creatures reflects and expresses these eternal relations.

What these relational terms (like Father, Son, begetting, and proceeding) mean in the context of the Trinity is mysterious. The early Christian theologians were very careful to insist that such terms don't mean exactly what they do in ordinary human relationships. The begetting of the Son is radically unlike the way human sons and daughters are begotten, since God is immaterial. And, they insisted that the terms Father and Son do not imply that these divine persons are male—being male, they thought, is a feature of bodies, and so can't apply to God who is not a body. They understood this language to be a matter of divine condescension, providing human language for the infinitely mysterious reality of God, inevitably stretching that language to the breaking point. The main point is that the distinctions between the persons are primarily in how they relate to one another, and the names by which the persons are known reflect this. The Father is the called Father, because of his relation to the Son, the Son is called the Son, because of his relation to the Father, etc. Below, we'll see that the names of the Seven seem to function quite differently than the names of the Trinity.

Before turning to the Seven, there is one more thing to notice about the religious function of the Trinity: understanding God as Trinity in this way shapes how Christians relate to God. Christian prayer in one basic form is addressed *to* the Father, *in the name of* the Son, *through* the Holy Spirit. Though it is also possible within trinitarian faith to pray to the Son or Spirit (and various biblical and liturgical prayers do just that), this particular way of identifying the God addressed signals that Christian prayer is an entry into the life of the Trinity, into the eternal relations of the persons to one another within the Godhead. To pray in a trinitarian way is to be drawn *into* the life of the Trinity, to join in the Son's speech to the Father, aided by the Spirit.

THE SEVEN CONTRASTED WITH THE THREE

So much for the Trinity. What of the Seven? One difficulty here is that we simply lack access to whatever history produced this religious tradition compared with what we know about Christianity. We don't have scriptures, academic theological treatises, conciliar dogmatic statements, detailed liturgies, or hymn books from the faith of the Seven. Any of these might provide clarity and nuance compared to what we see in the books or the show, where most of the characters are various kinds of laypeople. While we do see clergy and members of religious orders, we don't get scenes of them engaged in theological disputation or expounding their doctrine. Mostly they engage in conversation or prayer or ministry to laypeople. This is probably a good decision dramatically—a book or show about theologians doing theology does not seem likely to be very entertaining—but it leaves the real-world theologian who is curious about the intricacies of the theology of the Seven with comparatively little to go on.

We do have some clues, however. Like trinitarians, adherents of the Seven believe officially that there is one God, though like trinitarians, they believe there is also a kind of plurality in the one deity, perhaps to a greater degree than trinitarians, since it seems quite common for adherents to refer to the Seven as "the gods." This is even true for a cleric like Septon Meribald, who explains,

> One god with seven aspects. That's so my lady, and you are right to point it out, but the mystery of the Seven Who Are One is not easy for simple folk to grasp, and I am nothing if not simple, so I speak of seven gods.[8]

This is not a mistake medieval Christian priests would have been as likely to make in speech, given regular recitation of the Creed, which begins, *Credo in unum Deum*: I believe in one God.

What does this plurality in the God who is Seven consist of? In place of a Trinity of Father, Son, and Spirit, the Seven consists of the Mother, the Father, the Warrior, the Crone, the Smith, the Maiden, and the Stranger. According to the *Complete Guide to Westeros* series,[9] the Seven revealed itself to the Andal people in Essos shortly before they invaded Westeros, around 6,000 years before the events of the show. We don't have many details about this revelation, but it seems to have involved each of the Seven appearing in human form (in contrast to the Christian doctrine of Incarnation, where only the Son becomes human). The Seven each provide certain benefits to Hugor, the first king of the Andal people. Tyrion tells us that the Father provides a crown made of seven stars for Hugor, while the Maid provides him with a suitable wife. The Mother makes this wife fertile so that she bears King Hugor forty-four sons, the Warrior gives these sons strength for battle, and the Smith provides them with iron armor.[10]

The One who is Seven is thus supposed to have revealed itself as one deity in seven aspects (though from this story the basis for the deity's oneness remains obscure), each aspect associated with different qualities or concerns. The Father is associated with authority, justice, and wisdom; the Mother with love, mercy, fertility; the Warrior with courage, strength, and victory; the Smith with skill in artifice and building; the Maiden with beauty and innocence; the Crone with wisdom; the Stranger with death and the unknown. One thus prays to these different aspects of the deity depending on one's particular needs and station in life. This seems to be the main religious function of the plurality within the Seven for lay adherents. These names and images provide different ways to pray corresponding to different kinds of aid one might be seeking from the deity. The God who is Seven provides divine oversight of all normatively approved aspects and stations of human life. It thus serves to provide legitimacy to the overall structure of Westerosi society, including institutions relating to government, justice, the military, the family, productive labor, trade, and even death. All of these are situated as reflecting an easily identifiable aspect of the divine.

How does this picture compare with the Trinity? In labeling the Seven "one God with seven aspects," as opposed to seven distinct persons, it is difficult not to detect a kind of modalism. We can see this by noting a crucial difference in the way the Seven are distinguished as compared with the three in the Trinity. Whereas the persons of the Trinity are distinguished primarily in relation to *one another*, the Seven are distinguished by how they relate to *the world*. The Father, Son, and Spirit each fully share in every divine quality. It is not that the Father is stern, authoritative, and wise while the Son is friendly and kind. And so, Christians should not pray to the Father when needing justice and the Son when needing mercy. They are each supremely just, loving, merciful, and good, and they must all three be involved together in any action toward creatures. For Christians, it would be impossible to imagine receiving justice or protection from the Father alone. If one receives protection from the Triune God, then one is receiving protection from the Father, Son, and Spirit acting together in unity.[11]

In contrast, the fundamental revelation of the Seven involves actions that are distinct to each of the Seven. The Father, and not the Mother, created Hugor's crown; the Mother, not the Maiden, made Hugor's wife fertile; the

Smith, not the Warrior, made the iron armor for Hugor's sons. And in general, the names of the Seven simply do not seem to be names of relations to one another, but of relations to the world. In the Trinity, the Father is called Father because of his unique relation to the Son. If Christians came to see Jesus's Father as *their* Father, it is because they understand themselves to be united to Jesus by sharing in his Spirit, and in this way to become adopted sons and daughters alongside the Son (see Romans 8 for a basis for this idea in the New Testament). The Father in the Seven is so named because of how he is related to human beings in general, providing justice and authority, seemingly on analogy with certain stereotypical or normative features of fatherhood within the social worlds of Essos and Westeros—this is markedly different from early Christian conceptions of God the Father, which, recall, involved vigorous insistence that God's Fatherhood is radically different from human fatherhood and that all divine qualities belong equally to all three persons of the Trinity.

So, since these seven names seem to describe different aspects of God, different ways that the one God relates to the world at different times or to different individuals, it does seem like the Seven is essentially modalist. Christians avoid modalism by positing real rather than apparent distinctions between the persons; "Father" and "Son" aren't masks or roles God takes on toward us, but real relations within the Godhead. The Father is really distinct because he begets and isn't begotten. For the Seven, the Father and the Mother and the rest seem to be related to one another by simple identity—the one named Father really is the same as the one named Mother, just like the one my students call "Dr. Mahfood" is the same one my son calls "Dad" or my friends call "David." These are just different titles associated with different ways I happen to relate to different sets of people.

It would be interesting to ask a Westerosi theologian about this. Is it right to say that the Father is the same person as the Mother, just under a different name, or appearing in a different form, or playing a different role (as it could never be correct for a trinitarian to say the Father is the Son in a different mode)? Or is the word "person" inappropriate for some reason? What is the basis for saying these seven are one, anyway? Is it connected to some form of philosophical monotheism? If so, what does this monotheism look like? Is the Seven believed to be responsible for creating the world? If so, did it/ they create ex nihilo (i.e., from no preexisting material, as Christians believe of the Trinity)? Is the Seven omnipotent, omniscient, eternal, immutable, and so forth?

For ancient and medieval Trinitarians, the reason why the Father, the Son, and the Holy Spirit could not be distinguished by qualities like justice, kindness, strength, wisdom, and the like is because those things all go with being God. If the Son were not all-powerful, he would not be God and would not be worthy of worship. If the Father were not supremely kind and merciful, he would not be God. That is why they must each be all these things. For the same reason, they must each be involved in every divine action toward creation, because such actions belong to God as such. If the Son were not involved in the act of creation, he would not be God. In contrast, if the faith of the Seven is modalist, then this worry can be avoided: the one God is all of the things that the Seven are, because the Seven are just partial aspects of this one being. They don't point at *really* distinct referents, but just different aspects of the same single referent. "Father" is merely the name by which God's justice is praised or invoked, and "Mother" is the name by which God's mercy and fecundity is praised or invoked.

Modalism, therefore, seems like the most promising interpretation of the Seven given the evidence we have. Without clarification from theological treatises or dogmatic statements from within the faith of the Seven, we can't be sure, but this at least seems like a reasonable interpretation: the One who is Seven is one *person* who plays seven different *roles* corresponding to different qualities or aspects each belonging to the one person. The Father, Mother, Warrior, Maiden, Smith, Crone, and Stranger are not each the fullness of the deity, but rather represent aspects of the deity's one personality. On this interpretation (which could very well be contested within the faith of the Seven), each name captures just one slice of the one God rather than naming a person who is fully God.

This all suggests a further difference between the trinitarian theology of medieval Christendom and the theology of the Seven: the Seven appears to include some level of fragmentation or at least complexity within the divine being. Some of the different qualities and activities associated with the Seven aspects of the One seem fundamentally opposed to one another. The Seven seem to be irreducibly distinct parts of the divine personality. The Father is just while the Mother is merciful; the Warrior destroys while the Smith builds and preserves; the Father and Mother give life, while the Stranger is the face of death. Are these qualities and activities *inherent* to the One who is Seven? If so, and if the Seven were the creator of the world, we would have an explanation for why there is conflict, destruction, and death in the world, as well as life, love, and peace—these opposed pairs simply reflect different parts of the inner reality of the creator, mirrored in its creation. Or is the Seven the sort of being that exists within a world alongside hostile forces it must see as rivals and threats, and preexisting materials it is forced to work with?

Trinitarianism has thought of God in a radically different way, insisting that the divine essence which the Father, the Son, and the Holy Spirit each share is metaphysically simple, which is to say, it is not composed of parts. Christian theologians in the ancient and medieval world took this principle quite seriously, inferring that while we can't help thinking of God in terms of different qualities, every divine attribute refers to one identical reality, even if we don't always know how to reconcile them within our understanding. So, for instance, we normally think of justice and mercy as opposed to one another, but somehow in God they must be one reality. Mercy and justice must finally be one in God, even if we can't see how this could be the case. Relatedly, Christians have traditionally insisted that *evil* is not an aspect of God at all. Now, because the Triune God created everything that exists, everything that exists must reflect the image of the Triune God. It follows that evil cannot be a subsistent reality at all; it must simply be a *privation*, that is, a lack, a falling away from being. Death too, for trinitarians, is not an aspect of God, but a privation, a falling away from being into non-being. Christians do have a concept of the devil, an agent who sometimes seems in popular thought to be a great equal-and-opposite to God, but according to orthodox Christian teaching, even the devil is just a creature gone astray and become corrupt, in no way a rival to God.

Many questions arise. Is the God who is Seven simple or composed of parts? Are death, conflict, and the like an inherent part of the being of the Seven? Theologians of the Seven might say that their God really is simple, but insist, contrary to the Christian, that death and life can be integrated into a simple being just as Christians believe justice and mercy can be integrated. Or perhaps they would say that the Seven did not create everything that exists, but only some things, and that the Seven is one being alongside other rival beings opposed to it. If they do believe the Seven to have created the world, these theologians might well observe that they have a readier explanation than Christians for why there is so much conflict, death, and destruction in the world. The problem of evil would seem to be less pressing on this view for the Seven than for the Trinity, though the Christian may well respond by questioning whether a God who includes such opposed qualities within itself would be worthy of worship.

AUGUSTINE'S PSYCHOLOGICAL ANALOGY AND THE *IMAGO DEI*

I turn now to an important religious function of trinitarian reflection suggested by some of these last few observations: if the Triune God is the sole creator of the world from nothing, then coming to know the Triune God should reveal creation for what it truly is. Conversely, we should be able to find reflections of the Trinity within the created order. Perhaps this is one reason Christians have tended to seek analogies or images of the Trinity in created things. Christian theologians have usually insisted that no such analogy can be perfectly adequate, since the reality of God is transcendent and unique. Even so, the relationship between Creator and creation (and especially human beings, whom Christians understand to be created especially in the *imago Dei*, the image of God) suggests that such analogies should be possible (however imperfect), deepening our understanding of both God and the world. One particularly influential trinitarian analogy is St. Augustine's so-called "psychological" analogy. At this point, I will consider St. Augustine's example of finding an image of the Trinity within the structure of the human psyche, and then ask what it might be like to think of human beings as images of the Seven.

No post-biblical figure influenced the shape of medieval Catholic theology as profoundly and comprehensively as did St. Augustine of Hippo. Augustine lived in the fourth and fifth centuries (d. 430 CE) and produced an enormous body of work, including sermons, commentaries, theological treatises, as well as a classic spiritual autobiography written in the form of a prayer. In medieval Europe, Augustine's writings were assigned a level of authority that is difficult to overstate. One of Augustine's most important works is a treatise on the Trinity, called (fittingly enough) De Trinitate, or *On the Trinity*. Since he was writing in the early 400s, his understanding of the Trinity had taken on board the developments I sketched above: he thinks of the Triune God as one essence or being in three persons. While he does defend this set of claims from various objections, given his context in which these basic claims are mostly settled orthodoxy, it makes sense that he goes further, seeking to understand the Trinity in a deeper way by finding analogous trinities in human beings. Especially given Augustine's influence on medieval Catholic theology and spirituality, his sort of reflections here provide an interesting springboard for speculation about what sort of similar reflection the doctrine of the Seven might have inspired. For that reason, I will consider one aspect of Augustine's thought in some detail before returning to the Seven.

Augustine finds images of the Trinity especially within the human psyche. For the purposes of this chapter, I will focus on just one of these trinities: the mind, its understanding of itself, and its love of itself.[12] When the mind thinks of itself, Augustine suggests, the mind has an idea of itself, and yet the idea does not seem to be some other substance than the mind. The understanding is distinct from the mind—generated by the mind, perhaps even begotten, and yet of the same substance as the mind. The mind's understanding isn't something foreign to it, even though it can be distinguished (the mind is the thing doing the thinking which generates the understanding, and the understanding is the thing generated by the mind's thinking).

Augustine invites us to imagine the mind considering this understanding of itself, and finding this understanding delightful, loving it—not in a narcissistic, self-absorbed way, let's suppose, but simply enjoying a healthy sense that the mind itself is good and lovable. Just like the understanding, the mind's love seems to be distinct from both itself and from its understanding. Love seems to be something produced by the mind, perhaps flowing toward its understanding. And yet it is also something *of* the mind, not a different or foreign substance from it. The production of love seems to be different from the production of understanding; they are produced by different kinds of acts on the mind's part.

We can begin to see how this picture is similar to the Trinity. In this analogy, we have a set of three elements connected and distinguished by relations of origin: the mind generates its self-understanding, and in another way, its love. And yet, in another way, these things are simply one substance or essence, namely that of the mind itself. This is like the Trinity, the Father, the Son, and the Holy Spirit, all sharing the same essence the latter two receive from the Father, the Son begotten by the Father and the Spirit proceeding from the Father.

Now, the self-understanding of any actual human person is always partial, imperfect, and at some level inadequate to that person's total reality. No matter how many personality tests we take or how much introspection we do, we remain partially mysterious to ourselves. Perhaps this is a consequence of being finite. The mind can't contain a comprehensive understanding of itself without being bigger than itself (to use a rough metaphor), which is impossible. So, its understanding of itself would have to be *less* than its reality, and its love likewise would not correspond perfectly to what it is. In these ways, the psychological analogy as we've developed it so far is very different from the Trinity, because there, the Son and Holy Spirit must be *exactly* what the Father is in every way except, in that they come from the Father. The Son and Spirit can't be *less* than what the Father is.

But, Augustine suggests, imagine a mind which had a truly perfect understanding of itself. Its idea of itself would correspond exactly in every detail to the way it actually is. The mind's self-understanding in this case would be exactly like the mind itself, except for the fact of being generated by the mind rather than simply being the mind. And then imagine that the mind's love of itself were completely proportionate to what it is. That is, it would not think of itself as greater or less than it actually is. Such a mind would love itself just the right amount given what it truly is. Just like its self-understanding, the mind's love of itself would correspond perfectly to its reality in every way. In this idealized case, these three elements (the mind, its self-understanding, and its love of itself) would each share completely and perfectly in the reality of the mind, distinguished only in that the understanding and love are produced by the mind, each in their distinct mode of production.

Through this process of seeking a kind of trinity in the structure of the human psyche, Augustine finds both similarity and radical difference between the human person and the Triune God. The mind can be said to resemble the God who created it, but the similarity has to be qualified by noting the profound difference between the creature and God, since God is infinite and human beings are finite. Despite this qualification, though, this process of seeking the image of the Trinity in the human self undeniably shapes the believer's understanding of the human as well as perhaps deepening her understanding of the divine.

What might this psychological analogy suggest about humanity? If humanity is created in the image of the Trinity, it seems to follow that although we are radically different from God, composed of parts which *can* conflict with or fall short of one another, then perhaps we reflect the image of our creator to a greater degree to the extent that our parts relate harmoniously, producing a genuine unity. To be in the image of the Trinity is to be in the image of love, in which case love (considered not as a mere feeling, but as a movement involving both will and intellect) is the point at which humanity most resembles its creator.

To be created in the image of the Trinity is not to be created (for example) with a dark side and a light side always in conflict with one another. Augustine and the medieval Christians who followed him certainly thought that humans as they actually exist are infected and fragmented by sin, and thus *unlike* the God who created them—but this was precisely the problem to be solved by coming to know God. To be in the image of the Trinity, then, is to be created with parts that are all good in themselves. Although they may be out of their proper harmony with one another, they must at least in principle be capable of integration. And above all, for Augustine, the human mind reflects the image of the Triune God when it *knows and loves the Triune God*. For Augustine, this is the best thing we can do with ourselves, the path from fragmentation back to wholeness. Knowing God is the path to true knowledge of self, and genuine self-knowledge points toward God. When the self truly knows and loves God, as Peter Drilling puts it, "The self knows and loves itself as it is known and loved by God into existence, into redemption, and into union."[13] For Augustine, this knowledge and love of the Triune God is what restores human persons to the image of the Trinity, which is what they were created to be.

HUMAN SELF AS *IMAGO SEPTEM*?

We can now see that one crucial religious function of the concept of God as Trinity in medieval Christianity was to shed light on the nature of human persons. Faith in the Trinity implies some things about what humans are and what they may hope to become, because of the related claim that humanity is created in the image of the God revealed as Trinity. It is unclear (at least to this reader) whether the faith of the Seven teaches that the Seven created the world, or created humanity in its image, but it seems reasonable to guess that the answer is at least a partial yes. If the answer is yes, then the Seven could fill a similar role to the Trinity in motivating reflection on the nature and purpose of human beings. Since my question has been how the Seven can serve as a religious analog to the Trinity, I will assume that for adherents of the Seven, the God who is Seven is responsible for creating human beings in its own image (though not necessarily that this deity created the world out of nothing).

What would it be like, then, to think of humans as created in the *imago Septem*—the image of the Seven—instead of the image of the Triune God? What sort of analogies would a Westerosi St. Augustine have explored in a hypothetical treatise *De Septem*? What purposes might believers imagine the Seven created them for? What sort of persons would devout Westerosi believers aspire to become if they understood themselves to be made by and in the image of the Seven? We can only speculate, but such questions are an invitation to imagine how the faith of the Seven might have shaped the self-understanding of Westerosi people, in comparison and contrast to how faith in the Trinity helped shape the self-understanding of medieval Christians.

Recall first that the names and qualities of the Seven specify not primarily relations to one another, but relations to the outside world. The Warrior does not seem to apply his strength at arms to any of the Seven, nor does the Father's justice seem to be exacted to any of them. The Smith doesn't seem to practice his arts on any of the other aspects of the Seven, but on some external material he uses to build. These actions in particular seem to imply something outside of and even opposed to the Seven on which to act. What use is a Warrior without enemies to fight? Perhaps the Warrior fights to protect the others, and the Father enacts justice upon those who offend the others, and the Smith creates works of artifice which he gives to the others, but even then, fighting, enacting justice, and building seem to require direct objects outside of the deity. Even the Father and Mother (whom one might be tempted to think of as analogous to the Father in the Trinity) do not seem to be depicted as Father and Mother *of* the other five but rather Father and Mother toward human beings.

Perhaps, whereas St. Augustine finds the clearest image of the Trinity in the interiority of the human soul relating to itself, a Westerosi theologian would find the clearest image of the Seven in a person who relates appropriately and effectively to the world around her. The *imago Septem* seems to entail that the human person exists in a world that necessarily includes hostile and unjust forces arrayed against her, innocents in need of protection, and intransigent matter in need of skilled manipulation and ordering into useful objects. Indeed, in the aspect of the Stranger, it seems to imply that death itself is a necessary part of humanity reflecting the image of its creator. The person who fully reflects the *imago Septem* would respond to such a world with justice, mercy, intelligence, innocence, courage, and wisdom in appropriate measure depending on the situation. For the trinitarian Augustine, the core problem of humanity is a kind of disharmony and fragmentation within the human self as it turns away from its loving Creator. For an adherent of the Seven, the core problem might be how to relate to a complex and partly hostile external world.

Another, perhaps more natural way, to envision humanity in the image of the Seven would be to think not just of an individual person but of a society. The Seven could be imaged not so much by one person displaying all the various qualities associated with them, but by a community including representatives of each one—fathers, mothers, warriors, maidens, and such—relating in proper order. Different human persons would imitate and stand for one or more of the Seven aspects of the deity depending on their stations in life, the community itself flourishing through harmonious relations within and effective responses to challenges from without.

Not surprisingly, Christians have also developed social images of the Trinity (although this approach was less common in Latin-speaking Christianity, thanks in part to the influence of Augustine). But even then, the image of the Trinity looks quite different from the image of the Seven. A community imaging the Seven would seem to need enemies to fight, an external world of materials to act on, and the reality of death to contend with. The crucial qualities of a society imaging the Trinity would, in contrast, have to do primarily with relations *within* the community. Such social relationships would not depend on the existence of external forces. The ultimate solution to problems posed by external others would (if the Trinity is one's example) have to be a matter of drawing the other *into* the community rather than overcoming them by force, since this is what the Triune God does with humans—inviting them into his own life, God makes enemies into friends. The continuing existence of enemies or other intransigent external objects may be an ongoing reality in fact, but it cannot be a strict necessity within the trinitarian picture.

To the extent that these speculations are correct, it seems the faith of the Seven would support a quite different understanding of self and world than faith in the Trinity. For the trinitarian, the world happens to include hostile elements, but this is a defect, a corruption of reality that pulls it away from the full image of God. The core problem to be addressed is the existence of corruption within the self, which is a consequence of turning away from the Creator. The self is then healed by grace turning it back toward its Creator, coming to reflect it fully in the way it was intended. It makes sense, then, that medieval Christians, by and large, treated the contemplative life—the life of the monk and the nun, devoting as much time as possible to prayer and meditation—as the highest spiritual calling, the fullest possible embodiment of the truths of its religious faith.

The adherent of the Seven, on the other hand, would perhaps see the world itself as inherently fragmented, necessarily including hostile forces arrayed against her. She comes to reflect the image of her deity by responding well to this world, perhaps by embodying within herself all the virtues of the Seven in appropriate measure and at the appropriate time, or by embodying the aspect or aspects of the Seven corresponding to her station in life. The solution to the fundamental problem, then, is a well-ordered society in which people play their roles effectively. The focus of a devout adherent to this faith may well be more exterior than interior; unlike medieval Christians, she will be less likely to think of the contemplative life as a higher calling than the active life. No, for her, the highest calling will be the life of activity within the community, playing a direct role in society's flourishing over against the forces which challenge it.

CONCLUSION

Despite surface similarity, it turns out that the faith of the Seven offers a quite different vision of God than the Trinity. The idea of the Seven could not have arisen within orthodox Christianity as a satisfactory theology, because it runs afoul of central commitments of Christian orthodoxy. The Seven do not appear to act together in absolute unity toward creation the way the Trinity does, but are distinguished precisely by their distinct and sometimes opposing acts toward creatures. The way the Seven are understood is likely to veer into modalism: these Seven seem to be manifestations of one underlying deity, who appears in these different ways at different times, whereas the Father, Son, and Holy Spirit are one in act and being but are really distinct in relation to one another. Moreover, the diverse acts associated with each of the Seven suggest internal conflict and complexity within the divine being, which is opposed to the simplicity and unity of the essence the Trinity are understood to share. And, finally, the Seven as they're presented seem to imply that evil and death are fundamentally part of the divine being rather than a privation or falling away from God's being.

Hand-in-hand with this different vision of God, the faith of the Seven suggests a fundamentally different vision of humanity and therefore of the spiritual orientation of human persons. The spirituality following from the theology of the Seven seems likely to be external and social, rather than interior and contemplative.[14] For the individual Westerosi, reflecting the image of the Seven will mean playing one's role within society well, enabling society to flourish in the face of the challenges presented by a hostile world. It will involve embodying the virtues appropriate to one's particular station in life, to serve as part of a well-ordered whole. Of course, medieval Christianity also found a positive place for diverse active vocations and the virtues associated with them, but in medieval Europe, it usually envisioned the contemplative life as the highest calling, even if it meant forgoing a more materially useful role in society.

Ultimately, the idea of the Trinity as the Creator of the universe suggests hope of a final eschatological end to conflict and fragmentation (between self and God, within the self, and between human individuals and communities). The life of contemplatives devoted to prayer and meditation, which often involved little obvious contribution to the political and economic goods of society, functions as a visible sign of that eschatological hope. If the religion of the Seven provides a hope like this, it at least seems to be less clearly underwritten by that religion's picture of God. The religious focus of adherents within the faith of the Seven seems likely to be more squarely on this life, and on making a contribution to the material flourishing of the community within which one lives.

We have had to arrive at these conclusions by speculating a great deal about what technical theologians of the Seven might say in response to decidedly Christian questioning. A learned Septa or Septon, or a close look at some primary religious texts, could quickly shed some light on our questions and correct our misunderstandings. Perhaps clergy or theologians might explain to us the ways in which popular Westerosi piety falls short of representing sound theology (certainly a theology of the Trinity derived from popular medieval piety would look different than what we get from reading bishops and theologians). Perhaps the Westerosi theologians would explain why the Seven are really distinct rather than modes of one underlying subject (or perhaps they'd affirm modalism as correct). Perhaps they could give us a strategy for maintaining the absolute simplicity of the One who is manifested as the Seven. Maybe these Seven aspects are only how God is revealed *given* the fallen and fragmented state of the world rather than who the One truly is in itself, and the latter can only be known mystically, through contemplative practice, and thus perhaps there's a way adherents of the faith of the Seven could view the contemplative life as a highly valuable religious good. Without more material evidence to work with, we can only guess.

Fictional worlds are always reflections of our own world, and so they provide unique opportunities to understand our own world better by trying to understand them. In the faith of the Seven, Martin has given us an interesting, imperfect (and all the more interesting for being imperfect) reflection of medieval Christianity, with the Seven as reflection of the Trinity Christians worship. My hope, therefore, is that by engaging in this imaginative exercise we will have deepened our understanding of the real-world religion of

Christianity, the fictional religion of the Seven, and the people (real and fictional) who shape and are shaped by them.

NOTES

1. In this section, I attempt to tell the story of the early development of the Trinity with a view to the key theological premises that arose through that process. Given the purpose here is to give a sense of the medieval Catholic understanding of Trinity, the way I tell the story is decidedly shaped by the (Latin-speaking) Catholic reception of the patristic material. For a much more detailed look at these developments, see Jaroslav Pelikan, *The Christian Tradition: A History of the Development of Doctrine, Vol. 1: The Emergence of the Catholic Tradition* vol. 1, 5 vols. (Chicago, IL: University of Chicago Press, 1975), 172–225. Key primary sources for these early debates can be found in translation in William C. Rusch, ed., *The Trinitarian Controversy*, Sources of Early Christian Thought (Philadelphia: Fortress Press, 1980) and Edward Rochie Hardy, ed., *Christology of the Later Fathers*, The Library of Christian Classics v. 3 (Philadelphia: Westminster Press, 1954).

2. This commitment does not exclude the existence of other spiritual powers which could be called gods, but none could be a rival to the one true God, the God of Israel.

3. Tanner, *Decrees of the Ecumenical Councils, Volume I: Nicaea I - Lateran V*, 5.

4. Ibid.

5. Bettenson and Maunder, eds., *Documents of the Christian Church*, 28.

6. For two classic and influential medieval statements of this conception of what it is to be God, as well as how the Father, Son, and Holy Spirit are to be understood as distinct persons yet each fully God, see Anselm of Canterbury, *Proslogion*, and Thomas Aquinas, *Summa Theologiae*, I.q2-12, 27–43.

7. Eastern and Western Christianity would later divide into what we now know as Roman Catholicism and Eastern Orthodoxy when, in the West, the Nicene-Constantinopolitan Creed was revised to say that the Spirit proceeds from both the Father and the Son, whereas Eastern Orthodox Christianity rejected this addition. Below, my analysis of St. Augustine's psychological analogy for the Trinity, Augustine's characteristically Western view will be reflected, in which the Spirit proceeds from both the Father and the Son.

8. Martin, *A Feast for Crows*, 370.

9. For a summary of the segment, see "The Old Gods and the New (Complete Guide to Westeros)." *Game of Thrones* Wiki. Accessed June 27, 2019. https://gameofthrones.fandom.com/wiki/The_Old_Gods_and_the_New_(Complete_Guide_to_Westeros).

10. Tyrion recalls this story from *The Seven-Pointed Star*, the faith of the Seven's sacred text. See Martin, *A Dance with Dragons*, 79–80.

11. In this respect, the Seven plays a role more like the medieval cult of saints. Medieval Christians (along with modern Catholic and Orthodox, as well as some Protestants) would venerate and communicate with particular saints who had died, believing those saints to be in a position to pray for them. Different saints would be

associated with different aspects of human life, professions, situations, problems, illnesses, etc. Prayers to saints function this way, but the trinitarian persons do not.

12. Augustine of Hippo, *De Trinitate*, IX.

13. Drilling, "The Psychological Analogy of the Trinity: Augustine, Aquinas, and Lonergan," 326.

14. To be fair, the interior focus of medieval Christianity is somewhat exaggerated in this chapter due to singling out St. Augustine for attention—other medieval examples would round out this picture to a significant degree. Still, it is not wrong to say that medieval Latin-speaking Christianity (certainly under Augustine's influence) tended to see the contemplative life as the highest spiritual calling.

BIBLIOGRAPHY

Bettenson, Henry, and Chris Maunder, eds. *Documents of the Christian Church*. 4th edition. Oxford ; New York: Oxford University Press, USA, 2011.

Drilling, Peter. "The Psychological Analogy of the Trinity: Augustine, Aquinas, and Lonergan." *Irish Theological Quarterly* 71, no. 3–4 (August 1, 2006): 320–37. https://doi.org/10.1177/0021140006075751.

Hardy, Edward Rochie, ed. *Christology of the Later Fathers*. The Library of Christian Classics, v. 3. Philadelphia: Westminster Press, 1954.

Martin, George R. R. *A Dance with Dragons*. A Song of Ice and Fire 5. New York, NY: Bantam Books, n.d.

———. *A Feast for Crows*. Bantam Spectra trade paperback edition. A Song of Ice and Fire 4. New York, NY: Bantam Dell, 2007.

Pelikan, Jaroslav. *The Christian Tradition: A History of the Development of Doctrine, Vol. 1: The Emergence of the Catholic Tradition*. Vol. 1. 5 vols. Chicago, IL: University of Chicago Press, 1975.

Rusch, William C., ed. *The Trinitarian Controversy*. Sources of Early Christian Thought. Philadelphia: Fortress Press, 1980.

Tanner, Norman P. *Decrees of the Ecumenical Councils, Volume I: Nicaea I - Lateran V*. Washington, DC: Georgetown University Press, 1990.

Part IV

DISPATCHES FROM ESSOS

PLURALISM AND ORIENTALISM IN THE WORLD OF ICE AND FIRE

Chapter 8

Is Hinduism Present in *Game of Thrones*?

Jeffery D. Long

HINDUISM IN *GAME OF THRONES*: AN OVERVIEW

A number of elements of Hinduism can be discerned in the epic fantasy works of George R. R. Martin. This does not mean that Hinduism has exerted a major influence on Martin, at least consciously. One, however, who is knowledgeable of Hindu thought and practice can discern some fascinating resemblances between aspects of Hinduism and concepts found in Martin's works.

In this chapter, I shall first discuss, invoking Tolkien, the relationship between the secondary world of a good, believable fantasy story and our "real," primary world, with reference to Martin's highly effective incorporation of religion and religious diversity into the world of ice and fire. I shall then move on to ways in which Hinduism can be discerned in this world. Given that this world is not only modeled on medieval Europe but also on the way medieval Europeans perceived their world as a whole, various cultures from Essos, the eastern continent, can be seen to reflect orientalist projections onto the cultures of Asia that continue to mark Western perceptions of the "mysterious East." *Orientalism* is a term that refers to the tendency, noted famously in the work of scholar Edward Said, of Western scholars, particularly of the colonial period, to project negative stereotypes onto the cultures of other regions of the world. These stereotypes often reflect aspects of Western culture itself about which many Westerners are uncomfortable. Imagining "the Orient" as chaotic, uncivilized, and in need of "rational" governance serves to justify Western domination. The terms *orientalism* and *orientalist* were long used simply to denote the study of non-Western cultures and scholars who engaged in it. Said, though, redefined orientalism as "a kind of Western projection onto and will to govern over the Orient."[1]

To the extent that orientalism, or its Westerosi analogue, is reflected in the implied gaze of Martin's text, some of the events, characters, and images from his works that might seem to reflect Hindu influence are very negative, and actually reflect not so much the realities of Hinduism, but rather, exoticizing stereotypes of Hindu thought and practice. This is not a criticism of Martin so much as an effect of the way his world is constructed. The point is not that Martin should have tried to represent Hinduism better in his work, because the purpose of his work is not to represent Hinduism, or any religion of our world. The point is that medieval and early modern European views of Hinduism and India play out in Martin's Essos in expectedly negative ways.

Other dimensions of Martin's work, however, which focus on the culture and religions of Westeros, reflect Hinduism in positive ways that are quite unexpected. This is especially the case with regard to the religion of the Seven—a faith overtly modeled on medieval Christianity, but that actually includes a strong Hindu theological dimension—and the religion of the Old Gods of the men of the North. Hinduism is present in Martin's world, in other words, where one might least expect to find it—not in distant Essos, but in Westeros itself. After presenting a brief overview of Hindu thought and practice, I will turn to a discussion of some of these Westerosi connections with Hinduism.

A STRANGE QUESTION?

Like many works in the fantasy genre, George R. R. Martin's *A Song of Ice and Fire*—along with the HBO television series, *Game of Thrones*, based upon it—is set in a world that is, in myriad ways, inspired by or evocative of medieval Europe. The scenery, clothing, technology, political and social systems, the beliefs and attitudes of the characters, and a host of other details are clearly modeled upon a medieval European environment.[2]

A first reaction to the question, "Is Hinduism present in *Game of Thrones*?" could thus be one of puzzlement. "Why should Hinduism be present in *Game of Thrones*? Isn't Hinduism practiced mainly in India, a country with which medieval Europe had hardly any contact?"

A second reaction might be to say "No," because no religion of our "real," or primary world, is present, in its totality, in the world of *Game of Thrones*. For all this world's resemblances to medieval Europe, Christianity, Judaism, and Islam are also not, properly speaking, present there either, much less Hinduism. *Game of Thrones* is, after all, a fantasy series, not a work of history, sociology, or anthropology. Extensive influence from, and commentary upon, Christianity can be discerned in this series, but not actual Christianity, which is set in our world. Having Christian, Jewish, Muslim, or Hindu characters in *Game of Thrones* would connect it directly to our world and break the artistic spell by which the reader (or viewer) is convinced that she is experiencing a different world entirely—one with resemblances to our world, but clearly distinct from it.

Influences, though, from our world can certainly be discerned in the world of ice and fire, as can commentary on actual history, and even, arguably, on contemporary events and issues (such as climate change), for Martin has drawn freely from his prodigious knowledge of history, culture, and religion in his crafting of this world. Though medieval Europe has certainly exerted a massive influence on his imagination, it has not limited it in a way which would prevent him from drawing on a vast range of ideas and images in developing his stories or from playing freely and creatively with those influences upon which he has drawn. Why, then, should it not be possible, at least in principle, to discern elements of Hinduism in Martin's richly detailed and artfully crafted literary universe?

Such discernment can take at least two forms. One would be to establish that some specific elements of Martin's imaginary world possess a Hindu provenance, such as through an interview in which Martin says, "Yes, this particular idea comes from Hinduism." Another would be to note the resemblances between specific aspects of the world of ice and fire and aspects of Hinduism, without necessarily claiming that these resemblances are deliberate or represent a conscious design on Martin's part.

My method in this chapter will be to follow the latter course. As far as I can tell, there has not been any extensive influence of Hinduism or Hindu thought on Martin's literary creation. As an exercise in creative interpretation, though, numerous connections can actually be found between Hinduism and *Game of Thrones*. It may or may not be the case that these connections, whether consciously or otherwise, have played a role in the tremendous popularity of *Game of Thrones* in India, where it has drawn a massive and enthusiastic audience.[3] It does, however, show the depth of Martin's creativity that connections of this kind can be made between his literary universe and an ancient religious and philosophical tradition that is itself rich with multiple worlds and perspectives. To see elements of Hinduism in *Game of Thrones* sheds light on both of these cultural phenomena: on *Game of Thrones*, but also on Hinduism.

RELIGION IN THE WORLD OF ICE AND FIRE: THE INNER CONSISTENCY OF REALITY

As J. R. R. Tolkien, a well-attested influence on George R.R. Martin, writes in his celebrated essay, "On Fairy Stories": "It is at any rate essential to a genuine fairy-story . . . that it should be presented as 'true.'"[4] A good fantasy, according to Tolkien, must have "the inner consistency of reality."[5] Tolkien is, of course, famed for the lengths to which he went to ensure that his own works possessed this quality of believability: the internal consistency, as well as the richness of detail, that attaches to "real life" history. Tolkien's Middle-earth therefore comes with languages, chronologies of kings, histories, maps, and even such close details as the phases of the moon as his characters make their journey.[6]

The world of George R. R. Martin's *A Song of Ice and Fire* is similarly rich. It is, indeed, arguably richer even than Tolkien's standard-setting efforts with regard specifically to the question of religion. As A. Ron Hubbard and Anthony Le Donne observe:

> Tolkien (the devout Catholic) dug deep with mythology and language. And there's no doubt that certain biblical types bleed into *Lord of the Rings*. But where are the churches, monasteries, and temples in Middle Earth [*sic*]? The hobbits have seen Gandalf perform magic for decades; why isn't there a shrine venerating him in the Shire? Better yet, Eru is clearly the Divine Creator of Arda. Where is Thingol's ritual devotion? Why doesn't Fëanor develop the Valinor Tree cult that opposes the eagle religion of Manwë? The answer to all of these questions, of course, is that Tolkien wasn't giving us a religious sociology. This simply wasn't his intention. As irony would have it, it took a proudly lapsed Catholic [Martin] to give us a fantasy landscape with robust, textured, and compelling religious pluralism.[7]

By "religious pluralism," Hubbard and Le Donne are referring to religious diversity—to the fact that many religions exist. In some contexts, this term refers to a positive value being given to religious diversity, as well as to positive engagement, in the form of dialogue and mutual appreciation across religious boundaries, or even to the idea that there are many true religions, which are all valid ways of seeking to achieve the ultimate goal of human existence—what Christians call salvation.[8]

Tolkien's works are certainly rich with theological implications–even whimsical children's works like *The Hobbit*. As Hubbard and Le Donne point out, Tolkien was a devout Catholic. In sharp contrast, though, with his friend C. S. Lewis, he did not try to give theological instruction in his fantasy works.[9]

Religious diversity also is not a strong feature of Tolkien's universe. Religiously, it seems that Middle-earth is dualistic. There is the true religion of Eru (the Creator), the angelic Valar, the Elves, and those humans who remain faithful to them, and the false religion of those who follow the evil Morgoth. Neither of these religions is really fleshed out or presented in any great detail.

Martin has surpassed Tolkien in developing a world rich with religious diversity, and each religion is described in some detail—though some more than others; for, as with Tolkien, Martin's primary goal is to tell his readers a good story, not to write about the sociology of religion. Religion is presented in the service of the story. Thus, the details of the religions of the world of ice and fire are given inasmuch as these have an impact on the characters and the narrative that Martin is trying to relate.

The most prominent religions of Martin's world include the Faith of the Seven, the worship of the Old Gods of the North, the religion of the Drowned God of the Ironborn, and, of course, the religion of R'hllor, known to his followers as the Lord of Light, but more commonly known as the Red God.

It is also understood in Martin's world that every culture will have its distinctive religious beliefs and practices. We see some of these in depth, like the religion of the Dothraki, while we get only a glimpse of others, like the religion of the Lhazareen, as the needs of the story dictate. There are mysterious religions particular to secret societies, such as the worship of the Many-Faced God by the Faceless Men, the cult of assassins joined, for a time, by Arya Stark. And there are skeptics, such as Tyrion Lannister and Sandor Clegane, who question the existence of otherworldly beings and a larger meaning of life.

Finally, given that *A Song of Ice and Fire* is a fantasy series, the world in which it occurs is a place where magic is real, though it is much more understated than in Middle-earth. Dragons really do exist, as do White Walkers, Children of the Forest, giants, and greenseers, the latter of whom are not only clairvoyant, but at least one—the Three-Eyed Crow, or Three-Eyed Raven—has the ability to see anything that has ever occurred in the past, and even, it seems, to reach back in time and intervene in past events. The existence of magic and beings of an otherworldly nature enhances the religious dimensions of Martin's work, as strange creatures can easily become objects of worship—as the White Walkers apparently are for Craster, who offers them his newborn male children. Unusual powers might be seen as a sign of divine favor, or even of divinity itself, on the part of the person who possesses those powers. The Three-Eyed Crow, or Raven, certainly seems to be godlike in his ability to look into and manipulate the past, and Melisandre's blood magic has definite, concrete effects, such as bringing out the deaths of Stannis's rivals to the Iron Throne.

All told, the religious texture of Martin's world appears to be no less rich than that of our own. Regarding religious diversity, Martin truly gives his literary universe "the inner consistency of reality." As in our world, there are many religions. Their adherents can and do come into conflict with one another. And, whether or not they are true, in terms of their claims and worldviews being correct descriptions of reality, they do shape the lives and decisions of those who practice them, including kings and queens, whose choices, in turn, shape the course of history and affect the lives of millions. At the very least, then, they can be seen as essential to the social construction of the realities, not only of those who adhere to them but of all who live in the world in which they operate as sources of moral values and other assumptions basic to human existence. And given, again, that magic and otherworldly beings are indisputably real elements of Martin's world, some of the religions of this world have the capacity to be true in a literal sense as well. White Walkers and Three-eyed Crows exist, as may R'hllor,[10] though whether any of these entities should be regarded as divine—that is, worthy of worship, or rightly seen as a being of ultimate significance—would be a matter for theological reflection and debate.

MARTIN'S MODEL: THE "REAL" MEDIEVAL EUROPEAN WORLD AND ITS IMAGINED "EXOTIC OTHER"

To return briefly to Tolkien's essay "On Fairy Stories," in addition to asserting that a good fantasy must have "the inner consistency of reality," Tolkien also points out that the "secondary world" in which the fantasy story occurs will inevitably draw upon the "primary world" which the author and the reader inhabit: what we conventionally think of as the "real" world. The more alien the fantasy elements of a story are to our conventional reality, the more difficult it is to make them believable—to give them that inner consistency. In Tolkien's words:

> [I]t is found in practice that "the inner consistency of reality" is more difficult to produce, the more unlike are the images and the rearrangements of primary material to the actual arrangements of the Primary World . . . Anyone inheriting the fantastic device of human language can say *the green sun*. Many can then imagine or picture it. But that is not enough . . . To make a Secondary World inside which the green sun will be credible, commanding Secondary Belief [or what some might call effective suspension of disbelief], will probably require labour and thought, and will certainly demand a special skill, a kind of elvish craft. Few attempt such difficult tasks. But when they are attempted and in any degree accomplished then we have a rare achievement of Art: indeed narrative art, story-making in its primary and most potent mode.[11]

In other words, the more radically different the elements of a fantasy story are from things in our primary world, the more difficult it is to make them believable. Giving "the inner consistency of reality" to that which is normally incredible requires "special skill, a kind of elvish craft," which Tolkien's and Martin's fans would certainly agree both authors possess in abundance. This also means, though, that weaving elements of the primary world into one's story can be a great help in making it believable.

The elements of the primary world that are the chief sources of Martin's inspiration, and which he then rearranges creatively to develop the world of *Game of Thrones*, are drawn chiefly, as already mentioned, from medieval Europe. As Carolyne Larrington elaborates:

> Like Tolkien's Middle-earth, *Game of Thrones/A Song of Ice and Fire* constructs its fantasy out of familiar building blocks: familiar, that is, to us medieval scholars. These blocks are chiseled out of the historical and imaginary medieval past, out of the medieval north, with its icy wastes, its monsters and its wolves; out of the medieval west, with its recognisable social institutions of chivalry, kingship, its conventions of inheritance and masculinity; out of the medieval Mediterranean, with its hotchpotch of trading ports, pirates, slavers and ancient civilisations; and out of the medieval fantasies of the exotic east, where Mongol horsemen harried fabled cities of unimaginable riches, and where bizarre customs held sway among strange tribes on the edges of the known world—and even beyond.[12]

The last element Larrington mentions is of particular interest to us as we explore the question of the presence of Hindu elements in the world of ice and fire. Martin's world is not only based upon medieval Europe, as it existed historically, but also upon the ways in which medieval Europeans perceived their world as a whole. Westeros is certainly based upon medieval Europe—and upon medieval Britain, in particular. Their geographic outlines strongly resemble one another, though Westeros, as a continent, is considerably larger than the Isle of Britain. The Wall appears to be inspired by Hadrian's Wall separating England from Scotland, and the Wildlings beyond it by the Picts and Scots of the Roman period. The men of the North also have cultural affinities with Scotland and northern England, while the cultures of the kingdoms of the South, with their courtly codes of chivalry, are closer to southern England and continental Europe. Dorne appears akin to medieval Spain or Morocco—and indeed, some of *Game of Thrones* has been filmed in Morocco. Similarly, the Free Cities on the west coast of the eastern continent, Essos, resemble medieval Mediterranean city-states, like Venice, and share cultural and geographic proximity to the more distant east.

Much of Martin's world, however—the further eastern region of Essos—is based not so much on the medieval realities of Asia as it is on medieval European perceptions of Asia: that is, on the "medieval fantasies of the exotic east" that Larrington mentions. Martin's world as a whole bears strong resemblances not only to medieval Europe but to the world as medieval Europeans believed it to be.

HINDUISM AND INDIA IN REALITY AND IN MEDIEVAL FANTASY

How did Hinduism and the land where it has mainly been practiced, India, figure into the world of medieval Europe? And what is the relationship of the perceived Hinduism and India of the medieval European imagination to the Hinduism and India of reality?

I mention early modern as well as medieval European perceptions because Martin, again, is mainly interested in telling a good story. He does not, therefore, restrict his imagination unduly to the world of medieval Europe, in spite of its being his primary inspiration. Knowledge of both Hinduism and India, and Asia as a whole, was extremely limited in medieval Europe. It is evident that some of the ideas and images on which Martin draws for his depictions of the cultures of further Essos come not from the medieval period, but also draw upon early modern travelers' tales, as European merchants and missionaries began to make their way to such distant destinations as India, China, and Japan.

One can, of course, have a spirited debate over when, precisely the medieval period ended and the modern period began. These are very broad terms, and the characteristics often associated with either modernity or medieviality did not emerge simultaneously across Europe, but sooner in some places than in others. I am using the term "early modern" to refer to the phase of European history in which exploration and colonization of the rest of the world began in earnest.

We are discussing Hinduism in conjunction with India because the two, while distinct, are, in many respects, inseparable. Even the words *Hinduism* and *Hindu*, used to denote a religion and a practitioner of that religion, respectively, refer, in their origins, to the Indian subcontinent. *Hindu* is the Persian pronunciation of *Sindhu*, the old Sanskrit name of the river that flows through what is today Pakistan, and which was called, by the Greeks, the Indus. *Hindustan* became the name of the land on the other side (from Persia, or Iran) of the *Hindu* river, and the people of that land came to be known as Hindus. When the British came to India, they took up this same terminology, and further coined the word *Hinduism* (adding the English suffix *-ism* to the word *Hindu*) to denote the religions native to India. *India* itself is the Greek name for Hindustan, derived from *Indus*. Hindus, on the other hand, have traditionally referred to Hinduism as *Dharma*, or *Sanātana Dharma*—the eternal way of life—and to India as *Bhārata* or *Bhārata-varṣa*, the land ruled in ancient times by the legendary king, Bharata.[13]

Hindu thus basically means *Indian*, in its origins, and *Hinduism* something like *Indianism*. Many Indians, however, do not practice the Hindu religion (the second-most practiced religion in India being Islam, with a considerable following), and a growing number of people in the modern period who practice Hinduism are not Indian by either citizenship or ethnicity, due both to Hindus from India immigrating to Western countries and to Hindu spiritual teachers attracting non-Indian followers. The terms *Hindu* and *Indian* are thus gradually becoming more distinct, though the two nevertheless remain linked in the minds of many. Even today, roughly 95 percent of the world's Hindus live in India, where they make up roughly 79 percent of the population. Close association between Hinduism and India is thus inevitable.

It is also the case that, although Hinduism has a philosophy that claims universal relevance, much of its practice is closely centered on India and its sacred geography. To make a pilgrimage to a holy river or temple associated with an important event in Hindu sacred literature are important practices, greatly valued by Hindus to the present—even among those who have made their homes in, or who hail originally from, other parts of the world.

To medieval Europeans, both India and Hinduism were largely unknown. Among educated Europeans, the only firsthand report of India, for many centuries, was the *Indika* of Megasthenes (c. 350–290 BCE), a Greek ambassador to the court of the Indian emperor, Chandragupta Maurya, who reigned from 321 to 297 BCE. Megasthenes recorded both things that he witnessed directly and things which were only hearsay, carefully distinguishing one from the other. It is interesting, though, that some of the most fantastic creatures Megasthenes describes, like a tribe of humanoids with no heads, and faces in their torsos, or a species of giant ants with the habit of digging for gold (and jealously guarding it from thieves) were taken by medieval Europeans to be real, while other creatures he described, such as snakes that could swallow a deer whole, or birds that could talk (pythons and parrots) were widely regarded as inventions of the author's imagination. This gives us an idea of the accuracy of knowledge about India in medieval Europe!

The travelogue of the famed Italian adventurer, Marco Polo (1254–1324) gives a more up-to-date and accurate picture of India in the medieval period. But Polo, too, was widely disbelieved by his contemporaries. It is only with the sea voyage of Vasco da Gama (1497–1499) that regular contact between India and Europe is established, and more accurate accounts of Indian culture and religion begins to filter into European consciousness. Even from this time, though, there are a good many distortions and cultural miscommunications. Scholars of Hinduism even today will often point to the orientalist tropes and exoticizing distortions in the work not only of earlier generations of scholars, but even in contemporary scholarly writing and popular culture.[14]

The India of the medieval and early modern European imagination was, as Larrington says, a place of "fabled cities of unimaginable riches . . . where bizarre customs held sway among strange tribes on the edges of the known world."[15] Indeed, the fabled wealth of India was exactly why Europeans like Vasco da Gama and his contemporary, Christopher Columbus, sought a sea route to trade with the fabulously wealthy Indians. When Columbus reached the isles of the Caribbean, mistakenly thinking he had reached India, he labeled the indigenous people "Indians"—a name that has stuck to the present day. India's fabled wealth was also not entirely mythical. For much of history, both India and China held a considerable proportion of the world's wealth. Both countries were also more advanced, technologically, than Europe at the time. The relative physical comfort of the wealthy classes in Essos, in contrast with the dreary castles and impoverished villages of Westeros, is a not wholly inaccurate representation of the contrast between life in medieval Asia and life in medieval Europe. The fabulous wealth of the city of Qarth is perhaps an evocation of medieval views of Asian prosperity.

Regarding "bizarre customs," bizarreness is, of course, in the eye of the beholder. It may be useful at this point to get a sense of what Hinduism actually teaches, and what its practice involves, before turning to possible Hindu elements in the world of ice and fire.

A QUICK OVERVIEW OF HINDU PHILOSOPHY[16]

Depending on how one defines the word *Hinduism*, this term refers either to one of the oldest—perhaps *the* oldest—of the world's religions or to the relatively recent development of the merging together of numerous traditions native to the Indian subcontinent, which share a common reverence for a set of ancient texts known as the *Vedas*.

The word *Veda* means "wisdom" in the ancient Sanskrit language in which these texts were composed. The *Vedas* are among the most ancient scriptures in the world and are *the* most ancient scriptures of a religion that is still in practice today (ancient Egyptian and Sumerian religion having died out long ago). Due to its association with the *Vedas*, Sanskrit became and remained a sacred language and a language of high culture for many centuries after it ceased to be spoken in everyday life. It thus plays a role in South Asia akin to the role traditionally played in Europe by Latin, at least until the rise of the dominance of English (in both Europe and India).

Modern scholarship locates the composition, or at least the compilation, of the Vedic texts between 1500 and 1000 BCE, though many Hindu scholars claim they are much older even than this. The oldest known civilization in India, and one of the oldest in the world, was the Harappan or Indus Valley civilization, which was at its technological height from 2600 to 1900 BCE. It is possible that elements of this civilization and its culture are preserved in the *Vedas*, as well as the culture of Indo-European migrants who likely began entering India around the time of the decline of the Harappans. It was once believed that these migrants had violently invaded and destroyed the Harappan civilization, but this view is now generally rejected. Harappan civilization declined mainly due to geological changes, such as earthquakes and the drying up and changing courses of rivers. Its culture did not die out, but blended with that of the pastoral Indo-Europeans, the result of this blending being the religion of the *Vedas*.[17]

The philosophical core of the Vedic literature is presented in a set of texts composed in the first millennium BCE, roughly between 800 and 200 BCE. This same period saw the rise of both Jainism and Buddhism in the Ganga, or Ganges, river valley: the region to which the weight of Indian civilization shifted after the decline of the Indus civilization. The Vedic texts of this period, which were also composed mainly in the Ganges region, are called the *Upanishads*, a name which means *secret wisdom*. They communicate a philosophy known as *Vedanta*, which literally means the end or aim of the *Vedas*, or the aim of all wisdom.

According to Vedanta, the basis of all existence, the ground of being, which has become this whole universe, from which the universe has emerged and to which it will return, is a field of pure consciousness called *Brahman*. All things, ultimately, are manifestations of Brahman, which is, in its own nature, infinite being, consciousness, and bliss. We, ourselves, are also Brahman, in the core of our being. Brahman as Self—the Self of all beings, and of each individual—is called the *Atman*. There is *Atman* in the sense of the world-soul: the Self of all beings, or universal Self. This is also known as the *Paramatman*, or Supreme Self. This is what Hindus understand to be God: the Supreme Being who lovingly coordinates the events of the universe in order to lead all beings to a realization of their true nature—as one Upanishadic prayer says, "from the unreal to the real, from darkness to light, from death to immortality." There is also *Atman* in the sense of each individual soul, which is also known as the *Jiva*, or life force. Each *Jiva* can be seen as a spark or "piece" of the universal Brahman (although, technically speaking, Brahman does not have parts).

The human condition—and the condition of all living beings—is that we are each an eternal and immortal soul that has misidentified itself with a physical body. This is due to *Maya*, a kind of deluding veil of ignorance that keeps us from realizing our true nature as Brahman. Once this veil is lifted and we realize our true nature, we become free from all limitations. This, however, takes a long time: more than a single lifetime. Our current lifetime is only the current chapter of a story that has been unfolding forever. We will continue to be reborn—to identify with another body—until we realize our true nature and achieve ultimate freedom, or *Moksha*.

As explained by the Supreme Being Himself, in one of the Hindu scriptures, the *Bhagavad Gita*, which is basically a summary of the *Upanishads*:

> Never was there a time when I did not exist, nor you, nor all these kings; nor in the future shall any of us cease to be. As the embodied soul continually passes, in this body, from boyhood to youth, and then to old age, the soul similarly passes into another body at death. The self-realized soul is not bewildered by such a change . . . That which pervades the entire body is indestructible. No one is able to destroy the imperishable soul . . . For the soul there is never birth nor death. Nor, having once been, does he ever cease to be. He is unborn, eternal, ever-existing, undying and primeval. He is not slain when the body is slain . . . As a person puts on new garments, giving up old ones, similarly the soul accepts new material bodies, giving up the old and useless ones . . . Knowing this, you should not grieve for the body.[18]

This is not only the human condition, but is, in fact, the condition of all living beings. *Human* is a species: a type of body in which the soul can incarnate, with which it can identify over the course of that body's lifetime. But the soul itself is pure awareness. The same soul can possess a human body in one lifetime and a body of another species in another lifetime.

It is important to note that this process of rebirth is very different from the concept of the resurrection of the body found in Christianity (and evoked in Jon Snow's resurrection by the Red Woman, Melisandre). In resurrection, a body that was once dead is returned to life: the soul is re-united with the body in which it previously dwelled. In rebirth, or reincarnation, the soul takes on a new body, almost like putting on a new set of clothes, to use the *Bhagavad Gita*'s image, or like a driver getting out of one car and into another. This difference in beliefs is also connected with the ways in which different religions handle the bodies of the deceased, with religions that await a resurrection typically engaging in burial, and religions that affirm rebirth engaging in cremation (because the old body is no longer needed).

The ultimate aim of life, according to Vedanta, is the realization of our true, divine nature as Brahman and consequent release from the cycle of rebirth, to which we are bound by the actions we undertake out of desire. Desire-infused action, or karma, attracts new experiences to the soul, propelling it into the cycle of rebirth if the body dies with karmic effects yet unfulfilled (which is normally the case).

Realization of our nature occurs through the practice of the *Yogas*. *Yoga* here refers not to stretching in a gym (though it can certainly include that), but to spiritual discipline. The Yogas are of four basic types. There is the Yoga of Action, which means doing good selflessly, without any desire for a result. There is the Yoga of Knowledge, which means cultivating knowledge of the true nature of reality through a path of intellectual inquiry. There is the Yoga of Devotion, the most popular path, which involves self-surrender to the Supreme Being. Finally, there is the Yoga of Meditation, in which one turns one's attention from the external realm of Maya and focuses inward to realize the Self directly.[19]

It is in the Yoga of Devotion, or *bhakti*, that the many deities for which Hinduism is famous become relevant. It is difficult even to conceive of the infinite Brahman, much less relate to it in a loving, devotional way. One needs to relate to a person: an infinitely loveable person, a being of pure love with whom one has a relationship of complete dependence. For us to approach the divine reality, the divine reality needs to take on a personal form, which, according to Hinduism, the divine does, for our benefit. Because we are all different, we will all relate to the divine reality differently. The divine reality, being infinite, takes on infinite forms: again, for our benefit. These many forms are the Gods and Goddesses of Hinduism—and of all religions, at least according to some Hindu schools of thought.[20] Hinduism, rather like the Faith of the Seven, is neither strictly monotheistic nor polytheistic but has aspects of both of these. It is *panentheistic*, seeing the divine presence everywhere, within all beings, and potentially taking on any form in order to aid devotees on the path to liberation. The divine is, in another sense, both one and many in Hinduism. There is one supreme, infinite divine reality. But this reality appears in infinite ways. Like Hindu deities, the Seven are frequently referred to as "gods" or "the gods," but they are also referred to as the "seven faces of god."[21]

In regard to the Yoga of Meditation—the source of the famous stretching exercises, which were essentially designed to calm the body and make it a fit vehicle for meditation—there are some systems of Hindu meditation that involve focusing on subtle energy centers in the body known as *chakras*. The energy in these centers is believed to aid the process of meditation. One of these centers is believed to be located just above the space between the eyebrows and is often known as the *third eye*. Some of the Hindu deities—in particular, Shiva, the Lord of the Cosmic Dance of Creation and Destruction, and Lord of Yoga, as well as his wife, Shakti, the Mother Goddess and underlying energy of creation—are depicted as having this third eye open, a state which represents spiritual illumination. Does this remind us of a certain raven in the world of ice and fire?

TRADITIONAL INDIAN SOCIETY: FACTS AND STEREOTYPES

As already hinted, two important Hindu concepts—the idea of one divinity in many forms and the idea of the third eye—can be seen in the religions of

Westeros. What, though, of the exotic cultures of Essos, where one might expect to find Hinduism in Martin's literary world?

More than the profound concepts of Vedanta philosophy, what seem to be more present in the cultures of Essos are precisely the kinds of stereotypes one would expect medieval and modern Europeans to have of the "mysterious East." These stereotypes are not based on Vedanta, which was unknown in Europe until the last couple of centuries—though echoes of Vedantic concepts can be discerned in Platonic and Neoplatonic philosophy, as a result of ancient Greek contact with the Indian subcontinent. They are based, rather, on foreign perceptions of traditional Indian society.

The priestly community tasked with the preservation of the *Vedas* and the performance of the religious rituals enjoined in these texts is known as the *Brahmin* community. There is some evidence that, in the early Vedic period, the pursuit of a career was a matter of choice and personal aptitude.[22] Certainly by the period of the *Upanishads*, though, the dominant custom was to distribute social tasks, including Brahminhood, on the basis of birth. Indian society was arranged into a hierarchy of birth-based groups called *Jatis*, a term later translated as *castes*. The Brahmins were regarded as the most ritually pure of these groups, due to their duty of learning and teaching the *Vedas* and communicating with the deities through sacred ritual. Rulers or nobles came next, followed by craftsmen, merchants, and farmers, and then by servants or menial laborers. Finally, there were those whose jobs were regarded as being so impure as to require them to live separately from the rest of society as so-called untouchables.

This system has long been a source of fascination for non-Hindus, although it is not all that different from similar, birth-based occupational hierarchies across the globe. Surnames like Baker, Miller, and Smith attest to the fact that European society was also once organized on similar lines. The chief distinction in European society was that between nobles and common people—Martin's noble houses and "small folk." The fascination of the Indian system probably lay with its intricacy, as well as its persistence even into the modern period, as well as with the fact that it was given a religious justification. From a Hindu point of view, the circumstances of one's life are the result of one's previous actions–one's karma, both from earlier lives and from this life. If one combines this view with an assumption that one naturally ought to follow the trade of one's family, as well as with the assumption that one trade is better than another, one arrives at the view that one's career choice *and* social position are a result of one's good or bad karma.

The capacity for such a tradition to be experienced as oppressive, especially by those whom it regards as impure, is clear, and has been extensively documented. It is also, however, a system that lends itself to being stereotyped; for the kind of simplistic explanation I have given to it here is often taken to mean that this system is observed in precisely this way in all times and places by the Hindu community. The reality, though, is vastly more complex. It is important to note that this system has been contested in a variety of ways by diverse groups throughout India's history. There are entire Hindu communities and traditions that reject the notion of caste or that invert it in various ways.[23] Swami Vivekananda, a widely respected modern reformer and teacher of Vedanta says quite bluntly that: "[C]aste is simply a social institution, which after doing its service is now filling the atmosphere of India with its stench."[24] Many contemporary Hindus view caste as an embarrassment.[25] This rejection of caste prejudice is not simply a result of modern or European influence, as a Westerner might expect. The idea that one's career choice and social position are determined by karma can be, and has been, critiqued on the basis of Hindu principles.[26] This assumption ignores, for example, the fact that one's karma is still being formed, at each moment, by one's choices in the present. One can therefore reshape one's karma with different kinds of choices.

THE EXOTICIZED ORIENT OF ESSOS

A number of European stereotypes of Indian society, or elements of Indian society viewed as exotic by Europeans, can be discerned in several of the incidents, characters, and concepts in the world of ice and fire, based in the continent of Essos.

One of the most dramatic of these is the episode in which Daenerys Targaryen enters the funeral pyre of her deceased husband, Khal Drogo, carrying with her the dragon eggs given to her as a wedding gift, and sensing that the flames will not destroy her, but that they, in fact, play an important role in the fulfillment of her destiny:

> She had sensed the truth of it long ago, Dany thought as she took a step closer to the conflagration, but the brazier had not been hot enough. [This is the brazier into which she had placed the dragon eggs, with no discernible effect upon them.] The flames writhed before her like the women who had danced at her wedding, whirling and singing and spinning their yellow and orange and crimson veils, fearsome to behold, yet lovely, so lovely, alive with heat. Dany opened her arms to them, her skin flushed and glowing. *This is a wedding, too*, she thought.[27]

Ultimately, Daenerys emerges from the flames unharmed, and in the company of three newly hatched baby dragons.

This scene evokes two Hindu images. One, which has become a major object of Western interest, but has never, in reality, been a mainstream Hindu practice, is the image of *Sati*. Sati is a practice—historically confined to upper-caste Hindus in Rajasthan and Bengal until being outlawed in the nineteenth century—in which a widow immolates herself upon the funeral pyre of her deceased husband. The banning of the practice by the British came about thanks to intensive lobbying by the Hindu reformer, Ram Mohan Roy (1772–1833). The practice is named after a goddess, Sati, the wife of Shiva, who did not immolate herself on a funeral pyre, but had herself burned alive in protest against her father, who had insulted her husband. Shiva is inconsolable after Sati's death. Sati, however, reincarnates as the goddess Parvati, and marries Shiva again, later giving birth to two important deities: Ganesha, known for his elephant head, and Kartikkeya, a warrior deity who rides into battle on a peacock.

This scene, however, even more closely evokes an image less known in the West, but well-known to Hindus, drawn from the *Ramayana*, a Sanskrit epic regarded by many as a scripture on par with the *Vedas* themselves. In the *Ramayana*, the hero, Rama, an incarnation of the god Vishnu, who preserves the order of the universe, rescues his wife, Sita from the clutches of the demonic being, Ravana, who has abducted her. Sita is herself a goddess: an incarnation of Vishnu's wife, Lakshmi. After a lengthy battle, in which Rama calls on such allies as an army of intelligent apes and other talking animals, Ravana is finally vanquished and Sita rescued.

Shockingly, however (not only to Western sensibilities, but to many Hindus), upon meeting and reuniting with Sita after she has been in captivity for many months, Rama insists that Sita prove she has remained faithful to him while dwelling in the home of another man. Sita calls upon Agni, the god of fire, to prove her faithfulness. She enters a fire and walks through it, coming out unharmed. It is later explained that Rama never doubted Sita, but that, as the ruler of his kingdom, his citizens might gossip and raise doubts about his queen's fidelity, thus undermining their faith in their leaders. The test of fire is intended to dispel any such doubts. Many Hindus find even this explanation unsatisfactory, given what a beloved character Sita is. A medieval Hindi version of the epic which is actually better known by most Hindus than the original Sanskrit *Ramayana* claims that the real Sita was never captured by Ravana and that the entire battle has been carried out simply to destroy this evil being. An illusion of Sita walks into the fire, and it is the real Sita, unscathed and never abducted, who emerges from the other side.

The resemblances of the scene of Daenerys entering and emerging unharmed from the fire of Khal Drogo's cremation with her baby dragons and the scene of Sita emerging unharmed from her test of fire are quite suggestive. Sita is a living goddess, a divinity in human form. Daenerys, too, the Unburnt,

Mother of Dragons and Breaker of Chains, takes on something of the nature of a goddess for her followers. In later scenes, when she liberates the slaves from the cities of Slavers' Bay, they hail her as "Mother," a common way to address Hindu goddesses as well. In terms of the critique of orientalism, however, one can also note that this liberating goddess, in Martin's work, is a white woman, which plays into the orientalist trope of the "white savior."

Another, more stereotypical scene set in Essos, is the one involving the Warlocks of Qarth, when Daenerys enters their House of the Undying to rescue her dragons. The Warlocks are magic users, as their name suggests. Their lips are stained blue from their regular consumption of a drink called "shade of the evening." This drink seems to have psychedelic effects, as Dany's experience in the House of the Undying suggests, and is also believed, when consumed in sufficient quantities, to confer immortality. When a single, slender glass, or flute, of this drink is given to Daenerys, she asks, "Will it turn my lips blue?" The Warlock Pyat Pree replies, "One flute will serve only to unstop your ears and remove the caul from off your eyes, so that you may hear and see the truths that will be laid before you."[28]

The Warlocks evoke a stereotypical view of Brahmins as a sinister magic-using priesthood. Shade of the evening brings to mind the *soma* drink consumed by Brahmins in ancient times and mentioned in the *Vedas*. Soma is a plant thought by many to be a species of ephedra that would be crushed and mixed with milk to create a potent psychedelic drink which would enable Brahmins to commune with the gods. It may come from a time when Brahmanic practices developed from an even more ancient shamanism. By the historical period, soma was replaced by meditation.

Finally, the cities of Slavers' Bay may evoke, for some, an image of a caste-based society in which large numbers of people live in servitude to those at the top of the social system. Slavery, though, in the strict sense of ownership of one person or group of people by another, has been a relative rarity in Indian history. Caste is, if anything, closer to the medieval practice of serfdom, in which serfs were not technically owned by the nobility, but were born to be at their service—not unlike the small folk of Westeros in relation to the great houses. The society of Slavers' Bay is, historically speaking, more akin to the societies of ancient Greece and Rome—or the antebellum South—in this respect.

ONE GOD IN MANY: VEDANTA IN THE FAITH OF THE SEVEN

Interestingly, the closest resemblances to actual Hindu beliefs that one finds in the world of ice and fire are not to be found in Essos, Martin's equivalent of Asia as perceived in medieval Europe, but much closer to "home," in Westeros itself.

The Faith of the Seven, the dominant religion of Westeros, and particularly of its southern regions, is modeled closely on Christianity, and specifically, on the Roman Catholic faith. Martin is, in fact, on record as affirming this connection:

> The Faith of the Seven is very loosely modeled on the medieval Catholic Church. But, of course, with different elements . . . I'm no longer a practicing Catholic, but that was how I was born and raised. [The Catholic Church] has the whole concept of the Trinity, which was explained to be as: "it's three, but it's also one." Which kids can never get. It's like "okay, we have three gods."—"No, no, you don't have three gods, you have one God; he has three parts." . . . It was like the shamrock, you know, the three-leafed clover.[29]

Intriguingly, although the overt influence on Martin in developing the Faith of the Seven, including its theology, its institutional and social structures, and its relationship to political power was the medieval Catholic Church—quite understandably, given that Westeros as a whole is based on medieval Europe, and the world as a whole on the world as perceived by medieval Europeans—it is in the Faith of the Seven that a prominent element of Hindu theology can be discerned most clearly. This is the idea, mentioned previously, that divinity is one and many. The many deities of Hinduism—and indeed, of all the world religions—are forms or manifestations of the one, supreme Brahman, that is the ground of all being.

The Seven are understood to be different aspects of one supreme deity, much like the Holy Trinity of Christianity: "'One God in three persons: Father, Son, and Holy Spirit.' Martin expands this to seven: Father, Mother, Maiden, Crone, Warrior, Smith, and Stranger."[30] If one expands the number of aspects of the one divinity to infinity, one has something close to the Vedantic doctrine of the godhead. Hinduism, interestingly, also has its own variations of the Trinity and the Seven. There is the Trimurti, or "three forms" of Ishvara, the Supreme Being, made up of Brahma, the creator, Vishnu, the preserver of the cosmic order, and Shiva, who brings the world to an end at the end of each cosmic cycle so that it may be re-created anew at the start of the next cycle. It is also not uncommon to approach divinity in seven forms, though this is not formally stated in the tradition, to my knowledge: the aforementioned Brahma, Vishnu, and Shiva, with their respective spouses, Saraswati, goddess of wisdom, Lakshmi, goddess of prosperity and divine grace, and the mother goddess, known variously as Shakti, Devi, Uma, Parvati, Durga, and Kali, plus Ganesha. The eighth- to ninth-century reformer, Shankara (c. 788–820 CE), formalized a system of worship of five forms of the one divinity: Ganesha, Shiva, Shakti, Vishnu, and Surya, the Vedic sun god.

SOME STARK CONNECTIONS

The *Song of Ice and Fire* books and the television series *Game of Thrones* are, as already mentioned, highly popular in India, as they are globally. Anecdotally, many of my Hindu friends have compared the overall "feel" of Martin's works with the great Hindu epics, the aforementioned *Ramayana*, and even more so, the *Mahabharata*, an ancient tale of political intrigue and conflict between two branches of a royal family competing for control of a kingdom in northern India. In the *Mahabharata*, the characters are also engaged in a *game of thrones*: not for the Iron Throne of the Seven Kingdoms, but for the Lion Throne of Hastinapur. Each character in the *Mahabharata* possesses certain strengths and virtues and certain weaknesses. Its character's weaknesses make this story more relatable, many say, than the *Ramayana*, whose characters—the noble Rama, the virtuous Sita, the ever-faithful Hanuman—hew closer to a representation of archetypes or ideals than of actual human behavior. An atmosphere of tragedy hangs over both the *Mahabharata* and *Game of Thrones*, and no character is exempt from the possibility of death. Even Lord Krishna, who is Vishnu incarnate, dies a tragic death, and his people destroy themselves in a futile fratricidal conflict.

Interestingly, the *Mahabharata*, like *Game of Thrones*, also centers around five siblings—the Pandava brothers—who could be seen as analogous to the five Stark children. There is also a sixth, hidden Pandava, Karna, who is analogous, in many respects, to Jon Snow. Karna is the son of Kunti, the mother of the Pandavas. She bore him in her youth, before she was married, because she was given a special prayer, or *mantra*, that would enable her to summon any deity, who would then father a child with her. Curious whether it would work, she summoned Surya, the sun god, and gave birth to Karna, a child who was powerful and luminous like the sun. Ashamed, as an unwed mother, she put her baby on a raft on a river—not unlike the biblical Moses—from which he was rescued by a lowly charioteer. The charioteer and his wife raised Karna lovingly as their own. Accordingly, he is believed to be of humble birth, but he is actually the eldest child of Kunti, and so the heir to the throne. Unaware of his heritage, he is befriended by Duryodhana, the arch enemy of the Pandavas. His true parentage is revealed to him late in the story, by Krishna and by Kunti herself, in an effort to avert the war between Duryodhana and the Pandavas. Loyal, however, to Duryodhana, Karna, who is the true heir to the throne, refuses to reveal himself, fighting and dying for his friend.

Karna is not unlike the sixth Stark child, Jon Snow, who was thought to be a bastard, but is, in fact, Aegon Targaryen, the true heir to the Iron Throne. Because of his loyalty to Daenerys, Jon, like Karna, refuses to reveal his true identity and claim the throne which is rightfully his. In both cases, the loyalty of the tragic hero proves misguided. Karna's loyalty to Duryodhana leads to his own death on the battlefield where he is fighting against his own brothers, who do not know that he is one of their own. Jon's loyalty to Daenerys prevents him from stopping her descent into violent madness and ultimately forces him into the even more difficult situation of having to end her life to save the world. Both Duryodhana and Daenerys end up dead, as does Karna. Jon ends up permanently exiled to the Wall and the lands beyond it. The main discrepancy between the two stories, in regard to Jon and Karna, is that Jon is not actually forced by circumstances to be on the opposite side of his (adoptive) family—though it very nearly does come to this as Daenerys becomes more authoritarian. The analogy between *Game of the Thrones* and the *Mahabharata* would only be perfect if Jon had been raised by the Lannisters.

Another Stark child bears even more profound connections to Hinduism. A highly esoteric Hindu image is invoked in the beliefs of the men of the North, and in particular, in the character of the Three-Eyed Raven, or Three-Eyed Crow, who first draws Brandon Stark to him, and whose role Bran eventually assumes himself, in the television series. As Larrington points out, "In some forms of Hindu ascetic practice the interior third eye gives access to arcane knowledge of different kinds."[31] In Hindu practice, the third eye is the chakra, or subtle energy center, associated with wisdom and insight. Its opening is seen as the penultimate stage to the achievement of ultimate enlightenment. Shiva and Shakti are both depicted with their third eye opened, and there is a story of Shiva sending forth a blast of energy from this eye which destroys Kamadeva, the god of sensory pleasure and desire, when Kamadeva tries to distract Shiva in his practice of meditation.

The power of the Three-Eyed Raven is certainly godlike, encompassing both the ability to see anything that has happened in the past and to warg into other living beings and assume control of their bodies. In the Tantric system of Hindu practice, where the chakras are the most emphasized and elaborated upon, powers of this kind are also sought. Paranormal powers derived from yogic practice are known as *siddhis*, or perfections. The temptation to use them for evil is so great that the Buddha is said to have forbidden his followers from using them at all.

Bran, after becoming the Three-Eyed Raven, assumes a personality which, in many ways, matches the ways in which an enlightened being might behave in both the Hindu and Buddhist traditions. He exudes an air of profound detachment, as though his ability to see the entirety of the past has minimized any sense of urgency about the present. When Jaime Lannister apologizes to him for shoving him out of a window, causing the paralysis which afflicts his legs (and leading to his being known as "Bran the Broken"), Bran responds by telling Jaime that everything he has done has led to the present moment, in which Jaime has become a valued ally in the larger struggle with the White Walkers and their Night King. It is not so much absolution or forgiveness in the Christian sense, but more an affirmation, in a more Hindu or Buddhist sense, that all that happens does so for a purpose: that all of our previous choices have led to this present moment, just as the present moment is now creating the future. In his enlightened state, as the Three-Eyed Raven, Bran feels no resentment or anger toward Jaime; for even his paralysis has been a step in the process of his own enlightenment.

CONCLUSION

There is no evidence that Hinduism has played a prominent role in Martin's creation of the secondary world of *Game of Thrones*. While Hinduism may not have been an *influence* on Martin—and, to the extent that some of the Hindu-like elements in the series are based not so much on deep knowledge of Hinduism as on medieval and early modern stereotypes of India, such as Daenerys's sati experience, as well as the Warlocks of Qarth and their soma-like shade of the evening—one can certainly discern significant elements of Hinduism, or overlaps with Hinduism, in the religions of Westeros. The theology of the Faith of the Seven sounds like Vedanta, in terms of seeing the one in the many and the many as one. Brandon's mystical experiences, his understanding of time and causation, and the imagery of the third eye resonate with important dimensions of Tantric yoga.

Part of the popularity of Martin's work worldwide must rest with the fact that it truly seems to have something for everyone. Even a series based on medieval Europe can, given the creativity of its author, resonate with themes of an ancient religion of faraway India. Hinduism is indeed present in *Game of Thrones*.

NOTES

1. Edward Said, *Orientalism* (New York: Pantheon Books, 1978), p. 95.
2. The specifics of medieval European life and history upon which Martin draws are very well presented in Carolyne Larrington's *Winter Is Coming: The Medieval World of Game of Thrones* (London: IB Tauris, 2016).
3. Priyanka Bhadani, "GoT's Popularity Is a Pan-India Phenomenon," *The Week* (September 3, 2017).

4. J. R. R. Tolkien, "On Fairy Stories," in *The Tolkien Reader* (New York: Ballantine Books, 1966), 42.

Ibid, 68.

5. Ibid, 68.

6. J. R. R. Tolkien, *The Lord of the Rings* (Boston: Houghton Mifflin, 1991), 1128–1132, 1141.

7. A. Ron Hubbard and Anthony Le Donne, *Gods of Thrones: A Pilgrim's Guide to the Religions of Ice and Fire, Volume One* (Middletown, Delaware: A. Ron Hubbard & Anthony Le Donne, 2018), 104–105.

8. See, for example, the "Pluralistic Hypothesis" of John Hick, which is most fully laid out in his *An Interpretation of Religion: Human Responses to the Transcendent* (New Haven, Connecticut: Yale University Press, 1989), as well as attempts to further deepen and go beyond Hick's hypothesis in David Ray Griffin's edited volume, *Deep Religious Pluralism* (Louisville, Kentucky: Westminster John Knox Press, 2005), not to mention my own work in this regard.

9. See the previously cited essay "On Fairy Stories," in which Tolkien articulates a theological vision in which the author of fantasy is a "sub-creator," the urge to create being a central characteristic of the Creator, in whose image we are made, and in whose creativity we thus participate. See also Humphrey Carpenter, *Tolkien: A Biography* (New York: Ballantine Books, 1977), 102–103.

10. Hubbard and Le Donne, 52.

11. Tolkien, "On Fairy Stories," 69, 70.

12. Larrington, 1.

13. Scholar Asko Parpola traces the first known usage of the word *Hindu* to the sixth century BC Persian emperor, Darius the Great. See Asko Parpola, *The Roots of Hinduism: The Early Aryans and the Indus Civilization* (New York: Oxford University Press, 2015), 3.

14. The term *Orientalism* to denote an exoticizing and "othering" style of writing by Western scholars describing diverse cultures was first coined by Edward Said, as discussed earlier, in the classic book of the same title. One recent example of a scholarly work that critiques the distortions of Hinduism in particular in both earlier and contemporary Western writing is Vishwa Adluri and Joydeep Bagchee, *The Nay Science: A History of German Indology* (Oxford: Oxford University Press, 2014).

15. Larrington, 1

16. What is provided here is by no means a thorough overview of Hinduism. I am providing some basic concepts, focusing particularly on ideas that are relevant to the world of ice and fire. Many good books on Hinduism exist, which I would recommend the interested reader to consult for greater detail. A very thorough yet easy to read text is Klaus K. Klostermaier's *A Survey of Hinduism* (Third Edition) (Albany: State University of New York Press, 2007). A brief and exceptionally clear guide to the central philosophy of Hinduism is Pravrajika Vrajaprana's *Vedanta: A Simple Introduction* (Hollywood: Vedanta Press, 1999).

17. See Parpola for the most thorough account of this process of cultural blending.

18. *Bhagavad Gita* 2:11b-13, 17, 20, 22, 25b. *Bhagavad Gita: As It Is*, with translation and commentary by A.C. Bhaktivedanta Swami Prabhupada (Los Angeles: Bhaktivedanta Book Trust, 1972), 21–24, 26–29.

19. See Vrajaprana, 15–35.
20. For an excellent elaboration on a prominent Hindu system of religious pluralism, see Ayon Maharaj, *Infinite Paths to Infinite Reality: Sri Ramakrishna and Cross-Cultural Philosophy of Religion* (Oxford: Oxford University Press, 2018).
21. George R. R. Martin, *A Game of Thrones* (New York: Bantam Books, 1996), 19, 78.
22. See Wendy Doniger, *The Hindus: An Alternative History* (Oxford: Oxford University Press, 2009), 103–134.
23. See Ramdas Lamb, *Rapt in the Name: The Ramnamis, Ramnam, and Untouchable Religion in Central India* (Albany: State University of New York Press, 2002).
24. Swami Vivekananda, *Complete Works*, Volume Five (Mayavati: Advaita Ashrama, 1979), 22–23.
25. Joyce Burkhalter Flueckiger, *Everyday Hinduism* (Chichester: Wiley Blackwell, 2015), 13-17
26. See Lamb.
27. Martin, 1996, 672.
28. Martin, *A Clash of Kings* (New York: Bantam Books, 1999), 525.
29. Martin, cited in Hubbard and Le Donne, 93.
30. Hubbard and Le Donne, 93–94.
31. Larrington, 91–92. It is interesting to note that the Three-Eyed Raven who draws Bran to him, Brynden Rivers—also known as Bloodraven—is a minor character in Martin's novel, *A Knight of the Seven Kingdoms*, which narrates the adventures of Dunk and Egg–Ser Duncan the Tall and his squire, who is really the crown prince in disguise, Aegon V Targaryen. Lord Bloodraven was forced to "take the black" and join the Night's Watch, eventually becoming its Lord Commander, and finally disappearing and becoming the Three-Eyed Raven, for the murder of Aenys Blackfyre, who had rebelled against the realm. In a sense, Lord Bloodraven prefigures Jaime Lannister's dishonor as the "Kingslayer" for having wrongfully murdered someone but having done so for the greater good of the realm. Bloodraven's interest in magic and the dark arts is mentioned in *A Knight of the Seven Kingdoms*, and it seems that this interest did not leave him when he was assigned to the Wall, with his quest for deeper knowledge eventually leading him to take on the role of the Three-Eyed Raven.

BIBLIOGRAPHY

Adluri, Vishwa, and Joydeep Bagchee. *The Nay Science: A History of German Indology*. Oxford: Oxford University Press, 2014.

Bhadani, Priyanka. "GoT's Popularity Is a Pan-India Phenomenon." *The Week* (September 3, 2017).

Carpenter, Humphrey. *Tolkien: A Biography*. New York: Ballantine Books, 1977.

Doniger, Wendy. *The Hindus: An Alternative History*. Oxford: Oxford University Press, 2009.

Flueckiger, Joyce Burkhalter. *Everyday Hinduism*. Chichester: Wiley Blackwell, 2015.
Griffin, David Ray, ed. *Deep Religious Pluralism*. Louisville, Kentucky: Westminster John Knox Press, 2005.
Hick, John. *An Interpretation of Religion: Human Responses to the Transcendent*. New Haven, Connecticut: Yale University Press, 1989.
Hubbard, A. Ron, and Anthony Le Donne. *Gods of Thrones: A Pilgrim's Guide to the Religions of Ice and Fire, Volume One*. Middletown, Delaware: A. Ron Hubbard & Anthony Le Donne, 2018.
Klostermaier, Klaus K. *A Survey of Hinduism*. Third Edition. Albany: State University of New York Press, 2007.
Lamb, Ramdas. *Rapt in the Name: The Ramnamis, Ramnam, and Untouchable Religion in Central India*. Albany: State University of New York Press, 2002.
Larrington, Carolyne Larrington. *Winter Is Coming: The Medieval World of Game of Thrones*. London: IB Tauris, 2016.
Maharaj, Ayon. *Infinite Paths to Infinite Reality: Sri Ramakrishna and Cross-Cultural Philosophy of Religion*. Oxford: Oxford University Press, 2018.
Martin, George R.R. *A Clash of Kings*. New York: Bantam Books, 1999.
———. *A Game of Thrones*. New York: Bantam Books, 1996.
———. *A Knight of the Seven Kingdoms*. New York: Bantam Books, 2015.
Parpola, Asko. *The Roots of Hinduism: The Early Aryans and the Indus Civilization*. New York: Oxford University Press, 2015.
Prabhupada, A.C. Swami Bhaktivedanta, trans. *Bhagavad Gita: As It Is*. Los Angeles: Bhaktivedanta Book Trust, 1972.
Said, Edward. *Orientalism*. New York: Pantheon Books, 1978.
Tolkien, J.R.R. "On Fairy Stories," in *The Tolkien Reader*. New York: Ballantine Books, 1966.
———. *The Lord of the Rings*. Boston: Houghton Mifflin, 1991.
———. *The Silmarillion*. Boston: Houghton Mifflin, 1998.
Vivekananda, Swami. *Complete Works*, Volume Five. Mayavati: Advaita Ashrama, 1979.
Vrajaprana, Pravrajika. *Vedanta: A Simple Introduction*. Hollywood: Vedanta Press, 1999.

Chapter 9

"To Reach the West You Must Go East"

The Empty Shadow of Postsecular Orientalism in A Song of Ice and Fire

Justin KH Tse

INTRODUCTION: *A SONG OF ICE AND FIRE* IN ORIENTALIST FANTASY

Edward Said's seminal insight in his classic *Orientalism* was that knowledges of the "Orient" were "imaginative geographies." Knowing about the "East," a region comprising half the world from about Turkey to China, is not the same as that which actually composes those places and the people who live in them. Orientalism, in other words, is the intellectual tradition that bases itself on fantasies that are projected upon geographical spaces. It has little to do with the everyday lives of those who are being imagined. And yet, as "imaginative" geographies, these imaginations are productive—they become the ideological engine by which the East, with the quotidian communities living in them, is integrated into the West.

It is this psychic integration—a colonizing one, really—of the imaginative Orient into the self-conception of the West that prompts what might be called Said's postsecular musings. For Said, the method by which orientalist imaginative geographies are integrated into an occidentalist self-conception is what he calls a "textual attitude," the "fallacy" that assumes "that the swarming, unpredictable, and problematic mess in which human beings live can be understood on the basis of what books—texts—say."[1] The implication is that the books, typically the classics of what is taken to be Eastern civilizations, become the source for understanding those cultures, resulting in a static conception of culture instead of attentiveness to the living, dynamic flow of practices, and their organic development. There is, Said then claims, a psychological reason behind this imaginative textuality. In fact, it is in his central argument:

> My thesis is that the essential aspects of modern Orientalist theory and praxis (from which present-day Orientalism derives) can be understood, not as a sudden access of objective knowledge about the Orient, but as a set of structures inherited from the past, secularized, redisposed, and re-formed by such disciplines as philology, which in turn were naturalized, modernized, and laicized substitutes for (or versions of) Christian supernaturalism.[2]

Said thus anticipates the arguments among scholars of the postsecular, whether in the vein of virtue ethics,[3] Radical Orthodoxy,[4] anthropologies of the secular,[5] philosophies of the "immanent frame" of modern temporality,[6] and critiques of racial formations and late-capitalist processes.[7] The general consensus in this scholarship holds that within the secular, there is an ideological gap, a phantom limb from the attempt to excise Christian conceptions of the supernatural.[8] Said's anticipated contribution to this line is that the resilience of "Christian supernaturalism" in the memory of the secular is why the West had to construct an East to be assimilated into its ego, its self-understanding. The Orient fills a spiritual void, its classics predating modern secularity and thus providing a glimpse into a world in the past where spirits and gods, heroes and ghosts were constitutive of civilizational glory. The postsecular, in other words, is already within secular consciousness, waiting to "bubble up," as the geographers Paul Cloke, Chris Baker, Callum Sutherland, and Andrew Williams put it, in spaces where it seems that the technocratic bureaucracy of the modern secular order has shut all of life into a Weberian iron cage.[9]

It is this social formation, this orientalist order of things, that I want to explore in George R.R. Martin's *Song of Ice and Fire*, with an exegesis rooted in the second book, *A Clash of Kings*, but moving across the series to develop the reflections.[10] In so doing, my aim is to contribute to the treatments of Martin as an anti-Tolkien disrupting the narrative arc of the fairy-tale happy ending with the brutal absurdity of everyday life, as it "incorporates and revises traditions that have become central to American mass-market fantasy."[11] On its face, *A Song of Ice and Fire* falls within the framework of the postsecular musings that are inherent to orientalism; it traces on its surface the plotline that Said charts in which the secular incorporates the East as a latent seed of supernatural memory that may become unrepressed at any moment. In this way, the world of Westeros might be said to function as a parallel universe to the one Said describes, literally, with the same orientalist formation that grids it into place. Magic, as far as those in the Seven Kingdoms are concerned, is from the East, from across the Narrow Sea. As

Martin described in a blog post about the publication of the atlas of Westeros, the maps are drawn from the perspective of the knowledge of the learned men of the Seven Kingdoms, the maesters of the Citadel. For them, what is in the East is already considered other, with Asshai being the furthest afield so that "past a certain point legends and myths will creep here. Here there be winged men, and such."[12] Brian Cowlishaw drives home a similar point in a treatment of Martin's maesters that mirrors Said's critique of orientalist knowledge: "Here, then, is the point about maesters' knowledge: it's all wrong. What they 'know' doesn't matter much, and what they *should* know, they don't."[13] Orientalism, as Said frames it, is a negation of knowledge on the part of those who claim to know. It is but a fantasy of what the East is, an imaginative geography that presumes more than it knows. It actually knows nothing.

My first move in this chapter will be to establish why I focus on *A Clash of Kings*. Following *A Game of Thrones*, the second novel definitively shifts the narrative along an East-West axis, revealing that the postsecular, the crisis of the secular in Westerosi society in which everything revolves around the "*game of thrones*" over which one wins or dies, comes from an Orient of sorts. I then trace three characters in *A Clash of Kings* who illustrate various dimensions of this postsecular orientalism: Melisandre, Daenerys Targaryen, and Arya Stark. The first, a priestess of the Lord of Light, brings to Westerosi shores the mythological figure of Azor Ahai, the Prince who was promised, who is said to be able to overcome the emergence of icy Others from the North. The second brings dragons, and the stories trace her development in the East, especially in her encounters with the mysterious Quaithe of the Shadow in Qarth. The third encounters the Faceless Man Jaqen H'ghar, who solicits three deaths from Arya and then gives her a coin to ensure her arrival in Braavos for her own training.

Each of these characters' eastward orientation, then, is integrated into the events that tear Westeros apart over the Iron Throne. My argument is that the integration of postsecular orientalism into Westeros is often construed as a search for meaning, but there is actually nothing to the magic. Its meaning is empty. This supernatural nothingness, so key to the emptiness of what Said describes as orientalism, ultimately undermines the East-West distinction, subverting the orientalist imaginary that the magical resurgence from the East has to mean something. In other words, as Quaithe tells Daenerys, "to reach the west, you must go east"—that is, there is in an ultimate sense of no distinction between these two directions because *A Song of Ice and Fire* may be sung within the structure of an orientalist fantasy. But in so doing, the imaginative geography falls apart. Ideologically speaking, Westeros cannot exist without the East. Indeed, its postsecularity is constituted by it. But as is typical of Martin's subversion of European fantasy genres, this orientalism also means nothing. The characters, though, do not know that.

THE OLD GODS AND THE NEW? THE SECULARIZATION OF "THE GAME OF THRONES" AFTER ROBERT'S REBELLION

The story in *A Clash of Kings* picks up from what might be considered postsecular stirrings at the end of the first novel, *A Game of Thrones*. The first novel begins with a glimpse of the Others, the "White Walkers" of the HBO show, that used to be the stuff of old wives' tales in the North and ends with Daenerys not only using Khal Drogo's funeral pyre to burn the sorceress Mirri Maz Duur alive for murdering him with her magic learned from the far East in Asshai, but also climbing into the flames and emerging unscathed with three dragon eggs hatched. With the re-emergence of magic in the world, *A Clash of Kings* undertakes a shift of geographical orientation. The fire that is part of the *Song of Ice and Fire* comes from the East. "He has a song," Daenerys later overhears her brother Rhaegar tell his wife Elia in the House of the Undying Ones in Qarth as he holds their newborn in his arms. "He is the prince that was promised, and his is the song of ice and fire . . . There must be one more . . . The dragon has three heads."[14] In an Eastern city, Daenerys hears the foreshadowing about "ice and fire," the re-emergence of the Others from the north placed on an axis with the fire of dragons from the East. It is the second novel that adjusts the orientation of the saga to fully include that which is eastward across the Narrow Sea and the postsecular fire that comes from that direction, the first hint of which is the birth of Daenerys's dragons.

The plot of the first novel *A Game of Thrones* moves by contrast from north to south. Centered on the adventures of Eddard "Ned" Stark as a man of honor, the initial story, as Martin tells it, begins in the north. From the beginning, the exposition introduces the Others, who kill two members of a ranger party from the Night's Watch, the order of men who have "taken the black" to watch for the return of the White Walkers from a Wall legendarily built by the ancestor of the Starks, Bran the Builder, to keep them north. Ned beheads the sole survivor of that group—the only one not turned into a blue-eyed wight that is destined to serve in an army of the dead—as a deserter from that Wall, which results in the discovery of direwolves that were thought to be extinct but then become pets for each of the Stark children. The emergence of the postsecular at this point seems to have a northward direction: "There's not a direwolf sighted south of the Wall in two hundred years," Theon Greyjoy, the Stark ward until he later betrays them, observes. The Stark home Winterfell's master of horse, Hullen, agrees: "Direwolves loose in the realm, after so many years . . . I like it not," as does their household guard captain Jory Cassel. "It's a sign," he says.[15] Others, wights, and direwolves: magic has awakened in the north, the stuff of old wives' tales for centuries, and it is presumably made of ice.

A Game of Thrones travels, then, on a north-south axis. The first glimpse that this directional pull is at work occurs in the godswood at Winterfell where Ned and his wife Catelyn converse. "Catelyn had never liked this godswood," the scene opens, and then explains that

> she had been born a Tully, at Riverrun far to the south, on the Red Fork of the Trident. The godswood there was a garden, bright and airy, where tall redwoods spread dappled shadows across tinkling streams, birds sang from hidden nests, and the air was spicy with the scent of flowers.

The northern godswood, by contrast, was a "dark and primal place, three acres of old forest untouched for ten thousand years as the gloomy castle rose around it."[16] There are thus old gods and new ones, the former in the north, the latter in the south. "Catelyn had been anointed with the seven oils and named in the rainbow of light that filled the sept of Riverrun": she belongs to the new gods, the Faith of the Seven, with worship that fills septs with the smoke of incense. Her husband Ned is, however, a Stark: "the blood of the First Men still flowed in the veins of the Starks, and his own gods were the old ones, the nameless, faceless gods of the greenswood they shared with the vanished children of the forest," the indigenous peoples of Westeros.[17] Not only is there a postsecular turn in the North with the emergence of the agency of ice—incidentally, also the name of Ned Stark's sword—but there is also a sense that Westerosi society is, at least in name, a devout one, serving the old gods and the new, making vows and oaths by their name, and running its society with them as a kind of civic theology.

Parallel to the theological axis of the old gods and the new that runs from north to south, the plot of *A Game of Thrones* travels in the same direction. The Stark bastard Jon Snow, seeing the success of his Uncle Benjen who took the black, travels north to take on a new identity that transcends the presumed illegitimacy of his birth. Jon becomes a member of the Night's Watch and is eventually dispatched as part of another ranger party to look for the Others as well as the "wildlings," the people who live north of the wall who are not subject to the laws of the rest of Westeros. The story of Jon Snow, in other words, covers the postsecular dimensions of the north as an attempt to narrate how it is that the agency of ice, muted for centuries, is now re-emerging. Meanwhile, the untimely death of Jon Arryn, Baratheon's first hand, propels the rest of the Starks to move south to King's Landing, but not before the child Bran Stark discovers the Lannister twins Jaime and Cersei, respectively, a kingsguard and the queen of Westeros, copulating in a tower at Winterfell. He is pushed by Jaime presumably to his death to prevent their secret from getting out, catalyzing a series of events, including an assassination attempt on the recovering boy, that results in the Starks arresting the "Imp" Tyrion

Lannister and attempting to try him for murder. Tyrion's champion triumphs in a trial by combat, freeing him to rejoin his dysfunctional, incestuous family. Moving south to become Hand to Robert Baratheon, Ned discovers the same dirty truth of the Lannister incest while investigating the king's bastards that the Lannister incest has produced three children presumably born of Robert Baratheon— Joffrey, Myrcella, and Tommen—all of whom are fair of hair, instead of black like the Baratheon line. But as Ned is about to break the news to Robert, the king dies in a hunting accident, gored by a boar while drunk. The succession automatically goes to the boy Joffrey.

The discovery that Joffrey and his siblings are not in fact of Baratheon's bloodline is especially significant because the House of Baratheon had usurped the Iron Throne, the ruling seat of the Seven Kingdoms, from the Targaryens, an ancient family that escaped the destruction of the eastern city of Valyria and arrived on Westeros with their dragons to conquer its houses, forcing them to swear loyalty to House Targaryen in perpetuity. The north-south axis of *A Game of Thrones*, in other words, is no accident. It is a creation of House Baratheon's usurpation, with hints that it does not quite hold, because there are also chapters that cover the adventures of Viserys and Daenerys Targaryen, the last remaining survivors of their house, in the East. The unity of the Seven Kingdoms under the Iron Throne has an orientalist twist. It was united by the "blood of the dragon," the descendants of Aegon Targaryen and his sisters Visenya and Rhaenys, who literally conquered Westeros with three dragons. By the time of "Robert's Rebellion," though, the dragon had become merely symbolic, and this despite the significance of real dragons in the early part of Westeros's history under House Targaryen. One thinks, for example, of the erstwhile Queen Rhaenyra over 150 years before the events of *A Song of Ice and Fire*. She was "delivered" as an "offering" to her half-brother's dragon Sunfyre during the period of civil war known as the Dance of Dragons, in which most of the dragons were killed in intra-Targaryen warfare.[18]

Their main steed reduced to symbols, the "blood of the dragon" had to find new expressions of dragon-ness. The "Mad King" Aerys II, the cause of the uprising, had a fascination with fire as a natural substitute for the magic of dragons that had become all-but-extinct. The fire of "the dragon," as the Targaryens were called, had become increasingly rare and hard to reproduce. Aerys II's grandfather Aegon V, the famous "Egg" who squired for the knight Duncan the Tall, famously died while trying to hatch dragon eggs with fire.[19] One might call this post-Dance of Dragons era a time of *secularization*. The world, as even the last few generations of the Targaryens knew it, was becoming increasingly disenchanted, the power even of the dragons reduced to such symbolic gestures that the later generations of the Targaryens were forced to substitute their connection to dragons with natural fire. When

Robert Baratheon vanquished Rhaegar Targaryen on the battlefield for allegedly kidnapping his betrothed Lyanna Stark and led an invasion of the capital city King's Landing, he did more than to take the Iron Throne for House Baratheon, ensuring that the only axis that held in Westeros was north to south, with no more East. If the fire of the dragon had been dying down to its last few smoldering embers, then Robert's Rebellion snuffed it out.

The world that Ned Stark enters in King's Landing eighteen years later as King's Hand is therefore totally secular, a place where political power in a purely temporal sphere is all there—and thus the ideal conditions to examine the spiritual vacuum that Said highlights as the context that orientalist fantasy must fill. When Ned tries to warn Queen Cersei that he knows of her sexual betrayals and that he will take action to have a rightful heir of House Baratheon's bloodline sit on the Iron Throne, she replies that he should have taken the throne for himself during Robert's Rebellion: "When you play the *game of thrones*, you win or you die. There is no middle ground."[20] There are no gods here, neither old nor new. There is only power, the kind that only humans wield. Nothing divine will save him; playing the *game of thrones* wrongly—with notions of honor that befit the traditions of the First Men and their old gods—he is beheaded on the Sept of Baelor, the seat of the new gods, though there really are no divinities at play here, neither old or new. In a discussion that Ned has before his execution with the spymaster Varys, he realizes that he has played the game wrong, that it was, as Varys says, his *"mercy"* that killed the king. "Gods forgive me," Ned says, to which Varys replies, "If there are gods . . . I expect they will," after which he concocts a plan for Ned to confess his treason and be spared.[21] He does, and there are no gods to forgive him; Joffrey has Ned executed on the spot. The conditional *if* in Varys's statement is theologically telling: Ned's execution is a purely atheistic moment—that if the gods had existed, mercy might too, but since they do not, the only thing is the game. This world is secular. The result of this execution is not divine retribution, but more politics in what is known in the second book as the War of Five Kings, with Joffrey attempting to hold on to his throne, Robert's brothers Stannis and Renly laying claim to it on the account that Joffrey is a bastard, while Ned's son Robb is declared an independent King in the north and Balon Greyjoy the Lord of the Iron Islands. Temporal power, it seems, is all there is.

Or is it? The first book ends with a cliffhanger, the possibility of the postsecular arising from the East, just like Said says it always does:

> As Daenerys Targaryen rose to her feet, her black *hissed*, pale smoke venting from its mouth and nostrils. The other two pulled away from her breasts and added their voices to the call, translucent wings unfolding and stirring the air,

and for the first time in hundreds of years, the night came alive with the music of dragons.[22]

The dragons are symptomatic of what seems to be a postsecular challenge to the secular Westerosian *game of thrones*. But to follow this logic would be to center the Targaryen conquest of Westeros as the pin that holds the threads of such orientalism together. *A Clash of Kings*, I hope to show, attempts to untie this knot by re-orienting the plot along an East-West axis, enabling precisely Said's analytic to apply to *A Song of Ice and Fire*. In this way, that which is across the Narrow Sea is inescapably constituting Westeros, even in the post-Targaryen era.

THE LIMITS OF THE RED PRIESTESS'S SHADOW: MELISANDRE OF ASSHAI

A Clash of Kings does not begin with the Targaryen overlords, though it does start at Dragonstone, the historic site where the Targaryens first arrived from Valyria and escaped its volcanic doom. The lengthy introduction is told from the perspective of Stannis Baratheon's advisor, Maester Cressen. Staking out his claim to the Iron Throne, his forces are encamped at Dragonstone, from which Stannis plots his campaign to rule the Seven Kingdoms. After sketches of innocent scenes of interaction with Stannis's daughter Shireen, Maester Cressen's true intentions are revealed. He has decided that a certain "red woman" has exerted far too much theological influence on Stannis's wife Selyse, turning her from the Faith of the Seven to the Lord of Light, from *gods* to a singular god. "Melisandre of Asshai," he describes her and specifying her eastern provenance, "sorceress, shadowbinder, and priestess to R'hilor, the Lord of Light, the Heart of Fire, the God of Flame and Shadow. Melisandre, whose madness must not be allowed to spread beyond Dragonstone."[23] To kill her, he prepares a poison "from a certain plant that grew only on the islands of the Jade Sea, half a world way." It is a specialty known by those east of Westeros:

> The alchemists of Lys knew the way of it . . . and the Faceless Men of Braavos . . . and the masters of his order as well . . . Cressen no longer recalled the name the Asshai'i gave the leaf, or the Lysene poisoners the crystal. In the Citadel, it was simply called the strangler.

Moving forward to the banquet where "Lord Stannis would feast his bannermen, his lady wife . . . and the red woman, Melisandre of Asshai,"[24] he puts it in both of their wines during a toast, only to discover as he shares it with her that it is only he who is choking to death, while "the red woman looked down on him in pity, the candle flames dancing in her red red eyes."[25] Attempting to remove this woman from the east whom he thinks has poisoned Selyse and Stannis's minds, Maester Cressen dies of the Eastern poison.

There are three references to what might be called a postsecular East, a fantasy of the orient as filling in the spiritual vacuum of the West, in this introduction. The first is that Stannis is appropriating Dragonstone in a post-Targaryen era. Claiming to be Robert's successor, Stannis gathers strength at Dragonstone, where Aegon and his sisters had planned the conquest of Westeros centuries ago. Stannis is not claiming Targaryen lineage; he is replacing them. But second, he replaces the Targaryen line with an Eastern claim as well, one that is also constituted by fire, though not that of the dragon. He relies instead on the counsel of the red priestess Melisandre, who has converted his wife Selyse in an effort to make him see that he is the fulfillment of the prophecy of her religion, of Azor Ahai, the same "Prince that was Promised" that Daenerys sees her brother Rhaegar referencing in the House of the Undying Ones and says that the "dragon has three heads." Stannis's fire is not Targaryen, though; from the perspective of Stannis's right-hand man, the erstwhile smuggler Davos Seaworth: "Dragonstone's sept had been where Aegon the Conqueror knelt to pray the night before he sailed. That had not saved it from the queen's men," a reference to Selyse, who in her religious zeal tore down the sept, removed its gods, and took their statues to the beach to be burned.[26] Just as Stannis needs no dragons, he requires none of the Targaryens' gods. He is Azor Ahai, as appointed by R'hillor, the Lord of Light, from the East. Melisandre says to herself, as the gods are burned and a ritual is performed where Stannis enacts the part of the prophesied hero:

> In ancient books of Asshai it is written that there will come a day after a long summer when the stars bleed and the cold breath of darkness falls heavy on the world. In this dread hour a warrior shall draw from the fire a burning sword. And that sword shall be Lightbringer, the Red Sword of Heroes, and he who clasps it shall be Azor Ahai come again, and the darkness shall flee before him.[27]

Stannis emerges as the chanting congregation names him Azor Ahai, and he picks up a sword on the beach and plunges it into the fire. Selyse, seeing her husband thus, goes into ecstasy. As Davos and his friend Salladhor Saan later tell the story, the plot points of the Azor Ahai myth are all to be found in this ritual. In "a time when darkness lay heavy on the world," Azor Ahai forged a "hero's blade" that failed to be tempered by water or the body of a lion. Calling his beloved wife to him, he plunges it into "her living heart," and it "is said that the cry of anguish and ecstasy left a crack across the face of the moon"—no wonder Selyse enters a trancelike state—"but her blood and her soul and her strength and her courage all went into the steel."[28] There are no dragons here, let alone three heads. Stannis, with Melisandre's help and Selyse's devotion, is appealing to an even more ancient prophecy, here simply given as a tradition from unnamed texts from Asshai (from which Melisandre also originates), to claim his place on the throne as Azor Ahai reborn. Burning the statues of the Seven in this very ritual, Stannis claims to replace the Targaryens forever.

But the third reference to the postsecular East in the opening of *A Clash of Kings* is perhaps the strangest of all. Melisandre's power is not symbolic, but real. The shadowbinder of Asshai survives the "strangler" poison whose Asshai'i name Maester Cressen had forgotten. No one survives it. Indeed, much later in *A Storm of Swords*, it is this same poison that kills Joffrey at his own wedding, strangling him to death when it is put into his wine. The point, though, is not that the poison of the strangler is from the East. In both the case of Maester Cressen and the assassination of Joffrey, it is administered with purely natural ingenuity, the former with a toast, the latter with an elaborate plan for Sansa Stark, alone in King's Landing, to take on as a personal knight the alcoholic Ser Dontos, who gifts her a hairnet with barbs of poison that the grandmother of the bride, Olenna Tyrell, plucks from her at the wedding and puts into the king's chalice. The postsecular marvel is that Melisandre, having taken this poison, does not die. Instead, her "red red eyes" come alive as she watches the maester perish.

For much of *A Clash of Kings*, Melisandre's mysterious allure as the embodiment of what Said might frame as a postsecular "oriental" is thus played up. At a parley when Stannis besieges the Baratheon family home of Storm's End, Renly Baratheon seems "amused" by his brother's sigil of the Lord of Light in flames. As this scene plays out in the HBO series, he even mocks Stannis with the very terms of the Azor Ahai myth. "You should kneel before your brother," Melisandre counsels Renly. "He is the Lord's chosen, born amidst salt and smoke." "Is he a ham?" Renly retorts ("Garden of Bones"). That very night, as the widow Catelyn Stark begs him to consider an alliance with her son Robb, Renly is beginning to make yet another joke "when a sudden gust of wind flung open the door of the tent." Catelyn "thought she glimpsed movement, but when she turned her head, it was only the king's shadow shifting against the silken walls." She sees "his shadow moving, lifting its sword, black on green, candles guttering, shivering, something was queer, wrong, and then she saw Renly's sword still in its scabbard, sheathed still, but the shadowsword." Renly utters one word, "Cold," before the steel protrudes from his throat and blood gushes out. Catelyn reflects:

> *The shadow*. Something dark and evil had happened here, she knew, something that she could not begin to understand. *Renly never cast that shadow. Death*

came in that door and blew the life out of him as swift as the wind snuffed out his candles.[29]

From joking about the postsecular, Renly is taken by surprise, killed by the shadow of the sigil that he mocked. It is later when Stannis attempts to take Storm's End from its castellan Ser Cortnay Pentrose that Davos discovers what that shadow is—"death in the form of Melisandre of Asshai."[30] Davos is given the task of rowing the red priestess to the castle walls, where she explains that while it was easy to assassinate Renly in a tent because he was "unprotected," "this Storm's End is an old place. There are spells woven into the stones. Dark walls that no shadow can pass—ancient, forgotten, yet still in place." She explains to Davos the relationship between fire and the shadow: "There are no shadows in the dark. Shadows are the servants of light, the children of fire. The brightest flame casts the darkest shadows."[31] Her bringing of the fire of the Lord of Light from the East—from as far as Asshai—is part and parcel of her work as an Asshai'i shadowbinder, then, as darkness in her theological conception is constitutive of the light, serving its brightness. With that, she goes into labor:

> And Davos saw the crown of the child's head push its way out of her. Two arms wriggled free, grasping, black fingers coiling around Melisandre's strained thighs, pushing, until the whole of the shadow slid out into the world and rose taller than Davos, tall as the tunnel, towering above the boat.

Looking at the shadow, he knows it, "as he knew the man who'd cast it."[32] As Renly's kingsguard Brienne of Tarth notes throughout her recounting of Renly's assassination, it is the face of Stannis, who has weaponized the postsecular orient to kill his enemies with the dark Asshai'i magic of shadowbinding, first his brother Renly, then Ser Cortnay.

The shock, then, comes at the conclusion of *A Clash of Kings*: the Azor Ahai in whose company is the red priestess shadowbinder of Asshai, who assassinates his enemies with shadows and burns the gods in a ritual enactment of the flaming sword of Lightbringer, is defeated by purely natural and secular pyrotechnics at Blackwater Bay. Defending King's Landing, Tyrion Lannister, acting as Joffrey's hand, assembles the alchemic wildfire from the days of the Mad King and prepares them to be launched at Stannis's naval fleet. The plan just about works, as Stannis's fleet is decimated and Davos loses all of his sons, though the Lannister patriarch Tywin has to ride in to save the day in a near-repeat of his sacking of King's Landing during Robert's Rebellion. Melisandre, it turns out, is only good for two things. First, she kills Stannis's enemies with the shadow, initially with the shadow babies, and then in *A Storm of Swords*, by using leeches to extract king's blood and cast them into the fire as tokens of the rival kings Robb Stark, Balon Greyjoy, and Joffrey Baratheon to be killed by circumstance. They all do die, Greyjoy from being pushed off a bridge, Stark at a "Red Wedding" where the Starks are slaughtered by the Freys with whom they had been allied at the time, and Baratheon at his own wedding with the strangler poison. Second, Melisandre, like others in the hierarchy of the Lord of Light, can bring people like Jon Snow back from the dead (if the sixth season of HBO show has correctly followed Martin's as yet unwritten sixth novel, *The Winds of Winter*), a feat first foreshadowed yet again in the third novel by another red priest Thoros of Myr repeatedly bringing Beric Dondarion back from the dead to lead the outlaw Brotherhood without Banners (and in the books only, Catelyn Stark as "Lady Stoneheart," who avenges the "Red Wedding"). But the limits of the postsecular orient lie at military strategy. Individual kings can be killed, but magic cannot win the Battle of Blackwater Bay. Indeed, therein lies the tragedy: the plot development in HBO's *Game of Thrones*'s fifth season has Stannis's daughter Shireen burned at Melisandre's behest in a bid to the Lord of Light to be on Stannis's woefully outnumbered side to take Winterfell in the north. He loses. And for his part in the sexual creation of the shadow that killed Renly, Brienne of Tarth, Renly's erstwhile kingsguard, executes him. Natural politics, it seems, cannot be defeated by the supernatural. Said is right. There really is nothing to orientalism.

Or is he? Might orientalism work with a strategist who is not Melisandre of Asshai, someone with a more legitimate claim to the postsecular orient?

TEXTS AND HOUSES OF THE SHADOW: QUAITHE ON DAENERYS TARGARYEN'S "POSTSECULAR ORIENTAL" IDENTITY

At least for Quaithe of the Shadow, the ability of a Qartheen firemage to conjure a ladder of fire in the middle of a bazaar, then climb it and disappear, is no coincidence, much less a cheap trick. It is, she says, because of the arrival of Daenerys Targaryen, the Unburnt *khaleesi* and Mother of Dragons, into the city that this man who "could scarcely wake fire from dragonglass" can achieve such fiery feats: "And now his powers grow, *Khaleesi*. And you are the cause of it."[33] As one of the three representatives of Qarth, Quaithe had, from behind her "lacquered wooden mask" and "in the Common Tongue of the Seven Kingdoms," told Daenerys that they "come seeking dragons."[34] Now Daenerys is in Qarth, her queenly presence literally lighting up the city, and it is in this very moment that Quaithe warns of danger. "You must leave this city soon, Daenerys Targaryen," Quaithe says, stepping back into the crowd as she provides her analysis of Daenerys's empowering presence on the firemage and her touch on Daenerys's wrist is rebuffed, "or you will never be permitted to leave it at all." Daenerys asks Quaithe where she should go, then, if not here. "To go north," Quaithe tells Daenerys, "you must journey south. To reach the west, you must go east. To go forward you must go back, and to touch the light you must pass beneath the shadow."[35] Daenerys immediately makes an orientalist assumption, the kind that Said suggests that those grasping at mental straws often do. She links Quaithe's mystical quality to her Asshai'i origins and interpreting her words thus. "*Asshai*, Dany thought. *She would have me to go Asshai*," assuming that Quaithe is counseling her to move East to raise funds or an army, both of which the subsequent novels do find Daenerys doing in the Slaver's Bay cities of Yunkai, Astapor, and Meereen, where she acquires the Unsullied soldiers, the translator Missandei, ships and monetary funds to finance her invasion of Westeros, and a reputation for being an idealist "Breaker of Chains." But Quaithe's response to Daenerys's thought reveals that the Mother of Dragons is wrong about why it might be important to go East. It is not to raise an army or funds. "What is there in Asshai that I will not find in Qarth?" Daenerys demands. The reply is, simply: "Truth."[36]

Daenerys, however, does not leave the city. Instead, she follows the Qartheen mages into the House of the Undying Ones, where she is nearly assassinated. Indeed, *not* following Quaithe's postsecular orientalist counsel, the advice to go East to search for who she truly is, sets up their relationship through the books. And yet, as Quaithe argues in the subsequent books, Daenerys's encounters in the House of the Undying Ones is very much an act of going East. Entering with her dragon Drogon, she has a number of visions, of a woman surrounded by four little men, of a scene of carnage in the aftermath of a feast, of Rhaegar saying that there must be one more child to complete the set of the dragon having three heads as the Prince that was Promised, of a hall of the Undying who honor her by name, of her brother Viserys and her healer Mirri Maz Duur who were burned to death. "A thousand years we knew, and have been waiting all this time," a wizard king who introduces himself as an undying one tells her. "We sent the comet to show you the way," to which a "warrior in shining emerald armor" adds, "We have knowledge to share with you . . . and magic weapons to arm you with. You have passed every trial. Now come and sit with us, and all your questions shall be answered." Drogon interrupts this scene, and a "handsome young man" jokes, "A willful beast . . . Shall we teach you the secret speech of dragonkind? Come, come."[37] There is something, this instructive scene posits, that links Daenerys with dragons, along with a certain kind of destiny for which these undying elders have waited long to show her. The direction here may not be literally East, but the words dovetail with Quaithe's counsel to find the truth about herself.

Quaithe's advice in *A Clash of Kings* then repeats in the subsequent novels, driving home the importance of her cryptic counsel for Daenerys's character arc. As Daenerys sails to Slaver's Bay to trick the masters into letting her conquer their cities and extract their resources, she considers all of her lessons in Qarth, including the assassination attempts made on her life by the warlock Pyat Pree, as well as the reality that the Dothraki, the nomadic warriors into whose ranks she had once married, were now alienated from her because of the death of her husband, the only attachment she had had to them. In that context, she remembers "Quaithe of the Shadow, that strange woman in the red lacquer mask with all her cryptic counsel. Was she an enemy too, or only a dangerous friend? Dany could not say."[38] There is something, though, in her more general reflections with her counselors, who advise her to listen to their wisdom instead of relying on her wits. Quaithe had advised her on going East to learn the truth of her identity. Just before Daenerys's ruminations on whether Quaithe is an enemy or friend, her advisors tell her the story of her older brother Rhaegar, who was much more inclined to book knowledge than the life of a warrior until "one day Prince Rhaegar found something in the scrolls that changed him. No one knows what it might have been, only that the boy suddenly appeared early one morning in the yard as the knights were donning their steel" and asked to be trained in combat.[39] Daenerys, of course, does know what he understood, having heard his words in the House of the Undying Ones. It was that his children would come to compose a composite "Prince that was Promised," the Azor Ahai of Melisandre's reading. The source, as the bookish Night's Watch brother Samwell Tarly, learns from the Wall's maester (who turns out to be Aemon Targaryen) in *A Feast for Crows*, is a text known as Colloquo Votar's *Jade Compendium*, "a thick volume of tales and legends from the east that Maester Aemon had commanded him to find."[40] In the fifth novel *A Dance of Dragons*, Jon says that he has read it:

> I looked at the book Maester Aemon left me. The *Jade Compendium*. The pages that told of Azor Ahai. Lightbringer was his sword. Tempered with his wife's blood if Votar can be believed. Thereafter Lightbringer was never cold to the touch, but warm as Nissa Nissa had been warm.[41]

Likely reading this text from the East, Rhaegar, as much as Melisandre with Stannis, also attempted to manufacture a fulfillment to this postsecular Eastern prophecy, a return of magical order to an increasingly secularized Westeros, a search for his truest identity in the supernatural constitution of that world in order to perfect his rule.

This impulse is similar, then, to Quaithe's counsel to Daenerys: she needs to know who she is, like Rhaegar and Jon Snow (who turns out to be Rhaegar's son), by moving East and passing under the shadow. While sleeping on her ship en route to Astapor, the first of the slave cities she conquers, she notices that she is not alone in the cabin. Asking whether it is one of her maidservants or advisors, a woman answers, in close proximity to Daenerys: "They sleep . . . They all sleep . . . Even dragons must sleep." She then sees a "shadow, the faintest outline of a shape," reminiscent of the one that killed Renly and Ser Cortnay, but it is not here to kill her. And then the counsel is repeated: "Remember. To go north, you must journey south. To reach the west, you must go east. To go forward you must go back, and to touch the light you must pass beneath the shadow." Daenerys decidedly rejects this advice:

> "*If I look back I am lost,* Dany told herself the next morning as she entered Astapor through the harbor gates. She dared not remind herself how small and insignificant her following truly was, or she would lose all courage."[42]

With this impulse to increase her numbers, she rampages across the slave cities, freeing the slaves who in each city reach out to her with the call of *Myssa*. *Myssa*, Daenerys as the mother who bought them freedom, is the maternal name of the "Breaker of Chains." It is an identity that is conjured out of weakness, manufactured to give herself courage to conquer and govern from a position of strength, not one that is acquired by seeking the truth in the East.

Quaithe's critique of Daenerys, then, is that she chooses to listen to those around her and to feign strength instead of going East to find out who she truly is, as her brother Rhaegar did. Quaithe thus reaches out to her yet again when she has conquered the last of the slave cities, Meereen, reminding her of their encounter prior to her conquering the first city, Astapor and telling her that it was not a dream but that she is also not technically there either. She comes again with counsel to remind her of the eastward direction of her identity:

> Hear me, Daenerys Targaryen. The glass candles are burning. Soon comes the pale mare, and after her the others. Kraken and dark flame, lion and griffin, the sun's son and the mummer's dragon. Trust none of them. Remember the Undying. Beware the perfumed seneschal.

Here, Quaithe provides a clue about what it means to move East. The movement may not be physical, just as it is Quaithe's shadow and not her in the room but may have happened already in the House of the Undying where her visions might inform her of who she is and from where she comes. As in books like *The Jade Compendium* and the legends of Asshai, so also in those memories: Daenerys must go East to find herself. Indeed, this time, Daenerys can repeat Quaithe's counsel—"I remember the way. I go north to go south, east to go west, back to go forward. And to touch the light I have to pass beneath the shadow"—before telling her that she is "half-sick of riddling" and commands Quaithe to tell her the truth, again striking a pose to shore up her insecure rule. "*Daenerys*," Quaithe says, cutting her off. "Remember the Undying. Remember who you are."[43] Daenerys is a bit more receptive when assassinations made on her make her flee the cities and wander aimlessly. Fleeting in and out of consciousness while considering the betrayals of both friends and enemies, Daenerys encounters Quaithe again, seeing her "mask" that is "made of starlight." Quaithe whispers one more time in Daenerys's ear, "To go north, you must journey south. To reach the west, you must go east. To touch the light you must pass beneath the shadow," and then provides an interpretive key again, through the stars: "Remember who you are, Daenerys . . . The dragons know. Do you?"[44]

There is something of Said's "textual attitude" here, the notion that one does not need to go to the East in order to know it, because it is available in texts and sites that can access it via technological communications, in this case, the warlock magic of the House of the Undying and Quaithe's shadow-binding. The East, the wisdom says, is constitutive of the West—of Westeros and Daenerys's designs upon it—but the catch here is that Daenerys constantly *rejects* this self-knowledge. She has dragons, but she does not know her true connection to them. Indeed, that she calls herself their "mother" is a form of false consciousness, too. "They are my children," she reflects, "and if the *maegi*"—a reference to the Asshai'i witch who killed her husband and condemned her to barrenness—"spoke truly, they are the only children I am ever like to have."[45] Quaithe's warning, by contrast, is that the people around her, quite possibly including this malpracticing healer that she burned, are deceiving her, that she cannot know what to do unless she knows what she is. The HBO show puts these words into the mouth of Olenna Tyrell, in her counsel to Daenerys about listening to Tyrion Lannister, who has become her hand since she herself landed on Dragonstone to conquer Westeros: "He's a clever man, your Hand. I've known a great many clever men. I've outlived them all. Do you know why? I ignored them. The lords of Westeros are sheep. Are you a sheep? No. You're a dragon. Be a dragon" ("Stormborn"). Mirroring her relationship with Quaithe, Daenerys does not listen to Olenna, preferring to heed Tyrion's advice to take the Lannister family home of Casterly Rock. The result is that the Lannisters outflank Daenerys and invade the castles of her allies, including Olenna Tyrell. The "Queen of Thorns," as the Tyrell matriarch is called, may have survived by not listening to men, but the dragon did not heed her counsel. In this way, Daenerys not heeding the advice to go East, to discover that she herself is a dragon, causes the death of Olenna Tyrell, in whose mouth was also the postsecular orientalist counsel of Quaithe.

But if the true relationship that Daenerys has with her dragons is not as their mother and if those around her are giving her bad counsel, then who is she, really? What does she have to find in Asshai, whether physically there or through texts about it? What is the "truth" about her, if there can be one, given what Said says about the emptiness of such an orientalist attitude? For this question, I engage a final character who might drop a hint about what in fact constitutes the East in terms of its integration in Westeros. After the beheading of Ned Stark, Arya Stark also ultimately reaches the West by going East in her own search for an identity.

VALAR MORGHULIS, VALAR DOHAERIS: ARYA STARK MUST BECOME NO ONE

In the confusion that takes hold of Westeros after the beheading of Ned Stark in *A Game of Thrones*, his daughter Arya becomes subjected to various wandering parties in a journey to north. In the aftermath of the execution, Yoren, the recruiter for the Night's Watch, takes Arya along, disguised as the boy Arry, along with a number of prison captives. They fall prey to Lannister soldiers, who incarcerate her and others into what amounts to be a haphazard concentration camp set up by the mercenary group, the Brave Companions, hired by the Lannisters at the eerie castle Harrenhal, famous for its tall burnt spires that had been roasted by dragonfire when its original inhabitant, Lord Harren, refused to bend the knee to House Targaryen. Escaping her captors, Arya comes into the company of the Brotherhood without Banners, and in time, Arya finds herself escaping with Sandor "the Hound" Clegane. In so doing, Arya maintains a north-south axis throughout most of *A Clash of Kings*, but for her encounter with the Faceless Man, Jaqen H'ghar, during her Harrenhal captivity.

The truth, of course, is that Jaqen H'ghar is with Arya for most of *A Clash of Kings*. He is among the prisoners from King's Landing marching to the Wall in the north, and along the route, Arya feels a sense of familiarity with him: "Something about the way he talked reminded her of Syrio"—her swordsmanship teacher from the free city of Braavos east of Westeros when she was living in King's Landing—"it was the same, yet different too." He introduces himself to her by name, "once of the Free City of Lorath. Would that he were home."[46] Imprisoned with two others, they are trapped when the abandoned town in which they are staying is set on fire, but they are saved by Arya. When Arya arrives at Harrenhal, she is surprised to find Jaqen among the Brave Companions. As she engages in her nightly ritual of counting off her newly developed kill list of persons who have wronged her and her family leading up to the execution of her father, Jaqen approaches her. The first thing he tells her is that he has always known that she is "a girl" and that he is there because a "man pays his debts. A man owes three." He is referring to him and the two other prisoners who were supposed to have died in the fire, and then, like the other postsecular characters from the East, begins to wax theological about yet another Eastern deity:

> "The Red God has his due, sweet girl, and only death may pay for life. This girl took three that were his. This girl must give three in their places. Speak the names, and a man will do the rest."[47]

With reference to "the Red God," it is tempting without further reading to conclude that Jaqen also serves R'hillor, the Lord of Light, with the red priests and priestesses. In killing the three persons named by Arya—two of the Brave Companions, before extorting him for freedom by naming him, Jaqen, as the third to be killed—Jaqen H'ghar effects what can be said to be an initial catechesis in the honor of this Red God. The first person whose name she gives, Chiswyck, falls off a walkway and breaks his neck; "some are saying that it was Harren's ghost flung him down." Arya realizes that she is the "ghost in Harrenhal": "*It wasn't Harren*, Arya wanted to say, *it was me*. She had killed Chiswyck with a whisper, and she would kill two more before she was through."[48] When she names the second, Weese, she regrets and wants to pick a better target, only to hear Harrenhal's portcullis slam down on him, as if it were an accident, but for Jaqen leaning from the tower: "When he saw her looking, he lifted a hand to his face and laid two fingers casually against his cheek."[49] She then twists the third request, making double sure that she can name anyone and then naming Jaqen H'ghar himself. "A girl will weep," he answers. "A girl will lose her only friend." She then tells him that he is not a friend if he does not help to free the captives of Harrenhal, to which they make a deal that she will unname him if he helps. "*I'm not an evil child*," she reflects. "*I am a direwolf, and the ghost in Harrenhal*."[50] What makes Arya able to trick Jaqen, in other words, is a sense of her own identity, that she is a Stark of Winterfell and the real ghost who is haunting Harrenhal by whispering names to be killed.

What Jaqen then shows Arya is that her knowledge is only partially complete. After freeing the captives, Arya tells him that he does not need to die, to which he replies, "I do. My time is done," ripping off his face to reveal a completely new identity. Arya is stunned: "'Who *are* you?' she whispered, too astonished to be afraid. 'How did you *do* that? Was it hard?'" He replies that it is "no harder than taking a new name, if you know the way," and then reveals the place to learn it: "Far and away, across the narrow sea." Yet again, the axis of *A Clash of Kings* shifts, even in Arya's character arc, from south to north in her journey, to the possibility of an Eastward shift. Giving her a "small coin," he then reveals the city to which she must go: "As well ask what good is life, what good is death? If the day comes when you would find me again, give that coin to any man from Braavos, and say these words to him—*valar morghulis*."[51] By revealing this place, Jaqen—or whoever this new person is, for as he continues, "Jaqen is as dead as Arry,"[52] insinuating that the taking of a new face is equivalent to the death of one's identity—suggests that Arya's entire arc has always had an Eastern bent, beginning with the First Sword of Braavos, her sword teacher in King's Landing, now to this possibility of shedding one's face altogether.

This "Red God," or in the subsequent books, the "Many-Faced God," of the temple of the Faceless Men in Braavos, offers a key to interpreting how the eastwardly mysticism in *A Song of Ice and Fire* might be interpreted: it is, if one were to search for meaning, *nothing*. The truth that one might go East to learn, whether in Braavos or Asshai, through texts or temples, is that the search for meaning in the supernatural, in the irruption of the postsecular in fire from the east, is futile. It is thus that both Melisandre and Daenerys are frequently wrong about the significance of their magical acts of fire, the former with inaccurate predictions about the future and the personification of Azor Ahai, the latter with her pretensions to queenship based on the postsecular fact that she is bringing dragons from the East. What Arya learns is that what is to be learned about the postsecular orient is that it, *pace* Said, has *nothing* to contribute to the politics, meaning-making, or self-identification of life in Westeros. The postsecular simply *is*, in the sense that the secularization of Westerosi politics into a "*game of thrones*" that one either wins or dies, is overdetermined. There is magic, there is fire, there are dragons, and there may even be winged men in Asshai. But in the end, all men must die.

CONCLUSION: THE EMPTINESS OF POSTSECULAR ORIENTALISM

The geographical framework of *A Song of Ice and Fire*, I have been arguing in this chapter, broadly dovetails with the overarching grid in Said's *Orientalism*. Positing that the postsecular is incorporated within the secular West by integrating the East, Said theorizes that there is often a theological colonization of the "Orient" through the imaginative geographies that frame it as exotically backward in its technocratic inabilities. Similarly, the shift in *A Clash of Kings* along an East-West axis from *A Game of Thrones* seems to follow this orientalist imaginary, framing the emergence of fire, be it from the Lord of Light or the dragons of the Targaryens, as coming from an eastward direction to be integrated into the Westerosian secular apparatus of the "*game of thrones*" in which one simply wins or dies.

But following Johnston, Bettis, Cowlishaw, and others who argue that Martin tends to subvert the narrative tropes that are typical of Western literary genres, orientalism is also subverted. The characters that are presented in *A Clash of Kings*'s re-orientation of the narrative toward the East seem to be working out their identities in relation to an eastern geography: Melisandre in relation to the religion of R'hillor and the arts of shadowbinding from Asshai, Daenerys in terms of what it means to have dragons, and Arya in her fascination with the ability of the Faceless Men of Braavos to change identities as they offer the gift of death to their assassination victims. But whereas in Said, postsecular orientalism always presumes an imaginative content that is incorporated into Western consciousness, Martin suggests that this integration is the reason for the misinterpretation of prophecies, mythologies, and character arcs. For Rhaegar, Melisandre, and Daenerys, Azor Ahai, the Prince that was Promised, has to mean something, the supernatural fueling their sense of destiny. Yet in the wake of trying to figure out what the ancient lore means for them via the methodologies of the textual attitude of orientalism, all that it caused was war and mayhem in Westeros. Jaqen H'ghar, however, shows Arya the way forward, which is what Quaithe is also trying to show Daenerys and what Melisandre's failures are supposed to mean: nothing, except that all men must die.

Free of a sense of destiny, the answer in High Valyrian is *valar dohaeris*, all men must serve. It is true, then, that one must go East in order to reach the West: one must see that there is nothing in postsecular orientalism, no one in the legends of Azor Ahai or the prophecies of the Prince that Was Promised, no meaning in shadowbinding or dragons, in order to be free of a sense of destiny. Such freedom would allow the characters to embrace the possibility that the word of the gods, whether R'hillor or the Many-Faced God, the old gods or the new, is not that they will usher the chosen into a fixed destiny, but that they will accompany all into the abyss. To touch the light, one must go under the shadow, for shadows are made by the brightness of light, and the meaning of the shadow being bound is that one discovers the truest destination of all flesh: death.

NOTES

1. Edward Said, *Orientalism*, 3rd ed. (London: Penguin, 2003), 93.
2. Ibid., 122.
3. Alasdair MacIntyre, *After Virtue: A Study in Moral Theory* (Notre Dame, IN: University of Notre Dame Press, 1984).
4. John Milbank, Catherine Pickstock, and Graham Ward, eds., *Radical Orthodoxy: A New Theology* (London and New York: Routledge, 1999); Catherine

Pickstock, *After Writing: On the Liturgical Consummation of Philosophy* (Oxford: Blackwell, 1998); *Repetition and Identity* (Oxford: Oxford University Press, 2013); John Milbank, *Theology and Social Theory*, 2nd ed. (Oxford: Blackwell, 2006); *The Suspended Middle: Henri de Lubac and the Debate Concerning the Supernatural* (London: SCM Press, 2005); *Beyond Secular Order: The Representation of Being and the Representation of the People* (Malden, MA and Oxford: Wiley-Blackwell, 2013); John Milbank and Adrian Pabst, *The Politics of Virtue: Post-Liberalism and the Human Future* (London: Rowman and Littlefield, 2016).

5. Talal Asad, Formations of the Secular: Christianity, Islam, Modernity (Stanford: Stanford University Press, 2003); Secular Translations: Nation-State, Modern Self, and Calculative Reason (New York and Chichester: Columbia University Press, 2018); Saba Mahmood, *Politics of Piety: The Islamic Revival and the Feminist Subject* (Princeton and London: Princeton University Press, 2005); *Religious Difference in a Secular Age: A Minority Report* (Princeton and London: Princeton University Press, 2015); Charles Hirschkind, *The Ethical Soundscape: Cassette Sermons and Islamic Counterpublics* (New York and Chichester: Columbia University Press, 2009); Hussein Ali Agrama, *Questioning Secularism: Islam, Sovereignty, and the Rule of Law in Modern Egypt* (Chicago and London: University of Chicago Press, 2012).

6. Charles Taylor, *A Secular Age* (Cambridge, MA: Belknap Press of Harvard University Press, 2007); Judith Butler, "Sexual politics, torture, and secular time," *British Journal of Sociology* 59, no. 1 (2008): 1–23; Justin KH Tse, "Grounded Theologies: 'Religion' and the 'Secular' in Human Geography," *Progress in Human Geography* 38, no. 2 (2014): 201–220; Joan Wallach Scott, *Sex and Secularism* (Princeton and London: Princeton University Press, 2017).

7. J. Kameron Carter, *Race: A Theological Account* (Oxford and New York: Oxford University Press, 2008); Gil Anidjar, *Blood: A Critique of Christianity* (New York and Chichester: Columbia University Press, 2014).

8. Slavoj Žižek, *The Fragile Absolute, Or Why is the Christian Legacy Worth Fighting For?* (London: Verso, 2000); *The Puppet and the Dwarf: The Perverse Core of Christianity* (Cambridge, MA and London: MIT Press, 2003); *Less Than Nothing: Hegel and the Shadow of Dialectical Materialism* (London: Verso, 2012); Slavoj Žižek and John Milbank, *The Monstrosity of Christ: Paradox or Dialectic?*, ed. Creston Davis (Cambridge, MA and London: MIT Press, 2009); Slavoj Žižek and Boris Gunjević, *God in Pain: Inversions of Apocalypse*, trans. Ellen Elias-Bursac (New York: Seven Stories Press).

9. Paul Cloke, Christopher Baker, Callum Sutherland, and Andrew Williams, *Geographies of Postsecularity: Re-envisioning Politics, Subjectivity, and Ethics* (London and New York: Routledge, 2019), 3.

10. The "social formation" as a colonizing order of things gridded together by an infrastructure of networked institutions has one of its best introductions as a concept in Gary Y. Okihiro, *Third World Studies: Theorizing Liberation* (Durham and London: Duke University Press, 2016).

11. Susan Johnston and Jes Battis, "Introduction: On Knowing Nothing," in *Mastering the Game of Thrones: Essays on George R.R. Martin's A Song of Ice and*

Fire, eds. Jes Battis and Susan Johnston (Jefferson, NC: McFarland and Company, 2015), 3.

12. George R. R. Martin, 'Maps! Maps! Maps!' *Not a Blog*, 30 October 2012. Accessed 2 April 2019, from https://grrm.livejournal.com/297016.html

13. Brian Cowlishaw, "What Maesters Knew: Narrating Knowing," in *Mastering the Game of Thrones: Essays on George R.R. Martin's A Song of Ice and Fire*, eds. Jes Battis and Susan Johnston (Jefferson, NC: McFarland and Company, 2015), 64.

14. George R. R. Martin, *A Clash of Kings* (New York: Bantam, 2011), 701.

15. George R. R. Martin, *A Game of Thrones* (New York: Bantam, 2011), 18

16. Ibid., 22.

17. Ibid., 23.

18. George R. R. Martin, *Fire and Blood* (New York: Bantam, 2018), 546.

19. See also, George R. R. Martin, *A Knight of the Seven Kingdoms* (New York: Bantam, 2015), 260, where the characters are reminded that the status of "Egg" as Aegon V Targaryen means, as Ser Duncan the Tall, or "Dunk," reflects, "*Of course they'd put a dragon egg in his cradle*"—one that they naturally have trouble hatching in a secular age after the Dance of Dragons.

20. *A Game of Thrones*, 488.

21. Ibid., 634.

22. Ibid., 807.

23. *A Clash of Kings*, 20.

24. Ibid., 21.

25. Ibid., 29

26. Ibid., 146.

27. Ibid., 148.

28. Ibid., 155.

29. Ibid., 502.

30. Ibid., 619, italics removed.

31. Ibid., 621–622.

32. Ibid., 623.

33. Ibid., 582.

34. Ibid., 202.

35. Ibid., 583.

36. Ibid., 583.

37. Ibid., 704.

38. George R. R. Martin, *A Storm of Swords* (New York: Bantam: 2011), 113.

39. Ibid., 111.

40. George R. R. Martin, *A Feast for Crows*, (New York: Bantam: 2011), 108.

41. George R. R. Martin, *A Dance of Dragons* (New York: Bantam, 2013), 159.

42. *A Storm of Swords*, 375.

43. *A Dance with Dragons*, 166.

44. Ibid., 1026.

45. *A Storm of Swords*, 107.

46. *A Clash of Kings*, 86.

47. Ibid., 465.

48. Ibid., 468–469.
49. Ibid., 556.
50. Ibid., 685.
51. Ibid., 691.
52. Ibid., 692.

BIBLIOGRAPHY

Agrama, Hussein Ali. *Questioning Secularism: Islam, Sovereignty, and the Rule of Law in Modern Egypt*. Chicago and London: University of Chicago Press, 2012.

Anidjar, Gil. *Blood: A Critique of Christianity*. New York and Chichester: Columbia University Press, 2014.

Asad, Talal. *Formations of the Secular: Christianity, Islam, Modernity*. Stanford: Stanford University Press, 2003.

———. *Secular Translations: Nation-State, Modern Self, and Calculative Reason*. New York and Chichester: Columbia University Press, 2018.

Butler, Judith. "Sexual politics, torture, and secular time." *British Journal of Sociology* 59, no. 1 (2008): 1–23.

Carter, J. Kameron. *Race: A Theological Account*. Oxford and New York: Oxford University Press, 2008.

Cloke, Paul, Christopher Baker, Callum Sutherland, and Andrew Williams. *Geographies of Postsecularity: Re-envisioning Politics, Subjectivity, and Ethics*. London and New York: Routledge, 2019.

Cowlishaw, Brian. "What Maesters Knew: Narrating Knowing," in *Mastering the Game of Thrones: Essays on George R.R. Martin's A Song of Ice and Fire*, eds. Jes Battis and Susan Johnston, 57–69. Jefferson, NC: McFarland and Company, 2015.

Hirschkind, Charles. *The Ethical Soundscape: Cassette Sermons and Islamic Counterpublics*. New York and Chichester: Columbia University Press, 2009.

Johnston, Susan, and Jes Battis. "Introduction: On Knowing Nothing," in *Mastering the Game of Thrones: Essays on George R.R. Martin's A Song of Ice and Fire*, eds. Jes Battis and Susan Johnston, 1–14. Jefferson, NC: McFarland and Company, 2015.

MacIntyre, Alasdair. *After Virtue: A Study in Moral Theory*. Notre Dame, IN: University of Notre Dame Press, 1984.

Mahmood, Saba. *Politics of Piety: The Islamic Revival and the Feminist Subject*. Princeton and London: Princeton University Press, 2005.

———. *Religious Difference in a Secular Age: A Minority Report*. Princeton and London: Princeton University Press, 2015.

Martin, George R.R. *A Clash of Kings*. New York: Bantam, 2011.

———. *A Dance of Dragons*. New York: Bantam, 2013.

———. *A Feast for Crows*. New York: Bantam: 2011.

———. *Fire and Blood*. New York: Bantam, 2018.

———. *A Game of Thrones*. New York: Bantam, 2011.

———. *A Knight of the Seven Kingdoms*. New York: Bantam, 2015.

———. 'Maps! Maps! Maps!' *Not a Blog*, 30 October 2012. Accessed 2 April 2019, from https://grrm.livejournal.com/297016.html.
———. *A Storm of Swords*. New York: Bantam: 2011.
Milbank, John. *Beyond Secular Order: The Representation of Being and the Representation of the People*. Malden, MA and Oxford: Wiley-Blackwell, 2013.
———. *The Suspended Middle: Henri de Lubac and the Debate Concerning the Supernatural*. London: SCM Press, 2005.
———. *Theology and Social Theory*, 2nd ed. Oxford: Blackwell, 2006.
Milbank, John, and Adrian Pabst. *The Politics of Virtue: Post-Liberalism and the Human Future*. London: Rowman and Littlefield, 2016.
Milbank, John, Catherine Pickstock, and Graham Ward, eds. *Radical Orthodoxy: A New Theology*. London and New York: Routledge, 1999.
Okihiro, Gary Y. *Third World Studies: Theorizing Liberation*. Durham and London: Duke University Press, 2016.
Pickstock, Catherine. *After Writing: On the Liturgical Consummation of Philosophy*. Oxford: Blackwell, 1998.
———. *Repetition and Identity*. Oxford: Oxford University Press, 2013.
Said, Edward. *Orientalism*, 3rd ed. London: Penguin, 2003.
Scott, Joan Wallach. *Sex and Secularism*. Princeton and London: Princeton University Press, 2017.
Taylor, Charles. *A Secular Age*. Cambridge, MA: Belknap Press of Harvard University Press, 2007.
Tse, Justin KH. "Grounded Theologies: 'Religion' and the 'Secular' in Human Geography." *Progress in Human Geography* 38, no. 2 (2014): 201–220.
Žižek, Slavoj. *The Fragile Absolute, Or Why is the Christian Legacy Worth Fighting For?* London: Verso, 2000.
———. *Less Than Nothing: Hegel and the Shadow of Dialectical Materialism*. London: Verso, 2012.
———. *The Puppet and the Dwarf: The Perverse Core of Christianity*. Cambridge, MA and London: MIT Press, 2003.
Žižek, Slavoj, and Boris Gunjević. *God in Pain: Inversions of Apocalypse*, trans. Ellen Elias-Bursac New York: Seven Stories Press, 2008.
Žižek, Slavoj, and John Milbank. *The Monstrosity of Christ: Paradox or Dialectic?*, ed. Creston Davis. Cambridge, MA and London: MIT Press, 2009.

Chapter 10

Comparative Worldview Studies and *A Song of Ice and Fire*: World Religions, Comparison, and Fictional Worlds

Nathan Fredrickson

In this chapter, I use *A Song of Ice and Fire* to model a comparative worldview studies approach to fictional worldviews, because such an approach may advance the study of both religious and nonreligious worldviews outside the well-known constraints of past frameworks and categories. Due to space limitations, I only examine a portion of the impressive array of worldviews found in *A Song of Ice and Fire*, but they are sufficient to characterize Martin's approach to fictional world- and worldview-making and its relationship to the trap of essentialist thinking. I apply common categories of worldview studies (*ontology, cosmology, epistemology, axiology,* and *praxeology*) to the fictional worldviews in *A Song of Ice and Fire*. These categories refer to fundamental problems encountered by even the simplest forms of life. Specifying the nature of a fictional worldview, through the use of these categories, facilitates comparison not only between fictional worldviews (including those that might typically be neglected, because they are not "religious") but also with the extradiegetic worldviews on which they are modeled and of which they thus constitute an extended part of worldview families.

The study of fictional religions has tended to reflect biases evident in the comparative "world religions" paradigm—for example, privileging certain highly popular works and interpreting them primarily through the lenses and categories of (almost exclusively Protestant Christian) theology and (Western) philosophy. In the field of religious studies, the world religions paradigm—together with the more general project of comparing religions—has been intensely criticized for its bias in favor of Christian (especially Protestant) categories, its privileging of certain traditions (the "big five") and neglect of others (indigenous religions, non-elite forms, secular worldviews, etc.), its connections to colonialist projects, its abstraction and neglect of particularity, and its conceptual incoherence.[1] However, the power and value of comparison and the importance of the kind of cultural literacy intended to be promoted by studying and teaching the "world religions" has led scholars to try to respond to the critiques and propose solutions.[2] One of the most effective solutions has been a proposed return to Ninian Smart's[3] call for "religious studies" to reformulate itself as "worldview studies," but on a more solid evolutionary foundation,[4] so that scholars might comparatively study a fully inclusive range of worldviews with categories that do not privilege some over others.[5] An added benefit, particularly within the context of studying fantastika, wherein one encounters a fabulous array of imagined beings with distinctive worldviews and ways of life, is that such a worldview studies paradigm helps avoid an excessive anthropocentrism that may hinder appreciation of an author's attempts to create, for example, the worldviews of sentient trees, dragons, and other nonhuman beings.

As stated above, five popular worldview studies categories are *ontology*, *cosmology*, *epistemology*, *axiology*, and *praxeology*. *Ontology* refers to the problem, faced by all living things, of identifying what exists in one's environment, and *cosmology* extends this, being a response to the deeper question of the nature of what exists: How do things relate to each other? What is their nature? Where do they come from? What is their purpose or end? In its fully developed sense, the category of cosmology seems to require the ability to communicate symbolically, but all animals need to come up with basic answers, implicit in their behavior, to the question of the nature of relevant things in their environment. An animate being will have different properties, a different nature—such as potentially being a predator—from an inanimate being, for example. *Epistemology* reflects the need to know, to answer the question of how relevant information about one's self and one's world may be discovered, and even to interrogate that knowing, to ask and answer the question of whether one's knowledge is valid.[6] *Axiology* answers the vital question of what matters to a living thing. What is important, valuable, special, or worthy of pursuit? And, finally, *praxeology* is a creature's answer to the question—emerging in relation to its knowledge of what exists and what matters for it—of how it should behave, what it should do. All together, an animal's responses to these questions constitute its *worldview and way of life*, and the questions are deeply interrelated. For example, reflecting on the epistemic problem of knowledge in *A Song of Ice and Fire*, particularly relative to the maesters, Cowlishaw states,

> [M]aesters are central to Westeros's edifices of power. Maesters are the individuals designated to *know*, when very few others know much of anything. Knowing is their raison d'être. They know more than the kings and lords they

serve. By the authority of their state-approved knowledge, they define the ontology and status of nearly everything and everyone in the kingdom.[7]

Thus, in the case of the maesters, power over the central problem of knowledge leads to power over other basic questions of existence, meaning, and value that structure behavior. Although *worldview* may be used as a shorthand for the expression *worldview and way of life*, one should keep in mind the full expression, thus helping one avoid an overly cerebral, vision-based, abstract, or belief-oriented interpretation of the worldview studies approach, which always includes the body, the environment, behavior, and unconscious cognitive processes.

Though all animals *implicitly* respond to the important questions that underlie the main categories of worldview studies, humans are able to explicitly articulate their answers. This capacity for symbolic representation, however, allows humans to externalize, criticize, and reform their worldviews, leading to a proliferation of worldviews, including fictional worlds and worldviews (and other "fictional" conceptual tools), that are available to humans to entertain and use.[8] Because human creativity is cumulative,[9] using available worldviews to fashion new ones, human worldviews possess family resemblances.[10] In the context of American religious multiplicity, Melton's[11] approach to the problem of categorization in his *Encyclopedia of American Religions* rather effectively groups religions according to their family resemblances, but his work is limited to "religions," ignoring many of the influential worldviews that Americans adhere to. The worldview studies approach both encompasses the full range of philosophies, ideologies (e.g., political and economic), mystical systems, academic theories, spiritualities, magical systems, and so on that are included in the comparative project and supplies useful categories for comparison and identification of family resemblances that do not privilege certain worldviews over others.

The inclusion of *fictional* worldviews in the already ambitious worldview studies project complicates things in interesting and uniquely challenging ways, opening the field of inquiry to the vast array of other fictional worldviews that may be potential contributors in the making of a given fictional worldview. Additionally, reflecting a complication that has become increasingly relevant in considering religious innovation relative to globalization (e.g., consumption of mass media representations of other worldviews, interaction of worldviews due to cosmopolitan pluralism, etc.), the makers of fictional worlds and worldviews innovate in an often highly unconstrained fashion. A given novel worldview maybe, say, a synthesis of (1) a fictional worldview from another influential fictional storyworld, (2) an academic theory of "religion," and three "real" religions—(3) one Asian, (4) one an American New Religious Movement, and (5) one from ancient Mesopotamia.

Unlike a real-world religion that may have a clear historical lineage that helps identify its familial relationship to a worldview family, identifying a fictional worldview's membership in a worldview family or families requires a broad literacy in both *fantastika* (an umbrella term for non-mimetic genres like science fiction, fantasy, and horror, in which the making of novel fictional worldviews tend to occur) and the range of "real" human worldviews.

The categories of "religious" studies have often been used to naturalize and further entrench the interests of the powerful, and one hopes that a more "objective" worldview studies framework, rooted in evolution and cognition, would help unmask the workings of power in systems of representation like Martin's. This leads me to address the question of Martin's representation of racial and ethnic essentialism—a problem that invites one to return to the Tolkienian worldview (as I often do in the worldview analyses below) as a foil for Martin's project and ask the question: does *A Song of Ice and Fire* have an overarching worldview that promotes some way of life, a mode, or manner of responding to or being in the world?

Yes. Under the section below on the Faceless Men, I express my agreement with Wittingslow that "it is the belief of the Many-Faced God that most closely cleaves to the metaphysics of Martin's universe."[12] I then argue for a more nuanced reading of how Martin constructs the worldview of the Faceless Men than that advanced by Wittingslow; however, Wittingslow's argument is quite relevant to the question of what manner of being in the world is promoted by exposure to Martin's storyworld.

Gierzynski's[13] *The Political Effects of Entertainment Media: How Fictional Worlds Affect Real World Political Perspectives* describes, in part, how exposure to *Game of Thrones*' persistent violations of the "just world script" leads to a measurable decline in belief in a just world. *Game of Thrones* evokes some of the most pressing problems of our age—the sense among many of a return to a kind of capitalist-corporate feudalism, the pressing threat of global climate change, and such—but responds, not with the Tolkienian spectacle and magic of an eucatastrophe but with the Lovecraftian apocalypse of mortality, of the inevitability of death. One might argue that the overall worldview advanced by Martin's complex storyworld enervates even while it enchants.

In this, it may be compared to two recent original words released by Netflix, *Black Mirror: Bandersnatch* (2018) and *Russian Doll* (2019), which illustrate alternative responses to human finitude. Like *Bandersnatch*'s multiverse of possible narrative pathways, Martin's abundance of contradictory worldviews evokes a postmodern sense of the constructedness or fictionality of the various perspectives and ways of being in the world supplied by different cultures. One is left without a metanarrative or master story,[14] and certainly without a "just world script," which lack is accompanied, for many, by a mood of passivity, cynicism, or depression.[15] Like the Tolkienian myth, and unlike the world of *A Song of Ice and Fire*, *Russian Doll* treats the serious problem of mortality as a reason to cherish life, to make a livable story for oneself, indeed, to have hope. Though both Tolkien and Martin are noteworthy in the degree of realism they bring to their fantastical worldmaking, the former tempers the tragedy of implacable loss and decline with the (Catholic) spectacle of enduring magic (i.e., grace and sacramentality)[16] and the hope of its ultimate resurrection better than before, while the latter, who also is drawn by concern with death to the tragic genre wherein great souls suffer greatly, lives in a godless ("pagan") world in which no deus ex machina can realistically intervene, in which all heroes die—and some rise colder and harder. In schools where character formation is part of the argument for religious studies or worldview studies courses, the effects works of fantastika might have on percipients may be decisive, or at least call for instructors' to provide critical interventions.

Having surveyed some of the worldviews and ways of life in Martin's *A Song of Ice and Fire* storyworld (to examine the details of particular worldviews of interest, see below), one may make at least four general conclusions relative to the project of worldview studies.

1. A complex work of mythopoeic worldmaking like *A Song of Ice and Fire* invites the kind of on-the-ground comparative worldview studies thinking that has long been promoted by "comparative religion." And it may even encourage readers to develop worldview literacy outside the storyworld. For this reason, works of fantastika may be especially well suited to the religious studies or worldview studies classroom, and, in addition to pedagogical applications, the scientific study of "religion" (and of "religious studies" as an academic discipline) would benefit from further examination of the specific effects reading and viewing works of fantastika may have on people.
2. Fictional worldview studies demands of scholars a broad worldview literacy that encompasses familiarity with contemporary, ancient, fictional, and academic-theoretical worldviews. This likely means the including fictional worldviews as part of a larger worldview studies project would promote collaborative and interdisciplinary efforts—the requisite expertise simply cannot dwell in a single scholar or, even, in a single department like gender studies, religious studies, or Black studies.
3. As a study of representations, fictional worldview studies cannot evade the problem of power and its relationship to symbolic expression and meaning making, a problem that resurfaces constantly as one attempts to analyze fictional worldviews. Martin's racial and ethnic essentialisms (see below) and promotion of a cynical worldview overall (as noted

above) provide a robust example of how unavoidable considerations of power are in such analyses.
4. Martin's storyworld contains many worldviews, displaying a "worlds within worlds" complexity that gives it an aura of reality, but Martin's worldviews are themselves unlike real-world worldviews. Outside of Westeros,[17] they are flat, dimensionless, lacking themselves the "worlds within worlds" property, the inner diversity that is ubiquitous in real worldviews. This reinforces racial and ethnic essentialism and is only counteracted by specific characterizations of individuals, who do constitute "worlds" within their larger social worlds.

WORLDVIEWS AND WAYS OF LIFE IN THE *GAME OF THRONES*

The following analyses of worldviews and ways of life in the storyworld of *A Song of Ice and Fire*/*Game of Thrones* is not comprehensive, but it does endeavor to be robustly representative of Martin's elaborate worldmaking. It draws heavily on Martin, García Jr., and Antonsson's *The World of Ice and Fire: The Untold History of Westeros and the Game of Thrones*.[18]

The Children of the Forest[19]

Worldview Families: Native American; Druid and Norse religion and myth; animism; influences from other fantasy storyworlds containing American Indian-related cultures; Tolkien's elven religion (with its underlying Christian-Norse elements)

Commentary:
The manner in which the children of the forest's worldview singularizes or centers on the weirwoods evokes the theme of the tree in Tolkien and, more generally, the environmentalist theme in seminal figures like Tolkien and Lewis that has exercised a powerful influence on fantastika in general.[20] The fact that the trees of the children of the forest are also associated with the sacrifice of blood and life points to a similar synthesis of Christian crucifixion and Norse conceptions of, for example, the world tree, the association of gods with trees, Óðinn's sacrifice of himself to himself by being hanged on the world tree,[21] and so on that may also be noted in Tolkien's worldmaking. In Tolkien, the light of the cosmic trees,[22] Laurelin and Telperion, captured by Fëanor in the silmarils, is intimately related to the light of the one God, Eru Ilúvatar, and there is a strong association of the descendants of Telperion, such as Nimloth, the White Tree of Númenor, and the four successive White

Table 10.1 Worldview of the Children of the Forest

Big Question	Worldview and Way of Life
Ontology and Cosmology	Details unknown (perhaps some account of the nature of the children themselves, the giants, and the old gods)
Epistemology	Empirical perception; greenseeing—for the greenseers, time is known in a non-linear fashion as a totality of past and present, with also a degree of prophetic foresight
Axiology	Nature; the "old gods" of nature, especially the weirwoods; song; simple technology (simplicity); magic; blood; the children of the forest themselves
Praxeology	Working dragonglass, wood, and bone to fashion tools and weapons; using weirwood and grass to make bows and flying snares; making clothing from leaves and bark; making simple homes, including tree towns; singing and playing music; worship of natural features ("the innumerable gods of the streams and forests and stones" (ibid., 6); carved faces in the weirwoods; blood sacrifice; magic of the greenseers (warging, communication with ravens; knowledge of past and future, telepathy, the Breaking, and the making the Others); fighting the giants and, later, the humans

Trees of Gondor, with divine favor of righteous human kingship. Tolkien's elves' close relationship with trees and trees' strong association with divine communion and favor, then, seem to have played a role in the construction of the children of the forest's worldview and way of life and, perhaps, help account for the fact that the death of the trees is linked to their doom. And Tolkien's deployment of sacred trees reflects an old European pagan-Christian synthesis. Cusack's[23] *The Sacred Tree: Ancient and Medieval Manifestations* may be the most useful work for reflecting on the primary source for the dynamic Martin describes between the children of the forest and the First Men and, later, between the First Men and the Andals, for Cusack explains how important sacred trees were to pre-Christian European peoples, how Christians attempted to destroy such pagan idols, and how they were eventually syncretized with Christian cosmology and worship.

The manner in which the children of the forest have melted away and—with sadness and regret, but not anger—have surrendered to the inevitability of human ascendance aligns with the trope of the vanishing Indian as part of the American frontier myth, as described in Michail Zontos's[24] essay, "Dividing Lines: Frederick Jackson Turner's Western Frontier and George R.R. Martin's Northern Wall." Zontos states:

> As Tom Holm argues, "by the early nineteenth century, many white Americans ... adhered to the idea that American Indians were mystically in tune with the wonders of the natural world." For this reason they used to call them "children

of the forest." This connection was for many Americans the reason that Native Americans, "along with the forests and streams, would be crushed under the advance of a 'civilized' society." (Holm 54)[25]

Zontos's focus is on the wildlings, whose worldview and way of life is discussed below, but the children of the forest, the giants, and the wildlings all evidently participate in the American narrative tradition that has constructed the colonized first peoples of the United States as savages (though, as in the case of the children of the forest, noble ones) who necessarily fade out of existence as "civilization" (i.e., white colonization) advances. The romanticized role played by the children of the forest, relative to Bran, resembles that played by the Indian spirit guides and guardians who appeared to Spiritualist mediums from the mid-1800s through the end of the century, consoling them and counseling them.[26]

Though many aspects of the concern with blood and its power in fantasy fiction have far more to do with its functions in the Christian worldview[27] than with its role in indigenous worldviews, the conflation of ideas of druidic human sacrifice and ideas of Indian blood magic[28] and human sacrifice may also be observed in fantastical works like Madeleine L'Engle's[29] *An Acceptable Time*, the final volume of her *Time Quintet*, which begins with the far more famous *A Wrinkle in Time* (1962). It describes druids as having come to America and produced a hybrid culture with the Native Americans. (Orson Scott Card's fantasy of an alternative colonial U.S., *The Tales of Alvin Maker* series, likewise emphasizes Indian use of blood magic, sacrifice, and animistic oneness with nature—including Indians' ability to hear the "greensong.") Martin similarly seems to have syncretized ideas of druidic tree worship and Native American "children of the forest," perhaps even drawing on Native American ideas of giants and magical little people.[30] Concerning the children of the forest's potential for destruction, see below under the sections on the merlings and the southern Lengii.

The children of the forest, who call themselves "those who sing the song of earth,"[31] venerate nature, particularly the weirwoods. Warging[32] and skinchanging resemble the use of the "wit" in Robin Hobb's *The Realm of the Elderlings* series, and the capacity of weirwoods to retain memory and extend consciousness displays suggestive similarities to Hobb's wizardwood (i.e., sea-serpent/dragon cocoon) and memory stone[33] in *The Realm of the Elderlings* series and, more importantly, similarities to the Eldar Trees of the Speck people in Hobb's *Soldier Son Trilogy*,[34] who, like the children of the forest, fight the colonizing humans to defend their way of life. The tragedy of the destruction of the weirwoods parallels the cultural genocide of the many Native American peoples who were displaced from the lands in which their stories were anchored and their ways of life located. The weirwoods literally give the children of the forest access, through their greenseers, to the memory of the world, so their destruction by careless, greedy humans is a threat to their very being, all their ancestors' "histories and prayers, everything they knew about this world."[35]

Racial essentialism, ubiquitous in fantastical texts and subjected to much scholarly analysis and critique, poses distinct problems for worldview studies. As illustrated by the apparent homogeneity and opacity of the giant and children-of-the-forest worldviews and ways of life, racial essentialism flattens and obscures the answers peoples themselves might supply to worldview questions. Othering and dehumanization (i.e., the reduction of humans to "animals") frequently accompany racial projects[36] that incline toward essentialism and racism. The most extreme and obvious case of this in Martin's storyworld is the Others,[37] whose worldview and way of life may be surfaced only by observation of behavior.[38] The dragons (like the wyverns,[39] ice dragons of the Shivering Sea,[40] sea dragons,[41] stone giants,[42] ice spiders,[43] centaurs,[44] tiger-people,[45] shrykes,[46] ghouls,[47] direwolves,[48] shadowcats,[49] basilisks, selkies and walrus-men, krakens and leviathans, grumkins and snarks, and most other intelligent supernatural beings), similarly, possess only an unarticulated (though perhaps not inarticulate),[50] implicit worldview and way of life.

The First Men[51]

Worldview Families: the children of the forest (and thus, as discussed above, the kind of hyperreal Druidism and stereotyped Indian culture circulating in popular fiction); Tolkien's unfallen Númenóreans; American colonists; Pragmatism

Commentary:
The First Men's [sic] eventual participation in the worldview of the children of the forest and, indeed, the worldview of the children itself suggest parallels with Tolkien's Númenóreans and the elven worldview they embraced (though in other respects, the Númenórean worldview, drawing on the model of the Roman Empire, is more obviously a model for the Valyrians). The situation illustrates Tolkien's lasting influence on the fantasy megatext.

Contact and alliance with magical beings is transformative in Martin's world. Valyrian interaction with dragons, as discussed below, gives their people unique powers and properties. Similarly, some special individuals among the First Men and their descendants, such as the northern people of Westeros above and below the Wall, seem to be able to skin-change due to their association with the children of the forest and their participation in the way of life that involves some people, as rare among skin-changers as skin-changers are among ordinary people, uniting with the immortal weirwoods as greenseers. This way of life destabilizes the separation of human and non-human life,

Table 10.2 Worldview of the First Men

Big Question	Worldview and Way of Life
Ontology and Cosmology	Abandoned previous cosmology focused on divine sexual union or combat between sky and sea for the animistic cosmology of the children of the forest
Epistemology	Ordinary means of knowledge (e.g., perception, inference, reliable sources) and supernatural means—greenseeing and warging/skinchanging (use of ravens to convey knowledge over long distances); runes
Axiology	Life and livelihood; old gods (especially godswoods and heart trees); guest right; the dead; freedom to elect rulers; sacred orders of the Green Men and the Night's Watch
Praxeology	Practices and techniques to support life and combat others; free worship of the old gods—without ritualism; having the heart trees of the godswoods observe significant life events; sharing bread and salt with guests and giving them gifts; burying the dead; electing leaders and respecting each person's voice; maintaining the life of the weirwoods by supporting the Green Men and protecting the living from the dead by supporting the Night's Watch

opening up new epistemic possibilities. Such an ability to take on multiple perspectives would tend to destabilize any dogmatic, totalizing tendencies (note the absence of ritualism) and encourage pragmatism and mutual respect (as in the case of guest right and free election of leaders). Leederman, in an essay entitled "A Thousand Westerosi Plateaus: Wargs, Wolves and Ways of Being," argues,

> Increasingly, *A Song of Ice and Fire* suggests that hegemonic knowledge alone cannot solve our problems; we must look back, to earlier eras now wreathed in legend, and sideways, to other species, for new conceptual tools and ways of being in the world. This supposition has in-canon support from the often incomplete (though admittedly dutiful) hegemonic monopoly of knowledge and specialization practiced by the maesters, whom Marin often portrays as unprepared and even dismissive of the world's greatest threats.[52]

The ludic capacity to entertain multiple perspectives,[53] which is vital for worldview studies, is cultivated by interacting with multiple stories, different narrative perspectives. The First Men stopped killing the children of the forest and started listening, and from the children they gained access to many other perspectives. Pragmatism has been described as the distinctively American philosophy. It is closely allied with the perspectivist capacity to entertain multiple viewpoints since different perspectives, like other conceptual instruments and models, may deal more effectively than others with various situations and problems. Pragmatism has been variously linked to Black Americans[54] and Native Americans,[55] and one might note a robustly ludic element in both Afrodiasporic and indigenous American worldviews, with their trickster figures, masks, sacred clowns, and other cultural technologies that perhaps helped them remain resilient and adaptive in the face of adversity. Whatever the case, the pragmatism of the First Men seems to draw on an American ideal.

The First Men—though possessing "cowboy" settler qualities (evident especially in the people of the North)—come to be identified far more strongly with the "Indian" traits of the children of the forest, eventually functioning as the wild natives themselves when the quasi-Catholic Andals invade (and, again, in the conflict between the wildlings and the Seven Kingdoms and in the case of lesser groups like the Vale mountain clans).[56] Whereas the First Men took on the worldview of the children of the forest with a modified agrarian way of life adapted to their new worldview, the Andals, after military conquest, eventually tolerated minor expressions of the First Men's worldview (without adopting it) and intermarried, resembling Spanish colonization patterns in America in contrast to British, which more closely resemble the Seven Kingdoms' dominant mode of relation to the wildlings.[57]

The worldview of the First Men has been largely retained by a number of groups, though modified somewhat by interaction with other worldviews and by changed ways of life. Such groups include the peoples of the Kings of Winter/Kings in the North[58] and, later, the Lords of Winterfell,[59] the mountain clans of the Vale,[60] the "stoneborn" of Skagos,[61] the Crannogmen of the Neck,[62] and the wildlings/free folk.[63]

The Dothraki[64]

Worldview Families: Mongolians; Plains Indians; some influence from Frank Herbert's Fremen culture in the *Dune* series and Tolkien's Rohirrim; Jogos Nhai?

Commentary:
Maester Yandel states, "[T]he Dothraki consider the earth to be their mother and think it sinful to cut her flesh with plows and spades and axes."[65] An extended (and widely contested)[66] analysis of the concept of Indians worshiping a Mother Earth goddess as an invention of Western scholarship may be found in Sam Gill's[67] *Mother Earth: An American Story*, focusing on a famous quote very similar to Maester Yandel's above. The Dothraki's gift economy, their devotion to horses, and other customs are modeled after plains Indians. In other respects, they are modeled after Mongolians.[68]

Table 10.3 Worldview of the Dothraki

Big Question	Worldview and Way of Life
Ontology and Cosmology	Born from the Womb of the World (compare the goddess(es) Mother Earth and/or the Mother of Mountains (moon is also a goddess and *khaleesi* of the sun)); the model of the ancient great *khals* of all the Dothraki; the horse god, whom the Dothraki worship and whom the *khals* join after death, lives as *khal* in heaven, and the stars are fiery horses ridden by his *khalasar* of the noble dead; there is a hell
Epistemology	Much special knowledge is preserved by the *dosh khaleen* and the barren female and eunuch male healers; prophecy
Axiology	Mother Earth; the Mother of Mountains; the sacred city of Vaes Dothrak; the *dosh khaleen*—the widows of dead *khals* who rule Vaes Dothrak; being manly; having and riding horses; *khals*; the foretold "stallion who mounts the world"; conquest—signaled by braided hair and bells; gifts; the bloodrider vow and relationship (The intensity of devotion to and identification with the life of the *khal* is unusual, and it involves a number of distinctive practices, comparable to the vows made by same-sex Christian saints and warriors to each other, with the relationship's suicidal end reminding one of *sati*.); honor
Praxeology	Gift economy; conquest; important acts like marriage and sex should happen under an open sky; burning the dead

Like Paul Atreides as messianic "Mahdi" of the Fremen under the guidance of his Bene Gesserit mother, Lady Jessica, the ancient Khal Mengo was advised in his conquest by his mother, the witch queen Doshi, uniting the khalasars and leading them in conquest of the Sarnori kingdoms.[69] The fact that the sacred city is governed by the widows of the khals similarly resembles the Reverend Mothers of the Bene Gesserits and the Fremen—an idea that has influenced much fantastical worldmaking,[70] such as, for example, Robert Jordan's Aes Sedai and Aiel Wise Women. Still, one may not need to resort to fantastical texts to account for this aspect of the Dothraki worldview. Larrington notes that Mongolian "widows had a great deal of authority on the death of their husbands and that the Emperor's mother was given the power 'to execute justice' in his absence."[71]

The Dothraki march of the defeated people of Sathar, in which three-quarters of them died, strikes one as an odd reversal of the Trail of Tears, and the inability of the Sarnori kingdoms to unite against the existential threat of the Dothraki until it was too late seems to be based on European colonization of Native Americans. Again, the Dothraki transforming from wild natives into a great, civilization-conquering force (n.b. the allusions to the way Josephus describes the Roman siege and destruction of Jerusalem in the description of the Dothraki conquest of Mardosh[72]) parallels Frank Herbert's Fremen.

Since the Dothraki ultimately came from further east, past the Bone Mountains, one might speculate that their worldview developed out of one that was, in ancient times, the common ancestor of the present worldview of the Jogos Nhai.[73] Though their physical form and preferred mounts are different, the Jogos Nhai share with the Dothraki a proud warrior culture and a tradition of gender-distributed roles (e.g., the *jhat* [war chief] and the moonsinger [priestess-healer-judge]). The Jogos Nhai seem to have been constructed in key ways as contrasting with the Dothraki, in part by adding features of the Huns (e.g., the head binding) and in part by adding other features of Native American cultures (e.g., the two-spirit or third- and fourth-gender roles). One should note that the Temple of the Moonsingers in Braavos is the foremost house of worship there due to the role moonsingers played in prophesying the location of Braavos, making the people who are the apparent standard-bearer of American values in Essos dependent in their founding history on the help of a people who sound a lot like Indians.

The Andals[74]

Worldview Families: Catholicism; Gnosticism; Neopaganism; Protestantism

Commentary:
The worldview of the Andals contains an inherent tension between this-worldly and otherworldly values. The Faith of the Seven promises and ratifies material prosperity, but at the same time, it expects to be the ultimate concern of the faithful. Over time, members of the Andal ruling class have exhibited varying degrees of devotion to the Faith. In the moment revealed by Martin's narrative, many—perhaps a majority—of the aristocracy have fallen into decadence and varying degrees of unbelief, and, as Larrington observes, in many ways, Martin's representation of "the Faith resembles the corrupt late medieval Church as seen through the eyes of satirists such as Chaucer."[75] That said, the Faith is of central importance in the lives of most ordinary people of Andal descent.

Martin has expanded the Christian notion of the Trinity, drawing on a distinctly Gnostic-Neoplatonic understanding of the one godhead (the pleroma), who in his ultimate oneness is, like the Stranger, unqualified and unknowable, and who emanates a gender-balanced array (syzygies) of male and female gods (aeons). The female deities are taken from the Neopagan "Triple Goddess,"[76] and the male gods affirm the central values of Andal civilization: the hierarchical relationship of obligations that secure justice, which are embodied in the ideal of righteous kingship, technoscientific power, and its military application. The decadence of many of the leaders of the Seven Kingdoms and of the Faith of the Seven has led to a Protestant-like reform movement of humble "sparrows" that is popularizing the kind of discipline that the Faith had typically concentrated in its religious orders. The Faith

Table 10.4 Worldview of the Andals

Big Question	Worldview and Way of Life
Ontology and Cosmology	The Seven Who Are One (Father, Warrior, Smith, Mother, Maiden, Crone, Stranger) dwelt among the ancient Andals and made Hugor of the Hill the first king, taught them to forge iron, and promised King Hugor and his descendants a great kingdom; faith in the Seven protects one from the wights
Epistemology	Sacred knowledge contained in *The Seven-Pointed Star*; High Septon speaks for the gods; the Father and the Crone are especially associated with granting wisdom; ecclesiastical court
Axiology	The number seven (as in the colors of the rainbow, an important symbol, and the seven sacred "wanderers" in the sky); kinship (kin-slaying is the gravest sin, and incest is especially repugnant); guest-right (see Larrington, *Winter Is Coming*, 34–38); kingship; warfare (e.g., the Faith Militant) and trial by combat; light
Praxeology	Worshiping the gods, the seven faces of the one deity, using candles, crystals, song, and prayer; individuals focus on the aspect of the deity most relevant to their concern, and some gods have groups that are specially devoted to them (e.g., the Silent Sisters tend the dead and are devoted to the Stranger; the Faith Militant are especially devoted to the Warrior); septs are the sacred seven-walled buildings wherein the gods are worshipped; septons preside over weddings (i.e., kinship-making), knighting (i.e., warrior-making), and the High Septon anoints the king; though much of the Faith supports the way of life of the aristocracy, other aspects of the Faith promote a simple way of life and service to the poor (e.g., the wandering septons, the holy brothers and sisters, the members of the monastic septries and motherhouses, and the reform movement of the "sparrows")

Militant, with its Warrior's Sons and Poor Fellows, is modeled after the Catholic military orders.

Wittingslow suggests, in essence, that the seven-faced god of the Faith of the Seven has been designed to reflect the structure of the psyche and its individuation in the social world of the Andals:

> Indeed, the seven figures [. . .] seem far more akin to primordial images or character archetypes such as one would find in the work of Carl Jung or, more strikingly, Joseph Campbell in his landmark analysis *The Hero with a Thousand Faces*. [. . .] [T]he two sexed triads in the Seven may be reflective of mankind's relationship with itself, as each triad preserves the gendered aspect of social rules apparent in Martin's universe. [. . .] Moreover, these norms are sufficiently pervasive that any perceived threat to those norms is treated with confusion, if not outright hostility. These roles are both socially informative and world-constituting.[77]

The structure of the pleroma in the Neoplatonic-Gnostic worldview family may be read as a kind of cosmological map, and knowledge of the ultimate reality—the divine mind in both its finite divisions and its ineffable infinitude—is both salvific and therapeutic due to the correspondence of the divine macrocosm and the divine soul as microcosm. As Wittingslow proposes, thinkers like Carl Jung and Martin Heidegger, who secularized the core logic of the Neoplatonic-Gnostic worldview, have promoted its enduring influence.

If there were space, one might consider the worldviews and ways of life of each of the orders of the Faith, the tensions and struggles between the Faith and the Crown, and related issues. Likewise, individual Andal peoples have variations of the basic Andal worldview and way of life that a more fine-grained analysis could unpack. For example, one may note a parallel with the myth of Hugor of the Hill in the way Garth Greenhand, the legendary High King of the First Men, is described as the father of many noble houses, and at the same time the story of Garth Greenhand promotes the values of the children of the forest and the First Men, in that Garth is tied to the fertility of the natural world.[78] This synthesis of Andal-First Men worldviews seems to have flowered in the Reach,[79] the realm of House Tyrell of Highgarden,[80] where the ideals of chivalry are celebrated in song. Other diverse Andal groups include House Tully of Riverrun,[81] House Arryn of the Eyrie,[82] House Lannister of Casterly Rock,[83] and the Stony Dornish.[84]

The Valyrian Dragonlords[85]

Worldview Families: the Ghiscari (compare the cities of Slaver's Bay); Rome; Tolkien's fallen Númenóreans; Feist's Valheru; Hobb's elderlings

Commentary:
It is significant that the only known names of pre-dragonlord Valyrian deities survive as names given to dragons: for example, Balerion, Meraxes, Vhagar, Syrax. The Valyrian dragonlords thought of themselves as being part dragon, an idea embodied in the popular Valyrian symbol of the sphinx, which in its Valyrian variety is half dragon and half human. One might speculate that the prominence of bloodmages in the Valyrian Freehold had to do with the use of blood magic to produce both the dragons (from wyverns) and the Valyrians themselves.[86] The Valyrian obsession with blood purity, in order to preserve the blood of the dragon, led to the practice of incest. The worldview of the Valyrian dragonlords is one of self-worship, prizing wealth, power, and mastery above all, and their magic-subjugated dragons perfectly embody this ideal of violent domination.

I suspect the name "Valyrian," which designates Martin's Dragon Lords, may allude to Raymond Feist's "Valheru," the godlike race of violent dragon riders[87] known for their conquest and enslavement of peoples throughout Feist's cosmos. Robin Hobb's elderlings, in her *The Realm of the Elderlings* series, are transformed from humans to become a new magical race due to

Table 10.5 Worldview of the Valyrian Dragonlords

Big Question	Worldview and Way of Life
Ontology and Cosmology	Descent from dragons, who themselves were born from the volcanic mountains called the Fourteen Flames
Epistemology	Natural means of knowledge as well as supernatural (the dragonlords seem to have access to special dragon-related knowledge. Cox notes an interesting example of this in the case of Daenerys: "Daenerys's perception of warmth in her dragon eggs is not available to others. She feels them as warm, nearly hot, and comes to believe that they are ready to hatch if they can be placed in a hot enough fire; but Ser Jorah Mormont attests that the eggs feel cool to the touch" (Edward Cox, "Magic, Science, and Metaphysics in A Game of Thrones," in *Game of Thrones and Philosophy: Logic Cuts Deeper Than Swords*, ed. Henry Owen Jacoby (Hoboken, NJ: Wiley, 2012), 136)): prophecy, glass candles
Axiology	Dragons; precious metal; magical power—blood and fire related; conquest; slaves; blood purity
Praxeology	Using magic to rule dragons and dragons and magic (e.g., Valyrian steel— the suggestion that the "last hero" (at the end of the Long Night following the Age of Heroes) defeated the Others with a blade of dragonsteel may imply that the forging of Valyrian steel draws on the kind of blood magic (perhaps combined with dragon fire?) suggested by Azor Ahai's murder of his wife, Nissa Nissa; this draws on a long tradition, in fantasy literature and more broadly, of ensouled swords and other objects) to conquer and enslave other humans in order to force them to mine for ore; incest to preserve the blood of the dragon

their interaction with dragons. Like Valyrians, they are able to use magic to manipulate stone, but their relationship with dragons is not one of mastery, but, rather, service and adoration.

With their dragon roads and instrumental use of religious tolerance to pacify their subject peoples, the Valyrians are obviously modeled after Rome[88]— though with a political organization (the "Freehold") more like during the Republican rather than the Imperial period. The Doom of Valyria and many aspects of Valyria itself seem to be modeled after Tolkien's Númenóreans[89] and the destruction of their homeland, the island of Elenna, which involved not only the island being swallowed up by the sea but also fire erupting out of the peak of the sacred mountain, Meneltarma. Tolkien's adaptation of the Atlantis myth, like Martin's, evidently also references the fall of Rome.[90]

The Valyrian dragonlords seem to have adopted much of the worldview and way of life of the Ghiscari Empire that they defeated (the Ghiscari axiology evidently included the founder of Old Ghis and the lockstep legions, Grazdan, the mastery of slaves including their use in fighting pits), the number 33, the harpy and graces, and the making of pyramids, and their cosmology included a concept of 'a fiery hell populated by demons;'[91] the Ghiscari way of life continues in some form in the slaver cities of Astapor (who created the

Unsullied as a synthesis of the ideal of the ancient lockstep legions with the use of castrated slaves),[92] Yunkai, and Meereen.[93] Their pursuit of wealth and power and subjugation of other living things reflect a materialistic, egocentric worldview. Though having intimate knowledge of magic as an instrument of power, the Valyrian dragonlords stopped worshipping their traditional gods, became self-obsessed, and thought of religion as an opiate to pacify and divide the subjects of their domination.

Eight of the Free Cities (excluding Braavos) should be included as members of the Valyrian worldview family, though in the case of the Lorathi, the Norvoshi, and the Qohorik one perhaps gains insight into the pre-dragonlord Valyrian worldview.[94] The Lorathi worldview retains some slight influence from the extinct eunuch-ascetic priests of Boash, the Blind God, who taught the equality of all living things and the value of darkness and negating the self. The Norvoshi have a theocracy, being ruled by the bearded priests of their god, whose name is a secret kept by initiates; their way of life includes wearing hair shirts and self-flagellation, and all Norvoshi are regulated by the three bells of the city, which tell them what to do and when. Thus, the bells are important sources of knowledge, as are the revelations from the priests. The Qohorik also descend from religious dissidents who rejected the religious tolerance and skepticism of the dragonlords, but their practice of blood sacrifice (to their god, the Black Goat) and blood magic (including their ability to work with Valyrian steel) seems to preserve Valyrian ways. The cities of Myr, Lys,[95] and Tyrosh—like the Pentoshi[96] and the Volantenes[97]—reflect the more mercantile, "secularized" worldview of the Valyrian dragonlords,[98] but the priesthood of R'hllor is also powerful.

The Targaryen rulers of Westeros adopted the Faith of the Seven from the Andals, but with some modifications (e.g., the Doctrine of Exceptionalism permitting Targaryen incest), and one might see a survival, though much diminished, of their ancient skill in fire magic in the Alchemists' Guild.

The Braavosi[99]

Worldview Families: Venice, Italian banking, and a general evocation of Renaissance and Enlightenment values; capitalism; the United States

Commentary:
In such Braavosi institutions and achievements as the Iron Bank, the Arsenal, and the Titan one observes the great power—economic and military—Martin attributes to a free people whose representative elect a Sealord to rule them. As a young nation, a melting pot of the world's cultures, that is at the same time the wealthiest and most powerful, with suggestions of global influence through its powerful Iron Bank and the threat of its great military strength,

Table 10.6 Worldview of the Braavosi

Big Question	Worldview and Way of Life
Ontology and Cosmology	The Braavosi story of its origin and nature marks it as both opposed to Valyrian slavery and yet connected to the Valyrian way of life shared by the diverse slaves of Valyria who escaped to found Braavos
Epistemology	Pluralistic acceptance of many perspectives and sources of knowledge
Axiology	Freedom and anti-slavery; tolerance; prosperity; the Uncloaking
Praxeology	Trading (including sex work) and banking; war in defense of people and values (especially anti-slavery); celebration of the Uncloaking; diverse worship

the model of an idealized United States is unmistakable, a United States that is the standard-bearer of Enlightenment values clothed in the garb of medieval and Renaissance Italy.[100] In fact, the Iron Bank may be regarded as the primary embodiment of the Braavosi worldview and an expression of the growing power of transnational banks and corporations in the contemporary world. Giles Gunn[101] in his recent work, *The Pragmatist Turn: Religion, the Enlightenment, and the Formation of American Literature*, has provided a fine analysis of how the spiritual imaginaries of Protestant religion and Enlightenment thinking shaped both the idea of America and the formation of the American canon of literature. Martin's work is an important contribution to this ongoing conversation.[102]

The Faceless Men[103]

Worldview Families: Zen Buddhism and martial arts[104]

Commentary:
Though the goal of self-emptying, self-negation, or self-surrender is hardly unknown in Western traditions like Christianity,[105] including both ancient Western traditions like Neoplatonism and a variety of strands of recent philosophy that analyze, deconstruct, and subvert the self and, especially under the influence of Heidegger, attribute a divine logic to death and human finitude,[106] it is generally associated with Asian worldviews. Before turning to the Asian worldviews that are Martin's likely models, it is worth noting that the "faceless" deity that is adored in the House of Black and White (albeit through the use of the many faces of a great multitude of icons) in some respects resembles the aniconic God of the great Western traditions. Cataphatic (i.e., ontotheological) Western theological traditions that claim to know the nature of God and of the human often call for the negation of

Table 10.7 Worldview of the Faceless Men

Big Question	Worldview and Way of Life
Ontology and Cosmology	The Many-Faced God is Death, the ultimate necessity, to whom all the slaves of the Valyrian Freehold (unknowingly) prayed, and his faceless servants gave the gift of death, first to the slaves themselves and ultimately to the Valyrian dragonlords (cf. George R. R. Martin, *A Feast for Crows* (New York: Bantam Books, 2005), 322)
Epistemology	Knowledge is arrived at through self-negation
Axiology	Death is the "gift"; the gift of Him of Many Faces may be found in the House of Black and White; self-negation (becoming "No One") and submission to fate
Praxeology	Devotees of the Many-Faced God may take the gift of death by drinking from the poisoned black pool in his temple; the gift may also be purchased for others from the Faceless Men at a price that is always high but payable; if a death is taken from the Many-Faced God, it must be repaid; practices of transformation and murder are cultivated

the fallen, prideful, independent self in order for it to conform to and reunite with the divine. In contrast, apophatic theological traditions, which identify the deity as transcendent and ineffably beyond being a mere being among beings, tend to construe both the Western God and the human beings who bear the divine image in terms of self-creative openness,[107] actively working to deconstruct or negate the limits of positive attribution.

In this light, one may submit that there is a tension in the worldview of the Faceless Men. As noted by Wittingslow, Jaqen H'ghar—like other devotees of the Many-Faced God when called on to give the gift of death—is unable to choose for himself whom he will kill: "as a faceless device of his god [. . .] he is but a passive tool acting in the service of fate or some other profound teleological force";[108] the worldview of the Faceless Men is deeply fatalistic:

> [O]ne must not forget that [the] correct answer to the phrase *Valar Morghulis* ("all men must die") is *Valar Dohaeris* ("all men must serve" [. . .]). Death and service are thus rendered as relevantly similar concepts (or even overlapping concepts, in the case of the Faceless Men): both are utterly inescapable, and in both cases a person must do their duty.[109]

Therefore, according to Wittingslow, the worship of death leads to fatalism and passivity, an absolute submission to both the ultimate inevitability and to the deterministic forces and factors that condition one's actions.

Wittingslow's interpretation of the worldview of the Faceless Men stresses fatalism because Wittingslow is focused on the question of free will, but this is only part of the picture. I would agree with Wittingslow that "it is the belief of the Many-Faced God that most closely cleaves to the metaphysics of Martin's universe,"[110] but the Faceless Men are not simply fatalistic instruments of death. Rather, they are attentive and creative, adaptive but active. For this reason, Jacoby's[111] interpretation of the Faceless Men is more comprehensive than Wittingslow's, pointing to parallels between the Faceless Men and the water dancers, on the one hand, and Taoism, Zen, and martial arts, on the other. Within the storyworld, elements of the Confucianism- and Taoism-related YiTish worldview seem to resemble the apparent worldview of the Faceless Men.

In this context, I shall return briefly to commenting on the worldview of the children of the forest and their equanimity in the face of their doom. First, I think it is pertinent that the symbol of Ser Brynden Rivers (i.e., "Lord Bloodraven") is a red-eyed, fire-breathing white dragon on a black field—the combination of white and fire with black and of a dragon with what seems very much like a weirwood may suggest, not the sinister fall into darkness of a Targaryen who should be allied with fire, but a nondualistic worldview like the Faceless Men.[112] Melisandre's interpretation of her vision—and other textual clues linking Brynden, Bran, and the children of the forest with darkness and the Others—would, then, be a dualistic flattening of a more complex worldview. Many Western critics over the years have accused Asian worldviews like Buddhism of pessimism and death-worship, but Martin seems to suggest of worldviews that it is worse to deny death (and the approaching cold) than to accept and even venerate it. Martin's foil to exhibit this truth seems to be Qarth, the decadent city that, in sharp contrast to Braavos, highly values slavery and blood purity, with its Sorrowful Men and Undying Ones being the very antithesis of the Faceless Men.

The Sothoryi/the Brindled Men[113]

Worldview Families: white supremacy and anti-African racism; Lovecraftian allusions (e.g., the ancient city of Yeen)

Commentary:
Note that whereas it would be challenging to describe a single worldview and way of life for all of Westeros or Essos, Sothoryos presents no such difficulties; rather, all the challenges come from its being so dominated by the gaze of the fictional author of *The World of Ice & Fire* that almost no worldview and way of life is revealed at all—and the one that is described is highly problematic.

Reflecting on the way Sothoryos is constructed, one immediately calls to mind critical works like Achille Mbembe's[114] *On the Postcolony* and Charles Mills's[115] *The Racial Contract*. Africans and Africa are often constructed and deployed as part of racial projects that function to create the white,

Table 10.8 Worldview of the Sothoryi

Big Question	Worldview and Way of Life
Ontology and Cosmology	Unknown; said to worship "dark gods"
Epistemology	Unknown; said to be stupid
Axiology	Unknown; said to value cannibalism and obscene rites
Praxeology	Unknown—claims of cannibalism and obscene rites

Euro-American West—its identity, its natural supremacy, its positive presence and value—through its opposite and negation, and part of this work is accomplished through a discourse that conceals the constant operation of race, making itself instead about abstracted "human" nature: this complex project of identity formation and maintenance insists on its universal character as enlightened, rational, compassionate, free while elsewhere *proving* this through the representation of its opposites. Classic works like Edgar Rice Burroughs' Tarzan stories well illustrate how fiction has participated in this racist undertaking, which organizes commerce, law, politics, and other domains as powerfully as any other worldview one can think of.

Sothoryos is an endless wilderness populated by exotic beasts and countless diseases:

> Whatever its true extent, the southern continent is an unhealthy place, its very air full of foul humors and miasmas [. . . .] Blood boils, green fever, sweetrot, bronze pate, the Red Death, greyscale, brownleg, wormbone, sailor's bane, pus-eye, and yellowgum are only a few of the diseases found here, many so virulent that they have been known to wipe out whole settlements.[116]

And its subhuman inhabitants are savage and bestial, having strong bodies with weak minds, and miscegenation[117] with them is fundamentally unnatural:

> [. . .] And the native races grow ever more savage and primitive the farther one travels from the coasts.
>
> The Sothoryi are big-boned creatures, massively muscled, with long arms, sloped foreheads, huge square teeth, heavy jaws, and coarse black hair. Their broad, flat noses suggest snouts, and their thick skins are brindled in patterns of brown and white that seem more hoglike than human. Sothoryi women cannot breed with any save their own males; when mated with men from Essos or Westeros, they bring forth only stillbirths, many hideously malformed.
>
> The Sothoryi that dwell closest to the sea have learned to speak the trade talk. The Ghiscari consider them too slow of wit to make good slaves, but they are fierce fighters. Farther south, the trappings of civilization fall away,

and the Brindled Men become very more savage and barbaric. These Sothoryi worship dark gods with obscene rites. Many are cannibals, and more are ghouls; when they cannot feast upon the flesh of foes and strangers, they eat their own dead.

[. . .] Tales of lizard men, lost cities, and eyeless cave-dwellers are commonplace.[118]

Can such an appalling construction be justified in an age that knows better? Martin, García Jr., & Antonsson's *The World of Ice & Fire* is framed as the work of Maester Yandel, thus reflecting Westerosi biases—indeed, such a use of a limited, individual, Westerosi point of view is ubiquitous in *A Song of Ice and Fire* (becoming more problematic when translated into the medium of TV). And perhaps the heavy-handedness in the case of the way the Sothoryi and Sothoryos are described is intended to provoke critical reflection. Throughout this comparative worldview analysis, I have noted how *A Song of Ice and Fire* variously "plays Indian,"[119] draws on Orientalist tropes and fantasies,[120] and otherwise indulges in an uncritical touristic delight in exoticism and spectacle, in which diversity and individuality is abstracted into essentialized homogeneity.

Historically, this has been a persistent problem with the various subgenres of fantastika, but it also illustrates a challenge unique to fictional worldview studies. Narrative focalization is an issue of enormous importance. Because almost all access to non-Westerosi worldviews and ways of life is filtered through Westerosi perspectives, they all must be thought of, first and foremost, as aspects of the Westerosi worldview—though this is not to say that no access to other worldviews is possible.

The Empire of Yi Ti[121]

Worldview Families: Confucianism; Taoism; Orientalism

Commentary:
Insofar as the first God-Emperor's longevity and wise, benevolent rule seems to be a result of his being the son of the Maiden-Made-of-Light and the Lion of Night, he seems to express the Chinese doctrine of the Mandate of Heaven, for his virtuous rule (compare the Confucian-Taoist value of *te*) reflects his being in harmony with and an expression of the harmonious union of co-constitutive opposites (compare the Confucian-Taoist ultimate principle of the *Tao* and the goal of identifying with its boundless vitality and wisdom by harmonizing the opposing energies or qualities of *yin* and *yang*). The Blood Betrayal represents a shocking violation of and rebellion against the social hierarchies and relationships of mutual respect and responsibility (rooted in

Table 10.9 Worldview of the YiTish

Big Question	Worldview and Way of Life
Ontology and Cosmology	God-on-Earth lived and ruled for 10,000 years as the first God-Emperor, the only-begotten son of the Maiden-Made-of-Light and the Lion of Night; each new emperor and empress had a shorter lifespan, until the heretical Bloodstone Emperor, in an act known as the Blood Betrayal, murdered his sister, the rightful Empress, turned his back on humanity by taking a tiger-woman as a wife and by practicing cannibalism; he also turned away from the veneration of his ancestors, the Maiden-Made-of-Light and the Lion of Night, instead worshipping a black stone that fell from the sky; the Maiden-Made-of-Light then turned away from the world, and the Lion of Night's unleashed wrath produced the Long Night, from which humanity was saved in some fashion by a woman with a money's tail (cf. George R. R. Martin, *A Game of Thrones* (New York: Bantam Books, 1996), 627) or a hero with a flaming sword
Epistemology	Ancient records of priest-scribes; competing God-Emperors; prophecy
Axiology	Maiden-Made-of-Light; Lion of Night; God-Emperor; Leng
Praxeology	Trade and taxation; war; led by various competing God-Emperors, governors, and generals

the value of "filial piety") that constitute the social order and that should be reflective of the cosmic order.

The YiTish worldview is also shared by the northern people of Leng,[122] and one might speculate regarding why Leng is regarded by the YiTish as "the great and holy isle."[123] It might be significant that the Lengii have a God-Empress and that the Blood Betrayal centered around a brother's (the Bloodstone Emperor's) refusal to submit to his sister, the YiTish Empire's first God-Empress, the Amethyst Empress. Even before the Amethyst Empress, each of the preceding God-Emperors' reigns were "shorter and more troubled";[124] could this have been due, at least in part, to an overly masculine imbalance, a turning away from the feminine rule of the Maiden-Made-of-Light? Taoism has a noteworthy preference, in contrast to Confucianism's patriarchal inclinations, to value feminine forces and symbols. But, drawing on The World of Ice & Fire, note that the southern Lengii worldview and way of life has Lovecraftian qualities that may suggest that the cult of the Bloodstone Emperor (and, by extension, the Church of Starry Wisdom) that ushered in the Long Night and ascendance of the Lion of Night may have been an extension of tendencies within the YiTish worldview rather than a complete heretical innovation. Thus, in the form of the Church of Starry Wisdom, a form of the YiTish worldview "persists to this day in many port cities throughout the known world."[125]

A great deal of "Westerosi" Orientalism is evident in how the YiTish are represented. For example, consider the following passage about one of the God-Emperors:

Lo Tho, called Lo Longspoon and Lo the Terrible, the twenty-second scarlet emperor, a reputed sorcerer and cannibal, who is said to have supped upon the living brains of his enemies with a long pearl-handled spoon, after the tops of their skulls had been removed.[126]

This representation resembles an infamous scene in *Indiana Jones and the Temple of Doom* (1984), a film widely critiqued for its Orientalist excesses, but its voyeuristic horror seems to have been enhanced by making it an expression of cannibalism, blending it with a scene in the movie *Hannibal* (2001). As Larrington states in another context,

> This exoticising attitude to the inscrutable east is by no means restricted to modern, or even colonial-era, Western thinking. Its roots go a very long way back, into the early romances about Alexander the Great and his campaigns of conquest in Asia.[127]

One might contest distinguishing modernity and the colonialist project of mastery, but the use of oppositional identity formation and domination-through-definition are ancient tools.

The Worship of R'hllor[128]

Worldview Families: Manichaeism; Zoroastrianism; sacred sexuality; the worldview seems to be connected to the Asshai'i and to the shadowbinders' practices

Commentary:
Though there is complex debate in the history of the study of Zoroastrianism regarding whether Zoroaster's reforms of the ancient Iranian worldview were originally dualistic in character or ultimately monistic and monotheistic (as in *Second Isaiah* 45:1, 7, written under the powerful influence of the Persian liberator and "messiah," Cyrus, or in the form of Zoroastrianism known as Zurvanism), Manichaeism, with its highly Gnostic dualism, in this respect seems more similar to the religion of R'hllor. Given the medieval character of Martin's storyworld, Larrington may be correct that Martin's primary Gnostic model is the Cathars.[129] However, Gnostic worldviews and ways of life (such as Mandaeanism, which still exists), and Manichaeism, which is most comparable to the religion of R'hllor in terms of its geographic extent in the ancient world, tend to be intensely ascetic, precisely due to their dualism that regards the world and the flesh as a corrupt and evil trap. Martin's construction of the Lord of Light as encouraging sex and bloody sacrifice (something the Gnostics found particularly repugnant and further proof of

Table 10.10 Worldview of the Devotees of R'hllor

Big Question	Worldview and Way of Life
Ontology and Cosmology	R'hllor, the god of light, fire, and (especially sexual) vitality, is in eternal conflict with the Great Other, the god of shadow, cold, and death; his messianic champion is Azor Ahai, with his flaming sword, Lightbringer, containing the sacrificed life of his wife, Nissa Nissa, and Azor Ahai is foretold to come again
Epistemology	Prophetic knowledge of past, present, and future may be discerned in flames by trained priests
Axiology	Fire; light; blood; innocence; sexual vitality; sacrifice
Praxeology	Red priests often specialize as warriors (e.g., the Fiery Hand) and sacred prostitutes; marriage is consecrated as a sharing of fire; the dead are given a last, fiery kiss; fires are burned at sunrise and sunset; priests gaze into flames for knowledge, and they practice blood sacrifice; in Volantis, all priests were acquired as slaves by the Temple of the Lord of Light and are thus tattooed

the Hebrew God's derangement and delusion) may be modeled after the representations found in orthodox Christian heresiology. In any case, the name of the messiah (called the Saoshyant in Zoroastrianism) in the religion of R'hllor, that is, Azor Ahai, seems to intentionally sound a bit like the name of God of Zoroastrianism, Ahura Mazda.

NOTES

1. Cf., e.g., Suzanne Owen, "The World Religions Paradigm Time for a Change," *Arts and Humanities in Higher Education* 10, no. 3 (2011): 253–68; Guy Stroumsa, *The Making of the Abrahamic Religions in Late Antiquity* (Oxford: Oxford University Press, 2015); Tomoko Masuzawa, *The Invention of World Religions, or, How European Universalism Was Preserved in the Language of Pluralism* (Chicago: University of Chicago Press, 2005); Thomas Idinopulos, Brian Wilson, and James Constantine Hanges, eds., *Comparing Religions: Possibilities and Perils?* (Boston: Brill, 2006); Kimberley C. Patton and Benjamin C. Ray, eds., *A Magic Still Dwells: Comparative Religion in the Postmodern Age* (Berkeley, CA: University of California Press, 2000); William E. Paden, *New Patterns for Comparative Religion: Passages to an Evolutionary Perspective* (New York: Bloomsbury Academic, 2016); Aaron W. Hughes, *Comparison: A Critical Primer* (Bristol, CT: Equinox Publishing Ltd., 2017); Richard King, *Orientalism and Religion: Postcolonial Theory, India and "the Mystic East"* (New York: Routledge, 1999).

2. For example, see Patton and Ray, *Magic Still Dwells*; Christopher R. Cotter and David G. Robertson, eds., *After World Religions: Reconstructing Religious Studies* (New York: Routledge, 2016); Philip L. Tite, "Teaching Beyond the World Religions Paradigm?" Religion Bulletin: The Blogging Portal of the *Bulletin for the*

Study of Religion (accessed on April 17, 2019, http://bulletin.equinoxpub.com/2015/08/teaching-beyond-the-world-religions-paradigm); Robert Jackson, "Inclusive Study of Religions and World Views in Schools: *Signposts* from the Council of Europe," *Cogitatio* 4, no. 2 (2016): 14–25.

3. Ninian Smart, "The Philosophy of Worldviews—that is, the Philosophy of Religion Transformed," *Neue Zeitschrift für Systematische Theologie und Religionsphilosophie* 23, no. 1 (1981): 212–24.

4. William E Paden, "Theaters of Worldmaking Behaviors: Panhuman Contexts for Comparative Religion," in *Comparing Religions: Possibilities and Perils?*, eds. Thomas Idinopulos, Brian Wilson, and James Constantine Hanges (Boston: Brill, 2006); A. F. Droogers, *Methods for the Study of Religious Change: From Religious Studies to Worldview Studies* (Bristol, CT: Equinox Publishing, 2013).

5. Ann Taves, Egil Asprem, and Elliott Ihm, "Psychology, Meaning Making, and the Study of Worldviews: Beyond Religion and Non-Religion," *Psychology of Religion and Spirituality* 10, no. 3 (2018): 207–17.

6. Cf. Erik Baldwin, "How Can We Know Anything in a World of Magic and Miracles?," in *The Ultimate Game of Thrones and Philosophy: You Think or Die*, eds. Eric J. Silverman and Robert Arp (Chicago: Open Court, 2017).

7. Brian Cowlishaw, "What Maesters Knew: Narrating Knowing," in *Mastering the Game of Thrones: Essays on George R.R. Martin's* A Song of Ice and Fire, eds. Jes Battis and Susan Johnston (Jefferson, NC: McFarland & Company, Inc., 2015), 59–60.

8. Cf. Robert N. Bellah, *Religion in Human Evolution: From the Paleolithic to the Axial Age* (Cambridge, MA: Belknap Press of Harvard University Press, 2011); Michael T. Saler, *As If: Modern Enchantment and the Literary Pre-history of Virtual Reality* (Oxford: Oxford University Press, 2012); Yuval N. Harari, *Sapiens: A Brief History of Humankind* (New York: Harper, 2015).

9. Cf. Anthony K Brandt and David Eagleman, *The Runaway Species: How Human Creativity Remakes the World* (New York: Catapult, 2017).

10. The idea of "family resemblance" was first used by philologists to talk about relationships among languages (regarding the Martin's use of language families, see David Peterson, "Language and Narration: The Languages of Ice and Fire," in *Mastering the Game*, eds. Battis and Johnston, 18–19), and it is helpful to keep in mind the fuzziness and bleeding, the mutual interdependence and continuity, suggested both by the metaphor of "family," with its genetic and, ultimately, evolutionary reference, and by its application to languages, to which human worldviews, as symbolically represented systems, may be compared. These are not stable, fixed categories defined by a necessary and sufficient essence; they share dynamic, overlapping similarities.

11. J. Gordon Melton, *Encyclopedia of American Religions* (Detroit: Gale, 2003).

12. Wittingslow, "'All Men Must Serve,'" 129.

13. Anthony Gierzynski, *The Political Effects of Entertainment Media: How Fictional Worlds Affect Real World Political Perspectives* (Lanham, Maryland: Lexington Books, 2018).

14. Cf. Jean-François Lyotard, *The Postmodern Condition: A Report on Knowledge* (Minneapolis: University of Minnesota Press, 1984).

15. Fredric Jameson's *Postmodernism, or, The Cultural Logic of Late Capitalism* (Durham: Duke University Press, 1991) makes an argument along these lines, and Martin's evident sympathy with Asian worldviews like Zen (see, above, the section on the Faceless Men) may be accounted for by a similar critique of western Buddhism made by Žižek (Slavoj Žižek, *The Puppet and the Dwarf: The Perverse Core of Christianity* (Cambridge, MA: MIT Press, 2003); Slavoj Žižek, "The Prospects of Radical Politics Today," in *The Universal Exception*, eds. Rex Butler and Scott Stephens (London: Continuum, 2006); Slavoj Žižek, *On Belief* (London: Routledge, 2002)).

16. Cf. Andrew M. Greeley, *The Catholic Imagination* (Berkeley: University of California Press, 2000).

17. The Sparrows, for example, arise within the broader Faith of the Seven as a realized worldview comparable to the complexity of "Protestantism" and "Catholicism" within "Christianity," but note that the abstraction "Christianity," which encompasses an enormous number of worldviews from Mennonites and Jehovah's Witnesses to Greek Orthodoxy, is never realized in the real world. Even the subworlds of contemporary Protestantism and Catholicism contain a staggering abundance of worlds within worlds.

18. *A Song of Ice and Fire* functions as an excellent example of robust mythopoeic worldmaking. Wittingslow contrasts Martin's storyworld with the influential work of Tolkien:

Instead of the totalizing mythology of Tolkien's account, we find in Martin a vision of the world that is fractured. For unlike Tolkien, there is no grand narrative, and certainly no single coherent oral history; whereas the main dispute in Tolkien is fundamentally a difference of opinion about how to order a commonly agreed-upon universe, the denizens of Westeros and beyond are incapable of even agreeing upon the boundary conditions of the debate. (Ryan Mitchell Wittingslow, "'All Men Must Serve': Religion and Free Will from The Seven to The Faceless Men," in *Mastering the Game*, eds. Battis and Johnston, 113).

This "fractured" world is produced by a proliferation of inconsistent worldviews.

19. Cf. George R. R Martin, Elio García, Jr., and Linda Antonsson, *The World of Ice & Fire: The Untold History of Westeros and the Game of Thrones* (New York: Bantam Books, 2014), 5–12, 19, 145, 175, 195, 204, 211, 222–223, 226, 235, 237. The children of the forest are possibly the same species as the "woods walkers" of Essos (cf. ibid., 287).

20. See Marc Di Paolo, *Fire and Snow: Climate Fiction from the Inklings to Game of Thrones* (Albany: State University of New York Press, 2018).

21. This powerful image is referenced in Robert Jordan's depiction of Matrim Cauthon's being hanged by the Eelfinn as the price for the supernatural gifts they grant him and in the construction of Brynden, as Larrington notes:

Brynden's one-eyed status, his connection with ravens and crows, and the tree system into which he seems to be physically incorporated link him suggestively with Odin. The god is a master of magic and wisdom. He knows spells and charms and the wisdom of giants and men, which he has gained through his wandering. And by hanging himself on the world-tree Yggdrasil as a sacrifice, "himself to himself" as the Norse poem "Sayings of the High One" tells us, suffering for nine days and nine nights with neither food nor drink, he wins the runes. These are not just a writing system, allowing the preservation and communication of knowledge; they also have magical properties over the material world. Odin knows much of the past, the present, and of the future too. (Carolyne Larrington, *Winter Is Coming: The Medieval World of Game of Thrones* (London: I.B. Tauris & Co. Ltd., 2016), 92).

Odin's knowledge is, indeed, tied to the two features Larrington points out at the beginning of the above passage: his "one-eyed status," having sacrificed one of his eyes to drink from Mimir's well, and his ravens, who bring him knowledge. Brynden also resembles the Greco-Roman god Hypnos/Somnus (Cantuse, "Bloodraven: Greek God of Sleep," *Meditations on* A Song of Ice and Fire (blog), last modified August 18, 2014, https://cantuse.wordpress.com/2014/08/18/bloodraven-greek-god-of-sleep/).

22. This image of a luminescent cosmic tree is suggestive of a much older Jewish (and Christian and, before both, ancient Mediterranean and West Asian) motif. The Tree of Life is generally known as an element of the story of Adam and Eve in Paradise, the garden of God on his cosmic mountain (cf. Ezekiel 28:13–14). It is a symbol of the wife of YHWH, Asherah, who may survive in the Hebrew-Christian-Jewish tradition, among other things, as the divine figure of Wisdom (cf., for example, Proverbs 3:18), the Gnostic Sophia, Israel and the church as the bride of God, the notion of the Shekhinah in Rabbinic Judaism, and the Virgin Mary, whom Tolkien references in figures like Galadriel and Varda due to his special devotion to her. Asherah and her symbols' (e.g., snakes and trees/poles) banishment from the Temple (cf. 2 Kings 18:4) could even be part of the background for the Genesis narrative. In any case, the Tree of Life was symbolized in the Temple (and the Tabernacle—a portable shrine that functions in the sacred narrative to assure God's presence even in exile in the wilderness—both of which were understood as the dwelling of YHWH), which was located on the peak of Mount Zion (understood as the cosmic mountain, Zaphon [cf. Psalms 48:2]), by a lampstand with almond-blossoms at the ends of its branches, the Menorah. The comforting image of its enduring light as confirmation of God's continued presence and favor, even in exile, is symbolized in the story of the burning "bush" (Exodus 3:1–4:17; cf. N. Wyatt, "The Significance of the Burning Bush," in *The Mythic Mind: Essays on Cosmology and Religion in Ugaritic and Old Testament Literature* [London; Oakville, CT: Equinox Pub., 2005]) and resurfaces more explicitly in the story of the Maccabees celebrated in the festival of Hanukkah. The expectation of two messiahs, or "anointed ones," that may be found, for example, in some Qumran documents and the *Testaments of the Twelve Patriarchs*, derives from an image in Zechariah 4 of a lampstand fed by two olive trees (cf. Revelation 11:3–4). Thus, the image of the lampstand became associated with messianic-royal ideology, and it may come as no surprise that Christians, too, draw on the symbols of the lampstand, the tree, and other related images, associating them with ultimate cosmological realities like the cross and the church (e.g., Revelation 1:20; 22:1–5). And the Tree of Life as a cosmological metaphor or map becomes explicit in Kabbalistic thought. Tolkien's association of divinely approved human kingship with the vitality of the White Tree on the heights of Minas Tirith seems to draw on aspects of this

complex tradition, which, as noted above, resonates with other mythic notions like Yggdrasil.

23. Carole M. Cusack, *The Sacred Tree: Ancient and Medieval Manifestations* (Newcastle upon Tyne: Cambridge Scholars, 2011).

24. Michail Zontos, "Dividing Lines: Frederick Jackson Turner's Western Frontier and George R. R. Martin's Northern Wall," in *Mastering the Game*, eds. Jes Battis and Susan Johnston.

25. Ibid., p. 105. Compare how the culture of the children of the forest is contrasted with the first (human) "civilization," that of the Fisher Queens and others, followed by the Tall Men—called the Sarnori by the Westerosi, a remnant of whom still survive in Saath—and their hero king, Huzhor Amai, who lived in the Palace With a Thousand Rooms in the city of Sarnath of the Tall Towers:

It was here amid these grasses that civilization was born in the Dawn Age. Ten thousand years ago or more, when Westeros was yet a howling wilderness inhabited only by the giants and children of the forest, the first true towns arose beside the banks of the river Sarne and beside the myriad vassal streams that fed her on her meandering course northward to the Shivering Sea (Martin et al., *World of Ice & Fire*, 287).

The text reflects the biases of its fictional author, Maester Yandel. The northward flowing river probably draws on the concept of the Nile, and Sallosh, the City of Scholars, the great library of which is burned in the Dothraki conquest, is obviously based on the burning of the library of Alexandria. But most other aspects of the construction draw on ancient Mesopotamia. The Fisher Queens seem to be inspired by the popular idea of an ancient matriarchal phase of civilization, and the hero king, Huzhor Amai, whose name sounds intriguingly like that of Azor Ahai, seems to be modeled after the epic story of Gilgamesh, which has exerted a powerful influence on a vast number of subsequent hero myths. Indeed, the messiah-story and Christ-figure may be understood as part of this narrative tradition (cf. Evan Rosa, "Jon Snow, a Misshapen Christ Figure," in *Ultimate Game*, eds. Eric J Silverman and Robert Arp). Was Azor Ahai named after Huzhor Amai, the son of the last Fisher Queen (perhaps alluding to the legend of Sargon of Akkad's birth, with the name *Sarnath* playfully evoking Sargon, the Buddha as Chakravarti [he gave his first sermon in Sarnath], and Lovecraft's mythos), or vice versa? Or should they be identified as the same person?

26. Molly McGarry, *Ghosts of Futures Past: Spiritualism and the Cultural Politics of Nineteenth-century America* (Berkeley: University of California Press, 2008).

27. This is discussed in more detail under the section on the First Men; cf., for example, Gil Anidjar, *Blood: A Critique of Christianity* (New York: Columbia University Press, 2016); Larrington, *Winter Is Coming*, 15.

28. For a more responsible scholarly discussion of blood magic in the cosmologies of indigenous North American peoples, see Barbara Alice Mann, *Spirits of Blood, Spirits of Breath: The Twinned Cosmos of Indigenous America* (New York: Oxford University Press, 2016). This source, though at times overly syncretistic, also provides a great deal of emic insights into various Native American peoples' ideas regarding the giants, little people, human spirits' movements and relations with other living beings, and other mythic supernatural beings.

29. Madeleine L'Engle, *An Acceptable Time* (New York: Farrar Straus Giroux, 1989).

30. John Bierhorst, *The Deetkatoo: Native American Stories About Little People* (New York: William Morrow and Co., 1998); Mann, *Spirits of Blood*; cf. Larrington, *Winter Is Coming*, 95, regarding the children of the forest's similarity the Icelandic *huldufólk*, the elf-like "hidden people."

31. Is this a reference to the world as a whole, as a *coincidentia oppositorum*, rather than simply soil? Ice and fire, as correlated terms, are sometimes used by Martin as a way of referring to the world as a whole, in both its good and evil (and other mutually conditioned) aspects, and this might be an interpretation of the "song of ice and fire," that the children of the forest's worldview encompasses and even venerates both light and dark, the positive and negative aspects of reality. The "song" that "the prince that was promised" is said to possess may, then, be a harsh knowledge, perhaps of a cosmological character, preserved by the children.

32. See Larrington, *Winter Is Coming*, 58–64; David Gordon White, *Myths of the Dog-man* (Chicago: University of Chicago Press, 1991).

33. The similarity of black stone and dragonstone in Martin's world to Hobb's memory stone invites a more extended comparison, which may be found below under the section on the Valyrian worldview.

34. The lifecycle of the Speck people and the Eldar Trees is quite similar to that of the Pequeninos, with their Mothertrees and Fathertrees that are capable of "philotic" (i.e., supernatural) communication, in Orson Scott Card's *Speaker for the Dead* (London: Legend, 1992).

35. George R. R Martin, *A Dance with Dragons* (New York: Bantam Books, 2011), 452.

36. Cf. Michael Omi and Howard Winant, *Racial Formation in the United States* (New York: Routledge/Taylor & Francis Group, 2015).

37. Cf. Martin et al., *World of Ice & Fire*, 11–12, 146.

38. For example, they seem to value conversion and conquest through the death of all outgroups, including the children of the forest, to whom one might speculate they would relate in complex ways; given the effects heat and cold have on them, they may have strong beliefs about ice and fire, winter and summer, but, again, one may only guess; they use tools, including magic, to advance their goals; they have natural and supernatural means of knowledge; and so on.

39. Cf. Ibid., 285.

40. Ibid., 294.

41. Ibid., 179.

42. Ibid., 299.

43. Ibid., 11.

44. Ibid., 287.

45. Ibid., 301.

46. Ibid., 303.

47. Ibid., 24, 286.

48. Ibid., 6–8.

49. Ibid., 7.

50. In a vision, Daenerys is tempted by the Undying of Qarth with a promise to teach the secret speech of dragons, and there are suggestions that ravens, too, have a secret language, the True Tongue, but this may be a memory of the use warging on ravens by the children of the forest to convey messages (Martin et al., *World of Ice & Fire*, 7; cf. Martin, *Dance*).

51. Cf. Martin et al., *World of Ice & Fire*, 6–12, 19–20.

52. T.A. Leederman, "A Thousand Westerosi Plateaus: Wargs, Wolves and Ways of Being," in *Mastering the Game*, eds. Battis and Johnston, 193. Regarding the limited knowledge of the maesters, see Cowlishaw, "What Maesters Knew."

53. Cf. Droogers, *Methods*.

54. For example, Cornel West, *The American Evasion of Philosophy: A Genealogy of Pragmatism* (Madison, Wis.: University of Wisconsin Press, 1989); Leonard Harris, *The Critical Pragmatism of Alain Locke: A Reader on Value Theory, Aesthetics, Community, Culture, Race, and Education* (Lanham, Md.: Rowman & Littlefield, 1999); Eddie S. Glaude, *In a Shade of Blue: Pragmatism and the Politics of Black America* (Chicago: University of Chicago Press, 2007).

55. For example, Scott L Pratt, *Native Pragmatism: Rethinking the Roots of American Philosophy* (Bloomington, IN: Indiana University Press, 2002); Bruce W. Wilshire, *The Primal Roots of American Philosophy: Pragmatism, Phenomenology, and Native American Thought* (University Park, PA: Pennsylvania State University Press, 2000); Sidner Larson, "Pragmatism and American Indian Thought," *Studies in American Indian Literatures* 9, no. 2 (1997): 1–10.

56. Martin has long been interested in such themes. See, for example, the fascinating parallels in his early short story, George R. R. Martin, "And Seven Times Never Kill Man," eds. Ben Bova et al., *Analog: Science Fiction, Science Fact* 95, no. 7 (1975), which features a dark parody of Christianity, the religion of Bakkalon, a god also referenced in *A Song of Ice and Fire*. Martin enjoyed reading westerns as a child (and much early SF recapitulates the themes and motifs found in westerns), which leads Zontos to argue that the similarities between the Night's Watch and their conflict with the wildlings, Jon Snow's narrative of captivity beyond the wall, the problem of wildling assimilation, and other features of how the wildlings are represented and the themes found in westerns are not accidental (cf. Zontos, "Dividing Lines," 95, 106, 108).

57. Cf. ibid.

58. Cf. Martin et al., *World of Ice & Fire*, 135–138.

59. Ibid., 141–143.

60. Ibid., 139.

61. Ibid., 139–140.

62. Ibid., 140–141.

63. Ibid., 147–149.

64. Cf. ibid., 288–293, 296–297, 304.

65. Ibid., 289.

66. Cf., for example, Ward Churchill, "Sam Gill's *Mother Earth*: Colonialism, Genocide and the Expropriation of Indigenous Spiritual Tradition in Contemporary Academia," *American Indian Culture and Research Journal* 12, no. 3 (1988):

49–67; Jace Weaver, *Defending Mother Earth: Native American Perspectives on Environmental Justice* (Maryknoll, NY: Orbis Books, 1996); Barbara Alice Mann, *Spirits of Blood, Spirits of Breath: The Twinned Cosmos of Indigenous America* (New York: Oxford University Press, 2016).

67. Sam D. Gill, *Mother Earth: An American Story* (Chicago: University of Chicago Press, 1987).

68. See Larrington, *Winter Is Coming*, 192–198.

69. The similarity to the word "Sardaukar" is likely accidental.

70. Perhaps Martin also alludes to *Dune* in his representation of the Ancient Guild of Spicers in Qarth, or perhaps Herbert and Martin simply developed their representations independently, with both drawing on history and Orientalist stereotypes (cf. ibid., 220–222).

71. Ibid., 16, 194.//
72. Martin et al., *World of Ice & Fire*, 290.
73. Cf. ibid., 304–305.
74. Cf. ibid., 17–20, 53–58, 151–152, 163.
75. Ibid., 134.
76. Cf. ibid., 132.
77. Wittingslow, "'All Men Must Serve,'" 115.
78. Cf. Martin et al., *World of Ice & Fire*, 207–209.
79. Cf. ibid., 209–213.
80. Ibid., 217–219.
81. Ibid., 156–160.
82. Ibid., 169–173.
83. Ibid., 196–205.
84. Ibid., 236–241.
85. Ibid., 13–27, 32, 214, 253, 257, 268.
86. Compare their practices on the Isle of Tears, Gorgossos (cf. Martin et al., *World of Ice & Fire*, 283).
87. Popularization of the trope of dragon-riding should probably be traced to Anne McCaffrey's "dragonriders" of Pern.
88. See Larrington, 2016, 214–215.
89. For example, the Valyrian glass candle is very similar to the Númenórean palantír.
90. For a number of other historical and legendary parallels and potential sources, see Larrington, *Winter Is Coming*, 211–214.
91. Cf. Martin et al., *World of Ice & Fire*, 278.
92. It is worth noting that the Unsullied have special knowledge (the true name of their special (axiology) existent (ontology), namely, the great goddess, called by many titles such as Lady of Spears, Bride of Battle, and Mother of Hosts, which may suggest her nature (cosmology)) and practices (such as purification in sea water (praxeology)); theirs constitutes a distinct and complex worldview and way of life in its own right. It seems to draw on the *Galli*, the eunuch priests of the ancient goddess Cybele.
93. Cf. Martin et al., *World of Ice & Fire*, 13–15. The Ghiscari worldview-family religion practiced in Meereen, with its valorization of harpies and graces, recalls the complex ideology of bloodguilt (e.g., the Furies) and justice (or even gracious mercy),

the ancient concern with blood-pollution or miasma of which the Ghiscari are so infamously illustrative, and its interest in refuge, salvation, and rectification. An array of ancient Mediterranean stories, from Aeschylus' *Oresteia* to the story of Cain and Abel and the entangled Hebrew legal ideals of the cities of refuge and the avenger of blood, evoke this problem and its attempted resolution. The Ghiscari seem to fear and venerate the Harpy while seeking the mediation and intervention of Graces.

94. Cf. ibid., 253–260.

95. Reflecting their values and practices, "many Lyseni worship a love goddess whose naked, wanton figure graces their coinage" (ibid., p. 264). Likewise, the Lyseni venerate Yndros of the Twilight, a deity who alternates sex and whose acolytes are capable of the same transformation, reminding one of the great creativity and influence of Ursula K. Le Guin's (1969) *The Left Hand of Darkness*, and, as with the love goddess and Yndros, the other Lyseni deities and their cults, such as Saagael (the Giver of Pain) and Pantera (the six-breasted cat goddess) seem to function primarily as decorative, exoticizing, Orientalist gestures.

96. The Pentoshi prince seems to be based on Sir James George Frazer's *The Golden Bough* (1890), with its concept of a sacrificial priest-king, the embodiment of a dying-and-rising god who is the consort of an earth goddess (cf. Larrington, *Winter Is Coming*, 165). This is a fine example of an academic theory of magic and religion feeding into the construction of a fictional worldview.

97. See ibid., 168 ff.

98. Cf. Martin et al., *World of Ice & Fire*, 261–270.

99. Cf. ibid., 271–276.

100. Regarding medieval models for the Iron Bank, see Larrington, *Winter Is Coming*, 152 ff.

101. Giles B Gunn, *The Pragmatist Turn: Religion, the Enlightenment, and the Formation of American Literature* (Charlottesville, VA: University of Virginia Press, 2017).

102. Along these lines, Larrington notes in passing regarding Daenerys's efforts to abolish slavery:

Can Daenerys win the battle for hearts and minds and establish a democratic, just rule in the cities whose populations she has liberated? In this respect the liberal dilemmas which she faces, with her superior military power and above all the growing threat from her dragons, are more reminiscent of contemporary flexing of American political and military muscle in the Middle East than of the kinds of experiences faced in the medieval world (*Winter Is Coming*, 200; cf., ibid., 201–202).

It is not hard to critique Daenerys as an earnest "white savior," taking up the burden of giving freedom and justice to benighted savage peoples who do not seem ready for the responsibility of self-government, and perhaps that is Martin's intention: to promote such a critical response. Still, privileged points of view in the narrative tend to mute the critical voices.

103. Cf. Van Eyghen, "The Many-Faced God"; Wittingslow, "'All Men Must Serve,'" 122–130; Henry Owen Jacoby, "No One Dances the Water Dance," in *Game of Thrones and Philosophy: Logic Cuts Deeper Than Swords*, ed. Henry Owen Jacoby (Hoboken, N.J.: Wiley, 2012).

104. One might also compare western traditions of assassins (cf. Larrington, *Winter Is Coming*, 157–160) and fictional works like Lian Hearn's *Tales of the Otori* trilogy, particularly the first book *Across the Nightingale Floor* (2002), to Martin's representation of the Faceless Men, the water dancers, and Arya Stark's narrative development.

105. For example, John Corrigan, *Emptiness: Feeling Christian in America* (Chicago: University of Chicago Press, 2015).

106. Cf. Thomas A Carlson, *Indiscretion: Finitude and the Naming of God* (Chicago: University of Chicago Press, 1999).

107. Cf. Thomas A Carlson, *The Indiscrete Image: Infinitude & Creation of the Human* (Chicago, Ill.: University of Chicago Press, 2008).

108. Wittingslow, "'All Men Must Serve,'" 125.

109. Ibid., 127.

110. Ibid., 129.

111. Jacoby, "No One Dances the Water Dance."

112. The association of the Naathi "Lord of Harmony"—the giant god of a golden-eyed people—with a "black-and-white" butterfly that brings a violent death (very similar to the Red Death that ended the abominations of Gorgossos—cf. Martin, García Jr., & Antonsson, 2014, 283) to all non-Naathi without the Naathi needing to engage in any violence may reflect a similar nondualistic worldview (cf. Martin et al., *World of Ice & Fire*, 282).

113. Ibid., 284–286.

114. Achille Mbembe, *On the Postcolony* (Berkeley: University of California Press, 2001).

115. Charles W. Mills, *The Racial Contract* (Ithaca, NY: Cornell University Press, 1997).

116. Martin et al., *World of Ice & Fire*, 285.

117. The Ibbenese are similarly described as being unsuitable mates for other humans:

Though the men of Ib can father children upon the women of Westeros and other lands, the products of such unions are often malformed and inevitably sterile, in the manner of mules. Ibbenese females, when mated with men from other races, bring forth naught but stillbirths and monstrosities. (ibid., 296)

This description seems to follow the anxious logic of Christian concern about Jewish blood taint. The Ibbenese—though in other respects modeled after the indigenous peoples of the northern circumpolar region of the world—are a disturbingly anti-Semitic creation, drawing, too, on the long history in fantasy literature of dwarves being depicted in ways that reference anti-Jewish tropes. The short, strong, hairy, bearded Ibbenese are further "characterized by sloping brows with heavy ridges, small sunken eyes, great square teeth, and massive jaws, seem[ing] brutish and ugly to Westerosi eyes, an impression heightened by their guttural, grunting tongue" (ibid., 295), and they "are a cunning folk—skilled craftsmen" (ibid.). "The Ibbenese [are] a notoriously avaricious and, yea, even niggardly people" states Maester Yandel (ibid., 297). In general, they voluntarily isolate themselves from other peoples—indeed, they are so antisocial that they avoid even each other whenever possible. And though once ruled by a God-King, now they "are governed by the Shadow Council, whose members are chosen by the Thousand, an assembly of wealthy guildsmen, ancient nobles, priests, and priestesses" (ibid., 296). The idea of a "Shadow Council" government in this context already charged with anti-Semitic elements seems to play rather lightly with the old (and dangerous) conspiracy theory of a secret Jewish cabal orchestrating the fall of Christian civilization and the institution of a communist/globalist/atheist order, and any implicit critique of the Israeli treatment of Palestinians suggested by the idea that "the Ibbenese extinguished [the] gentle race" of the indigenous Ifequevron, as the "woods walkers" (the children of the forest) are known, thus becomes hopelessly entangled in anti-Semitism.

118. Ibid., 286.
119. See Philip Joseph Deloria, *Playing Indian* (New Haven, CT: Yale University Press, 1999).
120. Cf. Edward W. Said, *Orientalism* (New York: Vintage Books, 1994).
121. Cf. Martin et al., *World of Ice & Fire*, 40, 300–303.
122. Cf. Martin et al., *World of Ice & Fire*, 306–307.
123. Ibid., 300.
124. Ibid., 301.
125. Ibid., 301.
126. Ibid., 302.
127. Larrington, *Winter Is Coming*, 7.
128. Cf. ibid., 176 ff.
129. Ibid., 2016, 176 ff.

WORKS CITED

Anidjar, Gil. *Blood: a Critique of Christianity*. New York: Columbia University Press, 2016.

Baldwin, Erik. "How Can We Know Anything in a World of Magic and Miracles?," in *The Ultimate Game of Thrones and Philosophy: You Think or Die*, ed. Eric J Silverman and Robert Arp. Chicago: Open Court, 2017.

Bellah, Robert N. *Religion in Human Evolution: From the Paleolithic to the Axial Age*. Cambridge, Mass.: Belknap Press of Harvard University Press, 2011.

Bierhorst, John. *The Deetkatoo: Native American Stories About Little People*. New York: William Morrow and Co., 1998.

Brandt, Anthony K., and David Eagleman. *The Runaway Species: How Human Creativity Remakes the World*, 2017.

cantuse. "Bloodraven: Greek God of Sleep." *Meditations on A Song of Ice and Fire* (blog), August 18, 2014, https://cantuse.wordpress.com/2014/08/18/bloodraven-greek-god-of-sleep/.

Card, Orson Scott. *Speaker for the Dead*. London: Legend, 1992.

Carlson, Thomas A. *The Indiscrete Image: Infinitude & Creation of the Human*. Chicago, Ill.: University of Chicago Press, 2008.

———. *Indiscretion: Finitude and the Naming of God*. Chicago: University of Chicago Press, 1999.

Churchill, Ward. "Sam Gill's Mother Earth: Colonialism, Genocide and the Expropriation of Indigenous Spiritual Tradition in Contemporary Academia." *American Indian Culture and Research Journal* 12, no. 3 (1988): 49–67.

Corrigan, John. *Emptiness: Feeling Christian in America*. Chicago: University of Chicago Press, 2015.

Cotter, Christopher R., and David G. Robertson. *After World Religions: Reconstructing Religious Studies*. New York: Routledge, 2016.

Cowlishaw, Brian. "What Maesters Knew: Narrating Knowing," in *Mastering the Game of Thrones: Essays on George R.R. Martin's A Song of Ice and Fire*, ed. Jes Battis and Susan Johnston. Jefferson, NC: McFarland & Company, Inc., 2015.

Cox, Edward. "Magic, Science, and Metaphysics in *A Game of Thrones*," in *Game of Thrones and Philosophy: Logic Cuts Deeper Than Swords*, ed. Henry Owen Jacoby. Hoboken, NJ: Wiley, 2012.

Cusack, Carole M. *The Sacred Tree: Ancient and Medieval Manifestations*. Newcastle upon Tyne: Cambridge Scholars, 2011.

Deloria, Philip Joseph. *Playing Indian*. New Haven, CT: Yale University Press, 1999.

Di Paolo, Marc. *Fire and Snow: Climate Fiction from the Inklings to Game of Thrones*. Albany: SUNY Press, 2018.

Droogers, A. F. *Methods for the Study of Religious Change: From Religious Studies to Worldview Studies*. Sheffield, UK: Equinox Publishing, 2013.

Gierzynski, Anthony. *The Political Effects of Entertainment Media: How Fictional Worlds Affect Real World Political Perspectives*. Lanham, Maryland: Lexington Books, 2018.

Gill, Sam D. *Mother Earth: An American Story*. Chicago: University of Chicago Press, 1987.

Glaude, Eddie S. *In a Shade of Blue: Pragmatism and the Politics of Black America*. Chicago: University of Chicago Press, 2007.

Greeley, Andrew M. *The Catholic Imagination*. Berkeley: University of California Press, 2000.

Gunn, Giles B. *The Pragmatist Turn: Religion, the Enlightenment, and the Formation of American Literature*. Charlottesville, VA: University of Virginia Press, 2017.

Harari, Yuval N. *Sapiens: a Brief History of Humankind*. New York: HarperCollins, 2015.

Harris, Leonard. *The Critical Pragmatism of Alain Locke: A Reader on Value Theory, Aesthetics, Community, Culture, Race, and Education*. Lanham, Md.: Rowman & Littlefield, 1999.

Hughes, Aaron W. *Comparison: a Critical Primer*. Sheffield: Equinox Publishing, 2017.

Idinopulos, Thomas A, Brian C Wilson, and James Constantine Hanges. *Comparing Religions: Possibilities and Perils?* Leiden; Boston: Brill, 2006.

Jackson, Robert. "Inclusive Study of Religions and World Views in Schools: Signposts from the Council of Europe." *Social Inclusion* 4, no. 2 (April 19, 2016): 14–25, https://doi.org/10.17645/si.v4i2.493.

Jacoby, Henry Owen. "No One Dances the Water Dance," in *Game of Thrones and Philosophy: Logic Cuts Deeper Than Swords*, ed. Henry Owen Jacoby. Hoboken, NJ: Wiley, 2012.

Jameson, Fredric. *Postmodernism, or, The Cultural Logic of Late Capitalism.* Durham: Duke University Press, 1991.
King, Richard. *Orientalism and Religion: Postcolonial Theory, India and "the Mystic East."* London; New York: Routledge, 1999.
Larrington, Carolyne. *Winter Is Coming: The Medieval World of Game of Thrones.* London: I.B. Tauris, 2016.
Larson, Sidner. "Pragmatism and American Indian Thought." *Studamerindilite Studies in American Indian Literatures* 9, no. 2 (1997): 1–10.
Leederman, T.A. "A Thousand Westerosi Plateaus: Wargs, Wolves and Ways of Being," in *Mastering the Game of Thrones: Essays on George R.R. Martin's A Song of Ice and Fire*, ed. Jes Battis and Susan Johnston. Jefferson, NC: McFarland & Company, Inc., 2015.
L'Engle, Madeleine. *An Acceptable Time.* New York: Farrar Straus Giroux, 1989.
Lyotard, Jean-François. *The postmodern condition: A report on knowledge.* Minneapolis: University of Minnesota Press, 1984.
Mann, Barbara Alice. *Spirits of Blood, Spirits of Breath: The Twinned Cosmos of Indigenous America.* New York: Oxford University Press, 2016.
Martin, George R. R. "And Seven Times Never Kill Man," ed. Ben Bova et al., *Analog: Science Fiction, Science Fact* 95, no. 7 (1975).
———. *A Dance with Dragons.* New York: Bantam Books, 2011.
———. *A Feast for Crows.* New York: Bantam Books, 2005.
———. *A Game of Thrones.* New York: Bantam Books, 1996.
Martin, George R. R., Elio Garcia, and Linda Antonsson. *The World of Ice & Fire: The Untold History of Westeros and the Game of Thrones.* New York: Random House, 2014.
Masuzawa, Tomoko. *The Invention of World Religions, or, How European Universalism Was Preserved in the Language of Pluralism.* Chicago: University of Chicago Press, 2005.
Mbembe, Achille. *On the Postcolony.* Berkeley: University of California Press, 2001.
McGarry, Molly. *Ghosts of Futures Past: Spiritualism and the Cultural Politics of Nineteenth-century America.* Berkeley: University of California Press, 2008.
Melton, J. Gordon. *Encyclopedia of American Religions.* Detroit: Gale, 2003.
Mills, Charles W. *The Racial Contract.* Ithaca, N.Y.: Cornell University Press, 1997.
Omi, Michael, and Howard Winant. *Racial Formation in the United States.* New York: Routledge/Taylor & Francis Group, 2015.
Owen, Suzanne. "The World Religions Paradigm Time for a Change." *Arts and Humanities in Higher Education* 10, no. 3 (2011): 253–68.
Paden, William E. *New Patterns for Comparative Religion: Passages to an Evolutionary Perspective.* New York: Bloomsbury, 2016.
———."Theaters of Worldmaking Behaviors: Panhuman Contexts for Comparative Religion," in *Comparing Religions: Possibilities and Perils?*, ed. Thomas A Idinopulos, Brian C Wilson, and James Constantine Hanges. Leiden; Boston: Brill, 2006.
Patton, Kimberley C., and Benjamin C. Ray. *A Magic Still Dwells: Comparative Religion in the Postmodern Age.* Berkeley, CA: University of California Press, 2000.

Peterson, David. "Language and Narration: The Languages of Ice and Fire," in *Mastering the Game of Thrones: Essays on George R.R. Martin's A Song of Ice and Fire*, ed. Jes Battis and Susan Johnston. Jefferson, NC: McFarland & Company, Inc., 2015.

Pratt, Scott L. *Native Pragmatism: Rethinking the Roots of American Philosophy*. Bloomington, IN: Indiana University Press, 2002.

Rosa, Evan. "Jon Snow, a Misshapen Christ Figure," in *The Ultimate Game of Thrones and Philosophy: You Think or Die*, ed. Eric J Silverman and Robert Arp. Chicago: Open Court, 2017.

Said, Edward W. *Orientalism*. New York: Vintage Books, 1994.

Saler, Michael T. *As If: Modern Enchantment and the Literary Pre-history of Virtual Reality*. Oxford; New York: Oxford University Press, 2012.

Smart, Ninian. "The Philosophy of Worldviews—that is, the Philosophy of Religion Transformed." *Neue Zeitschrift für Systematische Theologie und Religionsphilosophie* 23, no. 1 (1981): 212–24.

Stroumsa, Guy G. *The Making of the Abrahamic Religions in Late Antiquity*. Oxford: Oxford University Press, 2015.

Taves, Ann, Egil Asprem, and Elliott Ihm, "Psychology, meaning making, and the study of worldviews: Beyond religion and non-religion." *Psychology of Religion and Spirituality* 10, no. 3 (2018): 207–17.

Tite, Philip L. "Teaching Beyond the World Religions Paradigm?," Bulletin for the Study of Religion, August 19, 2015, http://bulletin.equinoxpub.com/2015/08/teaching-beyond-the-world-religions-paradigm/.

Tolkien, J. R. R., and Christopher Tolkien. *The Silmarillion*. London: HarperCollins Publishers, 2001.

Van Eyghen, Hans. "The Many-Faced God and Indian Philosophy," in *The Ultimate Game of Thrones and Philosophy: You Think or Die*, ed. Eric J Silverman and Robert Arp. Chicago: Open Court, 2017.

Weaver, Jace. *Defending Mother Earth: Native American Perspectives on Environmental Justice*. Maryknoll, NY: Orbis Books, 1996.

West, Cornel. *The American Evasion of Philosophy: a Genealogy of Pragmatism*. Madison, Wis.: University of Wisconsin Press, 1989.

White, David Gordon. *Myths of the Dog-man*. Chicago: University of Chicago Press, 1991.

Wilshire, Bruce W. *The Primal Roots of American Philosophy: Pragmatism, Phenomenology, and Native American Thought*. University Park, Pa.: Pennsylvania State University Press, 2000.

Wittingslow, Ryan Mitchell. "'All Men Must Serve': Religion and Free Will from The Seven to The Faceless Men," in *Mastering the Game of Thrones: Essays on George R.R. Martin's A Song of Ice and Fire*, ed. Jes Battis and Susan Johnston. Jefferson, NC: McFarland & Company, Inc., 2015.

Wyatt, N. "The Significance of the Burning Bush," in *The Mythic Mind: Essays on Cosmology and Religion in Ugaritic and Old Testament Literature*. London; Oakville, CT: Equinox Pub., 2005.

Slavoj Žižek, *On Belief*. London: Routledge, 2002.

———. "The Prospects of Radical Politics Today," in *The Universal Exception*, ed. Rex Butler and Scott Stephens. London: Continuum, 2006.

———. *The Puppet and the Dwarf: The Perverse Core of Christianity*. Cambridge, Mass.: MIT Press, 2003.

Zontos, Michail. "Dividing Lines: Frederick Jackson Turner's Western Frontier and George R.R. Martin's Northern Wall," in *Mastering the Game of Thrones: Essays on George R.R. Martin's A Song of Ice and Fire*, ed. Jes Battis and Susan Johnston. Jefferson, North Carolina: McFarland & Company, Inc., 2015.

Part V

THE NIGHT IS DARK AND FULL OF TERRORS

SEXUAL VIOLENCE, DEATH, AND THE REAL IN *GAME OF THRONES*

Chapter 11

Concupiscence, Coercion, and the Communion of Persons

Reading the Rape of Cersei

Susan Johnston

On April 20, 2014, HBO aired "Breaker of Chains," the 33rd episode of *Game of Thrones*, one notable for what Sonia Saraiya called "an even darker turn than usual"[1]: the rape of Cersei Lannister (Lena Headey) by her brother, Jaime (Nikolaj Coster-Waldau), in the cathedral sanctuary of Baelor's Sept, where the body of their son, Joffrey (Jack Gleeson), has been laid out. It is, Saraiya notes, "hyperbolically awful—a violation of Cersei's agency, a violation of the sanctity of the grand sept, a violation of the reverence that ought to be provided to a corpse."[2] Margaret Lyons of *Vulture* called it "a new low for the deeply violent series,"[3] and over at *Change.org*, Ashleigh Vereen started a petition demanding an apology for a scene she called "especially heinous."[4] For Jessica Valenti, the horror of the scene was exacerbated by episode Director Alex Graves' claim that "[u]ltimately, it was meant to be consensual":[5] connecting the scene to such notorious sexual assault cases as 2012's Steubenville High School rape case, the 2008 acquittal of musician Robert Kelly on child pornography charges, and Whoopi Goldberg's 2009 defense of Roman Polanski on statutory rape charges, Valenti argued that Graves was "making excuses for rapists."[6]

Christian audiences, too, have been raising concerns about the representation of sex and relationships in the series. As early as the first season, Carissa Smith condemned the sexual education of Daenerys by her serving maids, noting that after repeated scenes of her rape by new husband Khal Drogo, Dany "suddenly gains curiosity about how to please a man": laughable, "if it weren't for the sinister underlying message that rape turns out okay if the woman just learns to enjoy it."[7] While few would take the dramatic view espoused by Reformed Christian pastor John Piper, that to watch *Game of Thrones* is to "recrucify Christ,"[8] in this domain at least feminist and Christian bloggers have made common cause. Nor are Smith and Piper alone in their call for abstinence: *Guardian* columnist Valenti has written about her break from TV dramas, one inspired by the stress of repeated graphic depictions of sexual assault,[9] and indeed every new *Game of Thrones* outrage, from the Red Wedding to the rape of Sansa Stark, has brought renewed vows to quit the show.[10] Though some of these have been the work of heartbroken fans,[11] others have been the kind of principled stand taken by Jill Pantozzi and others at feminist webmag *The Mary Sue*.[12] For such feminist thinkers, the repeated deployment of rape as a plot device, especially when it is used to motivate a male character's development, reflects what Rebecca Pahle calls the "rape culture that places blame on women." Pahle says "it's institutionalized sexism that creates this worldview of women as objects, it's in many cases years and years of trauma and PTSD and ruined lives .... but ... very little ability or even *willingness* to address the emotional consequences upon the victims."[13] Such a view reads the objectification of women on screen as an instrument, in the first place, of male pleasure, and in the second of plot development; Pahle suggests that the effect is to "trivialize rape ... by including it as a point of character development,"[14] and specifically male character development at that: "him trying to force her back and make him whole again," as actor Nikolaj Coster-Waldau said.[15] While many Christians would concur with this view, it is compounded in striking ways by a "purity movement" that emphasizes the exclusive expression of sexuality inside heterosexual marriage:[16] in such a view, the untrammeled nudity and graphic sex of *Game of Thrones* is an enticement to an immorality whose consequences are felt in the dehumanization of both men and women. Thus does at least one strain of Christian sexual ethics find allies in feminism, despite the concern of many thinkers, including feminists, that the purity movement contributes to the subjection of women by situating them as a threat to male purity.[17]

These responses reveal some of the fault lines in modern thinking about the ethics of representing sex and sexuality, and in what follows, I want both to outline what I take to be these fissures and to propose some ways in which a specifically Catholic theology of sexuality can work to bridge them. Part of what viewers have found troubling here is the translation of an admittedly complicated but nonetheless consensual book scene into what seems, in justifiable ways, to be consistently interpreted as rape. In the book, where George R. R. Martin gives us a series of interlaced limited omniscient narratives, this scene is part of Jaime Lannister's point of view. This sworn and forsworn knight of the Kingsguard, slayer and betrayer of the Mad King, twin brother and lover of Queen Cersei, is back from a long stint as prisoner of war, followed by a traumatic hostage situation in which his sword hand was violently severed. Returning at last to King's Landing, a filthy, near-starved refugee, he finds Cersei in the Great Sept of Baelor, the heart of the Faith of the Seven, mourning the murder of King Joffrey, the illegitimate fruit of their incestuous adultery:

> She kissed him. A light kiss, the merest brush of her lips on his, but he could feel her tremble as he slid his arms around her. "I am not whole without you."
> There was no tenderness in the kiss he returned to her, only hunger. Her mouth opened for his tongue. "No," she said weakly when his lips moved down her neck, "not here. The septons . . ."
> "The Others can take the septons." He kissed her again, kissed her silent, kissed her until she moaned. Then he knocked the candles aside and lifted her up onto the Mother's altar, pushing up her skirts and the silken shift beneath. She pounded on his chest with feeble fists, murmuring about the risk, the danger, about their father, about the septons, about the wrath of gods. He never heard her. He undid his breeches and climbed up and pushed her bare white legs apart. One hand slid up her thigh and underneath her smallclothes. When he tore them away, he saw that her moon's blood was on her, but it made no difference.
> "Hurry," she was whispering now, "quickly, *quickly*, now, do it now, do me now. Jaime Jaime Jaime." Her hands helped guide him. "Yes," Cersei said as he thrust, "my brother, sweet brother, yes, like that, yes, I have you, you're home now, you're home now, you're *home*." She kissed his ear and stroked his short bristly hair. Jaime lost himself in her flesh. He could feel Cersei's heart beating in time with his own, and the wetness of blood and seed where they were joined.[18]

Discussing this scene, Alicia Lutes points out that although Cersei unmistakably greets Jaime's sexual overtures with protests, in the end she does consent.[19] But that Cersei seems at first to initiate their intimacy, but then to withdraw her consent, "murmuring about the risk, the danger, about their father, about the septons, about the wrath of gods," before finally urging Jaime on, is a not-insignificant point if, like Amanda Marcotte, you see the book scene as "rough [but] consensual."[20] The simple past tense of the book passage, which enables us to occupy the scene both as something happening and as something that has already happened, to be both in the moment Cersei refuses and the one in which she assents, complicates our reading. George R. R. Martin reminds us that

> [i]n the novels, Jaime is not present at Joffrey's death, and indeed, Cersei has been fearful that he is dead himself, that she has lost both the son and the father/lover/brother. And then suddenly Jaime is there before her. Maimed and changed, but Jaime nonetheless. Though the time and place is wildly

inappropriate and Cersei is fearful of discovery, she is as hungry for him as he is for her.[21]

But even if we disagree with Martin's view of the scene, and see Cersei's belated response as compliance rather than consent, this scene is tonally rich in a way the television scene seems not to be. What is more, sexual compliance is not coercion, however much it elides the will and autonomy, indeed the dignity, of the one complying.

The television scene is, for many viewers, less ambiguous. Entering Baelor's Sept where the body of King Joffrey lies in state, Jaime sends the honor guard away. His twin is there, mourning their son:

CERSEI: It was Tyrion. He killed him. He told me he would. "The day will come when you think you are safe and happy, and your joy will turn to ashes in your mouth." That's what he said to me. You saw it. You saw Joff point at him just before—.
JAIME: I don't know what I saw.
CERSEI: Avenge him. Avenge our son. Kill Tyrion.
JAIME: Tyrion's my brother. *Our* brother. There will be a trial, we'll get to the truth of what happened.
CERSEI: I don't want a trial. He'll squirm his way to freedom given the chance. I want him dead. Please Jaime, you have to. He was our son, our baby boy.
   [*Cersei and Jaime embrace. Cersei kisses him, then pulls away.*]
JAIME: You're a hateful woman. Why have the gods made me love a hateful woman?
   [*Jaime initiates another embrace; Cersei appears to resist*]
CERSEI: Jaime, not here, please. Please. Stop it.
CERSEI: Stop. Stop.
JAIME: No.
CERSEI: Stop it!
CERSEI: Stop.
   [*Jaime pulls Cersei down to the floor and initiates intercourse*]
CERSEI: It's not right. It's not right.
JAIME: I don't care.
CERSEI: Don't, don't.
JAIME: I don't care. ("Breaker of Chains").

Reading this scene as a translation from the page means grappling with the shift away from the novel's focalization of this scene through Jaime's point of view, which mingles the events he observes and participates in with his own vision of those events.[22] Film, by contrast, focalizes through the camera, and here, the camera enters the Sept with Jaime and thus begins by presenting "correlatives of the mental and emotional dispositions" of this temporary protagonist.[23] The scene concludes, however, "from outside," mediating Jaime's perspective through an anonymous and external point of view.[24] Absent here is the attention and sympathy the novel has earned for Jaime as a point of view character[25] through his various captivities and his rescue of Brienne of Tarth from certain violation; likewise cast out is the way that, watching "with the character's eyes and will," we are "inclined to accept the vision presented by that character."[26] This is not to claim the primacy of the source text, but because *Game of Thrones*, as an explicit adaptation, trades on its relationship with the original it both converses with and contests, these changes have drawn considerable attention. In the end, they mean that the reader takes up the question of this act quite differently from the viewer, because she has been drawn into the novel's quite different economies of sex and power.[27] Where, for example, in the novel, Cersei's first impulse on Jaime's return is to enlist his sympathies in Tyrion's prosecution for Joffrey's murder, the show opens its fourth season with Jaime already in King's Landing, grappling with the loss of his hand and what seems to be the loss of Cersei's love ("Two Swords"). Rather than arriving after Joffrey's murder, Jaime is, on the screen, a guest of honor at the high table and thus a witness at Joffrey's ill-fated wedding ("The Lion and the Rose"). It is not merely the difficult external mediation of the camera that drains this scene of its strained and terrible intimacy. Given this change in the timeline, Cersei's early coolness toward his return, and her urgent pleading for Jaime to pre-empt the trial by killing Tyrion, the charge of rape makes more sense on the screen rather than less. Thus, for example, Sonia Saraiya remarks that while "[r]ape is a complicated plot device . . . it's not inherently problematic"; what is problematic is the translation of an apparently consensual scene into one that seems not to be.[28] And while Director Alex Graves may insist that the scene *is* ultimately consensual and thus relatively faithful, David Benioff, one of the two showrunners, confesses in the episode's video diary that

> [i]t becomes a really kind of horrifying scene, because you see, obviously, Joffrey's body right there, and you see that Cersei is resisting this. She's saying no, and he's forcing himself on her. So it was a really uncomfortable scene, and a tricky scene to shoot.[29]

For Rebecca Pahle, such a departure from the source text sustains critique of what she calls the "show's problem with using sexual violence against women for shock value."[30] Such views do rely on the conversation between the adaptation and its source, for it is the absence of prior consent from the small screen that supports the claim the rape is unmotivated in terms of story, destroying the redemption arc of a character both book and screen audiences were avidly following.[31] From season 1 to season 4, series followed book in an arc that traces Jaime from our first encounter with him as the glamorous, arrogant Kingslayer, illicit lover of his twin sister, the queen, and like her willing to murder a child to keep this terrible secret ("Winter Is Coming"), to the broken survivor of Robb Stark's war and Vargo Hoat's pointed and peculiar cruelties.[32]

Yet this arc proposes that even as Jaime falls, he rises, beginning what seemed briefly to be the complicated conversion that could make of his chivalry something more than "silk ribbons tied round the sword."[33] I have discussed this idea in more detail elsewhere, in work focused on the books and predating not just the rape of Cersei but Jaime's acquiescence to her increasingly paranoiacal tyranny (see, for example, "The Winds of Winter"),[34] and indeed the final episode of season 7, "The Dragon and the Wolf," shows at last the anticipated break between Jaime and his sister and the beginning of his new life, as he rides north alone to the Winter War. "I'm not that person anymore," says Jaime to Bran, apologizing for crippling him, shortly after telling Sansa that he will *not* apologize: "We were at war. Everything I did, I did for my House and family" ("A Knight of the Seven Kingdoms"). The ambivalence expressed in this episode remains at the core of Jaime's story, as the final season shows, poised on the knife-edge of the man Brienne sees in him and the one he recognizes in himself, who knows his own history and is imprisoned by it:

BRIENNE: You're not like your sister. You're not. You're better than she is. You're a good man and you can't save her. You don't need to die with her. Stay. Stay with me. Please. Stay.
JAIME: You think I'm a good man. I pushed a boy out a tower window, crippled him for life, for Cersei. I strangled my cousin with my own hands, just to get back to Cersei. I would have murdered every man, woman, and child in Riverrun, for Cersei. She's hateful, and so am I ("The Last of the Starks").

Here, of course, Brienne stands in the place of the viewer, pleading with Jaime to be the character we have been drawn to sympathize with, and his abandonment of her feels like his abandonment of us. In this way, we read his return to Cersei as a kind of betrayal of that sympathy, just as the scene in Baelor's Sept betrays both the ethical sensibilities and the narrative ones that drew critics and fans alike into sympathy with a rapist.

The dirty laundry of this unfolding reception history is begrimed further by Director Alex Graves' insistence, *contra* that of the showrunners, that the scene is "facebook complicated," but that Cersei is ultimately an enthusiastic participant:

> What was talked about was that it was not consensual as it began, but Jaime and Cersei, their entire sexual relationship has been based on and interwoven with risk . . . she's sort of cajoled into it, and it is consensual. Ultimately it was meant to be consensual. . . . The consensual part of it was that she wraps her legs around him, and she's holding on to the table, clearly not to escape but to get some grounding in what's going on. And also, the other thing that I think is clear before they hit the ground is she starts to make out with him. The big things to us that were so important, and that hopefully were not missed, is that before he rips her undergarment, she's way into kissing him back. She's kissing him aplenty.[35]

Laura Hudson, at *Wired*, says outright what other culture journalists merely hint at: "Encouraging people to imagine that Cersei secretly wants it, even as she is pinned down and screaming 'no' next [to the] corpse of her son, is encouraging people to think like rapists."[36] This is a big claim, but a significant one, and I am not prepared to dismiss the notion that this hugely popular and critically acclaimed series might work to shore up a culture whose grasp on the very notion of consent is loose at best. And here we might remark the difference between *Game of Thrones*' treatment of rape and that of the first season of the Netflix series *Jessica Jones* (2015). In *Jessica Jones*, season 1, her adaptation of the first four volumes of writer Brian Michael Bendis and artist Michael Gaydos' *Alias* (magazines #1–28), creator Melissa Rosenberg has been lauded for getting "exactly right" what most shows get wrong about rape, "from the legal loopholes that revictimize survivors to the confusion surrounding terms of consent to the psychological trauma that may never quite disappear."[37] This treatment is not inconsistent with the source text, although in *Alias*, Bendis and Gaydos simultaneously eschew the rape backstory for their Jessica Jones, while making it very clear, in the Purple Man story arc, that Killgrave's torture of Jessica using his mind control abilities was indeed a species of sexual coercion and that the ongoing trauma she experiences reflects that of rape survivors, even without physical rape. Jessica tells Luke Cage,

> What he did instead was—He fucking made me stand there and watch him fuck other girls. Telling me to *wish* it was me. Telling me to *cry* while I watched. [. . .]These— these college girls he would pull off the street. [. . .] But when there *weren't* any girls around, on a rainy night with nothing to do . . . he would make me *beg* him for it. Beg him. He'd just sit there and at his "request" I would beg him for it—I would beg him to fuck me. I would beg him 'til I cried. You hear me? You get where this is going? Eight months![38]

Verity Trott has compared the television series with the comic book, highlighting the ways in which both comic and TV series locate sexual violence in the ordinary and the everyday.[39] But Rosenberg's work in particular, Trott argues, works to deconstruct myths such as "stranger-danger" and the image of the vulnerable, weak female victim which work to normalize and indeed to "regulate" rape.[40] Bendis chose, as Trott notes, "to distance Jessica's narrative from the clichéd cheap ploy of illustrating a female character's experience of sexual violence, and instead attempts to draw out the complexities surrounding these issues and the humanisation of both the victim and the perpetrator."[41] For Rosenberg, however, the choice both to insist that Jessica's abuse included physical rape and not to show that rape on screen heightens this critique of the appalling ordinariness of sexual violence. Nor can we evade the gendering of this treatment. Brian Michael Bendis has said that his treatment of Jessica's abuse was informed both by his own situation as a man and by the prevalence of rape in comic books:

> I just thought as a man, that's not my road to go down. That's not my place. There was something going on in comics where there was just a lot of raping going on . . . And I thought there was a much more complex and dangerous road to go down that doesn't have that in it, and as a male creator, do that: teach by example. And at the same time, Melissa and all the writers—a lot of which are female—absolutely have every right in the world to take that material and go there, because that's the world that they live in.[42]

This is not to straightforwardly contrast the female-helmed *Jessica Jones* with Benioff and Weiss's *Game of Thrones*; both shows adapt male-authored source texts, and both make considerable use of male writers on individual episodes. Indeed, in "AKA WWJD?" and "AKA Smile," the two episodes which most clearly both unpack Jessica's thralldom and rape, and link that sexual coercion to the male attitudes which perpetuate such traumas, male writers Scott Reynolds and Jamie King played a prominent role. Rather, I want to note that both men and women have the capacity and indeed the experience to tell stories about rape in ways that critique rape culture. From this perspective, for example, Laura Hudson's view of the rape of Cersei is rather different from the perspective of Alyssa Rosenberg, for whom such scenes are of a piece with George R. R. Martin's "story about the consequences of rape and denial of sexual autonomy."[43] Rosenberg, therefore, sees the television series' treatment of sexual violence as far from unmotivated or exploitative, arguing instead that "[i]n Westeros in particular, where the ability to kill is a sign of manhood and even of honor, it's sexual misconduct that signifies monstrosity."[44] Although Rosenberg's dissent on the matter of the meaning and importance of HBO's *Game of Thrones* is significant, she shares with those who condemn the show not just a clear sense that the root of the matter lies in sexual misconduct but also an understanding of that misconduct as turning, *simpliciter*, on the matter of consent. The mention of sexual misconduct reveals the essentially contested ground of modern ideas of consent and of obligation, which seem to be both sufficient and insufficient to our notions of sexual ethics. Although this line of thinking is not by any means the whole of modern sexual ethics, as this reception history demonstrates, it is a significant part of it.

Though both novels and series are set in a medievalist world that ranges from the monasteries and feudal baronies of northern Europe[45] to the slave-soldiers of the Islamic world,[46] the sexual politics of the Martinverse are intermedial and interhistorical, in the sense that their audience is a modern one even while their temporal setting is the past. These works do not occupy a kind of timeless ahistorical space, in other words, but one where creators and audiences, rooted in the present riot of conflicting sexual ethos, are imagining a grittily benighted past. We are concerned, in Mariah Larsson's words, with "how the sex scenes in *A Song of Ice and Fire* (novels) and *Game of Thrones* (TV series) negotiate our modern understanding of sexuality and intimate relations... in another time and place."[47] This is so, I suggest, even if those modern understandings are naïve, confused, or wrongheaded; it may not be appropriate to judge the sexual actors of the Martinverse by modern standards of consent, but nor is it appropriate to say that such standards are *ultra vires*, for both series are trying to "align [themselves] with our contemporary ideas and conceptions of what sexuality might have been like in a different time and place."[48] For Larsson, for example, the marriages and sex scenes in *Game of Thrones* are overlaid by "ideas of gender equality, mutual pleasure, consent, and romantic love,"[49] but also by our modern perceptions of traditional and patriarchal marriage and the exigencies of pre-companionate marriage, where women were bartered as part of "financial and reproductive arrangement[s], used to forge alliances, combine wealth, and ensure rightful heirs."[50] Looked at from this perspective, Cersei's loveless marriage to Robert Baratheon and her efforts to evade its strictures might have garnered her our modern sympathies, and we might even have cheered her transgression, but that she transgresses the patriarchal system with her own twin brother places her beyond a pale both historical and modern.

In this way, we may say that the rape of Cersei foregrounds the ways in which sexual coercion and consent have become flashpoints in modern culture. Although legal understandings of sexual assault differ dramatically in the historical world approximated by *Game of Thrones* and in the world of its modern viewers,[51] the commonplace understanding of the audience derives from English common law, in which, as legal historians Decker and Baroni note, "a conviction of rape required evidence that the perpetrator used force or threats of force against the victim."[52] In such a view, it is not merely the absence of consent—which might be said to characterize the book scene—but what the criminal statutes typically call "forcible compulsion"[53] that typifies rape. Whether this scene involves forcible compulsion or some other kind and whether this common-law standard is adequate to our understanding of this specifically human failure is, of course, the issue, and the rape is further complicated by the intermedia storytelling which characterizes the Martinverse. I argue that these responses to the rape of Cersei too often erode what I take to be the Christian perspective of George R. R. Martin's fantasy series by reducing its complex sexual ethics to a starveling vocabulary of mere consent, a perspective that in the end, far from challenging toxic sexualities, of which sexual objectification is but one form, is complicit with them. Indeed, the reception of this scene reflects both the problem of adapting Christianity from page to screen and the problem of Christianity's absence from the screen. Sexual ethicists both secular and religious have struggled, it seems to me, with an ethics that, on the one hand, enables the *expression* of unfettered and mutual desire, and, on the other, fosters such expression in ways that are *consistent* with human flourishing and community stability: intimacy in the midst of a committed romantic relationship. Historically, these two imperatives have co-existed in a tension that has tended to be resolved in favor of commitment, but at the expense of both desire and romance, at least for women.

More recently, an increasingly individualistic North American culture has tended to emphasize sexual expressiveness and sought to articulate it as an individual freedom without sacrificing the mutuality that is at the heart of human sexuality, though both individual freedom and mutuality have more often been determined by the powerful than the powerless. And while at least one important strand of contemporary Christian sexual ethics, the evangelical sexual purity movement, has responded to this expansion of sexual expression outside of marriage with a renewed articulation of the deep meaning both of sex and of marriage, as well as the vital bounds of both,[54] recent scholars have suggested that practically speaking, purity culture works to control women's sexuality in particular and to restrict their freedoms in ways that foster ideas that women are responsible for the sexual violence of men.[55] But it is in the climate of such discussions that, in an effort to extend both freedom and mutuality, psychologists and sociologists have sought to distinguish sexual compliance—voluntary but unwanted sex, in the absence of specific or immediate pressure—from the sexual coercion of nonconsensual unwanted sex.[56] Legal theorists, debating such distinctions in the context of calls for affirmative consent, have favored caution. As Schulhofer put it in 1998: "The harm of *unwanted* sexual intimacy is extremely serious, but freedom to pursue *mutually desired* relationships is important as well."[57] Yet rape scholarship, in all fields, continues to long for the coming of a new millennium in which "the law really respects the woman's right to decline sex."[58] This longing has found popular expression in works like Jaclyn Friedman and

Jessica Valenti's 2008 *Yes Means Yes: Visions of Sexual Power and a World Without Rape*, with its call for consent "given freely and enthusiastically";[59] because, as Katz and Tirone remark, "black and white conceptions of consensual sexual behavior obscure the gray area of sexual compliance common in women's lives,"[60] they tend both to "confound consensual unwanted sex (sexual compliance) with nonconsensual unwanted sex (sexual coercion)."[61] This is the view, in fact, that a public intellectual like Laurie Penny promotes when she writes that "sexist fairy tales about what constitutes consent infect judges and juries just as much as the general public."[62] Penny writes very hopefully about the need for a shift in the culture of the modern West, one which will change not just the way we speak and talk about sexuality and sexual autonomy but one which will give house room to the frail and contingent power she calls "women's only real power . . . the power of sexual refusal."[63] This is the power that is under attack, Penny contends, because it is the only power women have that has the potential to erode the position of powerful men: "It is about power. It is about the insistence that women's bodies are public property, and women's words, women's autonomy, women's agency do not matter."[64] Only when the words and experiences of women don't matter can they be silenced in order to protect the sexual authority of men.

This clarion call has gone largely unheeded in the rush to condemn HBO and the *Game of Thrones* showrunners for the rape of Cersei, a kind of decency league blacklisting that perpetuates precisely the black-and-white conception of sexuality and consent that Katz and Tirone condemn. But it is in fact in the "gray area of sexual compliance" that George R. R. Martin's original scene casts the most light. Noting the book's transition from Cersei's "no," from her "pound[ing] on his chest" to her "Hurry . . . quickly, quickly, now," Donna Dickens remarks:

> Is this consent? Yes. Is this coerced consent and therefore questionable in a court of non-Westeros law? Probably. Is this not enthusiastic consent and really unethical by our standards? Definitely. But! It gives a subtle, distinct tonal shift to this scene and pulls it out of rape territory and into 'wow these people are irredeemably screwed up seriously y'all need Westeros Jesus.[65]

Now, Dickens may err in refusing to acknowledge the consequences of the uneasy kinship between sexual coercion and coerced compliance outlined by modern thinkers, but it is worth noting, too, her insistence that the flaw lies in the relationship itself, not merely in the work of the moment. For to take account of sexual ethics in such moments, useful though it is, is to neglect exactly what Dickens calls for, though she speaks tongue-in-cheek: a revitalized Christian anthropology of the body and its meanings. For what is absent from the calculus of consent and compliance—what is the power to which enthusiasm must be raised?—is the recognition that Jaime violates not just Cersei's body but the covenant that ought to characterize intimacy and mutuality. The small screen can only dramatize this void through Jaime's active coercion, a coercion rightly condemned as rape, but Martin's text takes on a brokenness well beyond this violation. When Cersei kisses Jaime, she tells him "I am not whole without you" but "[T]here [is] no tenderness in the kiss he return[s] to her, only hunger."[66] Jaime's concupiscence here fractures the fragile wholeness between them that Cersei claims, but we know, too, as indeed so does the television viewer, that this wholeness itself is already illusory. Their own hunger for each other has already shown forth its destructive power, in the broken bodies of young Bran Stark and of the realm. The world well lost for love indeed; brother and sister have sacrificed others, over and over again, to their own appetites. The wholeness that they would claim—first Cersei, then Jaime—must be known by its fruits: not a life-giving wholeness, but instead a death-dealing abyss. This, finally, is the lesson of Jaime and Cersei's shared death in the crypt as the Red Keep and King's Landing falls around them, the ruined city in the end the lasting legacy of their shared conviction that "Nothing else matters. Only us" ("The Bells"). Such a view is far indeed from a Christian anthropology of sex and the person, beginning as it would first from the premise that a human person is not incomplete, wandering helplessly while she seeks her "other half,"[67] but an end in herself, sufficient both to her own purposes and to God's. Cersei's sense of incompleteness, then, directed as it is toward Jaime, is like his raw hunger a desire that misses its mark and thus is sinful: the love that killed a city.

> What is it then that this desire and this inability proclaim to us, but that there was once in man a true happiness of which there now remain to him only the mark and empty trace, which he in vain tries to fill from all his surroundings, seeking from things absent the help he does not obtain in things present? But these are all inadequate, because the infinite abyss can only be filled by an infinite and immutable object, that is to say, only by God Himself.[68]

This does not mean that we were meant to be alone. Outlining his Christian anthropology in the Wednesday audiences from 1979 to 1984, John Paul II addresses the second account of the creation of man in the Hebrew Scripture, Genesis 2, which he calls "the oldest description and record of man's self-understanding."[69] It is in this ancient description that we first find the problem of solitude raised: "It is not good that the man should be alone; I want to make him a help similar to himself."[70] The separate accounts of the creation of man and woman and of their shared fall from innocence into history and sin which follow, point to a double meaning of this solitude, "*one deriving from man's very nature*, that is, from his humanity ... and *the other deriving from the relationship between male and female.*"[71] This is so, John Paul II suggests, because the second account of creation follows a first which does not differentiate its accounts: "male and female he created them."[72] Here, male and female are placed together in their first happiness, in Eden, in union with themselves and with God. Linked as it is to the rest of the story of creation, from formlessness to a good earth teeming with life, this first account is one that forges man as the object of God's creation but distinct from it, made in God's "own image" and called in His name to "subdue" and "rule" it.[73] Critically, too, this understanding of creation emphasizes a world made good. Though this account recognizes the importance of original sin as introducing concupiscence, and the sin and separation it entails, into the world, it does not imagine either the material world or the human person to be fundamentally corrupt. In this sense, it differs from the purity movement, whose evangelical roots include a Calvinist emphasis on the "total depravity" of human life, seen both in an individualistic emphasis on "personal human sinfulness" and in a cultural belief that "all of society was fallen."[74]

Humankind, like the world, is made good. Male and female, they are nonetheless unique in creation, and it is this element, says John Paul II, that is picked up in the second account of creation, when Adam ("man") surveys the living world and finds no one like himself:[75] "Thus, *the created man* finds himself from the first moment of his existence *before God* in search of his own being."[76] His solitude, in this way, is the fruit of his self-knowledge and his entrance into subjectivity, what John Paul II calls "*the first delineation* of the human being *as* a human *person*, with the proper subjectivity that characterizes the person.*"[77] Critically, Adam's solitude must be understood, in other words, in two senses: most famously, of course, in his aloneness as a human person, which the God of this second account calls "not good."[78] But it must also be understood in terms of man's sufficiency: made in the image of God, Adam is constituted as a person and thus a subject of the covenant, of the relationship with God, one who may be commanded and indeed command.[79] This form of man's solitude is, indeed, "very good";[80] in it, "[m]an is 'alone': this is to say that through his own humanity, through what he is, he is at the same time set into a *unique, exclusive, and unrepeatable relationship with God himself.*"[81] It is only in this prior sense of man's sufficiency as a "partner of the Absolute"[82] that man is capable of forming other covenantal relationships; only thus can he realize the nuptial meaning of the body, in the transforming relationship with another person. Thus is the goodness of creation fully realized.

It need hardly be remarked that John Paul II's understanding of Genesis, here, though consistent both with the Hebrew and Christian scripture and Catholic teaching of sex and sexuality, nonetheless diverges from many traditional accounts which have used the apparent belatedness of Eve to fuel theologies of obligation and compliance. In this way, too, the good world of Genesis has become the sorrowing and sorrowful source of concupiscence, a hungry world of consumption where the pretense of bodily sovereignty coexists with the breaking of corporeal boundaries and the shocking awareness of the fragility of that autonomy. It is particularly valuable, then, to recall the ways in which sexual compliance violates a covenantal understanding of the spousal body and the human wreckage that this violation entails. In this sense, it is vital that the television audience overlooks Jaime and Cersei in Baelor's Sept just as Bran overlooked them at Winterfell, the terrible voyeurism that led inexorably to Jaime's attempt at a concealing murder: "The things I do for love," he said, before pushing the boy out the window ("Winter is Coming"). Bran reprises this theme when the two meet again before the Battle of Winterfell, and in so doing strikes at what James Hibberd calls the core of Jaime's character.[83] For to say that Jaime Lannister has done hateful things for love is to excuse none of them, including the rape of Cersei; it is to indict a hateful love.

John Paul II contended, in the Christian anthropology that came to be known as his *Theology of the Body*, that we are subjects not only through self-consciousness and self-determination but through our bodies, which *"permit [us] to be the author of genuinely human activity."* He says, "in this activity" —which explicitly includes sexual activity, which too is genuinely human—"the body expresses the person. It is thus, in all its materiality [. . .] penetrable and transparent, as it were, in such a way as to make it clear who man is (and who he ought to be)."[84] For Martin, the battered, broken, often profoundly violated subjects of this fallen world are nonetheless capable of just such action, though fallen as we are we may need this language of a personhood, both beyond the body and united with it, that is, *ensouled*,[85] to see the ways that Jaime and Cersei's willed and willing union has desecrated not just their sept and world, but themselves. Martin traces in these two a debasement in which their appetites, little by little, lead them away from each other precisely in their coming together; thus it is that Martin's scene, oscillating between something like refusal and something like consent, reveals in the end the profound loneliness of those who deploy each other merely as tools to satisfy their own hungers.

I'm contending, here, that Martin's representations of sex and the sexualized body are undergirded by a very Catholic theology of the person, a theology that critics both secular and religious have struggled with in a world where our vocabulary of transgression and of human worth have thinned to ideas of consent and obligation. I noted above the efforts of ethicists to distinguish between compliance and coercion, efforts I propose could only be enhanced by supplementing our ideas of agency and autonomy with those of dignity and mutuality. This may be the beating heart of the theology of the body; as John Paul II indicates, the dignity of the human person is inseparable from that person's capacity to make a gift of the self in sexual intimacy. It is a sin, in this view, to treat persons as objects *even when they consent to their own diminishment.* The sexual compliance exacted like a toll from human persons who ought to be capable of covenant is such a diminishment. And here it is vital to distinguish John Paul II's theology from the purity movement with which it has sometimes been intertwined. As Valenti contends in *The Purity Myth*, though feminist and pro-woman porn culture does exist, the bulk of porn and purity culture have made a fetish not just of women's bodies but their subservience.[86] Nor has the promise of a dignified and sexual personhood that John Paul II holds out preserved Catholics from the purity movement's focus on the bodies of women. Jessica Valenti indicts the "Pure Fashion" shows, which originated with Catholic moms and teen leadership groups, both for their associated etiquette classes and the "misleading purity rhetoric" suggesting "that somehow it's 'good' girls who wear these modest clothes and bad girls who don't."[87] John Paul II's idea of purity, however, emphasizes the limits of the vocabulary of moral purity that Valenti finds so off-putting, acknowledging both the "dirtiness" which the analogy of "purity" invokes,[88] and condemning this widespread understanding as wrongheaded because of its focus on the external and the material.[89] Nor does this language of uncleanness confine itself to sexual uncleanness, for as John Paul II notes, "every moral good is a manifestation of purity and every moral evil a manifestation of impurity."[90]

It is in this context, too, that we must understand both John Paul II's condemnation of sexual utilitarianism, "a civilization of production and of use, a civilization of 'things' and not of 'persons,' a civilization in which persons are used in the same way that things are used,"[91] and Valenti's complaint that this opposition to unfettered sexual freedom is motivated by the desire to control women.[92] For Valenti, of course, John Paul II's emphasis on a contrarian "civilization of love," of which "*the family is the centre and the heart*"[93] is simply a tactic of "pathologizing sex" by "[p]ositioning unmarried, nonprocreative sex as dirty and immoral."[94] Yet it is fair and perhaps vital to note that John Paul is here concerned with contrasting the selflessness of mutual self-giving that is the aim and end of marriage with the "*freedom without responsibilities*"[95] precisely with the subordination of person to pleasure which characterizes the civilization of use, where "woman can become an object for man, children a hindrance to parents, the family an institution obstructing the freedom of its members."[96] And it is clear from his subsequent *Letter to Women* (1995) that this notion of an obstructive institution is to be understood both as chastising the hedonism which would see the family as a barrier to its own freedom and the self-centeredness which creates of the family a barrier to human flourishing. There, he both condemns the historical marginalization of women and their reduction to servitude[97] and the "perversion[s]" exemplified by "the long and degrading history . . . of violence against women in the area of sexuality" and "systematic exploitation of sexuality."[98] It should be clear from this development of his ideas that John Paul II sought to articulate an idea of the human person in which agency and autonomy are not diminished by mutuality and communion but integral to it; in such a view, of course, both violent coercion and the underground violence of compliance are perversion indeed.

Likewise, the interlaced perspectives of George R. R. Martin's novels condemn sexualities of coercion, possession, and objectification, in part by expressing the consequential absence of "communion between the persons."[99] And it might in fact seem that by developing this same scene as rape, HBO has in the end revealed that same coercion, possession, and objectification. Surprisingly enough, the television series which brought us "sexposition," whose representations of human worth vacillate between Cersei's bitter knowledge that "they hurt little girls everywhere in the world" and the spectacularization of lesbian sexuality for the delectation of an explicitly male gaze, though it has struggled to speak a language of violation and toxic sexuality outside of mere consent, revealed in its final season a more complex and fruitful understanding. "Breaker of Chains" Director Graves may have been seeking such a language, gesturing ham-handedly toward the scene as one in which consent *emerges*, but the screen—and the scene's reception—reflect the confusion of our own secular sexuality. It was left to "The Bells" Director Miguel Sapochnik to bring awful clarity to David Benioff and D. B. Weiss's script, as Jaime and Cersei die clutching each other in the ruins of the Red Keep's crypt; sans ideas of covenantal intimacy, shared personhood, and mutuality, these impoverished ideas of agency in the end bring ruin to us all.

NOTES

1. Sonia Saraiya, "Rape of Thrones." *AV/TV Club*, April 20, 2014.
2. Ibid.
3. Margaret Lyons, "Yes, Of Course That Was Rape on Last Night's *Game of Thrones*," *Vulture*, April 21, 2014.
4. Ashleigh Vereen, "Publicly Acknowledge and Apologize for 'Breaker of Chains' rape scene." *Change.org*.
5. Jessica Valenti, "When you call a rape anything but rape, you are just making excuses for rapists," *The Guardian*, April 24, 2014; Denise Martin, "Breaking down Jaime and Cersei's Controversial Scene with Last Night's *Game of Thrones* Director," *Vulture*, April 21, 2015.
6. Valenti, "When you call a rape anything but rape."

7. Alan Noble, "Sex and Thrones: Four Christian Views on Sex in *Game of Thrones*," *Patheos*, June 27, 2012.

8. Hayley Olson, "Christians Who Watch *Game of Thrones*, Nudity are 'Recrucifying Christ,' says John Piper." *Christian Post* 20 (June 2014); Tony Reinke. "Twelve Questions to Ask Before you Watch *Game of Thrones*." *Desiring God*, June 20, 2014.

9. Jessica Valenti, "Why do women love *The Walking Dead?* It might be the lack of rape scenes," *The Guardian*, June 12, 2014; Josephine Tovey. "*Game of Thrones*: Fans 'quit' show after controversial rape scene," *Stuff Entertainment*, May 19, 2015.

10. Ani Bundel, "Editorial: On the Rape of Sansa Stark and Quitting *Game of Thrones*," *Winteriscoming.net*, May 19, 2015.

11. James Hibberd, "HBO Defends *Game of Thrones*," *EW.com*, June 13, 2011.

12. Jill Pantozzi, "We Will No Longer Be Promoting HBO's *Game of Thrones*," *The Mary Sue*, May 18, 2015.

13. Mary Sue Staff. "A Frank Discussion of *Game of Thrones*'s Rape Scene and Its Epidemic of Sexual Violence." *The Mary Sue*, April 24, 2014.

14. Rebecca Pahle, "Here's What the Writer and Director of *Game of Thrones*' Controversial Rape Scene (Plus GRRM) Have to Say About It," *The Mary Sue*, April 22, 2014.

15. Ibid.

16. Kailla Edger, "Evangelicalism, Sexual Morality, and Sexual Addiction: Opposing Views and Continued Conflicts," *Journal of Religion and Health* 51 (2012): 164.

17. Ibid., 168; Sarah Moon and Jo Reger, "'You are not your own': Rape, Sexual Assault, and Consent in Evangelical Christian Dating Books," *Journal of Integrated Social Sciences* 4, no. 1 (2014); Kathryn R. Klement and Brad J. Sagarin, "Nobody Wants to Date a Whore: Rape-Supportive Messages in Women-Directed Christian Dating Books," *Sexuality and Culture* 21 (2017).

18. George R. R. Martin, *A Storm of Swords* (New York: Bantam, 2000), 700–1.

19. Alicia Lutes, "Let's Talk about that Cersei / Jaime scene from *Game of Thrones*," *Nerdist*, April 22, 2014.

20. Amanda Marcotte, "The Director of Sunday's *Game of Thrones* Doesn't Think That Was Rape," *XX Factor, Vulture*, April 21, 2014.

21. Pahle, "Here's What the Writer and Director of *Game of Thrones*' Controversial Rape Scene (Plus GRRM) Have to Say About It."

22. Mieke Bal, *Narratology: Introduction to the Theory of Narrative*, trans. Christine van Boheemen (Toronto: University of Toronto Press, 1985), 104.

23. Markus Kuhn and Johann N. Schmidt, "Narration in Film," *The Living Handbook of Narratology*, January 22, 2013, revised May 12, 2014, para. 29.

24. See Ibid., 29.

25. Bal, *Narratology: Introduction to the Theory of Narrative*, 105.

26. Ibid., 104.

27. But see Seymour Chatman (1980) for the argument that in film narrative "we can see through one character's eyes and feel through another's heart." "What Novels Can Do That Films Can't (And Vice Versa)." *Critical Inquiry* 7, no. 1 (1980), 140.

He notes film's capacity to "inspire identification" with its protagonists such that "we tend to identify even when the character appears to us in a completely frontal view" (140). Chatman's perspective would seem, for example, to counter Laura Mulvey's influential view that the cinematic gaze is that of the male voyeur, its eroticized object the woman, displayed as spectacle. See "Visual Pleasure and Narrative Cinema," *Screen* 16, no. 3 (1975), 11–12. What is more, this erotic spectacle is one Mulvey associates with sadism: "pleasure," she remarks, "lies in ascertaining guilt (immediately associated with castration), asserting control and subjecting the guilty person through punishment or forgiveness" (Ibid., 14; for a discussion of the ongoing relevance of this particular claim, see Sopie Mayer, "Demanding a New Story: Visual Pleasure at Forty and Narratives of Non-Violence," *Feminist Media Studies* 15, no. 5 [2015], 888–92). And while film scholars from Ellis (1982) to Wheatley (2015) have cautioned against the unproblematic adoption of Mulvey's idea of a normatively heteromasculine gaze for television in particular, this scene in particular seems to resist any attempt to associate it with a female gaze or indeed with female desire. See John Ellis, *Visible Fictions: Cinema, Television, Video* (London and New York: Routledge, 1982), 142; Helen Wheatley, "Visual Pleasure and Narrative Television," *Feminist Media Studies* 15, no. 5 (2015), 898. And here, too, we might note the alignment with the Christian purity movement, which likewise associates female nudity with a persistently and problematically desiring male gaze.

28. Saraiya, "Rape of *Thrones*."

29. David Benioff, quoted in Pahle, "Here's What the Writer and Director of *Game of Thrones*' Controversial Rape Scene (Plus GRRM) Have to Say About It."

30. Ibid.

31. Donna Dickens, "*Game of Thrones* 'Breaker of Chains' Episode Breaks Fans' Hearts Instead,"*Hitfix*, April 21, 2014.

32. Martin. *A Storm of Swords,* 342–51; "Walk of Punishment" S3.03.

33. Ibid., 385.

34. Susan Johnston, "Grief Poignant as Joy: Dyscatastrophe and Eucatastrophe in *A Song of Ice and Fire*," *Mythlore* 31, no. 1/2 (2012), 148–50.

35. Denise Martin, "Breaking Down Jaime and Cersei's Controversial Scene with Last Night's *Game of Thrones* Director," *Vulture*, April 21, 2014.

36. Laura Hudson, "That *Game of Thrones* Scene Wasn't a 'Turn-On,' It Was Rape," *Wired*, April 21, 2014.

37. Sadie Gennis, "How *Jessica Jones* Got Rape Stories Right," *TV Guide*, Dec. 3, 2015.

38. Brian Michael Bendis and Michael Gaydos, "Purple, Pt. 2 [*Alias* #25]," in *Jessica Jones: Alias* (New York: Marvel Entertainment, 2015): 4:n.p.

39. Verity Trott, "'Let's start with a smile': Rape Culture in Marvel's *Jessica Jones*," in *Superhero Bodies: Identity, Materiality, Transformation*, edited by Wendy Haslem, Elizabeth MacFarlane and Sarah Richardson (New York: Routledge, 2019), 51.

40. Trott, 48; she is indebted here to Catherine MacKinnon's foundational analysis of rape and rape culture. See "Feminism, Marxism, Method, and the State: Toward Feminist Jurisprudence," *Signs* 8, no. 4 (1983), 651.

41. Trott, 53.

42. Laura Hurley, "*Jessica Jones* added a new element to the show from the comics—here's how the creator feels," *Business Insider*, July 1, 2016. Melissa Rosenberg has likewise noted the prevalence of rape on television, remarking in an interview

> It's lazy and dull storytelling, if nothing else. We have this rich, complex female lead and we are looking at what happened to her from her perspective. We were not going to do that thing where it's about how the hero's wife and child were killed and how his wife was raped—and it's all about how he has to get revenge because that was "his woman." We are not doing that. We are looking at the aftermath of what happened to her from *her* viewpoint. See Maureen Ryan, "*Jessica Jones*' showrunner Melissa Rosenberg talks about her tough heroine," *Variety*, November 20, 2015.

43. Alyssa Rosenberg, "Act Four: *Game of Thrones* has always been a show about rape," *Washington Post*, May 19, 2015; See also; Amanda Marcotte. "The Director of Sunday's *Game of Thrones* Doesn't Think That Was Rape"; Caroline Frost, "*Game of Thrones*: 'Breaker of Chains' Review: The 'Most Shocking Sex Scene Ever' Between Jaime and Cersei Lannister—Really???" *Huffington Post UK*, April 22, 2014.

44. Alyssa Rosenberg, "Men and Monsters: Rape, Myth-Making, and the Rise and Fall of Nations in *A Song of Ice and Fire*," In *Beyond the Wall: Exploring George R. R. Martin's A Song of Ice and Fire*, ed. James Lowder (Dallas: Smartpop - Benbella Books, 2012), 17.

45. Brian Pavlac, ed., *Game of Thrones versus History: Written in Blood* (Malden, MA: Willey Blackwell, 2017); Carolyne Larrington, *Winter is Coming: The Medieval World of Game of Thrones* (London: IB Tauris, 2016).

46. Robert J. Haug, "Slaves with Swords: Slave-Soldiers in Essos and in the Islamic World," In *Game of Thrones versus History: Written in Blood*, ed. Brian A. Pavlac (Malden, MA: Wiley Blackwell, 2017), 111–21.

47. Mariah Larsson, "Adapting Sex: Cultural Conceptions of Sexuality in Words and Images," *Women of Ice and Fire: Gender, Game of Thrones, and Multiple Media Engagements*, ed. Anne Gjelsvik and Rikke Schubart (New York: Bloomsbury Academic, 2016), 17.

48. Ibid., 19.
49. Ibid., 21.
50. Ibid., 19.
51. John F. Decker and Peter G. Baroni, "'No' Still Means 'Yes': The Failure of the 'Non-consent' Reform Movement in American Rape and Sexual Assault Law," *The Journal of Criminal Law and Criminology* 101, no. 4 (2012), 1082.
52. Ibid., 1083.
53. Ibid., 1083.
54. Kailla Edger, "Evangelicalism, Sexual Morality, and Sexual Addiction: Opposing Views and Continued Conflicts," 164.
55. Jessica Valenti, *The Purity Myth: How America's Obsession with Virginity is Hurting Young Women* (New York: Seal Press, 2009); Kathryn R. Klement and Brad J. Sagarin, "Nobody Wants to Date a Whore: Rape-Supportive Messages in Women-Directed Christian Dating Books"; Sarah Moon and Jo Reger,"'You are not your own': Rape, Sexual Assault, and Consent in Evangelical Christian Dating Books."

56. See, e.g., Susan Sprecher, Elaine Hatfield, Anthony Cortese, Elena Potapova, and Anna Levitskaya, "Token Resistance to Sexual Intercourse and Consent to Unwanted Sexual Intercourse: College Students' Dating Experiences in Three Countries," *Journal of Sex Research* 31, no. 2 (1994), 130-1.

57. Stephen Schulhofer, *Unwanted Sex: The Culture of Intimidation and the Failure of Law* (Cambridge, MA: Harvard University Press, 1998), 184, quoted in Vivian Berger, "Defending Sexual Autonomy: Rev. of Stephen J. Schulhofer, *Unwanted Sex: The Culture of Intimidation and the Failure of Law*," *Criminal Justice Ethics* 20, no. 1 (2001), 50.

58. Berger, "Defending Sexual Autonomy: Rev. of Stephen J. Schulhofer, *Unwanted Sex: The Culture of Intimidation and the Failure of Law*," 50.

59. Jaclyn Friedman and Jessica Valenti, *Yes Means Yes: Visions of Female Sexual Power and a World Without Rape* (Berkeley, CA: Seal Press, 2008), 8.

60. Jennifer Katz and Vanessa Tirone, "Going Along With It: Sexually Coercive Partner Behavior Predicts Dating Women's Compliance with Unwanted Sex," *Violence Against Women* 16, no. 7 (2010), 740.

61. Ibid., 731.

62. Laurie Penny, *Bitch Doctrine: Essays for Dissenting Adults* (London: Bloomsbury Circus, 2017), 299.

63. Ibid., 301.

64. Ibid., 302.

65. Donna Dickens, "*Game of Thrones* 'Breaker of Chains' Episode Breaks Fans' Hearts Instead."

66. Martin, *A Storm of Swords*, 700.

67. Plato, *The Symposium*, trans. Walter Hamilton (Harmondsworth: Penguin Classics, 1951), 58-63.

68. Blaise Pascal, *Pascal's Pensées*. Introduction by T. S. Eliot. Urbana, Illinois: Project Gutenberg, 2006. Retrieved February 26, 2019. http://www.gutenberg.org/ebooks/18269: sec. VII, 425.

69. John Paul II (Karol Wojtyla), *Man and Woman He Created Them: A Theology of the Body*, trans. Michael Waldstein (Boston: Pauline Books and Media, 1997), 3:1, 137.

70. Genesis 2:18, qtd. John Paul II, *Man and Woman He Created Them: A Theology of the Body*, 5:2, 146. Waldstein has relied throughout his translation on his own direct translations of the edition of scripture used by John Paul II in preparing the Wednesday audiences, *La Sacra Bibbia: Edizione Ufficiale della CEI (Conferenza Episcopale Italiana)*, (Padova, 1971). Throughout this discussion I have used the translations of Genesis as they appear in *Man and Woman Created He Them*.

71. Ibid., 5:2, 147.

72. Genesis, 1:27.

73. Ibid., 1:27–8.

74. Mark Knight and Emma Mason, *Nineteenth-Century Religion and Literature: An Introduction* (Oxford: Oxford University Press, 2006), 128.

75. Genesis 2:19–20.

76. John Paul II, *Man and Woman He Created Them: A Theology of the Body*, 5:5, 149.

77. Ibid., 5:6, 150.

78. Genesis 2:18.

79. Ibid., 2:15–7.

80. Ibid.,1:31.

81. John Paul II, *Man and Woman He Created Them: A Theology of the Body*, 6:2, 151.

82. Ibid., 6:2, 151.

83. James Hibberd, "*Game of Thrones* Recap: Mistakes, Tragedy, and Fury," *EW.com*, May 5, 2019.

84. John Paul II, *Man and Woman He Created Them: A Theology of the Body*, 7:2, 154.

85. Reinhard Hütter. "The Spiritual Character of the Sense-Appetite and Its Acts, the Passions." In *L'Animale Umano: Procreazione, Educazione e le Basi della Società / The Human Animal: Procreation, Education, and the Foundations of Society: Proceedings of the X Plenary Session, 8–20 June, 2010* (Vatican City: Pontifical Academy of Saint Thomas Aquinas, 2010), 87.

86. Jessica Valenti, *The Purity Myth: How America's Obsession with Virginity is Hurting Young Women*, 96; see 66–91 for a fuller account of this claim.

87. Ibid., 49.

88. John Paul II, *Man and Woman He Created Them: A Theology of the Body*, 50:4, 328.

89. Ibid., 50:3, 327–8.

90. Ibid., 50:4, 328.

91. John Paul II, *Letter to Families [Gratissimam Sane]*. The Holy See. February 2, 1994, sec. 13.

92. Jessica Valenti, *The Purity Myth: How America's Obsession with Virginity is Hurting Young Women*, 57.

93. John Paul II, *Letter to Families*, sec. 13.

94. Jessica Valenti, *The Purity Myth: How America's Obsession with Virginity is Hurting Young Women*, 193.

95. John Paul II, *Letter to Families*, sec. 14.

96. Ibid., sec. 13.

97. John Paul II, *Letter to Women [Mulieris Dignitatem]*. The Holy See. June 29, 1995, sec. 3.

98. Ibid., sec. 5.

99. John Paul II, *Man and Woman He Created Them: A Theology of the Body*, 14:4, 183.

BIBLIOGRAPHY

Bal, Mieke. *Narratology: Introduction to the Theory of Narrative.* Translated by Christine van Boheemen. Toronto: University of Toronto Press, 1985.

Bendis, Brian Michael, and Michael Gaydos. *Jessica Jones: Alias*, vols. 1–4. New York: Marvel Entertainment Inc, 2015.

Berger, Vivian. "Defending Sexual Autonomy: Rev. of Stephen J. Schulhofer, *Unwanted Sex: The Culture of Intimidation and the Failure of Law*." *Criminal Justice Ethics* 20, no. 1 (2001): 45–52. https://doi-org.libproxy.uregina.ca/10.1080/0731129X.2001.9992100.

Bundel, Ani. "Editorial: On the Rape of Sansa Stark and Quitting *Game of Thrones*." *Winteriscoming.net.* May 19, 2015. Accessed May 8, 2018.

Chatman, Seymour. "What Novels Can Do That Films Can't (And Vice Versa)." *Critical Inquiry* 7, no. 1 (1980): 121–40. www.jstor.org/stable/1343179.

Decker, John F., and Peter G. Baroni. "'No' Still Means 'Yes': The Failure of the 'Non-consent' Reform Movement in American Rape and Sexual Assault Law." *The Journal of Criminal Law and Criminology* 101, no. 4 (2012): 1081–169. https://link-gale-com.libproxy. uregina.ca/apps/doc/A283591886/EAIM?u=ureginalib&sid=EAIM&xid=b20ec1c3.

Dickens, Donna. "*Game of Thrones* 'Breaker of Chains' Episode Breaks Fans' Hearts Instead."*Hitfix.* April 21, 2014. Accessed May 3, 2018. https://uproxx.com/hitfix/game-of-thrones-breaker-of-chains-episode-breaks-fans-hearts-instead/.

Edger, Kailla. "Evangelicalism, Sexual Morality, and Sexual Addiction: Opposing Views and Continued Conflicts." *Journal of Religion and Health* 51, no. 1 (2012): 162–78. https://doi-org.libproxy.uregina.ca/10.1007/s10943-010-9338-7

Ellis, John. *Visible Fictions: Cinema, Television, Video.* London and New York: Routledge, 1982.

Ferreday, Debra. "*Game of Thrones*, Rape Culture, and Feminist Fandom." *Australian Feminist Studies* 30, no. 83 (2015): 21–36. https://doi-org.libproxy.uregina.ca/10.1080/ 08164649.2014.998453

Friedman, Jaclyn, and Jessica Valenti, eds. *Yes Means Yes: Visions of Female Sexual Power and a World Without Rape.* Berkeley, CA: Seal Press, 2008.

Frost, Caroline. "*Game of Thrones*: 'Breaker of Chains' Review: The 'Most Shocking Sex Scene Ever' Between Jaime and Cersei Lannister—Really???" *Huffington Post UK.* April 22, 2014. Accessed May 3, 2018. www.huffingtonpost.co.uk.

Gennis, Sadie. "How *Jessica Jones* Got Rape Stories Right." *TV Guide.* December 3, 2015. Accessed September 10, 2020. www.tvguide.com.

Haug, Robert J. "Slaves with Swords: Slave-Soldiers in Essos and in the Islamic World." In *Game of Thrones versus History: Written in Blood*, edited by Brian A. Pavlac, 111–21. Malden, MA: Wiley Blackwell, 2017.

Hibberd, James. "*Game of Thrones* Recap: Mistakes, Tragedy, and Fury." *Entertainment Weekly.* May 5, 2019. Accessed June 26, 2019. https://ew.com.

———. "HBO Defends *Game of Thrones*." *Entertainment Weekly.* June 13, 2011. Accessed May 15, 2018. https://ew.com.

Hudson, Laura. "That *Game of Thrones* Scene Wasn't a 'Turn-On,' It Was Rape." *Wired.* April 21, 2014. Accessed May 3, 2018. www.wired.com.

Hughes, Sarah. "*Game of Thrones* recap: season four, episode three—'Breaker of Chains.'" *The Guardian.* April 21, 2014. www.theguardian.com.

Hurley, Laura. *Jessica Jones* added a new element to the show from the comics—here's how the creator feels." *Business Insider.* July 1, 2016. Accessed September 10, 2020. www.businessinsider.com.

Hutter, Reinhard. "The Spiritual Character of the Sense-Appetite and Its Acts, the Passions." In *L'Animale Umano: Procreazione, Educazione e le Basi della Società / The Human Animal: Procreation, Education, and the Foundations of Society: Proceedings of the X Plenary Session, 8–20 June, 2010, 82–109.* Vatican City: Pontifical Academy of Saint Thomas Aquinas, 2010.

John Paul II [Karol Wojtyla]. *Letter to Families [Gratissimam Sane]. The Holy See.* February 2, 1994. Accessed February 22, 2019. www.vatican.va/content/vatican/en.html.

———. *Letter to Women [Mulieris Dignitatem]. The Holy See.* June 29, 1995. Accessed February 22, 2019. www.vatican.va/content/vatican/en.html.

———. *Love and Responsibility.* Translated by H.T. Willetts. New York: Farrar, Straus, and Giroux, 1981.

———. *Man and Woman He Created Them: A Theology of the Body.* Translated by Michael Waldstein. Boston: Pauline Books and Media, 1997.

Johnston, Susan. "Grief Poignant as Joy: Dyscatastrophe and Eucatastrophe in *A Song of Ice and Fire*." *Mythlore* 31, no. 1 (2012–13): 135–56.

Katz, Jennifer, and Vanessa Tirone. "Going Along With It: Sexually Coercive Partner Behavior Predicts Dating Women's Compliance with Unwanted Sex." *Violence Against Women* 16, no. 7 (2010): 730–42. https://doi-org.libproxy.uregina.ca/10.1 177/ 1077801210374867.

Klement, Kathryn R., and Brad J. Sagarin. "Nobody Wants to Date a Whore: Rape-Supportive Messages in Women-Directed Christian Dating Books." *Sexuality and Culture* 21, (2017): 205–23. http://dx.doi.org.libproxy.uregina.ca/10.1007/s12119 -016-9390-x.

Knight, Mark, and Emma Mason. *Nineteenth-Century Religion and Literature: An Introduction.* Oxford: Oxford University Press, 2006.

Kuhn, Markus, and Johann N. Schmidt. "Narration in Film." In *The Living Handbook of Narratology.* January 22, 2013, revised May 12, 2014. https://www.lhn.uni -hamburg.de/.

Larsson, Mariah. "Adapting Sex: Cultural Conceptions of Sexuality in Words and Images." *Women of Ice and Fire: Gender, Game of Thrones, and Multiple Media Engagements*, edited by Anne Gjelsvik and Rikke Schubart. New York: Bloomsbury Academic, 2016.

Larrington, Carolyne. *Winter is Coming: The Medieval World of Game of Thrones.* London: IB Tauris, 2016.

Lutes, Alicia. "Let's talk about that Cersei / Jaime scene from *Game of Thrones*." *Nerdist.* April 22, 2014. Accessed May 10, 2018. https:/nerdist.com.

Lyons, Margaret. "Yes, Of Course That Was Rape on Last Night's *Game of Thrones*." *Vulture*. April 21, 2014. Accessed May 3, 2018. www.vulture.com.

MacKinnon, Catherine. "Feminism, Marxism, Method, and the State: Toward Feminist Jurisprudence," *Signs* 8, no. 4 (1983): 635–58. https://www.jstor.org/stable/3173687.

Marcotte, Amanda. "The Director of Sunday's *Game of Thrones* Doesn't Think That Was Rape." *XX Factor*. April 21, 2014. Accessed May 3, 2018. https://slate.com.

Martin, Denise. "Breaking Down Jaime and Cersei's Controversial Scene with Last Night's *Game of Thrones* Director." *Vulture*. April 21, 2014. Accessed 16 May 2018. www.vulture.com.

Martin, George R.R. *A Storm of Swords*. New York: Bantam, 2000.

Mary Sue Staff. "A Frank Discussion of *Game of Thrones's* Rape Scene and Its Epidemic of Sexual Violence." *The Mary Sue*. April 24, 2014. Accessed May 15, 2018. www.themarysue.com.

Mayer, Sophie. "Demanding a New Story: Visual Pleasure at Forty and Narratives of Non-Violence." *Feminist Media Studies* 15, no. 5 (2015): 888–92. https://doi-org.libproxy.uregina.ca/10.1080/14680777.2015.107527

Moon, Sarah, and Jo Reger. "'You are not your own': Rape, Sexual Assault, and Consent in Evangelical Christian Dating Books." *Journal of Integrated Social Sciences* 4, no. 1 (2014): 55–74. http://jiss.org/archive/4-1.php.

Mulvey, Laura. "Visual Pleasure and Narrative Cinema." *Screen* 16, no. 3 (1975): 6–18. https://doi-org.libproxy.uregina.ca/10.1093/screen/16.3.6.

Noble, Alan. "Sex and Thrones: Four Christian Views on Sex in *Game of Thrones*." *Patheos*. June 27, 2012. Accessed February 19, 2019. www.patheos.com.

Olson, Hayley. "Christians Who Watch *Game of Thrones,* Nudity are 'Recrucifying Christ,' says John Piper." *The Christian Post*. June 20, 2014. Accessed February 19, 2019. www.christianpost.com.

Pahle, Rebecca. "Here's What the Writer and Director of *Game of Thrones'* Controversial Rape Scene (Plus GRRM) Have to Say About It." *The Mary Sue*. April 22, 2014. Accessed May 3, 2018. www.themarysue.com.

Pantozzi, Jill. "We Will No Longer Be Promoting HBO's *Game of Thrones*." *The Mary Sue*. May 18, 2015. Accessed May 4, 2018. www.marysue.com.

Pascal, Blaise. *Pascal's Pensées*. Introduction by T.S. Eliot. Urbana, Illinois: Project Gutenberg, 2006. Accessed February 26, 2019. http://www.gutenberg.org/ebooks/18269.

Pavlac, Brian, ed. *Game of Thrones versus History: Written in Blood*. Malden, MA: Wiley Blackwell, 2017.

Penny, Laurie. *Bitch Doctrine: Essays for Dissenting Adults*. London: Bloomsbury Circus, 2017.

Plato. *The Symposium*, translated by Walter Hamilton. Harmondsworth: Penguin Classics, 1951.

Reinke, Tony. "Twelve Questions to Ask Before you Watch *Game of Thrones*." *Desiring God*. June 20, 2014. Accessed February 19, 2019. www.desiringgod.org.

Rosenberg, Alyssa. "Act Four: *Game of Thrones* has always been a show about rape." *Washington Post.* May 19, 2015. Accessed May 15, 2018. www.washingtonpost.com.

———. "Act Four: *Game of Thrones* Review: Breaker of chains, Breakers of will." *Washington Post.* April 20, 2014. Accessed May 15, 2018. *washingtonpost.com.*

———. "Men and Monsters: Rape, Myth-Making, and the Rise and Fall of Nations in *A Song of Ice and Fire*." In *Beyond the Wall: Exploring George R.R. Martin's A Song of Ice and Fire*, edited by James Lowder, 15–27. Dallas: Smartpop - Benbella Books, 2012.

Rosenberg, Melissa, creator. *Jessica Jones.* "AKA WWJD?" 1:08. Directed by Simon Cellan Jones. Written by Scott Reynolds and Jenna Reback. *Netflix.* November 20, 2015.

———. *Jessica Jones.* "AKA Smile." 1:13. Directed by Michael Rymer. Written by Scott Reynolds, Melissa Reynolds, Jamie King, and Jenna Reback. *Netflix.* November 20, 2015.

Ryan, Maureen. "*Jessica Jones*' showrunner Melissa Rosenberg talks about her tough heroine. *Variety.* November 20, 2015. Accessed September 10, 2020. https://variety.com.

Saraiya, Sonia. "Rape of *Thrones*" *AV/TV Club.* April 20, 2014. Accessed May 3, 2018. www.avclub.com.

Schulhofer, Stephen. *Unwanted Sex: The Culture of Intimidation and the Failure of Law.* Boston: Harvard University Press, 1998.

Sprecher, Susan, Elaine Hatfield, Anthony Cortese, Elena Potapova, and Anna Levitskaya. "Token Resistance to Sexual Intercourse and Consent to Unwanted Sexual Intercourse: College Students' Dating Experiences in Three Countries." *Journal of Sex Research* 31, no. 2 (1994): 125–32. DOI: 10.1080/00224499409551739.

Tovey, Josephine. "*Game of Thrones:* Fans 'quit' show after controversial rape scene." *Stuff Entertainment.* May 19, 2015. Accessed January 15, 2019. www.stuff.co.nz.

Trott, Verity. "'Let's start with a smile': Rape Culture in Marvel's *Jessica Jones*," in *Superhero Bodies: Identity, Materiality, Transformation*, edited by Wendy Haslem, Elizabeth MacFarlane and Sarah Richardson. New York: Routledge, 2019: 47–58.

Valenti, Jessica. *The Purity Myth: How America's Obsession with Virginity is Hurting Young Women.* New York: Seal Press, 2009.

———. "When you call a rape anything but rape, you are just making excuses for rapists." *The Guardian.* April 24, 2014. Accessed May 2, 2018. www.theguardian.com.

———. "Why do women love *The Walking Dead*? It might be the lack of rape scenes." *The Guardian.* June 12, 2014. Accessed November 6, 2017. www.theguardian.com.

Vereen, Ashleigh. "Publicly Acknowledge and Apologize for 'Breaker of Chains' rape scene." *Change.org.* Accessed May 13, 2018.

Wheatley, Helen. "Visual Pleasure and Narrative Television." *Feminist Media Studies* 15, no. 5 (2015): 896–9. https://doi-org.libproxy.uregina.ca/10.1080/14680777.2015.1075276.

Chapter 12

Valar Morghulis

Late-Modern Imaginaries of Death and Nihilism in Game of Thrones

Andrew D. Thrasher

Is Death the True God? Certainly *Game of Thrones* displays a pluriformity in defining Death through its various depictions: the Many-Faced God, the nothingness and death, and the fight between the living and the dead. While Death is certainly deified in *Game of Thrones* as the Many-Faced God, the complexities of the role of death in *Game of Thrones* can be described through the existential theology of the Heideggerian "Being-towards-death" and Paul Tillich's "courage to be" as primary resources for understanding the theological role of Death in *Game of Thrones*. Described by Arya Stark's service to the Many-Faced God and the experience of the nothingness of death by Jon Snow and Baric Dondarrion, death is the inevitable telos and possibility of existence. But it also signifies an imaginary of late modernity where the nihility of death implies the irrelevancy of theological resources to find meaning, purpose, and significance in the face of death. Whether the Many-Faced God or the Lord of Light is the true God, what rules is the sovereignty of death. And the sovereignty of death is the reality of *Game of Thrones*: death is expected. Death is anticipated constantly. In *Game of Thrones*, we must truly *dare* to hope that anyone survives. Within the world of *Game of Thrones*, we may either embrace the nothingness of death as my own most possibility and fight the living dead to live or become enslaved to the will of the Night King through the negation of our death.

In this chapter, I will to unpack in *Game of Thrones* how death is a reflection of late-modern culture, embodied through the re-enchantment of death in the fight between life and death. Not merely does *Game of Thrones* demonstrate a late-modern existential theology of death, but it does so by conveying the nihility of death as the ultimate end of existence in the fight between the living and the dead. I will argue that George R. R. Martin not merely deifies Death but informs a late-modern imaginary of the nothingness that inevitably awaits us in the absence of salvation and implies for us an existential theology where the will to death becomes a choice to fight death for life even when death is the inevitable outcome of life. But what triumphs? The Night King's sovereignty over death, or the Lord of Light's power over death? Both are enacted through the giving of life to the dead, and here is the paradoxical re-enchantment of death: are we to fight against the living dead or for the living that inevitably die? What purpose is there if all die? It is at the crux of death's nihility that we begin to see death as an imaginary of late modernity.

If the Many-Faced God is the God of Death as Arya Stark's initiation into the faceless men signifies, in the balance is not merely what is owed to death, but death itself. The Many-Faced God signifies not merely Death as God, but death as the telos of existence. This signifies that all anticipate their death or are anticipated by death, but also via Heidegger, Death becomes not merely the enemy but that which authenticates our existence as Being-towards-death. Even if death is our end and we fight against it, we all inevitably die. But the paradox is that we must fight and struggle with the nothingness of death, insofar as we fight against the negation of death and fight for life in the inevitable face of death. The battle between the Lord of Light's anointed and the Night King not only signifies two types of sovereignty over death but the battle for two types of life in the face of death: enslavement to the will of the Night King and the negation of our death or the courage to fight for life in the inevitable anticipation of death's nothingness.

Throughout this chapter, I seek to do two things. I describe through the lenses of Martin Heidegger and Paul Tillich how the sovereignty of Death in *Game of Thrones*, particularly in the story of Jon Snow, displays an existential theology that unpacks the nihility of death as a governing paradigm to a late-modern imaginary implicit within *Game of Thrones*. Second, I seek to unpack late-modern culture more theoretically to show how *Game of Thrones* both reflects contemporary late-modern imaginaries and re-enchants late-modern society through its theological analyses of nihilism and death.

IMAGINARIES OF DEATH: WHEN *GAME OF THRONES* MEETS EXISTENTIAL THEOLOGY

This part of the chapter lays out an existential theology of death in *Game of Thrones* by analyzing the character of Jon Snow through the lens of Martin Heidegger and Paul Tillich. If one is familiar with *Game of Thrones*, the futurity of death is always anticipated. With the anticipation of death within *Game of Thrones*, we are left to wonder who will die next. Throughout the show, from the death of Ned Stark to the Red Wedding through the death of Missandei, Martin and the writers of *Game of Thrones* always keep the audience wondering who will die next. Within this existential anticipation of death, there are striking Heideggerian and Tillichian themes. Between Heidegger's idea of Being-towards-death and Tillich's the 'courage to be,' I argue below that *Game of Thrones*, particularly in the storyline of Jon Snow, sheds light on a theology of death and nihilism in *Game of Thrones*.

Being-Towards-Death in *Game of Thrones*

Beginning with a Heideggerian view of death, Judith Wolfe argues that Martin Heidegger's philosophy of human existence is eschatological, "because it envisions the possibility of authentic existence as dependent on a certain existential relation to one's future."[1] In *Game of Thrones*, the character development of Jon Snow demonstrates a Heideggerian spin on an existential theology defined by the anticipation of death as the inevitable end of all life. By identifying death as the inevitable possibility of all existence and that we must fight for life despite death's inevitability, Baric Dondarrion tells us that "death is the enemy. The first enemy, and the last." Furthermore, Dondarrion tells us that "the enemy always wins. And we still need to fight him."[2] As Dondarrion speaks with Jon beyond the Wall, it is revealed that though they don't know why the Lord of Light wants them alive, it is clear that Jon has purpose when he mentions the Night's Watch vow: "I am the shield that guards the realms of men." Death becomes not only the inevitable possibility but must existentially be anticipated as my *ownmost* possibility: I will die, and I must face it for me to authentically exist in the world in such a way that gives account to my individual existence as set apart from the crowd of beings.[3]

In confronting the Night King and seeking to guard the realms of humanity, Jon actualizes his ownmost possibility. Not only is Jon assassinated by his own men for betraying the loyalty to the Night's Watch by letting the Wildlings settle south of the Wall,[4] but Jon experiences the nihility of death. Dondarrion tells us that there is no other side, and Jon tells us it is "nothing."[5] Jon, in Heideggerian terms, confronts his ownmost possibility authentically in how he fights for the living in rallying the Kingdoms of Westeros together to fight the Night King, and in turn anticipates again the inevitable possibility of nothingness.[6] Wolfe states that "death, as the horizon of possibility as futurity, is also its negation."[7] Conor Cunningham furthers this in his account of Heidegger when he comments on the nihilism of death in Heidegger's understanding of Dasein-(being-here/there)-in-the-world as anticipating its own death:

> Dasein recalls its nothingness in understanding itself as being-toward-death ... So the nothingness of Being is revealed by the Being-towards-death of Dasein. Dasein understands that its death defines it. Death is, in this, an echo of what is already, because Dasein has death as a result of its nothingness. Death allows Dasein to understand itself as nothing ... In doing so, death (as nothing) is not only definitive of Being-there but is constitutive. In this sense, death can be understood as Being, as the advent of Being. We know that Being is only correctly, concernfully approached when its nothingness becomes manifest. Consequently, death reveals this nothingness, but it does so as the advent of being. Death speaks the nothingness which Being is, and does so as the beginning rather than the end of Being. The nothingness of death makes manifest Being qua Being; only with death do we know that Being is *there* ... Dasein, in understanding death, can comprehend its own nothingness, and so begin to approach Being in an ontological manner, which means precisely, for Heidegger, to approach Being as nothing. We can think of Being as Death, as long as we do not misplace the event of death ... If Death is essential or constitutive, it must be there from the beginning, as that beginning.[8]

Dasein must face death as its ownmost possibility to become nothing, to realize its own nothingness. By meeting the inevitable nothingness of its existence, Dasein, or even Jon Snow, must confront the reality that

> death is what [Jon] must face if [he] is to come into an authentic relation to [his] own being and this existential "anticipation" of death is therefore the condition for being able to understand the meaning of Being as such.[9]

This entails that Jon Snow must wrestle with the reality of death as the ownmost possibility of his Being.

Emmanuel Falque highlights that "according to Heidegger, three modalities of 'being-toward-death' or of 'being-toward-the-end' allow us to turn away from the anxiety before death." He identifies within Christianity each of the three modalities, and I argue that all three can also be found within *Game of Thrones* in the story of Jon Snow. He identifies these three modalities as: (a) "resignation into disappearance" to allow the appearance of others in and after my own dissipation; (b) "the certainty of resurrection" in the sense of diversion or passing around an obstacle to obtain the goal; and (c) the "heroism of achievement" by putting one's mark on the world as the "finishing touch on life via an act of death" when we die for the sake of others.[10]

When Mance Rayder says that Jon "wants to be a hero,"[11] Jon's storyline within *Game of Thrones* certainly demonstrates that he embodies each of Falque's modalities of Heidegger's being-toward-death. Jon demonstrates the resignation to disappearance in his relationship with Daenerys, especially after they find out his true identity as the heir of the Iron Throne and his oft repeated mark, "I don't want it."[12] Jon's story represents the certainty of resurrection as he anticipates the hatred of the Night's Watch when he lets the Wildlings through Castle Black, because he passes around their hatred,[13] by his goal of protecting the living from the Night King (though he both dies by the hands of his brothers and is resurrected by the Lord of Light).[14] Last, Snow conveys a heroism of achievement when he kills Daenerys to protect others from her madness at risk of his own life, which ends with banishment to the Nights Watch (or rather by joining the Free Folk beyond the Wall).[15]

When Jon is resurrected by the prayer of Melisandre to the Lord of Light, before the Battle of the Bastards, he tells her not to bring him back a second time, implying his desire to bypass the problems of this world and dwell in the darkness and nihility of death. After his resurrection, we not only find that something is missing in his character, but as he searches for purpose, he resigns his role as Lord Commander in allowing Ed to lead the Night's Watch. We find the redemption of his character when he struggles with the despair and meaninglessness of life in the face of death: he authentically lives toward fighting for the living as his purpose. In affirming the purpose of his being before the threat of non-being, death becomes constitutive of Jon Snow's identity. Douglas Davies argues that the "theme of being and non-being is of fundamental significance" in how humans take it "as a frame for this life and the way in which [we] grasp [and] sense of it, and [how we] set out to live it" in the face of the futurity and certainty of death.[16] Jon Snow grappled with the ownmost possibility of his death in ways that conveys the reality of a life that has experienced death and struggles to make sense of life under the inevitable horizon of death.

But the reality of death is complex throughout the story of Jon Snow. Not only has he come back from death, but he must fight the possibility of becoming the living dead. These two scenarios of the possibility of death both contribute to his authenticity in facing death and the call to fight the Night King. Just as Jon experiences the nothingness, the darkness, and nihility of death, he also resists the Night King in his resolve and courage to unify the living to fight the Night King. If anything, Jon Snow would rather be dead so that he would not have to suffer the responsibilities of life and war with the living dead. Rather, in affirming his purpose in fighting against the Night King and rallying Westeros to fight the living dead, he not only anticipates the possibility of death, but he anticipates the possibility that all living creatures could become enslaved to the will of the Night King. By being thrown into life, Jon Snow must radically affirm the meaning of his existence in the face of nothingness and horror.

From Anticipation to Courage: Facing Death

If a theology of death in *Game of Thrones* may adopt a Heideggerian assist in understanding the inevitable possibility of death, then the turn in Jon Snow's storyline from the anticipation of death to the courage to fight the living dead may be a turn supported by the existential theology of Paul Tillich. Commenting on Heidegger's notion of death, George Pattison states that, "In resolutely running towards (anticipating) it [Jon Snow] allows death to be seen for what it is and we see ourselves in the light that our ineluctable mortality throws retrospectively upon the rest of our lives."[17] By facing death and exposing the Lords of Westeros to the living dead, Jon Snow radically throws the possibility of the enslavement to and the negation of death upon their consciences.[18] In a sense, though death is everywhere and inevitable in *Game of Thrones*, Jon Snow throws the lords and ladies of Westeros into the possibility of the negation of their ownmost being, the negation of their own death in becoming slaves to the will of the Night King.

In facing death and the negation of death as a possibility of existence, Jon Snow confronts the reality of death by fighting against the Night King. The Night King not only has the power of necromancy, but in that power, he has the power to negate and enslave death to his will to forget all memory and life. When Brandon Stark and Samwell Tarly reflect on why the Night King seeks to kill the Three-Eyed Raven, they reflect on the idea that death is the negation of not just life, but of memory: death is the forgetting of life.[19] By confronting the nihility of death as forgetting, life represents memory and unveils reasons to live courageously in the face of death, if only to protect others from the inevitable possibility of death. To wipe out all life, the Night King's goal is to wipe out all memory of life. If he is successful in enslaving all of the dead to his will, not only would this be a negation of death, but it would also be the negation of life and the memory of life. For the Night King, the logical end of all life is death. The courage of Jon Snow is to fight against the logical extreme embodied in the Night King's goal to get rid of memory and life: to fight for life.

As Jon courageously and single-mindedly seeks to unite the remaining armies of the Seven Kingdoms to contest the armies of the living dead, he demonstrates a central idea found within the thought of Paul Tillich: the courage to be. For Tillich, the courage to be is found in the face of the anxiety and meaninglessness of life. Douglas Davies, commenting on Paul Tillich's "courage to be," states that the arising of

> the phenomenon of anxiety, [is] a powerful notion in theology, especially the anxiety resulting from the awareness of our "having to die." It is the impact of knowing that there is an insistence upon our having to die that is the root of

anxiety. In that awareness we experience "non-being . . . from the inside."[20] Such anxious knowing would be overwhelming were it not for "courage." And it is this very notion of courage that resounds throughout Tillich's approach to death. Each of the categories of [Tillich's] thought reflects a combination of anxiety and courage and furnishes an arena of and for human life providing an opportunity for the individual to exercise courage and face the recognized anxiety. One should not flee in the face of anxiety but find the courage to engage it, even when what lies before us is death itself.[21]

In courageously facing of the eschatological—and existentially meaningless—certainty of his death, Jon Snow defies courageously the anxiety of its inevitability as one of the two ownmost possibilities of life: to die and be forgotten, or to become enslaved to the will of the Night King and eliminate all life and memory. Death, as such, embodies the nihility of memory and is the nihilation of all life. The question is, do we courageously fight for life, even against its nihility as an authentic being-toward-death or do we resign our anxiety to death never to be remembered in the negation of death by the Night King? Facing the resolve of death, Jon Snow unlocks his authenticity and resolutely affirms himself against the nihility of death. Paul Tillich states, commenting on Heidegger, that this resolution allows us to affirm that

> *we* must be ourselves; *we* must decide where to go. Our conscience is the call to ourselves . . . It calls us to ourselves out of the behavior of the average man, out of daily talk, the daily routine, out of the adjustment which is the main principle of the conformist courage to be as a part. But if we follow this call we become inescapably guilty, not through moral weakness but through our existential situation. Having the courage to be as ourselves we become guilty, and we are asked to take this existential guilt upon ourselves. Meaninglessness in all its aspects can be faced only by those who resolutely take the anxiety of finitude and guilt upon themselves.[22]

For Paul Tillich, the heart of being is meaninglessness and despair: both its face and facing it results in a faith facing the possibility of non-being and the dialectical affirmation of its own being before the threat of non-being. Douglas Davies says that for Tillich, "this kind of despair requires a courage, courage that expresses the power of being . . . Even despair depends upon a certain power of being and it is that power of being that enables someone to embrace meaninglessness."[23] Whether this power of being is the affirmation of Being-itself for Tillich or an existential affirmation of being in the face of meaninglessness, despair, and death, the fact of affirming death as one's ownmost possibility is itself an affirmation and sacralization of death's meaningfulness. When Jon Snow challenges the Night King, the inevitable certainty of death's possibility makes him affirm life as the realm within which he "lives, moves, and has his being."[Acts 17:28] Tillich argues that this takes courage—an existential courage that affirms meaning in the face of despair and death. Tillich states that:

> Courage is the self-affirmation of being in spite of the fact of non-being . . . Courage always includes a risk, it is always threatened by non-being, whether the risk of losing oneself and becoming a thing within the whole of things or of losing one's world in an empty self-relatedness. Courage needs the power of being, a power transcending the non-being which is experienced in the anxiety of fate and death, which is present in the anxiety of emptiness and meaninglessness, which is effective in the anxiety of guilt and condemnation. The courage which takes this threefold anxiety into itself must be rooted in a power of being that is greater than the power of oneself and the power of one's world. Neither self-affirmation as a part nor self-affirmation as oneself is beyond the manifold threat of non-being. Those who are mentioned as representative of these forms of courage try to transcend themselves and the world in which they participate in order to find the power of being-itself and a courage to be which is beyond the threat of non-being.[24]

For Jon Snow, the courage to be is in his affirmation of life against the inevitable nihility of death. Anticipated in all of life is the inevitable end of life: Death. And if death is the forgetting of all memory, the nihilation of life, then to fight the Night King implies not only the courage of self-affirmation and to be remembered, but it also implies that in the face of despair and the meaninglessness of life, Jon Snow affirms life against the threat of its extinction.

Absolute Faith and the Sovereignty of Death

Building on Tillich's idea of the courage to be, his idea of absolute faith may also be found in the storyline of Jon Snow. The first element of absolute faith is the *experience* of the power of being before the threat of non-being. By *affirming* himself in the face of death, Jon Snow dialectically affirms his being in the face of his non-being which is Tillich's second element of absolute faith. The second element must first confront non-being—one's death, despair, and meaninglessness—to affirm one's being in the experience of non-being. Jon Snow fits within this second category of absolute faith insofar as he has dwelled in the darkness and nihility of death and fights against the Night King. In his affirmation of fighting for the living, both against the living dead and despite the inevitability of death, Jon Snow radically affirms his purpose in the face of the inevitability of death as the universal, first, and last enemy. The third category for absolute faith is primarily the *acceptance* of being accepted.[25] Because of Jon's complex storyline, it could be argued that the third step of absolute faith is only achieved in his relationship to the Free Folk, as he is rejected by the Night's Watch, rejects his birthright for his love of Daenerys, and is rejected by the North who favored Sansa Stark.

Jon Snow, leading the North as the White Wolf against the living dead, had to not only rally the North behind him and contest Ramsey Bolton at the Battle of the Bastards, but had to accept the reality that not only must the North be united, but that they would need the southern kingdoms to fight against the Night King. By accepting the role of authority, he in turn accepts the faith of the North in him to lead them against the living dead. That is, by facing not only the inevitability of death and affirming his meaning in spite of the meaninglessness, he accepts his responsibility in leading the North against the living dead because he saw not only his ownmost possibility for death, but the possibility of the negation of all life and death in the power of the Night King. Thus, the fight between the living and the dead entails not only the inevitable possibility of death but the possible condition of the negation of death through the enslavement to the will of the Night King.

In facing the two possibilities of death, does Jon Snow follow the Lord of Light's predetermined path to fight the dead, prophetically called to by Melisandre? What is revealing of Jon Snow's willingness to fight the dead does not seem to be belief in the Lord of Light. Rather, his fight against the Night King is couched in his Night's Watch vows of guarding the realms of humanity, whether or not he acknowledges the power of the Lord of Light in bringing back the dead. This implies not only that belief in the Lord of Light is irrelevant—the gods don't matter is a telling theme throughout *Game of Thrones*—despite his power to raise the dead to life. It also implies that unbelief in the power of the gods, specifically the Lord of Light, is also irrelevant even if the Lord of Light has the power to bring the dead to life.

Let me clarify: The *belief* in the Lord of Light is almost irrelevant to sovereignty of the Lord of Light and the predestination of the Lord's Anointed. This means one can live serving him even without consciously knowing that they may be serving his purposes of fighting the Great War between the living and the dead. It is almost black and white: If you are alive you must fight, if you are dead you may inevitably become enslaved to the will of the Night King. Whereas belief or unbelief are irrelevant to the purposes of the Lord of Light, what Jon Snow makes apparent is that in the face of the horror of the living dead, he uses his free will to live and fight the dead. This speaks not merely to the sovereignty of the Lord of Light but to the irrelevance to human belief in his purposes. But it also speaks to the sovereignty of human will and the human commitment to something greater than himself. But what does the sovereignty of the Night King signify? That in death as the absence and negation of free will to the determinism of the will of the Night King—to kill the living, negate memory, and enslave death—we lose all that we are in the subversion to the will of the Night King. It is this that Jon Snow and the living must fight.

GAME OF THRONES AND LATE-MODERN IMAGINATION

Numerous theologians and philosophers in recent years have articulated a code word for understanding how we imagine ourselves within the world. Between Charles Taylor's social imaginaries,[26] Graham Ward's cultural imaginaries,[27] and James K. A. Smith's cultural liturgies,[28] we find a strand in which we are beginning a shift between understanding worldviews to understanding how we imagine ourselves as experiencing the world. Whereas a worldview is a lens through which we *see* the world, an imaginary is how we imagine ourselves *experiencing* in-the-world. The difference is subtle, but crucial in understanding how *Game of Thrones* displays how we imagine our experience of late modernity.

Late-Modern Imaginaries

If modernity is ruled by universal, objective reason and the scientific method undergirded by a representational[29] and foundational epistemology,[30] and post-modernity is characterized by the radical doubt in universal reason,[31] the concern for the question of otherness, the turn from objective truth to subjective feeling[32] and expressive individualism,[33] and the search for meaning in a world where we expect meaning but find meaninglessness,[34] late modernity is the culmination of the nihilism implicit within the hubris of reason to disenchant the world of the divine and the culmination of the meaninglessness of the postmodern emphasis on subjective feelings and the search for meaning. Undergirding each of these is what Ward has articulated as the simulacra of virtual reality,[35] where there is no depth to existence, nothing behind reality, but rather what is represented within it seeks its own transparency and collapses within itself as it merely is without any transcendent reason for *why* it is or a ground *on* which it is. Equally so, Smith has characterized late modernity as governed by a consumer gospel where materialism and the next best thing shapes our desires and hearts after the immanence of this-worldly goods.[36]

Taylor states that a social imaginary is the way in which "people imagine their social existence, how they fit together with others, how things go on between them and their fellows, the expectations that are normally met, and the deeper normative notions and images that underlie these expectations."[37]

Taylor goes further to say that a social imaginary is bound within common narratives and understandings of the whole society with common practices and notions of legitimacy. In the context of social imaginaries, we find a difference in the conditions for belief between the modern and pre-modern conception of transcendence and the self. Tied to the social imaginary of the modern mindset is not merely the gradual disembedding of a pre-modern identity from its participation in transcendence but also that *how* identity is embedded has changed, been replaced and displaced by a secular order governed by the market economy, citizen state, and public sphere.[38]

Furthermore, Ward articulates that our cultural imaginary is governed not by modern disenchantment but by the religious re-enchantment of Western culture through the pluralistic construction from marketplace spiritualities, contemporary literature, pop culture, and film. Hearkening to the reality that Christianity is now no longer the dominant worldview in the West and is now an optional extra in the pluralistic milieu of late modernity, how we imagine ourselves as existing within the world not only yearns for transcendence but seemingly abuses traditional religious beliefs in creating new religions. Late modernity is characterized by the distrust in democratic values and integrity, the globalization of the market economy, spirituality, and technocracy, and the pluralistic re-enchantment of Western spirituality through mass media, film, and pop culture.[39] But it is not merely that we create our own religious beliefs that give us purpose, meaning, and significance, but that we are shaped by cultural norms and expectations that help articulate what we believe and how we relate with others. Paul Tyson is apt: We have never been disenchanted. Merely what has enchanted us has changed: from God to reason to consumerism—and there is an implicit enchantment in daily, ordinary, everyday life that speaks of the charged sacralization and de-secularization of ordinary life.[40] If a late-modern cultural imaginary implies a latent religiosity that re-enchants our imagination, then I argue below that *Game of Thrones* offers us important reflections upon the implicit cultural and religious imaginaries of death within late modernity.

Game of Thrones and the Nihilism of Belief

So how does *Game of Thrones* reflect late-modern re-enchantment? It depicts re-enchantment in several ways. George R. R. Martin reinvents a medieval world to help us imagine death and experience a new world while eerily reflecting the stark reality of the nihilism of death and our pop-cultural consumption of the living dead. He also creates a world marked by religious pluralism where questions of absolute truth and the true God are deferred and delayed in a world where religious belief in God is irrelevant to God's ability to act within the world. *Game of Thrones* depicts secular re-enchantment in such a way that reflects late-modern belief—if God is an optional extra, why believe in him unless he agrees with me, is for me, or helps me cope? The ego-centricity of late-modern society implies that secular belief may believe in a God, but his presence, sovereignty, or power in the world is unsurprisingly irrelevant to daily life. It is as if we either believe in God, but distrust and don't quite believe what that entails, or rather that in our unbelief we are entirely ignorant to the content of belief and how that may shape our perspective on reality and how we imagine ourselves as existing within the world. At one extreme is indifference and the other, fanaticism.

Game of Thrones creates a late-modern imaginary that reflects our own experience of the embrace of meaninglessness in the affirmation of our self-experience of and in the world—whether God or the gods matter or even whether we believe or not in their power, presence, or sovereignty. Late-modern belief implies the virtual nihilism of belief or the fanaticism of sycophants: We can believe what we want at the expense of the theological depth to the nature of God or the gods. Late-modern belief neglects how this may shape how we perceive the world, see through the lens of, and apply imaginatively, how God's perspective may shape our reality. The nihilism of belief does not entail the negation of belief. Rather the nihilism of belief entails absence and/or irrelevancy of belief in how it shapes our daily life. It implies the turn toward the irrelevance of belief or unbelief in daily life where we float within an imagination that distorts truth and lacks the integrative substance of belief in daily practice. This does not mean we don't believe anything. Rather it means that what we believe tends to have no effect on how we perceive, practice, live in, and imagine the world through the lens of belief.

In turn, death and nihilism underlies the reality of the world of *Game of Thrones* in such a way that demonstrates the underlying beliefs and imaginations of late-modern culture by reflecting the horror of, and fascination with, death and the existential affirmation of ourselves in the face of it. If *Game of Thrones* depicts a late-modern imaginary, it truly reflects and shapes how we view the world in such a way that demonstrates the emptiness and irrelevancy of God to daily life while re-enchanting our world with a fascination with death and a capturing of new experiences through popular culture. In the face of death, despair, and meaninglessness that craves depth and meaning, *Game of Thrones* affirms to our imagination a consumerism of death that reflects that which we fear most but also that which actualizes who we are in the crucible.

It is thus in the courage to face death as we anticipate its inevitability that we may authentically become human. The late-modern obsession with death sheds light on our ultimate concerns. And yet, it also displays through our obsession something close to the heart of being human. If we could articulate a late-modern cultural imaginary, then it clearly reflects an existential concern with death and nihilism. This existential concern is not only existential. It also implies theologically what we are ultimately concerned with and how we think about death and the underlying concern, whether by fear or courage, by anticipation or resolve, or even by anxiety or meaninglessness, with the emptiness of death and the courage to face nihilation. Death overshadows not only late-modern imagination and its fascination with death and nihilism, but throughout this chapter, I have argued that *Game of Thrones* not only embodies a pop-cultural instance of late-modern culture. It also demonstrates something of how we religiously imagine death and nihilism within late modernity. It is within the anticipation of death, facing it courageously in the midst of anxiety of its meaninglessness that *Game of Thrones*, especially through the storyline of Jon Snow, portrays insights into late-modern religious and cultural concerns.

Game of Thrones highlights how we may be authentically human before the anxiety of death and nihilism. It also affirms a faith that produces meaning and purpose before the anxiety that death and nihilism allow us to face. It is thus in the resourcement of Martin Heidegger and Paul Tillich's existential theology that we may understand a theology of death and nihilism in *Game of Thrones*. Furthermore, this chapter has argued that the emphasis on death and nihilism in *Game of Thrones* sheds light on our late-modern cultural and religious concerns that in turn re-enchant our imagination and our imaginaries of how to courageously make sense of life in the midst of meaninglessness and anxiety, death and nihilism.

NOTES

1. Judith Wolfe, *Heidegger and Theology* (New York & London: Bloomsbury T & T Clark, 2014), 85.

2. Alan Taylor, "Beyond the Wall," DVD, *Game of Thrones* (Burbank, CA: HBO, August 20, 2017).

3. In my analysis of Heidegger's ontology, I have argued that central to Heidegger's understanding of "authenticity" is to confront one's *ownmost* possibility of being: Death. C.f. Andrew D. Thrasher, "Relationality and Everyday Meaning: An Ontological Dialogue Between Jean-Luc Nancy and Raimon Panikkar" (Master's Thesis, Fairfax, VA, George Mason University, 2014), 11–12.

4. C.f. David Nutter, "Mother's Mercy," DVD, *Game of Thrones* (Burbank, CA: HBO, June 14, 2015).

5. Alik Sakharov, "The Climb," DVD, *Game of Thrones* (Burbank, CA: HBO, May 5, 2013); Daniel Sackheim, "Oathbreaker," DVD, *Game of Thrones* (Burbank, CA: HBO, May 8, 2016).

6. Jon Snow says to Melisandre before the Battle of the Bastards, "If I do [fall in battle], don't bring me back," then orders her not to bring him back after she says she

must try. From this it could be said that Jon desires to be relieved of the duties of life in the nihility of death. C.f. Miguel Sapochnik, "Battle of the Bastards," DVD, *Game of Thrones* (Burbank, CA: HBO, June 19, 2016).

7. Judith Wolfe, *Heidegger and Theology*, 86.

8. Conor Cunningham, *Genealogy of Nihilism* (New York: Routledge Taylor & Francis Group, 2002), 138–9.

9. George Pattison, "Death," in *The Oxford Handbook of Theology and Modern European Thought*, ed. Nicholas Adams, George Pattison, and Graham Ward (Oxford: Oxford University Press, 2013), 204.

10. Emmanuel Falque, "Suffering Death," in *The Role of Death in Life: A Multidisciplinary Examination of the Relationship between Life and Death*, ed. John Behr and Conor Cunningham (Eugene, OR: Cascade Books, 2015), 47–48.

11. Daniel Minahan, "Valar Dohaeris," DVD, *Game of Thrones* (Burbank, CA: HBO, March 31, 2013).

12. Miguel Sapochnik, "The Bells," DVD, *Game of Thrones* (Burbank, CA: HBO, May 12, 2019).

13. It should be noted that Jon was hesitant in that he sought council with Maester Aemon. C.f. Jeremy Podeswa, "Kill the Boy," DVD, *Game of Thrones* (Burbank, CA: HBO, May 10, 2015).

14. C.f. David Nutter, "Mother's Mercy," DVD, *Game of Thrones* (Burbank, CA: HBO, June 14, 2015); Jeremy Podeswa, "The Red Woman," DVD, *Game of Thrones* (Burbank, CA: HBO, April 24, 2016).

15. David Benioff and D. B. Weiss, "The Iron Throne," DVD, *Game of Thrones* (Burbank, CA: HBO, May 19, 2019).

16. Douglas Davies, *The Theology of Death* (London: T & T Clark, 2008), 101.

17. George Pattison, "Death," 206.

18. Jeremy Podeswa, "The Dragon and the Wolf," DVD, *Game of Thrones* (Burbank, CA: HBO, August 27, 2017).

19. David Nutter, "A Knight of the Seven Kingdoms," DVD, *Game of Thrones* (Burbank, CA: HBO, April 21, 2019).

20. Paul Tillich, *The Courage to Be*, 215; opt cited in Douglas Davies, *The Theology of Death*, 101.

21. Douglas Davies, *The Theology of Death*, 101.

22. Paul Tillich, *The Courage to Be*, 2nd ed. (New Haven: Yale University Press, 1952), 148-9.

23. Douglas Davies, *The Theology of Death*, 103.

24. Paul Tillich, *The Courage to Be*, 155.

25. Ibid., 177.

26. Charles Taylor, *Modern Social Imaginaries* (Durham: Duke University Press, 2004); Charles Taylor, *A Secular Age* (Boston: Harvard University Press, 2007).

27. Graham Ward, *Cities of God* (London: Routledge, 2001); Graham Ward, *Cultural Transformation and Religious Practice* (Cambridge, UK: Cambridge University Press, 2005); and Graham Ward, *The Politics of Discipleship* (Grand Rapids, MI: Baker Academic, 2009).

28. James K. A. Smith, *Desiring the Kingdom: Worship, Worldview, and Cultural Formation*, vol. 1, 3 vols., Cultural Liturgies (Grand Rapids, MI: Baker Academic, 2009);

James K. A. Smith, *Imagining the Kingdom: How Worship Works*, vol. 2, 3 vols., Cultural Liturgies (Grand Rapids, MI: Baker Academic, 2013); James K. A. Smith, *How (Not) to Be Secular: Reading Charles Taylor* (Grand Rapids: Eerdmans, 2014); James K. A. Smith, *You Are What You Love: The Spiritual Power of Habit* (Grand Rapids, MI: Brazos Press, 2016); James K. A. Smith, *Awaiting the King: Reforming Public Theology*, vol. 3, 3 vols., Cultural Liturgies (Grand Rapids, MI: Baker Academic, 2017).

29. John Milbank, *Beyond Secular Order* (Oxford: Wiley-Blackwell, 2013).

30. Stanley Grenz and John Franke, *Beyond Foundationalism: Shaping Theology in a Postmodern Context* (Louisville: Westminster John Knox Press, 2001).

31. Stanley Grenz, *A Primer on Postmodernism* (Grand Rapids, MI: William B. Eerdmans Publishing Company, 1996).

32. C. S. Lewis, *The Abolition of Man* (New York: Harper Collins Publishers, 2001); Anthony C. Thistleton, *Interpreting God and the Postmodern Self: On Meaning, Manipulation, and Promise* (Grand Rapids, MI: William B. Eerdmans, 1995).

33. Stanley Grenz, *The Social God and the Relational Self: A Trinitarian Theology of the Imago Dei* (Louisville: Westminster John Knox Press, 2001); Charles Taylor, *Sources of the Self: The Making of the Modern Identity* (Cambridge: Harvard University Press, 1989); Taylor, *A Secular Age*.

34. Taylor, *A Secular Age*, 583.

35. Graham Ward, *Cities of God*, 60–61.

36. Smith, *You Are What You Love*, 46–53.

37. Taylor, *Modern Social Imaginaries*, 23.

38. Charles Taylor, *Modern Social Imaginaries*, 69–162.

39. Graham Ward, *Politics of Discipleship*, 37–158.

40. Paul Tyson, "Escaping the Silver Chair: Renewed Minds and Our Vision of Reality" (Lecture, September 28, 2018).

BIBLIOGRAPHY

Benioff, David, and D. B. Weiss. "The Iron Throne." DVD. *Game of Thrones*. Burbank, CA: HBO, May 19, 2019.

Cunningham, Conor. *Genealogy of Nihilism*. New York: Routledge, 2002.

Davies, Douglas. *The Theology of Death*. London: T & T Clark, 2008.

Falque, Emmanuel. "Suffering Death." In *The Role of Death in Life: A Multidisciplinary Examination of the Relationship between Life and Death*, edited by John Behr and Conor Cunningham. Eugene, OR: Cascade Books, 2015.

Grenz, Stanley. *A Primer of Postmodernism*. Grand Rapids, MI: Eerdmans, 1996.

———. *The Social God and the Relational Self: A Trinitarian Theology of the Imago Dei*. Louisville, KY: Westminster John Knox Press, 2001.

Grenz, Stanley, and John Franke. *Beyond Foundationalism: Shaping Theology in a Postmodern Context*. Louisville, KY: Westminster John Knox Press, 2001.

Heidegger, Martin. *Being and Time*. Translated by John MacQuarrie and Edward Robinson. New York: Harper Collins Publishers, 2008.

Lewis, C. S. *The Abolition of Man.* New York: Harper Collins Publishers, 2001.
Milbank, John. *Beyond Secular Order.* Malden, MA: Blackwell Publishing, 2013.
Minahan, Daniel. "Valar Dohaeris." DVD. *Game of Thrones.* Burbank, CA: HBO, March 31, 2013.
Nutter, David. "A Knight of the Seven Kingdoms." DVD. *Game of Thrones.* Burbank, CA: HBO, April 21, 2019.
———. "Mother's Mercy." DVD. *Game of Thrones.* Burbank, CA: HBO, June 14, 2015.
Pattison, George. "Death." In *The Oxford Handbook of Theology and Modern European Thought*, edited by George Pattison, Nicholas Adams, and Graham Ward. Oxford: Oxford University Press, 2013.
Podeswa, Jeremy. "Kill the Boy." DVD. *Game of Thrones.* Burbank, CA: HBO, May 10, 2015.
———. "The Dragon and the Wolf." DVD. *Game of Thrones.* Burbank, CA: HBO, August 27, 2017.
———. "The Red Woman." DVD. *Game of Thrones.* Burbank, CA: HBO, April 24, 2016.
Sackheim, Daniel. "Oathbreaker." DVD. *Game of Thrones.* Burbank, CA: HBO, May 8, 2016.
Sakharov, Alik. "The Climb." DVD. *Game of Thrones.* Burbank, CA: HBO, May 5, 2013.
Sapochnik, Miguel. "Battle of the Bastards." DVD. *Game of Thrones.* Burbank, CA: HBO, June 19, 2016.
———. "The Bells." DVD. *Game of Thrones.* Burbank, CA: HBO, May 12, 2019.
Smith, James K. A. *Awaiting the King: Reforming Public Theology.* Vol. 3. 3 vols. Cultural Liturgies. Grand Rapids, MI: Baker Academic, 2017.
———. *Desiring the Kingdom: Worship, Worldview, and Cultural Formation.* Vol. 1. 3 vols. Cultural Liturgies. Grand Rapids, MI: Baker Academic, 2009.
———. *How (Not) to Be Secular: Reading Charles Taylor.* Grand Rapids, MI: Eerdmans, 2014.
———. *Imagining the Kingdom: How Worship Works.* Vol. 2. 3 vols. Cultural Liturgies. Grand Rapids, MI: Baker Academic, 2013.
———. *You Are What You Love: The Spiritual Power of Habit.* Grand Rapids, MI: Brazos Press, 2016.
Taylor, Alan. "Beyond the Wall." DVD. *Game of Thrones.* Burbank, CA: HBO, August 20, 2017.
Taylor, Charles. *A Secular Age.* Cambridge, MA: Harvard University Press, 2007.
———. *Modern Social Imaginaries.* Durham: Duke University Press, 2004.
———. *Sources of the Self: The Making of the Modern Identity.* Cambridge, MA: Harvard University Press, 1989.
Thistleton, Anthony C. *Interpreting God and the Postmodern Self: On Meaning, Manipulation, and Promise.* Grand Rapids, MI: Eerdmans, 1995.
Thrasher, Andrew D. "Relationality and Everyday Meaning: An Ontological Dialogue Between Jean-Luc Nancy and Raimon Panikkar." Master's Thesis, George Mason University, 2014.

Tillich, Paul. *The Courage to Be*. 2nd ed. New Haven: Yale University Press, 1952.

Tyson, Paul. "Escaping the Silver Chair: Renewed Minds and Our Vision of Reality." Lecture presented at the Fall 2018 Mars Hill Areopagus Lecture, Charlottesville, VA, September 28, 2018.

Ward, Graham. *Cities of God*. London and New York: Routledge, 2000.

———. *Cultural Transformation and Religious Practice*. Cambridge, UK: Cambridge University Press, 2005.

———. *The Politics of Discipleship*. Grand Rapids, MI: Baker Academic, 2009.

Wolfe, Judith. *Heidegger and Theology*. New York and London: Bloomsbury T & T Clark, 2014.

Chapter 13

Hodor and the Transubstantiation of the Word Made Death

The Theological Real in Game of Thrones

Loraine Haywood

The closing scene in *Game of Thrones*, season 6 episode 5, ("The Door"), reveals the mystery behind the word/name "Hodor." In this scene, the characters of Bran, Meera, and Hodor leave the cave of the Three-Eyed Raven, trying to escape from the approaching undead army of Wights and White Walkers. Hodor's body is pressed firmly against a door that holds back both death and the dead—the metaphor/cliché of being at death's door. Meera takes Bran and escapes into the blizzard, calling out "Hold the door!" Bran is still in a trance, his consciousness travelling back in time to Wylis's past. Bran and Wylis (young Hodor) are standing in the Winterfell courtyard; they are caught in a gaze in liminal space. Bran merges the present escape with this impossibility, cutting across the void of time, and psychologically manipulating ("warging" into) Wylis/Hodor. He disrupts the symbolic order of young Wylis's life, causing a fissure—an intrusion of the Real. An intruder on the future who breaches the past, Bran acts as a bridge, opening a door to what should be held back. In the past, the young Wylis is traumatized by his encounter across the void in time and has a seizure where he conflates Meera's words "hold the door." What emerges from this liminal space is the word made flesh—"Hodor."

Game of Thrones season 6 unveils some of its mysteries as origin stories. In the beginning, the Night King was a man, transformed by the beings known as the Children of the Forest, stabbing him through the heart with Dragon Glass; Jon Snow is a trueborn child of the Targaryen/Stark lines, whose real name is Aegon; and Hodor used to be Wylis, a stable boy—and more importantly, an intelligible confidant of Lyanna Stark. These revelations are bookended by the "good news" of Jon Snow's resurrection, and the anticipation that he is a "Savior" set against an apocalyptic world where

301

the word that is made flesh is Hodor. *Game of Thrones* uses the themes of creation, nativity, apocalypse, prophecy, and resurrection to emulate biblical narratives, effectively resulting in the Gospel of Jon (Snow—recounting his nativity and resurrection) and the Revelation of Hodor (the unveiling of the mystery of the word).

The viewer of "The Door" has entered a psychological space exemplified by Bran's warging into the young Wylis and the older Hodor simultaneously. The revelation (the unveiling of the mystery of his utterance) of Hodor and the door shocks the viewer witnessing the scene. Because of Bran's perverted intrusion, Wylis has spent most of his life reliving the trauma of his death. The symptoms of this trauma are manifest in the repetitious chanting of the conflated word "Hodor"—a traumatic encounter with the Real of death. In this scene, the theological and psychological dimensions of human existence are warged into one another, mirroring a type of religious phenomenon where Hodor is literally transformed by "the Word."

This chapter confronts this Revelation of Hodor and theorizes that *Game of Thrones* presents the viewer with a Theological Real, a violent intrusion through religious practice. Discussion will focus on the use of biblical symbols and their appropriations drawing on the psychoanalysis of Sigmund Freud. Jacques Lacan's concepts of the gaze, voice, objects, and the Real taken up by film critics, such as Slavoj Žižek and Todd McGowan, is significant when considering Hodor's symptom.

LAY PSYCHOANALYSIS

Lacan turned to Freudian psychoanalysis to expand the language of the unconscious. Lacan developed a theory of the registers of human reality that he called the Imaginary, the Symbolic, and the Real. Film theorists use Lacan's theories to analyze films as lay psychoanalysts.[1] This is fulfilling Freud's insistence on the many cross-discipline uses of psychoanalysis in *The Question of Lay Analysis*.[2] Film theorists, such as Žižek and McGowan, consider Lacan's theory of the Real and the gaze critical elements for film studies.

As a guide to the Lacanian Real, McGowan gives a concise synopsis of Lacan's registers of human reality. McGowan explains that Lacan considers that a child who recognizes themselves looking in the mirror has an illusion of mastery over the image. This has been compared to film viewers. He states that Lacan considered that "the imaginary is the order of what we see, the symbolic as the structure supporting and regulating the visible world . . . the Lacanian Real is the indication of the incompleteness in the symbolic order."[3] Žižek, who uses Lacanian psychoanalysis, considers that language is the anonymous mechanism of the symbolic order . . . subjects are separated by the "wall of language."[4] It should be noted that in *Game of Thrones*, this same concept becomes an object. The Wall keeps the living within human reality using the symbolic order through laws and regulations in the political and social world. Žižek considers this "symbolic fiction [that] structures our reality and objects [that] symbolise power."[5]

The object of "The Wall" in *Game of Thrones*, which represents the symbolic order, has the same function of supporting its smooth running by attempts to keep out death and intrusions of the Real. In the character of the Night King, the viewer sees the intruder, the embodiment of death, as a breach in the wall of language; he does not speak, just as death has no voice.[6] This is one example of the Lacanian Real as the gap or void within the symbolic network that the viewer encounters as shocking. In film theory, Žižek considers that there is a "paradoxical status of those remnants and leftovers of the Real that elude the structuring of the signifier: gaze and voice."[7] These leftovers in *Game of Thrones* reside in the manifestation of the gaze of Bran (the conduit through which there is a transference of trauma), or the Night King's gaze (the abyss of death or trauma without a voice), the voice/word of Hodor (the traumatic symptom), and the ordinary object, the Door (Lacan's *objet a*). Hodor's word and the object become synonymous. Evans considers in Lacan's development of *objet a* that he at first borrows a Greek term *agalma*, an offering to the gods, and later the term is considered as implying "a surplus meaning."[8] The object of the door has a surplus meaning. It is the object of desire that allows an escape. But it is in the conflation of the words "hold the door," in the word of Hodor, his voice, that a surplus meaning is revealed to the viewer. It is a leftover of the Real of death. Only Bran can warg into Hodor. Only Bran can hold the door open to the past and the future and cause a traumatic irruption through the religious practices of the Children of the Forest and the Three-Eyed Raven.

Freud's method was a "talking cure"[9] where it was the patient's voice, their words, that would be necessary to understand symptoms manifesting a trauma. Julia Kristeva understands that "Freud is a specialist in transubstantiation . . . he hears flesh in the patient's associative speech."[10] The psychoanalytic treatment is here described in terms reminiscent of the Gospel of John: "the word made flesh" (John 1:14, KJV). In Freud's study on *The Question of Lay Analysis*,[11] the seemingly disparate concerns of theology and psychoanalysis he considered were connected through pastoral care and ministry. The psychoanalytical treatment, he argued, could be provided by non-doctors as a type of lay ministry.

For Žižek, Lacan's development of psychoanalysis involves the mysterious dimension of the Real. As an example of the Real, Žižek uses 1950s science fiction horror film, *The Invasion of the Body Snatchers* (1956), where an alien presence is detected and people are not behaving in what could be considered "normal" ways within the symbolic order. He states,

> The town has been taken over by aliens who have penetrated and colonized human bodies, controlling them from within . . . a tiny detail betrays their true nature . . . This detail is the Lacanian *object petite a,* a tiny feature whose presence magically transubstantiates its bearer into an alien.[12]

In *Game of Thrones*, the ordinary object of the door transubstantiates the *holder* into a "word," Hodor, who does not behave normally. This is augmented by the scene where Hodor is created via Bran's warging into him in the past at Winterfell. A tiny feature on Wylis's forehead, a cut, indicates that the subject is caught in the Real.

Game of Thrones transubstantiates Western Christian theology by warging in the Lacanian Real (an intrusion and disruption, such as death, fear, and anxiety) as the word. The failure of religious practice in prophecy and pastoral care of the individual is a regular theme employed to shock the viewer. In the various religions, prophecy and ritual magic operate in an underworld where the irruption of the Real is a "sign" of truth. Some violent occurrence is a sign of the working of the gods, such as the death of Rob Stark, Joffrey Baratheon, and Balon Greyjoy, after Melisandre's leech ritual. Žižek citing Lacan claims that "the truth arises from misrecognition."[13] The paradox is that these practitioners cause the condition in the future that is misrecognized as prophecy from the past. When Cersei visits Maggie the Frog, she is told she will be Queen until another one comes who is more beautiful and will take her throne. These prophecies work on Cersei's mind, and she acts with violence toward Tommen's wife. This sets the conditions that cause Tommen's suicide. The Mountain is only stationed outside his chambers to ensure Tommen is not in the Sept. The prophecies that guarantee the deaths of her children are read as signs that the prophecies are true. As two children are dead, this is a guarantee that the other will die as well. Cersei can misrecognize her own action or inaction in bringing the revelation to pass. "I was told all my children would die," and these are the conditions that enable her to seize The Iron Throne. Bran causes Hodor's symptom by simultaneously warging into Wylis and Hodor, causing the future condition where he will "hold the door" and sacrifice himself. Hodor is "the word" as a prophecy that was misrecognized in his past utterances, but Bran caused his sacrifice in the future. Maggie the Frog, Melisandre, Mirri Daz Durr, and Bran demonstrate the effects on the psychology of individuals who hear prophecy. They consider it as a bridge to the future, and this influences their lives as they are convinced that a "revelation" is true through misrecognition. This is demonstrated in the allure of the continuing application of the Azor Ahai prophecy of "the Prince that was Promised" and the reading of Prophetic signs.

The viewer confronts religious practice and prophecy as an unstable element in the human journey, a confrontation with the radical interpretations of "the word." For example, this is the case with Melisandre. On the beach at Dragonstone in season 2 episode 1 is where the word is burned into the flesh of the non-believers who will not convert to the Lord of Light. During this ritual sacrifice, she has Stanis pull a burning sword out of one of the burning statues to identify him as the "Prince Who was Promised." Dany's interaction with the witch Mirri Daz Durr speaks of mystery time in veiled speech when she declares a future time of impossibility where the Sun/Son rises in the West and sets in the East. Are we to recognize time going backward (2 Kings 20:11, KJV) as a return to the circumstances of the past or misrecognize the impossibility in her prophecy as a revelation of future events? Of course, we cannot limit her prophecy in this way since Dany was the "fire rising" in the West as her reign set in the East, but her death represented the conclusion to her rise. Or is Jon Snow or Bran the Son rising in the West? This is prophecy so veiled it could mean anything, and this is the problem. Only after an irruption of the Real of the future is the prophecy of the past revealed and read as a "Revelation" that has come to pass. The intrusion and disruption on everyday life is what Lacanian psychoanalysts consider a fissure in the symbolic order. The Theological Real is thus an irrupting violence inherent in these religious practices which tears away the illusion of wholeness in the symbolic narrative.

THE THEOLOGICAL REAL: ERUPTIONS IN RELIGIOUS PRACTICE

The Lacanian Real is a traumatic halt to the smooth running of the symbolic order that is sustained by our fantasy of reality. In Winterfell, when Bran travels back in time, Hodor is caught in a gaze that exchanges his symbolic identification, as a stable boy, and is transubstantiated into a future sacrifice. The voice speaks the truth in the conflation of the words "Hold-the-Door" arising from an encounter with the Real. Hodor's awareness of his mortality in violent death suddenly intrudes and irrupts his identity as Wylis, a stable boy. The television series *Game of Thrones* mimics religious practice, in that it is leading the viewer to read Hodor's language (word as symptom) as a revelation.

Psychoanalysis reads language and uses language and "the word" that is spoken as revelations in human reality. Initiates learn the signs, concepts, doctrines, and mysteries as a key to unlock their understanding. In a sense, this mimics theological discourse as the Bible is the doctrine of the "word of God" for it initiates, an established Western Christian symbolic order. Biblical narratives permeate Western society, entrenched in the social world and integrated into our symbolic order of rules and laws. The collision of these concepts found in *Game of Thrones* allows the viewer to cross a threshold into religious practice (a symbolic order) that is disrupted by the Lacanian Real (the irruption on Hodor's life) in a confrontation with the Real of death. The viewer can read Hodor's journey of sacrifice through an engagement with psychoanalytic theory and religious practices, particularly regarding the Children of the Forest. Their indigenous nature theology allows time travel in mysterious liminal spaces of the underworld of the cave, a type of unconscious level, and the magic of the Weirwood Tree. This is where the spoken word "Hodor" is manifested. This is mirrored in biblical texts that likewise use magic trees (Tree of Knowledge/Life) as sacred objects endowed with power of life and death in the divine/human odyssey.

Game of Thrones mirrors biblical texts by employing elements of Christology, fantasy, end of the world themes, and creation myths woven into a type of adaptation of the Book of Revelation and the Gospel of John. Nowhere is this more evident than in season 6. The viewer becomes a seer viewing mystery time in a revelatory cosmic vision. The ability to relate to these journeys is due to the influence on Western society of biblical narratives in the texts of the Gospel of John and the Book of Revelation. As such, the themes and stories of the Bible become symbolic keys that can be the basis for understanding how *Game of Thrones* uses theological concepts and the Lacanian Real.

The Revelation of Hodor is a psychological symptom of repetitious speech (the word) that was warged into him. This ordinary man represents the violence of religious practice that *Game of Thrones* continually exposes to the viewer as flawed and dangerous. This word throughout *Game of Thrones* has no obvious traumatic dimension, but the word that Hodor chants becomes synonymous with his identity as his name. Viewers accept the narrative that he is a simpleton. When the unknown relevance of his voice is translated through a biblical symbol on the cusp of psychoanalysis and theology, the Word does not just have meaning—it is the enigmatic leftover. The viewer experiences an irruption of the Lacanian Real as horror and shock. The Revelation of Hodor is that a perverted religious practice has caused a traumatic altering of language where the voice becomes the symptom of the irruption of the Real. Hodor as the Holder-of-the-Door, like Bran's role as the crippled Three-Eyed-Raven, are revelations as violent apertures at the intersection of psychoanalysis and religious phenomenon. Žižek claims that "authenticity resides in the act of violent transgression, from the Lacanian Real—the Thing Antigone confronts when she violates the order of the city."[14] Bran's warging is likewise a violation of a religious symbolic order (no one has been able to warg into a human being before). He is indoctrinated into time travel where he violates the order of time by warging into Hodor in the past and the future simultaneously. This results in perverted outcomes for Hodor.

Žižek claims that "for Freud, the pathological provides the key to the normal."[15] Hodor's repeated word became his name and a normal character trait that was a key to his symptom, a leftover of an irruption of the Real. This was misrecognized by the viewer who could not understand his symptoms. In the scene at Winterfell, the viewer can see that when the Real irrupts, it intrudes and disrupts everyday life leaving traces in the form of symptoms of trauma, such as reliving the trauma of death repeatedly. Hence, in Hodor's repeated word the viewer witnesses the symptoms of his trauma in the return of the repressed intruding on the normal (Lacan's symbolic order).

The series treats viewers as initiates into its revelations and mysteries, paralleling the journey of its characters through religious experiences as they are converted into biblical symbols. One of these symbols is the door. The journey into the Revelation of Hodor demonstrates psychoanalytic practice as it opens a door to the viewer's understanding. This supplies the key to his symptom as the Real, that likewise, disrupts the viewer. Hodor's repeated word/name is the result of the trauma of a religious encounter that opens the door to the abyss of death. This transubstantiation (the word made flesh) is the word made death—Hodor.

THE WORD

In the Book of Genesis, the word emerges from the abyss or void as an intermediary of speech creating a world. Lacan in *Speech and Language in Psychoanalysis* considers that "psychoanalysis has only a single intermediary: the patient's Word."[16] In the Gospel of John, Jesus Christ is an intermediary; the word made flesh dwelling among us. The Word is a metaphor for Jesus as subject.

In *Game of Thrones* season 6, these biblical narratives and Gospel structures form a framework for experiences with the Real irrupting within the religious experience. Various treatments of biblical symbols, prophetic visions, resurrection, and death along with the various religious practitioners are engagements in practices that intrude or upset the symbolic order of the lives of its characters. As a type of Gospel of John, the gospel of John Snow provides a frame for the viewer that unveils the Revelation of Hodor. This is an interesting parallel constituting a metanarrative for the prophetic or "word" of revelation. In the Gospel of John, "the Word" is a religious designation for the coming of Christ in the flesh as the Messiah and his teachings are the "good news." The preparation for this coming is manifested by a servant as "the voice of one crying in the wilderness" (John 1:23, KJV). This play between "word" and "voice" as divine incarnation drives the narrative of the "sign" (theological manifestation of divine intervention) or the "symptom" (the incarnation of the word in the flesh of Hodor). In *Game of Thrones* season 6, episode 5, there is a voice of one crying in the wilderness (Meera), proclaiming the advent of one who comes to sacrifice himself.

In *Game of Thrones*, this voice proclaims the necessity of the performance of a sacrifice so that Meera and Bran can escape. Leaving Hodor at the door, much like the word made flesh, Jesus, sacrificed on a tree. Hodor was transformed into a metaphor of the door, a signifying sacrifice on the threshold of worlds between life and death.

In the beginning, the words hold the door that were spoken and Hodor was created. His coming into being is revealed through a "revelation" of his word, like a biblical cosmic vision of revelatory time that intersects all linear time. In *A Voice and Nothing More*, Mladen Dolar considers that "in the beginning was a voice. In the beginning of psychoanalysis . . . the voice is a prime candidate for genesis of all sorts—the creation of the universe to start with."[17] Witnessing a genesis in Hodor's creation, season 6, episode 5 replicates the bookends of the Bible. In the episode "The Door," the creation and the apocalypse of Hodor are revealed. The word that creates Hodor destroys him. Hodor's traumatic encounter with Bran reveals Bran has a God-like ability to create "the word made flesh." Žižek clarifies that "When we speak . . . our speech activity is grounded on our accepting a complex network of rules . . . the same life-world . . . This symbolic space acts like a yardstick against which I measure myself."[18] When Hodor has a seizure (a symptom of the irruption of the Real), he is caught in the loop of trauma time that emerges from the liminal space. The symbolic space constituted by language now represents a wall for Hodor. The word he speaks is an unintelligible symptom that was warged into him and hidden from the viewer.

In *Game of Thrones,* people with special natural abilities can "warg" into animals, manipulating, controlling, and seeing what would otherwise be hidden by distance or perspective. Warging as a religious practice involves human-to-animal psychological control. This enables the mind to travel in the body of an animal host. The viewer is introduced to Bran's warging through his dire wolf Summer that he enters as he walks in the Godswood. There, he sees Summer's reflection in the pond instead of his own. As Summer jumps up on his bed, he sees himself, and this breaks the bond. The inherent violence in warging is that it leaves traces from the animal to the human. Bran tastes blood when Summer hunts and attempts to supplement his own hunger this way. In *Games of Thrones* season 3, warging is given a physical manifestation in its most violent representation. In the aftermath of the Red Wedding,

Rob Stark's dire wolf head is sown onto his body. As a physical representation, or metaphor, for warging, it betrays the violence of the transubstantiation of the self into another living thing. These intersections between human and animal in the series lead the viewer to the encounter with Hodor as the word of flesh in a Theological Real.

It is suggested in the series that because Hodor is "simple," Bran can warg into him, which is not the usual practice. The revelation of "The Word" to the viewer is that warging irreversibly altered his life, and this prevents Hodor's continuance as a human being in the symbolic order, and he becomes a dumb beast because he cannot breach the "wall of language." Žižek claims that "the anonymous mechanism of the symbolic order . . . the subject speaks, he is unbeknownst to himself, merely 'spoken', not master in his own house."[19] Žižek is arguing here that individuals are situated in the symbolic order through rules that must be followed in speech. However, the traumatic dimension of Bran's God-like warging causes Hodor as subject to be spoken through by the Real. The single word he speaks is the symptom of the Real that eludes translation until the impossible confrontation with death.

As a human animal sustained by language, and for whom language is a social necessity, Hodor's affliction isolates him. Hodor becomes like Balaam's ass. The donkey "spoke" (Numbers 22:28), and this revealed the unseen through "the word." When animals speak, it's traumatic because it is disordering the world, just as Bran's warging into a human being disorders his mind. Where there should be speech, there is only the word. Hodor, like the donkey, is the voice of prophetic trauma. God gave trauma a voice, just as Bran gives Hodor the word through opening the door to prophetic time in the trauma of the future. Bran's act of time travel and warging opens a door allowing the word through and constitutes a theology in the sense of the Lacanian formula: "the gods belong to the field of the real."[20] Bran's abilities are metaphysical manifestations associated with the "Gods" and Prophetic revelations, as an irruption of the Real through flaws in its theological practice as a perversion. Hodor's word is the residue of the prophetic truth in a revelation of death.

Hodor's repetitious speech of a single word initially has no apparent traumatic significance. Throughout the series, there is no mystery, purpose, or shadowy dimension to a word that makes no sense and comes to be identified with the speaker as his name. But he has sown the word "Hodor" in the hearts of the hearers, like the Parable of the Sower (Matthew 13:1–23, KJV). The viewer sees but does not perceive and hears but does not understand Hodor's word is mysterious speech, but once he is transfigured into a sacrifice, trauma is transferred to the viewer. For Lacan, this mystery of the voice as speech, as a symbolic exchange, he compared to the Trojan Horse, the symbolic gift concealing Troy's destruction. This metaphor, Žižek claims, is "a byword for favours that may seem beneficial but will damage the receiver."²¹ In Hodor's language, the viewer becomes entangled in the dubious gift of speech that conceals then reveals his trauma.

Just as the Trojans did not see the sack of Troy (an irruption of the Real in the sack of the city) in the gift of the horse, in *Game of Thrones* the viewer and "hearer of the word" does not hear a prophecy of death in the word Hodor, as Freud would hear flesh in the word. But it is in the image of his sacrifice as a transubstantiation into the door that the viewer both sees and hears the word. This engagement can be understood through the Freudian cross-discipline interpolation of psychoanalysis and religious practice and the further developments of Lacan. In Lacanian terms, it is an irruption of the Real, for the cutting into the flesh of Hodor is literally ending his symbolic identification as a human being. The viewer is caught in the violence of religious practice through revelation as a doorway to understanding. This is a consistent element in this television series where a series of mysteries are unveiled that shock the viewer as revelations.

Hodor's transubstantiation at the Door from the word to flesh is his body and blood given as a literal sacrifice. This emulates Christian religious practice of the transubstantiation of the flesh and blood of Jesus into the emblems of bread and wine in the Eucharist. The religious rite of the Eucharist opens a door to a mysterious transformation that crosses the boundaries of time. The transubstantiation of Hodor as the word, into the body and blood of a sacrifice, is the Eucharist at its purest. The mysterious transformation from Wylis as a stable boy is conflating a biblical theme; Jesus born in a stable, to Hodor, is the miracle tale. But Bran's birth is the heralding of Wylis's transubstantiation into sacrificial death that we can consider an irruption of the Lacanian Real.

Hodor moves from the darkness of the cave to the door as a boundary separating the inside from the outside. In the liminal space, at the threshold of "The Door," he is performing a religious rite. His symbolic identity, how he is known in the community at Winterfell, is transformed into the word. Wylis's seizure marks his transformation, literally between two deaths. At the door, Wylis/Hodor intersects time as he is renamed for death by his symptom emanating from the void of the mouth. This dissolves his symbolic identity in the past as the future trauma has become his identity and death. The viewer witnesses two deaths, death in the symbolic (he is no longer Wylis) and death as an irruption of the Real.

Žižek emphasizes a key to understanding the shock reveal of Hodor. He identifies "the place in which the Real interferes, it irrupts on the very boundary separating the 'outside' from the 'inside'."²² Not only are viewers witnessing this liminal boundary, but it also combines a psychoanalytic reading. The cave of the Three-Eyed Raven serves as an archetype of the underworld and the door the "visual symbol[s] of the movement between the two realms."²³ However, in *Game of Thrones*, there is a double irruption because the Real is "warged" into Hodor as he simultaneously stands at the door and is at Winterfell in the past. It is Bran that bridges time and opens the door between two worlds of being resulting in trauma. Moreover, this links the symptom with the order of time; the symptom has "returned from the future."²⁴ In this transubstantiation, the future is visiting the past like the Eucharist, the symbolic meal in the bread and water as the future remembrance of the death and sacrifice of Jesus (Mark 14:22–25, KJV). In *Game of Thrones*, however, there is no trace of Wylis in the word Hodor as the word has transubstantiated his flesh. For viewers, this is a missed reality that becomes a revelation. The hearers (the viewer) of the word come to understand that Hodor has been named for death as he manifests a psychological trauma, and his language is substituted by "the word." When the viewer hears the words "hold the door," there is an understanding of the traumatic function of the door as an ordinary object transformed into "the object of terror."²⁵ This ordinary object is endowed with supernatural power on the periphery of a binary between the light and the darkness. Freud considered the void of the mouth as a type of encounter with the terror of the "primordial flesh."²⁶ Hodor's voice emanating from the void is a miscommunication that leads to a misrecognition of the bearer of the word who is not a simpleton. The scene creates a symbolic key that unveils the mystery of the Revelation of Hodor illuminating the traumatic kernel of the Real of the voice.

GAME OF THRONES AND THE USE OF BIBLICAL SYMBOLS, THEMES, AND MOTIFS

Hodor's sacrifice is within a microcosmic view of his creation and his destruction compressing space and time into one episode. However, this sits within a broader biblical theme. Season 6 is bookended by a Christian configuration as the season begins with the resurrection of Jon Snow and ends with his nativity. This gives a biblical framework for Hodor's sacrifice and links the mystery of Hodor into the revealing word. Hodor is literally "the Word made flesh and dwelt amongst us" (John 1:14, KJV) and Jon Snow is the "truth set free" (John 8:32, KJV).

A REVELATION OF THE GAZE IN MYSTERY TIME

Bran's visions are the gaze through history to tell the story of the present tribulation. Both John the Revelator and Bran use time travel as a theological weapon to thwart power. The key to the story of "The Door" demonstrates tragic outcomes from the practice of time travel and warging. The Three-Eyed Raven reminds Bran that he "must learn" as they travel through mystery time, but he cannot control his visions and experiences time in overlapping flashes without order. Bran is unable to grasp their significance.

The Three-Eyed Raven takes Bran through a mysterious doorway that leads to the past of Winterfell. In the courtyard, the returning gaze of Wylis is a confirmation that he sees Bran and past, present, and future enter an eternal realm. During this exchange, the viewer sees in the flesh of Wylis a mysterious cut on his forehead. This small detail is Lacan's *object a*, a piece of the Real alerting the viewer to a fracture in the order of time and the symbolic order. This setting is an intersection, and the suggestion is that the cut returns from the future as an emblem of his transubstantiation. Bran and Wylis are locked in an impossible gaze in a transference of trauma across time. This liminal space in a reciprocal gaze highlights the space between two worlds.

Bran's appearance at Winterfell to the young Hodor is the advent of death outside the symbolic order of time. In this Revelation of Hodor, past, present, and future collide causing an encounter that fractures the order of time by an irruption of a theological practice. The mystery of Bran's travelling back in time is that it causes an impossible cosmic shift. The television viewer, Hodor, Bran, and a third God's eye (from above) are a multiplying gaze in the courtyard at Winterfell. This all-consuming view is the gaze of the "Revelator" in God-time, the timelessness of a space for the Real, from the remoteness of the cave. The viewer encounters the psychological effects of the religious practice of warging as an intrusion on the mind, and its psychological effects irrupt as trauma time.

Game of Thrones employs "mystery time" much like the *Book of Revelation* that veils and constructs another reality for the persecuted and politically oppressed. John wrote Revelation from a remote site in the Roman Empire to provide a "protest narrative" against Imperial power.[27] Similarly, the Three-Eyed Raven and Bran are working in the underworld causing an irruption of the Real that suspends the symbolic order of law and rules that would otherwise govern human behavior and history. To display the power of "greensight," the Three-Eyed Raven reveals to Bran that symbolic power and time are not obstacles in the role of the religious practitioner whose all-consuming gaze is God-like and interfering. Bran's warging into Hodor is a lesson he has to learn as it is a perversion of this gift, a threshold that should not have been crossed. Remembering Hodor's fear of the crypts at Winterfell, witnessed in season 2, the viewer is able to see the trauma of the future. It is only in the future that the past behavior of Hodor, who feared the crypts, is understood as it paralleled "the Door" to the cave.

As a guide to prophecy and its links to events using psychoanalysis, Mary Ann Doane explains that in Freudian psychoanalysis, trauma is the consequence of the non-assimilation of an event. She says that this "has its psychal impact years later, after the fact. But the event somehow persists, in semiotic limbo, as a kernel of the real that awaits only a second event whose collision with the first generates readability."[28] The effect of this "kernel of the Real" is an interruption as trauma time. For Bran and Hodor gazing across the courtyard before Hodor's seizure, there is a pause before an irruption of the Real. This irruption is experienced as trauma and shock, a psychic break, for the viewer in the advent of a new reality that is impossible to comprehend except through a symbol: Hodor's spoken word. The Three-Eyed Raven speaks of time to Bran as a "past [that] is already written, the ink is dry" proven by the journey into the past at Winterfell. The journey into Hodor's past reveals that the symptom of trauma (the repeated word) returned from the future in Meera's call "hold the door."

In *the Sublime Object of Ideology*, Žižek quotes Lacan's theory in regard to the past and future and the symptom. He claims "the repressed content is returning from the future, and not from the past, the transference—the actualization of the reality of the unconscious—must transpose into the future, not into the past."[29] The psychoanalytic treatment is a "journey into the past," a working-through. The viewer journeys into the past, with Bran, where Wylis is transubstantiated and there is a transference of the trauma as the repressed content of the story that is revealed to the viewer.

CONCLUSION

It is only through an irruption in theological practice as the Real of death that we see flesh in the word of a name: the word Hodor. Our understanding of the word is revealed in a translated symbol "the door," as Hodor is sacrificed. This is discovered through a non-linear timeline, a "mystery time" as in the *Book of Revelation* and psychoanalysis which views the return of the repressed as the future trauma.[30] *Game of Thrones* employs a Theological Real through religious practices weaved within biblical mythical frameworks that are violent trauma narratives. Psychoanalysis considers intrusions of the Real as disruptions upon human reality that cause symptoms of trauma such as repetition. Hodor's chanting, his speech is the repeated word that is revealed as a testament of death. This Theological Real is demonstrated in Christ on the cross, the person and the object in the action of sacrifice. The symbol and word become one.

The framing of season 6 adopts a biblical Christian framework that we can understand as the Gospel of Jon (Snow) in which there is a "revelation" of Hodor as "the word made flesh." Even though this word was never originally perceived by viewers as a symbol of sacrifice, it is in the revealing word that a psychological trauma is realized. The viewer that is hearing the word "Hodor" does not comprehend its significance until the warging and time travel, as part of Bran's mystical or religious power, serves as an intrusion of the Real—a distorted perversion. This is something violent and perverted, like the sewing of the Wolfe's head onto the body of Rob Stark after the murderous Red Wedding, a physical manifestation of the fissure in the symbolic order in the violation of hospitality.

Hodor's trauma involves the biblical symbol of the door, the interplay of a door and sacrifice as in the body of Jesus. When Hodor sacrifices himself for Bran, it is a theological working through of biblical themes and symbols through the instruction of the voice—a voice crying in the wilderness (John 1:23, KJV) "hold-the-door." The Revelation of Hodor is a journey to the underworld in a narrative of the confrontation at death's door. This mirrors the *Book of Revelation*, a supernatural attempt to overthrow the power of the Roman Empire in "a life-or-death situation."[31] Hodor's death will pay for the life or escape of Bran and the preservation of his supernatural powers and Kingship.

In an allegorical representation for holding back death, Hodor is the one who can be sacrificed.[32] By holding the door, and death or the dead behind it, Hodor is trying to hold back an intrusion of the Theological Real, which is impossible. This void or gap in understanding is the confrontation with death where "the enemy always wins." His death trauma was warged into him causing a psychological break manifested by the word as symptom. What emerges from the Revelation of Hodor is that he is metaphor for the Real, as a symbol for the word of the truth of death in the irruption of a Theological Real that is consequently warged into the viewer. Hodor, like the viewer, is holding back the unconscious fight against mortality, fed by religious experience—the transubstantiation of "the word" made death.

NOTES

1. Todd McGowan, *The Real Gaze: Film Theory after Lacan*, Suny Serfies in Psychoanalysis and Culture (Albany: State University of New York Press, 2007), 28.
2. Sigmund Freud, "The Question of Lay Analysis," in *Collected Papers Vol. 10 Sigmund Freud*, ed. James Strachey (London: Hogarth Press, 1926).
3. McGowan, *The Real Gaze: Film Theory after Lacan*, 2–3.
4. Slavoj Žižek, *How to Read Lacan* (New York: W. W. Norton & Co, 2007), 65.
5. Ibid., 33.
6. Freud in his paper, *The Theme of the Three Caskets*, on fairy tale motifs, considered that "dumbness is to be understood as representing death" (296). *Game of Thrones* contains fairy tale elements and characters, such as imps, giants, wicked stepmothers (Catelyn Stark), magic, and dragons to warrant a comparison.

7. "The Undergrowth of Enjoyment: How Popular Culture Can Serve as an Introduction to Lacan," *New Formations* 9, no. Winter (1989): 7.

8. Dylan Evans, *An Introductory Dictionary of Lacanian Psychoanalysis* (London: Routledge, 2010), 125.

9. *How to Read Lacan*, 4.

10. Julia Kristeva, *Intimate Revolt: The Powers and Limits of Psychoanalysis*, trans. Jeanine Herman, vol. 2 (New York: Columbia Press, 2002), 65.

11. Freud, "The Question of Lay Analysis."

12. Žižek, *How to Read Lacan*, 67.

13. *The Sublime Object of Ideology* (London: Verso, 1989), 57.

14. Slavoj Žižek, "The Matrix or, the Two Sides of Perversion," in *The Matrix and Philosophy Welcome to the Desert of the Real*, ed. William Irwin (Chicago: Open Court, 2002), 6.

15. Slavoj Žižek and John Milbank, *The Monstrosity of Christ: Paradox of Dialectic?* (Cambridge: MIT Press, 2009), 280.

16. Jacques Lacan, *Speech and Language in Psychoanalysis*, trans. Anthony Wilden (London: The John Hopkins University Press, 1968), 9.

17. Mladen Dolar, *A Voice and Nothing More* (Cambridge: MIT Press, 2006), 128.

18. *How to Read Lacan*, 9.

19. Ibid., 40.

20. Jacques Lacan, *The Four Fundamental Concepts of Psychoanalysis* trans. Alan Sheridan (New York: Norton, 1978), 45.

21. Žižek, *How to Read Lacan*, 7.

22. "The Undergrowth of Enjoyment: How Popular Culture Can Serve as an Introduction to Lacan," 12.

23. Evans Lansing Smith, "Framing the Underworld: Threshold Imagery in Murnau, Coctequ, and Bergman," *Literature/Film Quarterly* 24, no. 3 (1996): 242.

24. Žižek, *The Sublime Object of Ideology*, 56.

25. Dolar, *A Voice and Nothing More*, 133.

26. Žižek, *How to Read Lacan*, 66.

27. Keller, *Apocalypse Now and Then*, 39.

28. Mary Ann Doane, *The Emergence of Cinematic Time: Modernity, Contingency, the Archive* (Cambridge: Harvard University Press, 2002), 140.

29. Žižek, *The Sublime Object of Ideology*, 56.

30. Ibid.

31. Keller, *Apocalypse Now and Then*, 38.

32. See Giorgio Agamden, *Homo Sacer: Sovereign Power and Bare Life*, trans. Daniel Heller-Roazen (Stanford: Stanford University Press, 1998).

BIBLIOGRAPHY

Agamden, Giorgio. *Homo Sacer: Sovereign Power and Bare Life*. Translated by Daniel Heller-Roazen. Stanford: Stanford University Press, 1998.

Bowman, John Wick. "The Revelation to John Its Dramatic Structure and Message." *Union Seminary Magazine* 9, no. 4 (1955): 436–53.

Doane, Mary Ann. *The Emergence of Cinematic Time: Modernity, Contingency, the Archive*. Cambridge: Harvard University Press, 2002.
Dolar, Mladen. *A Voice and Nothing More*. Cambridge: MIT Press, 2006.
Evans, Dylan. *An Introductory Dictionary of Lacanian Psychoanalysis*. London: Routledge, 2010.
Freeland, Charles. *Antigone, in Her Unbearable Splendor*. Albany: State University of New York Press, 2013.
Freud, Sigmund. "The Question of Lay Analysis." In *Collected Papers Vol. 10 Sigmund Freud*, edited by James Strachey. London: Hogarth Press, 1926.
Keller, Catherine. *Apocalypse Now and Then*. Minneapolis: Augsburg Fortress Publishers, 2004.
Kristeva, Julia. *Intimate Revolt: The Powers and Limits of Psychoanalysis*. Translated by Jeanine Herman. Vol. 2, New York: Columbia Press, 2002.
Lacan, Jacques. *The Four Fundamental Concepts of Psychoanalysis* Translated by Alan Sheridan. New York: Norton, 1978.
———. *Speech and Language in Psychoanalysis*. Translated by Anthony Wilden. London: The John Hopkins University Press, 1968.
McGowan, Todd. *The Real Gaze: Film Theory after Lacan*. Suny Serfies in Psychoanalysis and Culture. Albany: State University of New York Press, 2007.
Smith, Evans Lansing. "Framing the Underworld: Threshold Imagery in Murnau, Coctequ, and Bergman." *Literature/Film Quarterly* 24, no. 3 (1996): 241–54.
Spiegelman, Art. *In the Shadow of No Towers*. London: Viking, 2004.
Thompson, Leonard L. *Book of Revelation: Apocalypse and Empire*. Oxford: Oxford University Press, 1990.
Žižek, Slavoj. *How to Read Lacan*. New York: W. W. Norton & Co, 2007.
———. "The Matrix or, the Two Sides of Perversion." Chap. 20 In *The Matrix and Philosophy Welcome to the Desert of the Real*, edited by William Irwin, 240–66. Chicago: Open Court, 2002.
———. *The Sublime Object of Ideology*. London: Verso, 1989.
———. "The Undergrowth of Enjoyment: How Popular Culture Can Serve as an Introduction to Lacan." *New Formations* 9, no. Winter (1989): 7–29.
Žižek, Slavoj, and John Milbank. *The Monstrosity of Christ: Paradox of Dialectic?* Cambridge: MIT Press, 2009.

Index

Accursed Kings, The/Rois maudits, Les, 29
adaptation, 261, 264, 268
adultery, 259
Africa and Africans, 234–36
American colonization, and the First Men, 223, 225
Amnon, 25
Ancient Near East, 23, 63, 72–73
Andals, 151–52; worldview of, 227–29
Aniconism, and "faceless" god, 232
animism, 42; worldview of the children of the forest, 220–21
apophatic theology, 233
Arendt, Hannah, 138
Asshai, 193–94, 198–203, 205–7, 209–10, 238
Astapor, 19–20
Atlantis myth, 230
Augustine, 125, 128–34, 139, 155–58
axiology, 216; Andals, 228; Braavosi, 232; Children of the Forest, 221; Dothraki, 226; Faceless Men, 233; First Men, 224; Ghiscari Empire, 230; Valyrian dragonlords, 230; Worship of the Lord of Light, 239; YiTish, 237. *See also* worldview studies, categories of
Azor Ahai, 239

baptism, 90–91, 93–95, 97–98
Baratheon, Joffrey, 68, 71, 77, 257, 259–60
Baratheon, Robert, 265
Baroni, Peter G., 265
Barth, Karl, 139
Bathsheba, 24–26
Bendis, Brian Michael, 263–64
Benioff, David, 1, 30, 77–79, 261, 264, 267, 272, 297, 298
Bible, 12–13, 22–32, 63, 64, 85–87. *See also* Hebrew Bible; Old Testament
Black Americans, 225. *See also* pragmatism
Black Goat, the, 231
Blood Betrayal, the, 236–37
blood magic: Children of the Forest worldview, 222; Qohorik, 231; Valyrian, 229
bloodrider vow, 226
blood sacrifice, 238–39
Bloodstone Emperor, 237
Boash, the Blind God, 231
Bonhoeffer, Dietrich, 88–90, 93–95, 97–99
Braavosi, 29
Brienne of Tarth, 261–62
Brindled Men. *See* Sothoryi
Buddhism, 177. *See also* Zen Buddhism
Burroughs, Edgar Rice, 235

cannibalism, 236–37; Orientalism in fiction, 237–38
capitalism, 231–32
Card, Orson Scott: and construction of Children of the Forest, 222
caste, 180–83
Casterly Rock, 92
Cataphatic theology, 232–33
Cathars, as Gnostic model for religion of R'hllor, 238
Catholicism: Andal worldview, 227–28; military orders and the Faith Militant, 227–28
chakra, 179, 186
charisma, 46–51, 55
Children of the Forest, 171, 301, 303, 306; response to their doom, 234; trope of the "vanishing Indian," 221
Childs, Brevard, 24
chivalry, 262
Christians, 62, 64, 73, 90, 97–99, 170, 257–58; conservative, 2; critics, 2; progressive, 2
Church, 90, 93, 97–99, 184
Clapp, Rodney, 113
Clarke, Emilia, 2
colonization, patterns of relative to *Game of Thrones*, 225
comparison: problems with comparing "religions," 215–16; value of worldview studies for, 215
concupiscence, 268, 270
Confucianism, 234
Constantinople, First Council of, 148
cosmology, 216; Andals, 228; Braavosi, 232; Dothraki, 226; Faceless Men, 233; First Men, 224; Ghiscari Empire, 230; Valyrian dragonlords, 230; worldview of the worship of the Lord of Light, 239; YiTish, 237. *See also* worldview studies, categories of
Coster-Waldau, Nikolaj, 257–58
covenant, 23–24, 30, 268–70
creation: *Ex nihilo*, 153, 155; Goodness of, 155, 269–70; of man, 87, 268–69; Shiva's dance of, 179; of women, 269; of the world, 147, 150, 153, 155;
Cressen (maester), 198–200
cross, 88–90, 95
crucifixion, 93–95

darkness, value of, 234
David, King of Israel, 23–26, 28–31
Davies, Brian, 136–37
death, 146, 152, 154–55, 159–61, 283–95; as a gift, 233; as the Many-Faced God, 232–34
Decker, John F., 265
deconstructionism, 232–33
Derrida, Jacques, 73, 74
Deuteronomistic History, 23
Dickens, Donna, 267
dignity of the person, 260, 270–71
direwolves, 223
disciple(ship), 86, 88–89
divine simplicity, 154–55
Dondarrion, Beric, 16
Dosh Khaleen, 226
Dothraki, 18–19, 171
dragons, 48, 50, 52–54, 74, 171, 181–83, 223
Drogo, Khal, 18–19, 181–82, 257
Drogon, 18–20
Drowned God, 85–96, 171, 173–74, 176, 180–83
druids, and children of the forest worldview, 222

egocentric worldview, Valyrians as example of, 229, 231
election, 87
environmentalism, 220–21
epistemology, 216; Andals, 228; Braavosi, 232; Children of the Forest, 221; Dothraki, 226; Faceless Men, 233; First Men, 224; Norvoshi, 231; Relationship of maesters to, 216–17; Valyrian dragonlords, 230; Worship of the Lord of Light, 239;

YiTish, 237. *See also* worldview studies, categories of
essentialism, 215. *See also* racial essentialism
Essos, 18, 20, 167–68
Esther: Queen of Persia, 25–26. *See also* Hebrew Bible, Esther
ethnic essentialism. *See* racial essentialism
Eucharist, 76, 310–11
evil, 126–42, 170, 182, 186; privation view of, 155; the problem of, 21–22, 155
exceptionalism, 49–56
exoticism, 236

Faceless Men: as related to the YiTish worldview, 234; tensions in worldview of, 233–34; worldview as outgrowth of Valyrian slave worldview, 233. *See also* worldview, Faceless Men
family, 62, 68, 70, 76, 78, 89, 92, 271
fans, 11, 39, 57, 77, 173, 257–58
fantastika, 218; as especially suited to teaching worldview studies, 219; problem of essentialism in, 236
fantasy megatext: Tolkien's decisive influence on, 223. *See also* Tolkienian worldview
fatalism: in worldview of the Faceless Men, 233–34
Feist, Raymond, 229–30
Feminist critics, 257–59, 261, 263–65, 267
Feuerbach, Ludwig, 44–45
fictional worldviews, 217; challenge of including in worldview studies, 217; study of as requiring increased worldview literacy and collaboration, 218; as syntheses of other worldviews, 217;
fire, 239
Fire and Blood, 41
flaming sword, 237, 239

Fokkelman, Jan, 25
Former Prophets, 13
free will, 266, 291
Freud, Sigmund, 302–3, 307, 310–12
Frey, Walder, 62, 63, 65–72, 75–78
Friedman, Jaclyn, 266
frontier myth: and children of the forest, 221–22
Frye, Northrop, 85, 96, 99

Game of Thrones, 265; compared to *Black Mirror: Bandersnatch*, 218–19; compared to *Russian Doll*, 219; compared to Tolkienian worldview, 219; effects of exposure to worldview of, 218–19; problem of distorted Westerosi gaze when adapted to TV, 236; as promoting comparative worldview studies thinking, 219; and representation of contemporary problems, 218; worldview of, 218, 234
Game of Thrones (TV Show Episodes): "Battle of the Bastards," 78, 79, 285, 295–96; "The Bells," 17, 20, 268, 272, 287, 296; "Beyond the Wall," 12; "Blood of My Blood," 19; "Book of the Stranger," 19; "Breaker of Chains," 257–68; "The Climb," 285, 295; "The Door," 91; "The Dragon and the Wolf," 126, 262, 288, 296; "Eastwatch," 18; "Fire and Blood," 19; "Garden of Bones," 18, 139; "The Ghost of Harrenhal," 98; "A Golden Crown," 18; "Home," 88; "The House of Black and White," 21; "The Iron Throne," 17, 18, 287, 296; "Kill the Boy," 287, 296; "A Knight of the Seven Kingdoms," 16, 262, 288, 296; "The Last of the Starks," 262; "The Lion and the Rose," 261; "Mhysa," 68–69, 79; "Mockingbird," 21; "Mother's Mercy," 285, 287, 295; "And Now His Watch Is Ended,"

19, 98; "Oathbreaker," 285, 295; "Oathkeeper," 20; "The Old Gods and the New," 98; "The Rains of Castamere," 65–67, 76–77, 79; "The Red Wedding," 61–68, 258; "The Red Woman," 287, 296; "Sons of the Harpy," 127; "Stormborn," 18; "Two Swords," 261; "Unbowed, Unbent, Unbroken," 258; "Valar Dohaeris," 88, 286, 296; "Walk of Punishment," 127; "The Wars to Come," 128; "What is Dead May Never Die," 93; "The Winds of Winter," 20, 69, 78, 262; "Winter is Coming," 14, 17, 72, 270; "You Win or You Die," 18, 28, 77
Gaydos, Michael, 263
gaze, the, 258, 302–3, 311–12
Genesis, Book of. *See* Hebrew Bible
Giantsbane, Tormund, 16
Gleeson, Jack, 257
globalization, as adding to complexity of fictional worldmaking, 217
Gnosticism, 238; Andals, 227–29
God, 24, 26, 127–31, 134, 139, 268–69; Hindu concepts of, 177, 179, 182–86
God-Emperor of Yi Ti, 236
gods, pre-dragonlord Valyrian, 229
Graves, Alex, director, 257, 261–62
Green Men, the, 224
greenseeing, and epistemology, 221
greenseers: American fantasies about "Indians," 221–22; epistemology of the First Men, 223–24. *See also* Native Americans
Greyjoy, Aeron, 87–88, 91–92, 94–95
Greyjoy, Asha/Yara, 92
Greyjoy, Balon, 92
Greyjoy, Euron, 91
Greyjoy, Theon, 88, 92–93, 97–98
Grey King, 87

Haman, 25–26
Hannah, 23, 30
Hannibal, 238

Hauerwas, Stanley, 112
Hays, Richard, 86, 96, 99
Headey, Lena, 257
Hebrew Bible, 12–13, 22–32, 147
   Genesis, 268–70
   Deuteronomy
      27–30, 23
   Ecclesiastes (Qohelet)
      7:15, 23
   Esther
      4:14, 26
   Job, 27, 31
   Proverbs
      26:27, 29 28:6, 27
   Samuel
      1 Sam 2, 23, 30
      1 Sam 13–15, 35
      1 Sam 16, 25
      1 Sam 24, 25
      1 Sam 25, 25
      1 Sam 28, 25
      1 Sam 28–31, 25
      2 Sam 7, 29
      2 Sam 11, 25
      2 Sam 12, 25–26
      2 Sam 13, 25
      2 Sam 22, 23, 30
Heidegger, Martin, 232, 284–86, 288
Herbert, Frank: and construction of Dothraki worldview, 225–26
H'ghar, Jaqen, 70, 193, 207–10, 233
Hibberd, James, 270
Hinduism, 174–87
Hoat, Vargo, 261
Hobb, Robin, 222
Hodor, 301–14
Home Box Office (HBO), vii, 1, 28, 61, 75, 77–79, 168
horse god, the, 226
hospitality, 61–81
hospitium, 61–63, 65–72, 74, 75, 77
House of Black and White, 232–34
Hudson, Laura, 263–64
Hugor, 152–53, 228–29
human body: spousal meaning of, 269–70

Ignatius of Antioch, 90, 97, 99
imaginary, 284, 292–95
Imago dei, 155–61, 269
incest, 16, 25, 28, 39, 48, 52, 229, 259, 265, 268; doctrine of exceptionalism, 231
Indiana Jones and the Temple of Doom, 238
Iron Bank, 231–32
Iron Islands, Ironborn, 85–92, 94–98
Iron Throne, the, 171, 185, 186

Jainism, 177
Jerusalem Temple, 24
Jessica Jones, 263–64
Jesus/Christ/Messiah, 85–90, 93–95, 97, 307
Jewish people, 3, 24
Job, Book of. *See* Hebrew Bible
John Paul II, Pope, Saint, 271–72; *Theology of the Body*, 268–72
Jung, Carl: and construction of Andal godhead, 228–29

Katz, Jennifer, 267
Keck, Leander, 115
khal, 226
King Jr., Martin Luther, 113
King's Landing, 259, 272
A Knight of the Seven Kingdoms, 189–90
Koch, Klaus, 22–23, 26

Lacan, Jacques, 5, 302–10, 312–13
Lannister, Cersei, 16, 28–29, 78, 125, 127, 133, 257–72
Lannister, Jaime, 14, 16–17, 28, 69, 78, 257–72
Lannister, Tyrion, 19, 20, 68–69, 75, 77, 152, 260–61
Larsson, Mariah, 265
Last Hearth, 16
Leng, 237
L'Engle, Madeleine: and construction of the Children of the Forest, 222

Levenson, Jon D., 26
Lewis, C.S., 2, 85, 131–33, 170
Lhazar, Lhazareen, 19, 171
Lindbeck, George, 106–7
Lion of the Night, 236
Lofhink, Gerhard, 113
Long Night, the, 237
Lord of Light, 77–78, 171, 238–39, 283–85, 291
Lovecraft, H. P.: allusions to, including racism of, 234–37
Lutes, Alicia, 259
Luther, Martin, 85, 90, 97, 99
Lyons, Margaret, 257

maesters, 4, 193, 216–17, 224. *See also* epistemology
magic: instrumental use of by Valyrian dragonlords, 229, 231. *See also* blood magic
Mahabharata, 185–86
Maiden-Made-of-Light, 236
male gaze, 272, 274n27
Manichaeism, 128–31; as basis for religion of R'hllor, 238
Manning, Brennan, 104
Many-Faced God, 61, 67, 70, 71, 78, 171, 283–84
Marcotte, Amanda, 259
marriage: heterosexual marriage, 265–66, 270; marriage of Cersei and Robert, 265
martial arts, 232, 234
Martin, George R.R., vii, 1–5, 21, 28, 61–63, 71–73, 76, 78, 167–72, 174, 180, 183–85, 187, 189–90, 259–60, 264
materialism: of Valyrian worldview family, 231
McGowan, Todd, 302
Medievalism, 62, 65, 72, 78, 265
Megasthenes, 175
Mereen, 19–20
Meribald, 151
messianic figures, 237–39

Minear, Paul, 105, 109–10
Mirri Maz Duur, 19, 194, 203
Missandei, 27
modalism, 146, 149, 152–54, 161–62
Mongolians, and construction of the Dothraki, 225–26
monotheism, 147, 149, 153, 179
Mordecai, 26
Mormont, Jorah, 21–22
multiple perspectives, value of, 224
Muslims, 3

narrative focalization: problem of relative to study of fictional worldviews, 236
Nathan, the prophet, 24–25, 29
Native Americans: construction of the Children of the Forest worldview and way of life, 220–23; First Men, as cowboys and "Indians," 225; Plains "Indians," and construction of Dothraki worldview, 225–26; "Playing Indian," 236; pragmatism, 225; Trail of Tears, compared to Dothraki treatment of people of Sathar, 226
Neopaganism: and construction of female deities of Andal worldview, 227
Neoplatonism, 232; Andals' worldview, 227, 229
New Gods, The, 28, 64, 75, 78
Nicaea, Council of, 148
Nicene Creed, 148, 151
Niebuhr, Reinhold, 2, 98, 132–35; Augustinian Realism, 2
Night King, 16, 28, 125–26, 187, 283–85, 287–92
Night's Watch, 16, 68, 73, 77, 285, 287; worldview of, 223–25
nihilism, 283–90, 292–95
non-dualism, of the Faceless Men and of the Children of the Forest, 234
Norse religion, and children of the forest, 220–21

nudity, 2–3, 257
Númenóreans: First Men, 223; Valyrians, 223, 230. *See also* Tolkienian worldview

Objet petite a, 303
Old Gods, The, 67–68, 70–71, 73, 75, 77, 85, 98, 145, 168, 171
Old Testament, 64, 73, 86, 147. *See also* Hebrew Bible
ontology, 216. *See also* worldview studies, categories of
ontotheology, 232–33
Orientalism, 167–68, 183, 187–88, 190, 236
Original Sin, 268–69

Pahle, Rebecca, 258, 261
Pantozzi, Jill, 258
Paskin, Willa, 12
Patton, George S., 110
Paul, 86, 93–94, 148
Penny, Laurie, 267
personhood, 269, 271–72
Philistines, 25, 31
Piper, John, 2, 257–58
point of view: filmic point of view, 260–61; narrative point of view, 260–61
polytheism, 64, 179
pornography, 257, 271
postsecular, 191–95, 198–204, 206, 208–10
power: problem of relative to fictional worldview studies, 219–20
pragmatism: First Men, 224–25
praxeology, 216; Andals, 228; Braavosi, 232; Children of the Forest, 221; Dothraki, 226; Faceless Men, 233; Valyrian dragonlords, 230; Worship of the Lord of Light, 239; YiTish, 237. *See also* worldview studies, categories of
Prince That Was Promised, 3, 193–94, 199, 203–4, 210, 244n31, 305

Protestantism: and worldview of the "sparrows," 227–28
psychoanalysis, 302–3, 305–8, 310, 313
pure fashion, 271
purity movement, 258, 266, 271

Qarth, 18–19; as foil of Braavos, 234

racial essentialism, 218; relative to power, 219. *See also* racism
racism, 220; anti-African, 234–36; depiction of the Children of the Forest, 223; giants, 223; racial projects, 234–35; Sothoryi, 234–36. *See also* racial essentialism
Ramayana, 182–83, 185
rape, 2, 15, 25, 263–66, 272; rape, threatened, of Brienne, 261; rape as plot device, 258, 261; rape culture, 263–64; rape in English common law, 265–66; rape of Cersei, 257–72; rape of Sansa, 15, 78, 258; rape of Tamar, 2; rape trauma, 263–64
Rastogi, Nina Shen, 12
Rat Cook, 68–69, 77
Ratzinger, Joseph, 104, 108–10, 112
Rayder, Mance, 286
Real, the: Lacanian Real, 301–2, 306, 310–11; Theological Real, 302, 305, 309
reality, aura of in *Game of Thrones*, 220
Red Keep, 272
red priests, 239
Red Wedding, the, vii, viiin1, 18, 20, 22, 28, 61–81, 285
religion: instrumental use of by Valyrian dragonlords, 230–31
resurrection, 178, 302, 307, 311
revelation, 304–5; of the Seven, 152
R'hllor, 171
Richter, Sandra, 105
Rivers, Ser Brynden, 234
Robson, Mark Ian, 136–37, 140
Roman Catholic Church, 145, 156, 163, 170, 184

Romans, compared to Valyrians, 230
Rosenberg, Alyssa, 264
Rosenberg, Joel, 24–25
Rosenberg, Melissa, 263–64

sacrifice, 304, 309–10, 313–14
Said, Edward, 167, 188n14, 191–93, 197–203, 206–7, 209–10
Sapochnik, Miguel, 272
Saraiya, Sonia, 257, 261
Sati, 182, 187
Saul, King of Israel, 23, 25–26, 28–29
Schulhofer, Stephen, 266
secular, 29, 56, 112, 114, 192–94, 197–98, 201, 204, 209; secularity, 192; secularization, 194, 209, 293;
seer. *See* greenseers
self-negation, 232–33
Selmy, Barristan, 20–22
septons/septas, 87, 151, 162
Seven, the, 42–45, 64–65, 68, 70–71, 75, 77–78, 85, 87, 145–46, 148, 150–56, 159–63, 168, 171, 179, 180, 183–85, 187, 189–90, 228
sex, 2–3. *See also* sexual consent
sexual assault. *See* rape
sexual autonomy, 266–67, 270–71
sexual coercion. *See* rape
sexual compliance, 260, 266–67, 270, 272
sexual consent, 258–59, 261, 265–67, 270
sexual ethics, 258, 265–67; Catholic sexual ethics. *See* Theology of the Body
sexual exploitation, 2, 272
sexuality, 265; lesbian sexuality, 272; sacred, 238–39;
sexual misconduct, 264–65
sexual objectification, 258, 265–66, 271–72
sexual politics, 265
sexual utilitarianism, 270–71
Sita, 182–83, 185
skin-changers, 223

slavery: in Ghiscari-Valyrian worldview, 230–32
Smith, Carissa, 257–58
Snow, Jon, 15, 29–30, 73, 77, 178, 185–86, 283–92, 295–96
Solomon, King of Israel, 24
A Song of Ice and Fire, 73, 79–81, 168, 170–71, 173, 185, 264–65, 272; *A Clash of Kings*, 92, 96–99, 189–90; *A Dance with Dragons*, 96–97, 99, 151–52; *A Feast for Crows*, 92, 96–99, 151; *A Game of Thrones*, 28, 189–90; *A Storm of Swords*, 75, 77, 259, 261, 268; *Winds of Winter*, 69, 78
Sorrowful Men: as foils of the Faceless Men, 234
Sothoryi: and racism, 234–36
sovereignty, 46, 283–84, 288–89, 291, 294
sparrows (religious order/sect), 145. *See also* Protestantism
Sphinx, Valyrian, 229
Stark, Arya, 14–15, 17, 66–71, 76–77, 171, 283–84
Stark, Bran, 16–17, 68, 69, 186–87, 189, 234, 262, 268, 270, 288, 301–6, 308–14; and romanticized representation of Children of the Forest, 222
Stark, Robb, 65–69, 75–77, 92, 262
Stark, Sansa, 14, 15, 68, 258, 262
Storm God, 87, 96
subjectivity, 269
symptom, 302–11, 313–14

Tamar, 25
Tao (Confucian-Taoist ideal), 236
Taoism, 234
Targaryen, Aegon I, 40, 43, 45–46
Targaryen, Aerys II, 55
Targaryen, Daenerys, 13, 15, 17–21, 28–29, 31, 63, 67, 74
Targaryen rule, 41–56
Tarly, Dickon, 18
Tarly, Randyll, 18
Tarly, Samwell, 77, 288

Te (Confucian-Taoist ideal), 236
theology, 184, 187
Theology of the Body, 258, 267–72
third eye, 179, 186–87
Three-eyed Crow/Three-eyed Raven, 171–72, 186–87, 189
tiger-woman, 237
Tillich, Paul, 284–85, 288–91
time: perception of greenseers, 221
Tirone, Vanessa, 267
Tolkien, J.R.R., 2, 86, 167, 169–73, 188–90
Tolkienian worldview: Children of the Forest, 220–21; First Men, the, 223
tourism, through fiction, 236
transformation: as effected by contact with magical beings, 223; of the self as a practice of the Faceless Men, 233
transubstantiation, 304, 310–11, 314
trauma, 302–3, 307–14. *See also* rape trauma
Tree of Knowledge/Life, 306
trees: doom of the Children of the Forest, 221; sacred, 221; worldview of the Children of the Forest, 220–21; worldview of the First Men and the Andals, 221
Trimurti, 184
Trinity, the, 184; historical development of, 146–51; psychological analogies of, 155–58
tritheism, 149
Trott, Verity, 263–64

Umber, Ned, 16
Undying Ones, the: as foils of the Faceless Men, 234
United States: Braavosi as idealized representation of, 231–32
Unsullied, origins of, 230–31
Uriah, the Hittite, 24–25

Vaes Dothrak, 19
Valar Marghulis, 29
Valenti, Jessica, 258, 267

Valyrian steel, 230n2
VanArendonk, Kathryn, 11–12
Varys, 18
Vedanta, 177–81, 183–85, 187–88, 190
Vereen, Ashleigh, 257
voice, 302–3, 305–6, 308–9, 311, 314
von Rad, Gerhard, 26

warging, 301–2, 304, 306–9, 312, 314
water dancers, 234
Weber, Max, 47
weirwoods, 224
Weiss, D.B., 1, 30, 77–78, 264, 267, 272
Westeros, 18–20, 22, 29, 62, 65, 68, 70–71, 74, 77–78, 86–87, 96, 98–99, 145, 151, 153, 159, 161–62, 168, 173, 176, 179–80, 183–84, 187
white supremacy, 234–36
Willimon, William, 112
Winterfell, 15–17, 19, 29, 71–72, 92
Word, the, 305–11, 313–14
world-building, 3, 167–69, 174–75
The World of Ice & Fire: problematic gaze of fictional author of, 234, 236
"world religions" paradigm: problems with, 215
worldview: absence of depiction of, 223, 234–35; of Alchemists' Guild, 231; of Andals, 227–29; of Braavosi, 231–32; of Children of the Forest, 220–23; of Church of Starry Wisdom, 237; of Crannogmen of the Neck, 223–25; of Dothraki, as contrasted with Jogos Nhai, 226–27; of Faceless Men, 232–34; of Ghiscari Empire, 230–31; of House Arryn, 227–29; of House Lannister, 227–29; of House Tully, 227–29; of House Tyrell, 229; inner diversity within, 220, 229; of Jogos Nhai, 226–27; of Kings of Winter/Lords of Winterfell, 223–25; of Lengii (northern and southern), 237; of Lorathi, 231; of Lys, 231; of Myr, 231; of Norvoshi, 231; as not merely cerebral, 217; of Pentoshi, 231; of Qohorik, 231; of Skagos, 223–25; of Stony Dornish, 227–29; of Targaryens, 231; of Tyrosh, 231; of Vale, mountain clans of, 223–25; of Valyrian (dragonlords, and as dependent on worldview of the Ghiscari Empire, 229–31; pre-dragonlords, 231); of Volantenes, 231; Westerosi worldview as distorting perception of all others, 236; of wildlings, 223–25; of worship of R'hllor, and as contrasted with Gnosticism, 238–39; of YiTish, 236–38;
worldview families, 215; as due to cumulative nature of creativity, 217
worldview literacy: as necessary for study of fictional worldviews, 219
worldview studies, 215; avoidance of anthropocentric bias, 216; categories of, 215; example of more fine-grained analysis (within Andal worldview), 229; fictional, as requiring collaborative effort, 219; interrelationships of categories of, 216–17; as a more general and fair comparative framework, 217; relationship to study of power, 218; relative to pedagogy and character formation, 219; value of for cultural literacy, 216
Wright, N.T., 115

Ygritte, 36n35, 106–7, 111
yoga, 178–79, 187
Yunkai, 21

Zen Buddhism, 232, 234. *See also* Buddhism
Ziegler, Philip, 90, 97, 99
Žižek, Slavoj, 302–4, 306–10, 313
Zoroastrianism, 238–39
Zwingli, Ulrich, 90

About the Editor

Matthew Brake is the series editor for the *Theology and Pop Culture* series from Lexington Books and Fortress Academic. He also serves as the co-editor (with A. David Lewis) for the *Religion and Comics* series from Claremont Press. He has an master of divinity from Regent University, and master of arts in philosophy and interdisciplinary studies from George Mason University. Matthew has written numerous book chapters for the *Popular Culture and Philosophy* and the *Philosophy and Pop Culture* series. He has also written for the Ashgate series *Kierkegaard Research: Sources, Reception, Resources*. He also runs the blog *Popular Culture and Theology* at www.andtheology.com.

About the Contributors

Shaun C. Brown holds the PhD in theological studies from Wycliffe College and the University of Toronto. He is Associate Minister of First Christian Church (Disciples of Christ) in Garland, TX and adjunct professor at Johnson University and Hope International University. He is coeditor (with Amanda MacInnis-Hackney) of *Theology and Star Trek*, coeditor (with Taylor Ott) of *The Theological World of Harry Potter*, and author of *George Lindbeck and The Israel of God: Scripture Ecclesiology, and Ecumenism* (Palgrave Macmillan, 2021).

Nathan Fredrickson is a PhD candidate in the Department of Religious Studies at the University of California, Santa Barbara (UCSB), with an MA in religious studies from UCSB, an MA in classics from the University of Illinois at Urbana-Champaign (UIUC), and an MS in library and information science from UIUC. His dissertation is on the nature, conditions of genesis, and impact on identity-formation processes of fictional worldviews in "fantastika" (this being an umbrella term for genres like science fiction, fantasy, and horror). He has primarily published elsewhere on the value of using fiction, and especially fantastika, to teach people to think critically and compassionately about other worldviews as part of a general education curriculum that uses cutting-edge, evidence-based pedagogical methods.

Mollie Gossage is a highly caffeinated PhD student in cultural anthropology at the University of Wisconsin-Madison. She is currently conducting field research on tourism and visual culture at a national park in Sichuan, China. When she is not studying other people having fun, you might find her playing her own piano arrangements of emo songs at a local guesthouse or heading to the city to attend a metal concert or the next Magic: The Gathering prerelease event. If Mollie were to found her own Westerosi house, the sigil would be a turtle that has awkwardly flipped onto its back but still had a happy song in its heart, and the house words would be all of the lyrics to "Make Your Own Kind of Music." Mollie's goal as an aspiring social scientist is to help illuminate the invisible structures that bind us, and possibly break them, making her like a nerdy, more metaphorical Daenerys. She has found that engaging with complex fantasy worlds such as Martin's is a stimulating way to think through the possible roles of ritual and belief in society.

Loraine Haywood is an honorary associate lecturer in the School of Humanities and Social Science at the University of Newcastle, Australia, where she also completed her master of theology. She is an interdisciplinary higher degree research candidate in classics, human geography, and film. Her research focus includes embedded trauma and psychoanalytic geography, as outlined by Paul Kingsbury and Steve Pile. She explores the resonances of ancient myth, fairy tale, fables, and biblical narratives in texts to understand human experience and ontology. This is a similar approach to Sigmund Freud in his theories in psychoanalysis to form an analysis and find language with which to understand the unconscious and human trauma. She is also researching the implications of artificial intelligence embedded in social media platforms and biometrics that are a type of theological interface in human and social futures. Loraine's research draws on the theories of Jean Baudrillard, the psychoanalytic theory of Sigmund Freud and Jacques Lacan, and their development in social, cultural, and film theory by Todd McGowan and Slavoj Žižek. She has recently published book chapters and articles on *Game of Thrones*, the Desert of the Real, and the ancient mythic story of the Labyrinth of Crete in film.

Eric X. Jarrard is the Elisabeth Luce Moore Postdoctoral Fellow in Religion at Wellesley College. He holds a doctorate in Hebrew Bible from Harvard University. His research examines the reception history of the Bible, both ancient and contemporary, with a focus on the relationship between physical sites and historiography in biblical literature. In addition to a co-written monograph on the Bible and Hip Hop forthcoming in the Pop Culture and Theology series, he has been published in *Zeitschrift für die alttestamentliche Wissenschaft, Biblical Interpretation,* and the *Harvard Divinity Bulletin*.

Susan Johnston is an associate professor of English at the University of Regina, Canada. She is co-editor with Jes Battis of *Mastering the Game of Thrones* (McFarland, 2015), as well as articles on fantasy and other forms of popular culture, including "Grief poignant as joy: Dyscatastrophe and Eucatastrophe in *A Song of Ice and Fire*" (*Mythlore* 31, 2012), "*Harry Potter,*

Eucatastrophe, and Christian Hope" (*Logos* 14, 2011), and most recently "When Are We Ever At Home? Exile and Nostalgia in the Work of Guy Gavriel Kay," in *Canadian Science Fiction, Fantasy, and Horror: Bridging the Solitudes* (2019). She is presently working on the representation of sexual assault in nineteenth-century print culture.

Katy Krieger is a doctoral student at The University of Oklahoma where she studies early modern literature and culture. Her dissertation work focuses on early modern drama and conceptions of health, contagion, humoral theory, and medicine. Her other scholarship involves transcribing theatre and court-related records to better understand early modern economics. She serves as senior assistant director of first-year composition, teaches at The University of Oklahoma and Oklahoma City Community College, serves on the executive board of OU's Center for Literary Studies, and holds both the FYC Teaching and Service Award and the Provost's Distinction of Teaching.

Jeffery D. Long is the Carl W. Zeigler professor of religion and philosophy at Elizabethtown College, where he has taught since receiving his doctoral degree from the University of Chicago Divinity School in the year 2000. He is the author of *A Vision for Hinduism, Jainism: An Introduction, The Historical Dictionary of Hinduism*, and *Hinduism in America: A Convergence of Worlds*, as well as the editor of *Perspectives on Reincarnation: Hindu, Christian, and Scientific* and the coeditor of the *Buddhism and Jainism* volumes of the Springer Encyclopedia of Indian Religions. He edits the Lexington Books series, *Explorations in Indic Religions: Ethical, Philosophical, and Theological*. In 2018, he received the Hindu American Foundation's Dharma Seva Award for his work to promote accurate and sensitive portrayals of Hindu traditions in the American education system.

David Mahfood holds a PhD in systematic theology from Southern Methodist University, and currently serves as assistant professor of theology at Johnson University in Kissimmee, Florida. His scholarly research focuses on the doctrine of atonement as well as the Trinity, especially in the thought of Anselm of Canterbury and Thomas Aquinas. He also greatly enjoys science fiction and fantasy and is grateful for the unexpected opportunity to bring these interests together with theology.

Drew McIntyre is the Pastor of Grace United Methodist Church in Greensboro, North Carolina and an adjunct instructor in the Religion Department at Greensboro College. He holds an MDiv from Duke Divinity School and a Doctor of Ministry from United Theological Seminary (Dayton, Ohio). His writing has appeared in *Ministry Matters, Seedbed*, and the

International Journal of Public Theology, and he is working on a chapter for the upcoming *Theology and Batman* volume in the *Theology and Pop Culture* series.

Andrew D. Thrasher is a post-graduate researcher at the University of Birmingham, U.K. His doctoral research is on late modern, everyday imaginaries of belief and taps into philosophical theology, cultural studies, and sociology of religion. He teaches Asian religions and comparative religion at George Mason University, American University, and Tidewater Community College. He is a contributor to several volumes in the Theology and Pop Culture Book series, a coeditor of the volume, *Fantasy, Theology, and the Imagination*, and is a contributor to a Festschrift on Raimon Panikkar. He is also working on a manuscript connecting the thought of Raimon Panikkar to continental philosophy and evangelical theology.

Justin KH Tse is assistant professor of humanities (education) at Singapore Management University's Office of Core Curriculum and School of Social Sciences. He is lead editor of Theological Reflections on the Hong Kong Umbrella Movement (2016, coedited with Jonathan Y. Tan) and is working on a book manuscript titled The Secular in a Sheet of Scattered Sand: Cantonese Protestants and Postsecular Publics on the Pacific Rim (in preliminary agreement, University of Notre Dame Press). As an Eastern Catholic, he used to blog on Patheos and reads fiction in an attempt to save his soul.

Edgar Valles is PhD student at the University of Wisconsin–Madison in education policy studies. He is currently finishing his final years of research and writing; his project explores how a community organization in a low-income neighborhood negotiates the many forms of inequality facing students as they strive towards a more collegiate future. While on the surface this work may seem unrelated to fictional thrones and the games thereof, Edgar has always found that fantasy and science fiction are more than just an escape from one's immediate reality. Instead, they give us novel ways of imagining the human experience. *Game of Thrones* (both the books and TV series) is uniquely intense in its storytelling, but it is the complexity of its characters and human situations that have resonated with philosophy Edgar finds useful far beyond mere entertainment.

Mark Wiebe holds a PhD in systematic theology from Southern Methodist University. He is associate professor of theology at Lubbock Christian University in Lubbock, Texas. Mark is the author of *On Evil, Providence, and Freedom* (NIU Press, 2017), and has been published in *The Heythrop Journal* and *Stone-Campbell Journal*.

www.ingramcontent.com/pod-product-compliance
Lightning Source LLC
Chambersburg PA
CBHW021342300426
44114CB00012B/1050